Enchantments of the Clinic

Enchantments of the Clinic

Power, Eroticism, and Illusion in the Clinical Relationship

Carl P. Ellerman, PhD

JASON ARONSON
Lanham • Boulder • New York • Toronto • Plymouth, UK

Published by Jason Aronson
An imprint of Rowman & Littlefield Publishers, Inc.
A wholly owned subsidiary of The Rowman & Littlefield Publishing Group, Inc.
4501 Forbes Boulevard, Suite 200, Lanham, Maryland 20706
http://www.rowmanlittlefield.com

Estover Road, Plymouth PL6 7PY, United Kingdom

British Library Cataloguing in Publication Information Available

Library of Congress Cataloging-in-Publication Data

Ellerman, Carl P., 1943–
Enchantments of the clinic : power, eroticism, and illusion in the clinical relationship / Carl P. Ellerman.
p. ; cm.
Includes bibliographical references and index.
ISBN 978-0-7657-0778-9 (cloth : alk. paper) — ISBN 978-0-7657-0780-2 (electronic)
1. Psychotherapist and patient. 2. Sex. 3. Existential psychotherapy. I. Title.
[DNLM: 1. Psychotherapy. 2. Erotica. 3. Illusions. 4. Physician-Patient Relations. 5. Power (Psychology) WM 420 E45e 2010]
RC480.8.E45 2010
616.89'14—dc22 2010008090

∞™ The paper used in this publication meets the minimum requirements of American National Standard for Information Sciences—Permanence of Paper for Printed Library Materials, ANSI/NISO Z39.48-1992. Printed in the United States of America

In memory of beloved parents who prevailed against the odds in Slocum Hollow and, while prisoned in this precinct on the northeastern peneplain of the Appalachian plateau, created living images of the struggle and the virtue of Sisyphus.

We can only achieve our therapeutic purpose by increasing the power of analysis to come to the assistance of the ego. . . . No substitute for hypnosis has yet been found. . . . We must not overlook the fact that . . . the affectionate attitude . . . is the strongest motive for the patient's taking a share in the joint work of analysis.

—Freud, *Analysis Terminable and Interminable*

Socrates . . . is like the satyr himself; for Socrates too enchants and charms men, not with a flute, but with words. . . . But no one with any intelligence . . . can be expected to accept the notoriously poor arguments that fill the dialogues. . . . Socrates' arguments are more often fallacious than not, his tactics are frequently unfair, he repeatedly contradicts himself, and he sometimes seems more interested in confusing an issue than in clarifying it.

—Herman L. Sinaiko, *Love, Knowledge, and Discourse in Plato*

Contents

Abbreviations

The following symbols will facilitate identification of works of Freud cited in more than one chapter:

AS	*An Autobiographical Study*
CD	*Civilization and Its Discontents*
FI	*The Future of an Illusion*
FL	*The Complete Letters of Sigmund Freud to Wilhelm Fliess, 1887–1904*
GR	*Group Psychology and the Analysis of the Ego*
ID	*The Interpretation of Dreams*
IL	*Introductory Lectures on Psycho-Analysis*
NI	*New Introductory Lectures on Psycho-Analysis*
QL	*The Question of Lay Analysis*
TI	*Analysis Terminable and Interminable*
TT	*Totem and Taboo*

Preface

This work was initially undertaken as a meditative argument focused on the ambiguities of clinical and philosophic life, most notably, the irreconcilable conflict between the vocation, historical role, and activity of the psychotherapist and the vocation, historical role, and activity of the philosopher, each of whom uses persuasive language and speech to fight significantly different battles. Interest in this subject was generated by a dual set of life experiences: the experience of being a philosopher responsible for engaging in the life of mind, while teaching critical inquiry to students, and the experience of being a psychotherapist responsible for treating patients afflicted with every manner and form of psychopathology. But I was motivated to put critical thoughts to paper due to a nagging need to respond to the hasty conclusion in clinical quarters that the vocation of psychotherapists and the vocation of philosophers are indistinguishable, given the origin of psychotherapy in discrete elements of the Socratic mystique, such as the value of an examined life, the use of persuasive speech to engage in the subtle art of leading souls (*psychagogia*), and the attempt to elicit a curative change of mind (*metanoia*) in dialogical partners.

More to the point, for many years, while waging war against mental illness in the clinical trenches—a war of words whose weapons might include a quest for truth, healing myth, adaptive fiction, or life-affirming illusion, depending on the character and emotional requirements of my patients—I experienced a profound conflict between (a) the ancient Socratic quest, with its uncompromising ideal of truth and disturbing challenge to the uncritically accepted beliefs of dialogical partners, and (b) the modern Freudian quest, with its uncompromising ideal of well-being and remedial therapy undertaken to produce a remission of morbid symptoms in dialogical partners who are emotionally disturbed and in need of a healing intervention.

Due to wrong turns, unexpected detours, dead ends, and frequent flat tires—a grueling experience endured by authors whose written work is blessed with and burdened by discovery—I made a pragmatic decision to eliminate philosophic arguments that did not impact life in the clinical trenches directly. Still, surviving arguments scattered throughout this text, as well as autumn arguments put aside for another day, all relate to the fundamental Socratic question: "How shall I live?" These are the arguments of a man with himself, but all issue from deep roots: deep conflicts and dilemmas that are ineluctable aspects of the human condition. Not only the human need for meaning and the drama of being an absurd animal who finds meaning in a meaning-destructive quest for truth, but also the lucid experience of human suffering and the elusive experience of rational reconciliation with life and self and humanness.

Having made the decision to publish a clinical work with a critical philosophic subtext, I invented fictitious names to shield the identity of patients whose lives and words I used to make a fine point. I have also juggled a fact or two in an effort to reinforce my patients' anonymity. Nevertheless, in every case, I remained faithful to the human drama enacted in clinical consulting rooms where I engaged in the carnival of clinical practice. But I did not remain faithful to the original subtitle of this work. Rather, with a nudge from my editor and a concerted effort to achieve greater clarity and precision of meaning, "Variations on Erotic Themes of Freud" was forsaken in favor of "Power, Eroticism, and Illusion in the Clinical Relationship."

I say "forsaken," because I have always thought it was important to acknowledge intellectual debts; and the original subtitle was chosen to pay a huge debt to the early, pioneering, hypnotic-minded Freud, who was not only mindful of the importance of the clinical relationship, particularly libidinal aspects of this formal affiliation, but also responsible for formulating invaluable insights regarding the analyst's suggestive power and influence in the clinical confessional. I realize that Freud has not been fashionable in empirical circles for some time. In fact, with neuroimaging technology in hand and illuminating research in cognitive neuroscience yielding astonishing results in the twenty-first century, it is fair to say that foot soldiers of empirical science are literally lighting up the physical kingdom of the human brain, thereby gaining access to the neurochemistry of order and disorder in human thinking and behavior. So the sun has set on Freud and his successors, and on untold legions of dialogical therapists who either disparage or claim no allegiance to Freud, but still owe much to the formidable young doctor who established a pioneering practice of neurology in Vienna. For out of his rich mythopoeic imagination evolved an inimitable body of speculative thought, as well as a life-affirming process of dialogical treatment that created a thriving culture of mental health clinicians who currently have little understanding of their debt or respect for their professional roots. Orphans of time, vagrants of history, they have forgotten who they are and where they come from.

In addition to intellectual debts, I am mindful of the fact that at the last minute, when I faced a deadline that seemed impossible to meet, Tricia Smith, rights and permissions representative at Art Resource in New York, expedited the license to use a digitized image of Ridolfo Ghirlandaio's *Leda and the Swan* on the cover of the book. I had the pleasure of viewing Ghirlandaio's rendering of the ancient Greek myth in the Galleria Borghese in Rome some time ago and I was reminded of this gratifying experience during a lengthy search for a suitable image. Although I had fairly settled on Andre Brouillet's *A Lesson on Hysteria by Jean Martin Charcot,* after careful consideration, I chose Ghirlandaio's exquisite artwork not only because I found it enchanting, but also because the myth of Leda and her swan intersects with several themes of the book, not the least being that like Zeus, who changed his shape and masqueraded as a swan in order to seduce Leda, dialogical therapists may be seen as clinical shapeshifters who become transfigured by the phantastic perceptions of patients: a phenomenal state of affairs that gives therapists the power to enchant and purposefully lead their patients to some important change of mind, a significant insight or self-discovery, a life-altering transformation of existential circumstances, and a hope-filled remission of morbid symptoms.

With this in mind, I must acknowledge the crude fact that a work of this sort could not exist without mental disorders, lesser emotional impairments, and incalculable human suffering; in addition to these specters of death, I must also add death itself. But I am humbled by the trust and hard work of valiant patients who struggled against this tide and in so doing, taught me practically everything I know about enchantments of the clinic. I am particularly grateful to Sabrina, a "star" patient who gave me permission to use her remarkable "outside letters," as well as her untitled poem of despair and decision, without which revelation of the substance and intensity of clinical enchantments from the patient's point of view would have suffered irreparably. I am also grateful to Ben, a former patient whose newfound joy in life resulted in permission to use a confidential correspondence that reveals his cognitive-emotional condition, assimilation of his therapist's language and existential worldview, and captivating comparison of dialogical therapy to cocaine.

I am indebted to Suzanne Staszak-Silva, senior acquisitions editor at Rowman & Littlefield Publishers, for graciously opening a door by delivering my written work to Julie E. Kirsch, editorial director of Jason Aronson. I also wish to offer formal words of thanks to Julie Kirsch, not only for her interest in and understanding of the active interplay of psychotherapy and philosophy, but also for guiding me through the painstaking process of putting together a finished book in the aftermath of writing and discovery. I must also thank Abigail Graber, editorial assistant to Ms. Kirsch, for presenting me with the daunting task of reducing four hundred pages to three hundred words of descriptive copy for marketing purposes, thereby keeping me attuned to John Updike's enormously helpful prosaic vision of writing as the unending daily effort of developing one's craft. Last but not least, experience with the Rowman & Littlefield Publishing Group resulted in the fortunate experience of being placed in the capable hands of Julia Loy, a congenial and accommodating associate editor of production, whose help with the nuts and bolts of producing a finished book was invaluable.

My esteemed clinical partner, Jennifer Cornish Genovese, read parts of early drafts of the manuscript and offered enthusiastic encouragement, astute clinical commentary, and important insights regarding clinical readers. She also provided steadfast collegiality during challenging discussions of incest and heretical discussions of dogmas of the therapeutic, while tolerating, without complaint, my absence from the clinic when I was possessed by an urgent need to isolate and record onrushing thoughts. To my clinical associate, Marla Velky-Reger, an authentic warrior maiden as the meaning of her maiden name "Velky" or "Valkyrie" suggests, many thanks for undertaking clinical responsibilities in my place, thereby enabling me to use precious time to complete the final manuscript. To my adorable wife Theresa, *Cent Anni,* and abiding gratitude for years of loyalty, forbearance, and support; also, much appreciation for reading early portions of the manuscript and offering pragmatic observations about nonclinical readers and styles of writing.

Finally, I would be remiss if I failed to remember former students, particularly inmates incarcerated in the maximum security prison where I was privileged to teach philosophy and engage in challenging conversations of an existential nature. Whatever else I might say in fond remembrance of things past, I am grateful to these ill-fated men, not only for forcing me to communicate abstruse ideas clearly and concretely, but also for favoring me with trust, outlaw wisdom, and Socratic dialogue of the highest sort.

Introduction: The Clinical Trenches

A DEADLY DISENCHANTMENT

Eddie leaped out a window and plunged eleven stories toward the ground. During his freefall, as I consider the enormity of the moment and try to imagine the ungodly interval before his brain and body shattered, it must have seemed as if time stopped. You see, while hurtling inelegantly through space, arms and legs flailing about, searching instinctively for grounding or support, Eddie never saw the ground approaching, he never heard the breeze, the flight of birds, or the cacophony of street noise rise to a grotesque crescendo. In his final, frenzied, frozen moment Eddie never knew what hit him, for he was blind and deaf and deadly disenchanted.

Don't misunderstand! There was a time when he seemed enchanted with the clinic, coming week after week, faithfully for years, as though therapy would never end. He complained, all right, in fact he was a real whiner: "I'm tired of this shit, I can't take it anymore, therapy isn't helping." But after several suicide attempts and subsequent hospitalizations for depression during years of treatment with a number of capable clinicians, during our clinical encounter, Eddie gave every appearance of reconciling himself to blindness and to unrelenting physical illness. In due course he learned to move about the city freely using public conveyances, he got a decent job, he moved out of his mother's home and rented an apartment after acquiring many of the concrete skills a person needs to live independently. In fact, it seemed as if his depression finally remitted. Eddie fared so well that I was seduced by Plato's enchanting notion that "the cure of the soul" is "effected by the use of certain charms, and these charms are fair words."[1] I even entertained the bewitching fiction that fair words induce moderation in the soul in a way that leads to well-being and self-mastery. But this was evidence of my hubris, for Eddie was simply long-suffering and working on a deadly disenchantment.

Born prematurely and incubated fatefully, Eddie's immature retinal vascular bed was exposed to high concentrations of oxygen and he developed Retrolental Fibroplasia: a retinal disorder that left him legally blind. When he was twenty-eight years old, he became totally blind in the aftermath of cataract surgery and Glaucoma. Afflicted with Diabetes Mellitus, as well, he developed Peripheral Neuropathy: a syndrome of sensory, motor, reflex, and vasomotor symptoms that resulted in decreased sensation in his fingers and loss of sensation in his penis. To my surprise, Eddie once confessed that his inability to experience sexual pleasure was more tormenting than being blind. I was taken aback, having carefully considered how much vision profoundly impacts almost every aspect of a person's life; of course Freud said the same about sex and with my organs of sight and sex intact how was I to know. Although Eddie was able to achieve an erection, he couldn't feel a thing, except the awful feeling of not being a man. As a result of this distorted thinking he became a crazed animal who refused to seek the love, the intimacy, the emotional support of a female companion. Compounding these misfortunes, by the time he was forty years old, impaired sensation in his fingers made it increasingly difficult for him to read Braille. This was an enormous loss, since he was a bright, college-educated man who devoured the daily news and delighted in using his razor-sharp wit to cut a satirical swath through the absurdities of politics and government. Given his indomitable will and fair words that seemed to inspire a life-affirming celebration of the Spartan virtues of Sisyphus—the ill-fated mythic character forced to reconcile himself to the hopeless life of endlessly rolling a monstrous rock to the crest of a mountain in Hades—Eddie learned to compensate for his loss of reading by listening to audio tapes and TV news, until the Fates and the Furies became distempered and dealt a final crushing blow.

Initially, the constant ringing in his ears drove him nuts. As his hearing became increasingly impaired, his will to live collapsed, as if a fragile lust for life had been sucked into the vortex of an inescapable black hole. No sight! No sound! No penis! No touch! Nothing . . . save a massive boulder to push in concert with the curse of Sisyphus. But worse, for Sisyphus could see his boulder as he strained every muscle and sinew heaving his hellish rock toward that fabled mountain peak in the deathly underworld of Hades. Fearing closure of the sensate world, an inability to care for himself, and institutionalization in a dismal warehouse for human rejects, Eddie rejected the finer legacy of Sisyphus: the existential hero's reconciliation with and consequent overcoming of seemingly hopeless terms of existence. One morning soon thereafter, Eddie snubbed his nose at the gods and lesser mortals while leaping headlong from his apartment window: the charming apartment his healer's fair words encouraged him to seek.

In retrospect, during the hopeful years of our acquaintance when Eddie seemed enchanted with the clinic, I guided him through a process of existential therapy that resulted in a memorable psychic turn: a cognitive-emotional turn that evidenced a quickening of the indwelling spirit required to accept and manage sightlessness, chronic illness, loneliness, and other unforgiving aspects of his Sisyphean existence. Dwelling in his own private Hades, with psychotropic medication and a few fair words each week to work a minor miracle on his serotonin receptors, Eddie gave every appearance of sustaining the therapeutic work of dwelling in harmony with the imperfect realities inhabiting his wounded body and his tormented mind, as if he were another one of history's Sisyphean heroes: "conquerors," according to Camus, who "sometimes talk of vanquishing and overcoming. But it is always 'overcoming oneself' that they mean."[2]

Unfortunately, clinical experience suggests that the art of reconciliation is fragile, demanding, and uncertain, because it requires strength of character and a powerful will to persevere: the kind of spiny character and tenacious will Michelangelo displayed when toiling on his back year after year to create beauty on the Sistine Chapel ceiling. From time to time, the neuronal wiring that sustains a tenacious will becomes twisted in a knot too tight to be unraveled by the fairest words and the most potent psychotropic medications. This was the case with Eddie: a brave, long-suffering Sisyphean soul who became deadly disenchanted with myth, truth, and dialogical therapy, as well as all other aspects of the agonistic life of humans.

CLINICAL SPELLS, EROTIC ENCHANTMENTS

During our clinical acquaintance, Eddie often said that being deaf would be far worse than being blind and he prided himself on being a man of his word. As a result of this ambiguous virtue, Eddie's legacy is a mute confession of the gratification and the gravity of clinical speaking and hearing, particularly dialogical encounters informed by the fair words of psychological healers whose persuasive language, ideas, and speech have the capacity to captivate and charm countless men and women who cross the threshold of the mental health clinic seeking a dialogical cure for the emotional wounds of existence. Given his deadly disenchantment and the fact that the persuasive art of dialogical therapy is obscure, rather than transparent, Eddie's legacy is also a remainder of death that figured prominently in my uneasy decision to bring to public view my impressions of the enchantments of the clinic. This is a fascinating topic that brought me face to face with the early work of the pioneering Freud, an imaginative genius who once appeared to be so enchanted by the entrancing spells of hypnotic suggestion—entrancing spells facilitated by the erotically enriched relationship of doctor and patient—that he referred to clinical suggestion as a "miracle"; less than two years later, on 17 February 1889, to be exact, Freud's older, wizened teacher, the venerable neurologist and psychohypnotist Jean Martin Charcot, took a momentary pause from his experimental work with hysterically paralyzed patients to draft a letter to Freud in which he mentioned certain "advantages" of hypnotism, while also warning of "the dangers" (*FL*, 18n2, 20n3).[3]

Freud is out of fashion in scientific quarters these days and if one listens to eager college students aspiring to become psychological healers, one gets the impression that the pioneering psychoanalyst is hardly read at all; but if he is read, it is for historical perspective on the psychoanalytic origin of dialogical therapy, rather than for clues to worthy theory or effective clinical practice. Nevertheless, in 1889, when he took a momentary pause from his scanty clinical practice to read Charcot's warning, Freud was not blind to the dangers of clinical experiments. In fact, in a seemingly disenchanted mood, during a reflection on libidinal aspects of suggestion, he confessed to having felt a "muffled hostility to this tyranny of suggestion" (*GR*, 89).[4] "Tyranny" is a big word carrying the sense of power that is harsh, severe, and oppressive; and when Freud used this meaningful word with reference to clinical suggestion, he was referring to the wrath of jilted hypnotists and verbal "violence" visited on subjects who failed to become enchanted, spellbound, influenced, or controlled by therapeutic suggestion.

Although I cannot personally verify the tyranny of suggestion or the wrath of jilted therapists, experience in the clinical trenches, where I have had silent conversations with myself, as well as intimate conversations with colleagues, enables me to confirm that dialogical therapists of every manner and sort may become as disenchanted with unenchanted patients as unenchanted patients appear to be with ordinary therapists.

Mindful of the advantages and the dangers of clinical experiments, particularly human experiments involving therapeutic strategies and techniques that enhance the power and the influence of mental health clinicians, I am using the term "enchantment" throughout this work to capture the experience of falling under a spell, following medieval poets like Chaucer, who used "enchantment" with this connotation in mind. The intriguing notion of falling under a spell is also reminiscent of Plato's earlier classical reference to being charmed by fair words, specifically, the persuasive words of his philosophic mentor and dramatis persona, Socrates.

While dramatizing Socrates' persuasive manner of curing souls in *Meno*, an early dialogue that raised the formidable question, "What is virtue?" Plato compared Socrates to a stingray who numbs or paralyzes those who come in contact with it at sea. Reflecting on this aspect of his disturbing dialogical encounter with Socrates, Meno informed the beguiling philosopher that his mind and lips were numbed by their conversation, so numbed, that he is unable to reply to Socrates' penetrating questions, although he had spoken about virtue many times before. Humiliated by philosophic conversation that exposed his ignorance, Meno maintained that he had fallen under a paralyzing spell and he accused Socrates of practicing sorcery that rendered him helpless. Meno also advised Socrates rather ominously that if he ever left Athens and reduced others to perplexity the way he perplexes his dialogical partners in the streets and marketplaces of Athens, he is likely to be arrested and accused of being a wizard.[5]

Like Socrates, but for vastly different reasons, I have had the questionable experience of being called a wizard by a dialogical partner. In the clinical trenches, while engaged in the agonistic struggle against illness and death, hearing this startling word gave me pause and ample reason to reflect, not only on the art of dialogical therapy, but also on the idiosyncratic manner in which I engaged in the personal art of listening and speaking. I have taught Socrates to students of philosophy in a maximum security prison and in a respectable college on the East Coast; but I was never referred to as a wizard during philosophic encounters with felons or fresh-faced students. Therefore, as a philosophically minded pragmatic existential therapist responsible for the health and well-being of fellow humans, it falls to me to say that while keeping the rich notion of falling under a spell in plain sight, when I speak of enchantments of the clinic, I am referring to the animating hope of therapist and patient that their dialogical encounter will achieve a psychological healing or emotional cure: a remission of morbid symptoms, some purchase on well-being, a salutary change of cognitive-emotional state for which a fee is paid and accepted. This seductive hope, sometimes authentic, other times fanciful, is the raison d'être of dialogical therapy, the uncertain ground of the clinical relationship, the fertile soil in which the rich ensemble of entrancing language, captivating ideas, and charming speech is conceived and tested. But clinical experience also suggests that beneath the manifest surface of formal dialogical encounters, during the clinical struggle against emotional illness and death, other important variables are working or waiting in the shadows, one clear example being an enthrallment with clinical confession. The erotic experience of self-disclosure—the ambivalent yes and no of stripping, the enticing interpersonal game of evasion and invasion, the painful pleasure of denuding the self and giving oneself away—plays a unique and vital role in the daemonic underworld of secrets: sometimes guilty secrets, oftentimes shameful secrets, whose fateful disclosure facilitates the interpersonal process of dialogical therapy and the psychological healing that is the goal of clinical speaking and hearing.

The erudite postmodern philosopher Michel Foucault referred to the confession of secrets as a game of "capture and seduction" when he attempted to dissect the reciprocal relationship of power and pleasure informing a variety of confessional relationships; in fact, with medical and psychiatric examinations in mind, Foucault maintained that these confessional relationships were "mechanisms with a double impetus," by which he meant "*perpetual spirals of power and pleasure*": the kind of power involved in questioning and monitoring, watching and spying, searching-out and bringing to light, as well as the pleasure that comes from evading, fleeing, fooling, being scandalous or making a travesty of the power that questions, monitors, and spies.[6] Although Foucault examined the neuroanatomy of power like a skilled surgeon at the height of his power to cut to the gray matter of human motivation, on my reading, he failed to adequately dissect daemonic aspects of clinical confession. Given clinical experience and supplemental thinking that traverses terrain first trod by Theodor Reik, an ardent disciple of Freud whose work on the compulsion to confess I shall examine in chapter 3, "The Erotization of Confession," I am more inclined to speak of a triple impetus or *perpetual spirals of power, pain, and pleasure,* for this seems to more accurately capture the daemonic underside of human encounter in the clinical trenches, where the game of capture and seduction can become a serious game of direct, sometimes dire consequences. Whatever else I might say about enchantments of the clinic, one thing seems certain: there is a dialectic of power, pain, and pleasure in the clinical confessional and the fluctuating interplay of power, pain, and pleasure is capable of producing excitations and incitements that unfold on a field of erotic action and reaction, where the quest for psychological health and well-being meets capture and seduction—strategic players in a clinical game whose direct results are manifested in the life and death, the illness and health, of human beings and other strangers.

Digging deeper into the underworld of clinical experience, where the high-stakes game of persuasive dialogical therapy often is won or lost, I am mindful of the interesting way in which certain illusions of the clinical station enable an ordinary therapist to cast an unintentional spell that captivates and charms unsuspecting patients—not every patient, of course, but some unpredictably. In fact, clinical experience with a broad spectrum of fellow humans enables me to say that the provocative relationship of therapist and patient—the intimate, trusting relationship of clinical confessor and clinical confessant—may become hypnotically suggestive, such that a suggestible patient perceives the therapist as an "imaginary . . . object," to use a fruitful expression that captured the early clinical experience of Freud (*IL*, 454).[7] As the reader will see when I introduce clinical experience that not only confirms, but also is a variation on erotic themes of Freud, this illusion-dependent and illusion-making transformation of the therapist occurs during random erotizations of the clinic—erotizations an opportunistic therapist can use to facilitate the dialogical process of psychological healing, providing the erotization of the clinic, the erotization of the clinician (therapist-confessor), and the erotization of clinical confession are understood and managed well.

The awareness and use of clinical enchantments is not the exclusive province of Freud or an inherited fortune exclusively my own. In psychoanalytic circles, it is no secret that young Dr. Freud honed his skills with hypnosis and suggestion while studying with Charcot in Paris and Bernheim in Nancy, after which he found it reasonable to state: "My clients are sick people, hence especially irrational and suggestible" (*FL*, 446). I shall comment more thoroughly on this fascinating state of affairs in chapter 2, "The Erotization of the Clinician"; for now, suffice it to say that my heightened awareness of clinical spells and spellbound patients is remarkably consistent with the clinical experience of post-Freudian therapists, such as Jerome Frank, who reported that many demoralized patients "actively seek out and respond readily to a helper . . . in a state of heightened suggestibility."[8] Given the current popularity of cognitive-behavioral therapy as a concrete method for treating depression, anger, OCD, and a seemingly endless variety of emotional disorders, it is important to understand that when he reflected on the origins of his rational-emotive or cognitive therapy, Albert Ellis maintained that "man is not only a highly suggestible but an unusually *auto*suggestible animal." Having arrived at the crucial understanding that his patients were externally conditioned to believe irrational ideas early on, Ellis claimed that emotional disorders persist because self-defeating ideas are "internally . . . autosuggested"—a clinical state of affairs that enabled Ellis to develop a practical mode of psychotherapy premised on the principle that, "since suggestibility seems to be an almost ineradicable trait of human beings, we should not aim at destroying but modifying it so that man becomes more *intelligently* suggestible."[9]

Where I differ from Freud and post-Freudian clinicians like Frank and Ellis, who correctly conceived psychological healing as a function of dialogical suggestion and persuasion, is my predilection for placing charming words, libidinal fixations, enthrallments with confession, and other clinical captivations, under the encircling arc of enchantment, an engrossing cognitive-emotional state that includes perceptions of a fantastic sort—seductive perceptions informed and guided by the erotization of the clinic, clinician, and confession. Freud conceived this cognitive-emotional condition rather astutely when he described the hypnotic situation as "a group of two," while offering the following definition of suggestion: "A conviction which is not based upon perception and reasoning but upon an erotic tie" (*GR*, 127–28).

AN EROTIC TIE

Experienced clinicians will undoubtedly understand that I am being coy in this introduction to the enchantments of the clinic, like a male version of the coy mistress in Andrew Marvell's illustrious poem of a modest maiden who failed to seize the moment to have a sporting good time with her suitor. But if I were a marvelous writer pressed to devour time before expiring, I would simply confess the truth, to wit, my patients taught me everything I know about clinical enchantments and the erotizations of the clinical situation I am bashfully laying at the door of Freud. In full confession, many enchanted patients achieved a remission of symptoms or some form of psychological healing after crossing the threshold of the clinic and committing themselves to the difficult work of dialogical therapy. But I have been their eager student and they have been my unwitting teachers. Sabrina was noteworthy in this regard, due to the fact that some of her instruction came to me by means of extraordinary letters: "outside letters," as she called them, referring to illuminating confessional letters drafted, mailed, and read outside the formal clinical context.

When she crossed the threshold of the clinic, Sabrina was a forty-two-year-old married mother of four children. She had a baccalaureate in literature, but she was a closet intellectual, having forsaken graduate studies and a professional vocation to home-school her beloved children. A naturally beautiful, self-described "earth mother," Sabrina was experiencing a morbid depression and an emotional estrangement from her husband, Gerald, described as a powerful, alcohol abusive man, fourteen years her senior, who could be likened to a despot in a provincial American castle. Fearful of conflict, Sabrina tried to "avoid any show of anger," as if anger were the deadly plague that afflicted the Dark Ages.

During her psychosocial evaluation, in an important confession that announced her susceptibility to suggestion, Sabrina recalled a history of being controlled by others. Unfortunately, when she was a younger woman, she had no purchase on the perverse fact that the personal attributes that draw us to significant others often become the very attributes that later bring us grief. As a result, she failed to anticipate the demoralizing truth that she would gradually lose power and become a petrified self, performing "a silent little mouse routine" in a dreary marriage to a controlling man destined to acquire despotic power in his provincial castle. Adding to her oppression was the fact that Sabrina was committed to the interminable nursing of four children. I say interminable because Sabrina was a member of La Leche; as if she were one of the founding mothers, she nursed each of her four children for at least five years. I'll leave the precise math to the reader and simply say that prior to therapy Sabrina was a nursing mother for fifteen years. Whatever the equation, Gerald found Sabrina's full, round, lactating breasts very stimulating; consequently, he pursued her like a primitive animal in heat. Given her suppressed libido and consequent loss of an erotic self and body, Sabrina developed the habit of fellating her husband mechanically, rather than submitting to the dark ceremony of forced entry in the still of night. By all accounts, she wanted to end it, but she had become a "silent little mouse" who felt totally disempowered.

After spending eighteen years with a "cold," "decisive," "formidable," "quick to anger," "strong man," Sabrina awakened early one summer morning in anguish. Like many depressed people who lose themselves in empty marriages to lovers who become strangers, Sabrina awakened one morning to the sickness unto death: the kind of sickness conceived by Kierkegaard as an inability to authentically live and an inability to die.[10] In modern dress, this psychoreligious concept of *despair* translates nicely into the clinical concept of *demoralization* identified by Frank in *Persuasion and Healing*. Existential markers of demoralization—the most common mental state of persons seeking dialogical therapy—are powerlessness, hopelessness, helplessness, and isolation, with clinical symptoms of depression and anxiety being morbid sequelae.[11] Sabrina suffered the sickness unto death for another three months, after which she arrived in my office complaining of being "nothing but a tit!"

In retrospect, Sabrina was enthralled with clinical confession, nevertheless, her early outside letters revealed the game of capture and seduction and the strategy of evasion to invasion that characterizes the onset of therapy when patients are not yet able to trust a stranger with shameful secrets. Initially ambivalent about confession, a letter recounting a dream of disordering panic manifests Sabrina's reluctance to undress her psyche: an aversion to being seen and becoming truly known by her therapist-confessor. Phenomenological markers of ambivalence are the desire to cancel or not go to her clinical appointment, yet feeling maddened by the thought of not attending; the feeling of being bad in her therapist's presence; fear that I would reject her or turn my back after learning her secrets; admission of skimming the surface of secrets and hiding or trying to hide. Sabrina referred to this illuminating dream as "the Dr. E dream" and it was part of an early outside letter that arrived unexpectedly in the morning mail.

> Dr. E: I wake up in my dream and it's a wild morning. Mayhem. I'm thinking I just *can't* go to my appointment with you, but it's too late to cancel. I let time keep ticking away, but get into a panic about how to explain myself later. Suddenly you're there and I've got this "I've been bad" feeling, though I'm not sure/can't say what you're doing to make me have this reaction. Next thing I know it's another morning—quite near to a morning that did, in fact, occur. The weather or something has me thinking I may be unable to make my session and *that* threat has me nuts. Concerned when I get to your office, my image of you is sitting turned away from me.
>
> Just skimming the surface, I want to not "confess" this dream, but I'm too curious based upon where you guide me in this stuff. So here goes. Why wouldn't I just call you and say I couldn't go? It's like I'm hiding—or think I can try to hide. . . . So then getting to your office and you're turned away??? I'm lost here. It just ticks me off in general that dreams hold such significance.

After processing this dream during one of our regular weekly clinical hours, productive therapy proceeded apace until one day everything changed when I received a letter out of the blue: a loquacious letter confessing the secret that Sabrina had eroticized her therapist. Reporting a new "feeling of delight," as if she were in process of becoming enchanted; admitting that she was "impressed with" her therapist's "balanced brain," his clinical "work *and* art/literature/poetry"; Sabrina confided that "it would be fun to visit in a more . . . social atmosphere," musing, "perhaps one day." Referring to dialogical therapy in a mystical way, Sabrina mentioned a "painful growth of self-awareness" as a "lucky" experience, "tinged with life's mystery and strangeness." Then, with direct reference to having "felt a common bond that feeds a comforting familiarity," Sabrina confessed to experiencing a "tug of war" between "proper/improper, appropriate/inappropriate," in as much as the erotic tie or "bond" she experienced with her therapist "seems outside the therapeutic scope." Consistent with our clinical goal of creating an appropriately assertive authentic self to replace the depressed, disempowered "silent little mouse" who did not have the courage to speak, Sabrina ended this confession by writing boldly, "I'll also claim triumph in choosing perspective and not keeping my mouth shut, a rare occurrence as you know."

In another letter written while she was in New Orleans, Sabrina adumbrated a budding enchantment, not only borrowing a literary reference to the experience of being enraptured, but also referring to our dialogical work as a "heightened (?) experience":

> Dr. E: On my second day in New Orleans I was wishing I'd brought some books with me (I'd forced myself not to), and my Rilke poems was one. The sights,

> smells, sounds and songs in my head reminded me of Rilke. As I pursue eros—having had the opportunity to do so in New Orleans—I was mindful of Rilke writing about our inability to know why some things in life enrapture us.
>
> That I would wander so far astray from things I love . . . like poetry; but that I would waken one morning. That my turn of events would be thus (I've recently heard disappointing therapist stories, making my appreciation for landing in your office all the deeper) is gratifying. That things roll off you in such graspable ways. That the "things" are sometimes long neglected but beloved—it's . . . well I think it makes this whole process easier; a heightened (?) experience. I'm losing words now. You pick up stuff I can't yet name, and so I'm unstuck even more.

I would like to say that Sabrina's quizzing reference to a "heightened (?) experience" is not only reminiscent of Freud's observation regarding the suggestibility of the sick people he encountered in the clinical trenches, but also remarkably consistent with Frank's reference to the "heightened suggestibility" of the demoralized patients in his care. But this conclusion is unjustified, given the vague supporting evidence in this letter. On the other hand, the following extraordinary letter leaves little doubt about Sabrina's enchantment with the clinic, while also referring unequivocally to the hypnotic aspect of her dialogical encounter:

> Dr. E: Speaking of eros and enrapturement, I have a mental movie/reverie of all the times I've been in your office and was struck quite suddenly by some feeling for you personally (three times it was concern for your health—you just looked ill or wiped) and always, always that feeling would be drowned when you spoke. It is this, like, hypnotic atmosphere that you can induce? Your work is pretty awesome, and it's interesting that you manage to do it so well—make us feel so comfortable in therapy, so interested in figuring ourselves out, so dumbstruck at our fumblings and awakenings and then gushing in them. So that when an otherwise "normal" feeling pops into sight it's almost immediately pushed away if it had something to do with you. I often feel like I've forgotten manners, for God's sake. Is this something unique to me? No, I'm sure that this is a frequent occurrence in your office, and I guess I had to mention it by way of a thank you.
>
> I have this game of "how much I love you" with the kids. When they're three or so, until they're five, they're easily fascinated by the fact that I love them "past the stars" or "beyond the deepest forest'" or "deeper than the ocean." So my son, who is five, in his effort to "best" my love, said in his halting, groping for words voice: "Well Mama, I love you so much . . . that it's . . . more. I love you as much as God loves us!" I'll leave you with these words and the poem on the other side. Rest assured there are songs and poems and books and movies for which I'd pay dearly to share with you.

I would be remiss if I failed to openly state the fact that a dialogical therapist can become enchanted, not only with his own power, influence, and authority, but also with the confirmation of his charms, specifically, the fair words spoken to dialogical partners during the clinical hour. This self-enchantment may become unseemly when a therapist's narcissism is not tempered by the Freudian virtue of insight and Socratic virtues of self-examination and self-mastery.

Regarding these virtues, I can confirm the fact that Sabrina's perception of my "wiped" appearance was accurate. At the time, I was in the throe of something akin to a bipolar mania featuring a hyper-abundance of creative energy that resulted in my awakening at three o'clock every morning bursting with ideas that demanded outpouring on the printed page. Consequently, I developed the daily routine of rising and writing at an ungodly hour before driving to the clinic for a full day's work with patients. After returning home, having dinner, and spending some time with my sorely neglected spouse, I would research and write again until I was exhausted, usually collapsing in bed around 11:00 PM, eager to awaken again at three in the morning in full surrender to the ungovernable mania. The toll on health and appearance was considerable and Sabrina's perception was on the mark, but her inference that I was able to "induce" a "hypnotic atmosphere" was shaky, a state of affairs she openly acknowledged by placing a question mark, a symbol of wonderment, at the end of the telling sentence.

The fact is, I have never purposefully induced a hypnotic trance while working with patients in the clinical trenches, although I readily refer to clinical words as fair or charming and the mental health clinic as enchanted. For this and other reasons, not the least being my gradual awareness of the subtle enchantments of the clinic, I have come to believe that the hypnotic atmosphere experienced by Sabrina and other patients in my care has more to do with the auto-suggestibility of emotionally needy patients than with a hypnotic technique used purposefully by me. Indeed, I remember telling one patient that I had awakened very early that particular morning to do some writing, in response to her query regarding my weary appearance. When she asked what I was writing about, I responded, "enchantments of the clinic."

"I've never been enchanted!" she shot back, and this was true, although she benefited greatly from brief, solution-focused therapy and a little Prozac.

On the other hand, one truly enchanted patient who had previously eroticized the clinic telephoned my office one afternoon, and in a proverbial Freudian slip, stated: "I would like to make a date!" rather than saying more appropriately, "I would like to make an appointment."

Unbeknown to Sabrina, in *Symposium*, a masterfully crafted dialogue focused on different aspects of love, Plato used the character of Diotima to state that eros is a powerful daemon: an "impetuous, and energetic . . .

mighty hunter," "a master of . . . artifice, a "seeker after truth," who is "adept in sorcery, enchantment, and seduction."[12] I use this philosophic reference to acknowledge the fact that in days of yore, there was a prevailing understanding that when eros comes one's way, however innocent the appearance of eros may be, there is a great risk of being gripped by the volatile, uncontrollable power and influence Plato parsed as daemonic. Consistent with this understanding, earlier in *Republic*, Plato depicted the sexual love of beautiful, beguiling, irresistible, sometimes deceptive, treacherous, and evil Aphrodite, mother of eros, as an "insane" or madding pleasure, once again drawing attention to the daemonic aspect of eros.[13] Simply put, erotic love has been conceived historically as a powerful daemon that can take possession of a person in a way that transforms life inalterably for good or ill. Anger carries the latent power of the daemonic as well. Who can forget the good and kindly Dr. Jekyll, particularly the seemingly innocent way the daemonic erupted in his life, ultimately overtaking Jekyll and transforming him into the powerful, enraged, murdering monster, Hyde.

More to the point, like legions of men and women who create secret subterranean lives to compensate for a deathly existence issuing from an absence of life-fulfilling eros, Sabrina embraced erotic fantasy, initially by safe identification with fictional characters in literary books, and later, while in throe of a clinical enchantment, by writing outside letters that were a vital part of a daemonic adventure with her seemingly charming therapist-confessor. For a time, Sabrina's letters fulfilled compensatory needs for intimate communication; her correspondence also gave her a safe way to nurture and develop a powerful voice, becoming a creative force for the liberation and renewal of her forsaken intellectual, poetic, and erotic self. Sabrina's letters also became a launch pad for important therapeutic discussions during the formal clinical hour, during which time she demonstrated the fact that she was an inveterate confessant willing and able to thoroughly examine her thoughts, feelings, and words.

In spite of these gains, Sabrina's letters also revealed that she was possessed by a powerful daemon that threatened the success of therapy and her well-being at the same time. For example, when she came out of hiding and began to practice self-assertion in earnest, most notably at her writing desk in the still of night, she began to give voice to a madding pleasure. "I've felt strangely disconcerted all day," she wrote, as if she were experiencing an inchoate madness that lacked the pleasure of Plato's reference:

> The kids are tucked in and I'm ensconced with lap desk, tea, one ounce of scotch (for later!), and writing things. The most important items: gushing emotions, wonderments, and you.
>
> When you said today that I seemed contained I was genuinely surprised, and remained so until a while ago. I've thought a fair amount about where I

> fall on the "average patient" list, so I can't say I don't appreciate your words. And more. I've come to pick them apart, especially my being "contained." Because it's quite improbable that you misread me.
>
> You'll remember telling me about the gutsy woman who said something like, "if you knew what I was thinking you wouldn't talk to me." My question then (but I didn't ask because I thought there was only one answer) was, how do you go on from there? Or didn't you? I must ask it now. When I think of the number of people who must basically fall in love with you, and how you handle it, and how it will always happen, it's just maddening! Maybe I think part of being exceptional means I won't be a therapeutic statistic—and now I feel like one. Of course I'm contained! I decided a few weeks ago that I could continue therapy as a separate path from what I'm experiencing with this tidbit of you that I get. And now that pisses me off. I mean you know so much about me and I obviously read so much into what I have of you! What was I thinking? That I'd get through this therapy thing and I'd be able to have lunch with you? Meet you for coffee? Befriend you at the least? And then I try to pretend you're a woman. What then? Well in many ways it would all be easier. In most ways it'd be easier. So I'm left with these: awakening, in love, alone, rediscovering the world, joy, feelings—everything. Potential, dreams, fantasy, awareness of my capabilities, learning that I am not alone, that I take baby steps, that I can see where I need to "work" by looking at what (or whom) I'm avoiding! Obviously I could take this to the ends of the earth. Instead I'll consider using *my* guts and put this in the mail. I will sorely miss a visit next week. Or I'll think of this and want to pull it back.

Given certain dogmas of the therapeutic, I responded infrequently to Sabrina's letters, having inherited the questionable dogma that all the action between therapist and patient should take place during the clinical hour; however, from time to time, I mailed an encouraging or a probing response, believing it was important for Sabrina to continue writing and reflecting in order to sustain the empowering process of releasing herself from the annihilative habits of the silent mouse who believed she could not speak. Given her husband's rejection of her literary endeavors—one pertinent example being his devastating critique of a human interest story she planned to submit to National Public Radio—I was mindful of the possibility that Sabrina would experience a serious invalidation if I turned my back on a generous supply of letters received outside the formal context of face-to-face therapy. Most of all, while functioning as a pragmatic existential therapist, I am constantly focused on the demonstrable fact that patients are stuck in life, mired in self-defeating ways of existing, imprisoned by negative patterns of thinking, feeling, and behaving that paralyze the will, shrivel the spirit, petrify self-creation. In good part, my existential method amounts to pushing patients out of entrenched positions by coaxing, teasing, drawing, or pulling out of *pŏtentĭia*, decisions, choices, commitments, and concrete actions that generate movement toward the future, while begetting life-affirming self-creation. Practicing the therapeutic art of clinical midwifery with Sabrina, I challenged her to make a resolute commitment to asserting herself in her writing; I also challenged her to assert herself appropriately at home in direct verbal exchanges with her husband, not to mention a challenge to assert herself in the clinic during therapeutic dialogues with me. To say that this challenge was successful would be an understatement.

About one year after a formal termination of treatment, Sabrina called to arrange a visit to the clinic. Late one morning she arrived all flustered, having encountered construction and a detour that stole a good amount of precious time. When she caught her breath we sat in my office for an hour or so and Sabrina gave me the latest details of her life. Symptoms of depression had remitted and in a self-directed way, she continued the therapeutic process of becoming a stronger, self-determining woman committed to releasing her creative potential. She was no longer a silent little mouse, to say the least. She acquired a commanding voice in her home and she continued to sleep in a separate bedroom, this being a decision made previously in the clinic: a personal decision having to do with reclaiming ownership of her body. She was taking a course in creative writing, in fact, she was writing poetry in earnest and had become a member of a literary group for creative writers in her community. Her solid commitment to a poetic vocation was a life-affirming choice, fulfilling authentic potential she had forsaken many years ago when she chose the role of wife and mother and commenced a time- and self-consuming process of home-schooling four children. She showed me her most recent literary efforts and the poems demonstrated that she had acquired a powerful voice: a keen, incisive, electrifying voice used to identify and disclose the travail of women. The following poem recorded her tearful, early morning awakening to the sickness unto death, an existential state of despair that resulted in a fateful decision to pursue therapy: "Then I did finally see / Really *see* her / She was everywhere: There when I woke in the morning / And with me during the day, / even while I was well occupied. / When she was still with me by night's fall / She gave me pause. / When she inhabited my nights / I finally heard her screams / And worse, the dead silence that surrounded her. / She was in a vacuum of silence / And I decided to / Go / Get Her Out."

In my mind, Sabrina was fast becoming a wonderful poet and I encouraged her to think about publishing a collection of her work. As time grew short and our visit was fast coming to an end, Sabrina glanced away; then she turned to me and said: "I don't know if I love you or if I'm in love with the words!" Perhaps Sabrina would never know the difference between her former therapist and his fair words. Strange as it may seem, there may be no difference in the enchanted clinic. But I thought about her discriminating remark for quite some time as I have carried an indelible memory of an earlier outside letter in which she stated forthrightly: "You have an unnerving ability to ask a simple question that leads to a startling realization. This is part of your gift and power. But it's driving me towards mental health, so I'm glad of it." Whatever else I might say about this patient and her particular enchantment with the clinic, her telling words triggered an unforgettable recollection of Plato's enchanting notion that the cure of souls is achieved by the use of charms, these charms being the healer's fair words.

Since that time, I have often thought that in the aftermath of the Freudian revolution, use of the mental health clinic and clinical confession were twin compulsions of many women and men during the twentieth century. While listening to a vast array of clinical confessions that offered a stunning introduction to every conceivable human pathos—from copulation with animals (Zoophilia) to the fine art of pulling out one's hair (Trichotollomania)—I began to realize that certain manifest pleasures of the clinic—a trustworthy, intimate dialogical relationship, the hope of cure, healthy narcissistic self-examination, cathartic relief from the verbal expression of emotionally charged events—are the foundation of a potentially life-affirming, albeit daemonic enchantment. I also began to entertain the hypothesis that for many symptomatic patients, particularly those who use the intimate space of the clinical confessional for liberation from real or imaginary demons, in spite of difficult struggles in the trenches, the mental health clinic may be experienced as a spellbinding safe haven invested with the magical power to cure, as well as with the magical power to entrance, enrapture, captivate, or charm. But when I speak of clinical enchantments or refer to entranced, enraptured, captivated, or charmed patients like Sabrina, I am not referring to my isolated case alone. Rather, I am suggesting that dialogical therapists of all manner and sort, irrespective of gender, ethnicity, personality type, credentials, and professional status, have the potential to become powerful, influential, imaginary persons in the eyes of emotionally impaired patients.

The salient point of this remark is that there are many ways of being perceived and imagined, many ways of being enchanting, and many ways of becoming enchanted. As a result, dialogical therapists may wish to undertake the interesting and important adventure of becoming observing egos in order to discover the characteristic ways in which their idiosyncratic gifts, their presentation of self, the clinical milieu they design and inhabit, can put them in possession of the power of the wizard for the benefit of patients.

CLINICAL NIHILISM

Consistent with Charcot's warning regarding the danger of clinical practices involving suggestion—hypnotic suggestion arising from, enhancing, often exaggerating the persuasive power and influence of mental health clinicians—I shall state at the outset that the opportunistic use of clinical enchantments, including erotic ties with vulnerable patients, raises complex questions of clinical ethics, as well as serious philosophic questions regarding clinical collusion in creating a veritable *"desert of the real itself"*; the imaginary desert is celebrated cultural critic Jean Baudrillard's derisive image of a destructive postmodern condition in which "truth, reference, objective cause have ceased to exist."[14] Stationed in this desert as a student of the mental health clinic and a dialogical therapist struggling against emotional illness in the clinical trenches, I am focused on the fact that in the aftermath of the Freudian revolution, modern psychologizers became advocates of a nihilistic disvaluation of truth in clinical practice. Indeed, while working to achieve a "triumph of the therapeutic," to use an incisive construction of sociologist, cultural historian, and Freudian scholar Philip Rieff, "psychological man" participated in the cultural integration of a clinical nihilism produced by blind, but well-intentioned, dialogical therapists who rejected Freud's presumptive love of truth, while developing therapeutic strategies and techniques as if nothing were at risk in the lives of patients or in the destiny of Western culture, "beyond a manipulatable sense of well-being."[15] As a result of the clinical assault on the blessed trinity—the classical, medieval, and modern trinity of objectivity, truth, and referential reality—in "Aberrations," part III of the text, I conceive the dialogical therapist as a potentially dangerous, ethically vulnerable *therapeutic artiste*, whose strategic encounters in the postmodern clinic are aesthetic experiences in which objectivity, truth, and reality are obsolete or irrelevant, in spite of clinical posturing that reinforces in suggestible patients a blind trust in the honesty, truthfulness, and intellectual integrity of psychological healers who may be likened to sorcerer's apprentices.

Alternately put, in the postmodern clinic, the generative Freudian project of unearthing the truth of childhood experience, repressed truth thought to be the underlying cause of morbid symptoms, has been replaced by the aesthetic act of creating enchanting myths, tall tales, or good stories, whose meaning, coherence, and beauty will hopefully activate and reinforce a sense of well-being in suggestible patients—objectivity, truth, and historical reality be damned! Given this clinical state of affairs, Baudrillard's postmodern complaint that "the passion for reality and the passion for truth have gone" appears to be true; however, his sightless rejoinder, "all that remains is a duty to reality, a duty to truth," is wildly and dangerously mistaken.[16] In fact, in the postmodern clinic, where the dialogical therapist's language, ideas, and speech have lost mooring to the perennial quest for truth that issued in Freud's professed desire to provide an *"education to reality,"* however misguided that education might have been, an anarchistic loss of rules has found a fabulous home (*FI*, 49).[17] The result is potentially catastrophic when one considers the fact that the first principle of anarchism, "anything goes," is now responsibly honored in the clinical trenches. For example, after debunking the Freudian quest for truth—the archeological dig to uncover repressed truths of childhood experience—and replacing this method of clinical encounter with the aesthetic act of creating a captivating story—a clinical fiction whose enchanting meaning and beauty may work a psychological healing on patients seduced into believing they are embraced by truth—one sober, self-reflective clinical storyteller confessed the anarchistic truth and its consequences rather anxiously: "If interpretations are creative rather than veridical and if the analyst functions more as a pattern maker than a pattern finder, then we may be faced with a glaring absence of general rules. . . . It makes each analyst even more alone than he is already; if there are almost no guidelines, then the risk of going wrong is sizably increased."[18]

Prescinding from consideration of the gross seduction of patients—the fact that unsuspecting men and women are seduced into falsely believing that clinical fiction is truth—this depiction of the absence of rules is not an overstatement of the current clinical situation. In order to initiate a responsible countermovement to clinical nihilism, thereby hoping to reduce the sizeable risk of going wrong while engaged in therapeutic dialogue with clinic patients, some of whom are destined to become erotically enchanted, I shall propose a measured anarchism that challenges every rule, method, and presupposition, including venerable *dogmas of the therapeutic*. In fact, while reflecting on a clinical ethic that is neither ruthless nor unscrupulous, I shall identify myself as a pragmatic existential therapist whose measured anarchism keeps clinical options open, while refusing to accept the nihilistic conclusion that anything goes. As the reader will see in various chapters that include dramatizations of therapeutic work with symptomatic patients like Eddie and Sabrina, a measured anarchism strives to be a responsible consideration of the methods, goals, strategies, and techniques working or waiting in the shadows of a pragmatic mental health clinic that traffics opportunistically in the enchantments of patients: clinical enchantments based less on veridical perception and reasoning, than on imaginary perception and erotic ties.

THE CRAZED SPECIES

I anticipate the responsible criticism that any claim I make regarding the human estate will be distorted by the quality of the evidence, specifically, the clinical confessions of pathological patients. After all, these are sick, irrational, suggestible people, as Freud stated forthrightly: men and women whose mental illness separates them presumably from the broader society of humans perceived and accepted as normal. Addressing this criticism head on, I shall state unequivocally that the highly functioning professional population I have treated in my private practice, as well as the chronically ill population I have treated in the psychiatric service of an urban American hospital—excluding psychotic individuals whose purchase on shared reality is compromised by hallucination, delusion, or severe dissociative disorders—are a representative sample of your neighbors: the men, women, and children living next door. In fact, the patients whose lived experience I dramatize here and there throughout the text could be your surgeon, your primary care physician, your nurse, your dentist, or your pharmacist; your child's schoolteacher, sitter, college dean, or best friend; the policeman handing you a traffic ticket or the judge assessing the fine; the butcher in your supermarket or the person delivering your mail; the chief executive officer of an international corporation manufacturing a consumer staple you recently purchased; the architect who designed or the contractor who constructed your new home; the person selling you a dress, a suit, or a new pair of shoes; the waiter or waitress in your favorite restaurant; your florist, your insurance agent, your rabbi, minister, or priest—even your trusted, seemingly well-balanced therapist. At one time or another these individuals have all confessed their secrets while sighing on my sofa and bemoaning the Sisyphean rock they are straining to push in their own private Hades. But don't be dismayed, for *Homo sapiens* is a crazed species and practically anyone you have contact with while engaged in the daily grind could populate my caseload of patients. None are exempt from failed wishes, hopes, and dreams; all have discovered the worries and the woes of existence; each has a peculiar discontent, a particular anguish, a precious torment. In short, everyone has a boulder to push, a body that bleeds and dies, and complex human relationships to manage in life-affirming or self-defeating ways.

In this broad interpersonal context of appearance and illusion, nothing is as sane or as rational as it seems. Clinical experience suggests that a man or a woman can be crazed in their personal life, while functioning at an extremely high level professionally, such that any person who plays the complementary role of the "other" would never detect how crazed a person in their field of vision can be. A person's relationship to self and others can be irrational, while that person achieves *arête* or excellence in his professional life. This is one of the more intriguing findings of my clinical experience: a surprising discovery of appearance and illusion totally unexpected when I was a younger man full of hope and dream and promise. For example, I once treated a physician obsessed by the agonizing belief that his penis was quite small. Dr. Klein confessed that he often compared the size of his organ to the size of a patient's penis. The comparison often resulted in a rabid, mute critique of himself, as well as hostile feelings of jealousy firmly attached to the unsuspecting patient in his care. Given Dr. Klein's obsession, his tortured psyche, his hostility, a discerning person would not dream of trusting this physician with the grave responsibility for life and death. Those were my thoughts when I first heard his clinical confession. But Dr. Klein performed admirably in the operating theatre and he gave every appearance of success, earning much money, power, and prestige, despite the longstanding derangement he suffered while heaving a huge boulder in Hades.

Mind you, I am not saying anything new when I speak of Dr. Klein or other members of the crazed species. Rather, I am reflecting on and reporting my clinical experience, while restating in a personal way, critical observations made long before I saw light of day. For example, in 1909, Freud's disciple, Sandor Ferenczi—a Hungarian neurologist, dedicated psychoanalyst, and avid psychohypnotist—stated unequivocally:

> The fundamental differences, assumed before Freud's time, between normal and psychoneurotic do not exist. . . . It may be considered as settled that there are only quantitative differences between "normal" and "psychoneurotic" mental processes, and that the results of mental investigation of psychoneurotics are also applicable to the psychology of the normal. . . . If we go deep enough into the mental life of any human being (whether "normal" or neurotic) we can find again, apart from quantitative differences, the same phenomena. (*IT*, 44, 52, 57)[19]

Late in his career, a disillusioned Freud put this clinical observation in a harsher way: "A normal ego . . . is, like normality in general, an ideal fiction. The abnormal ego . . . is unfortunately no fiction. Every normal person, in fact, is only normal on the average. His ego approximates to that of the psychotic in some part or other and to a greater of lesser extent" (*TI*, 235).[20] Of course neither Freud nor Ferenczi were developing a new line of thought. When he was eighty years old, disenchanted with the human experiment and in no mood to mince words, Plato (428–348 B.C.) stated forthrightly: "Humanity is in a condition of public war of every man against every man, and private war of each man with himself."[21]

Consistent with my personal view of the crazed species and the observations of Plato, Freud, and Ferenczi, clinical experience suggests that there is much value in the unique human capacity to channel irrational thinking, feeling, and behavior into some constructive, life-affirming activity. When we fail to channel our idiosyncratic derangements effectively, free-floating irrationality may metastasize and consume the psyche like a malignant cancer. In truth, mastering the conflicts of life constructively, by giving emotional impairment and behavioral dysfunction form and shape in some creative, life-affirming activity, is easier said than done, but it is not impossible, even in cases of severe impairment, examples of which one might never imagine. For example, Isaac Newton, who holds a seat of honor in the pantheon of modern science and is rivaled by Einstein alone, was a depressed, lonely, solitary man who never knew his biological father, was abandoned by his mother early on, and never had an intimate relationship with a woman. As a youth, he had bloody fistfights with peers, not to mention threatening to burn down his mother's house and his mother with it; he physically abused a half-sister and he was given to bouts of despair occasioned by suicidal ideation and a solemn wish for his death.[22] Later, Newton managed to channel the energy of severe impairment into scientific activity that resulted in the creation of laws of mechanics that altered scientific investigation and the human experiment perceptibly. At the university, of course, while being taught to honor the prince of science who drafted the mechanical architecture of the modern world, my fellow students and I learned much about Newton's scientific achievements, a magnificent remainder of death unlike most others; but we never learned about Newton's emotional illness or his severe behavioral dysfunction. These things were of no consequence to the cadre of students studying the philosophy of science while enthralled with the rationalist pretensions informing the life of mind.

In this regard, I am embarrassed to say, when I was a naïve young man harboring certain rational expectations in an ivory tower removed from the dirty trenches of clinical practice, I assumed rather blindly that a successful, highly functioning person possessed a good indwelling spirit and was well ordered in the soul or the psyche. But this is not true! Being a crazed human being involved in disordered relationships with self and others is a hidden aspect of a grand illusion of power, success, and well-being enacted not by a few, but by many. When false appearances are undressed in the clinical confessional, the playing field of human experience is leveled: each person in the food chain, caught up in the daily grind, regardless of ancestry, education, and socioeconomic status, is uniquely crazed, as if we all succumb to one or another personal insanity or derangement. Sometimes the crazed state is trifling, as it was with Dr. Klein; other times, the crazed condition is severe, as it was with Isaac Newton, who was a disenchanted prince of destruction before he became an enchanted prince of empirical science.

GUIDING PRINCIPLES

Fortunately, when a dynamic interpersonal relationship develops within the clinical confessional, particularly when a patient is clinically enchanted, I am able to use clinical power and influence to redirect free-floating irrationality in life-affirming ways. Often, to be as frank as Freud, I am involved in the activity of "talking people into or out of things—which is what my occupation consists in" (*FL*, 18). Less disillusioned than Freud about the crude realities of dialogical therapy, I am not prepared to belittle my vocation or to state consequentially that my involvement in persuasive dialogical activity "robs me of the best time for work."

The fact is, there is an art to talking people into and out of things: a fine art whose development and effective use hinges on a variety of critical factors. Not only the educational preparation, intellect, depth of life experience, cultural interests, capacity for insight, values, and emotional disorders of the therapist, but also the aesthetics of the clinical environment and the therapist's presentation of self, including manner of dress, forms of speech, facial expressions, bodily gestures—countless incalculable factors comprising authentic and inauthentic elements of conduct, ambience, and appearance. Whether strategically fashioned or not, these personal and dramaturgical aspects of the clinician's art will guide the selective impressions and uncritically accepted inferences of patients, thereby setting the stage in advance of treatment, for the historical creation and enactment of the plot, reversals, and denouement of the seductive psychological drama Freud referred to in a belittling, prosaic way as "talking people into or out of things."

In this artful context of power, eroticism, and illusion, I happen to be a pragmatic existential therapist who values the clinical enchantments that give me the power to use fair words to persuade symptomatic patients to modify their distorted needs, destructive core beliefs, and self-defeating behaviors. Nevertheless, my Sisyphean struggle caters to a meager few, not to the many. Accordingly, there is little I can do to check the unfolding drama of the crazed species except to honor the Socratic dream of reason, while remaining faithful to the ideal of self-examination and self-mastery the antique dream of reason commends.

Given these Socratic scruples and my functional role as a pragmatic existential therapist responsible for revising the ponderous philosophizing and clinically vacuous psychologizing of pioneering existential forbears, my struggle to have a remedial impact on the agonistic life of patients in my care is a direct challenge to Camus' paradigmatic analysis of the Homeric myth of Sisyphus: a clinical and a philosophic challenge to the hopelessness reinforcing Camus' defeated view that reason is useless to a lucid mind enlightened by the absurdities of existence; on the other hand, my clinical work and my philosophic vision honor Camus' underlying thesis that on occasion, happiness and the absurd are harmonious, rather than inimical.[23]

NOTES

1. Plato, *Charmides,* trans. Benjamin Jowett, in *The Collected Dialogues of Plato,* Bollingen Series 71, ed. Edith Hamilton and Huntington Cairns (Princeton, NJ: Princeton University Press, 1969), 157a.

2. Albert Camus, *The Myth of Sisyphus and Other Essays,* trans. Justin O'Brien (New York: Vintage Books, 1961), 65.

3. Jeffrey Moussaieff Masson, trans. and ed., *The Complete Letters of Sigmund Freud to Wilhelm Fliess, 1887–1904* (Cambridge: The Belknap Press, 1985); cited in the text as *FL.*

4. Sigmund Freud, *Group Psychology and the Analysis of the Ego,* in *The Standard Edition of the Complete Psychological Works of Sigmund Freud,* vol. 18, trans. James Strachey, in collaboration with Anna Freud, assisted by Alix Strachey and Alan Tyson (London: The Hogarth Press and the Institute of Psycho-Analysis, 1975); cited in the text as *GR.*

5. Plato, *Meno,* trans. W. K. C. Guthrie, in *Collected Dialogues,* 80a–b.

6. Michel Foucault, *The History of Sexuality: An Introduction,* vol. 1, trans. Robert Hurley (New York: Vintage Books, 1990), 45.

7. Sigmund Freud, *Introductory Lectures on Psycho-Analysis* (Part III), in *Standard Edition,* vol. 16 (1963); cited in the text as *IL.*

8. Jerome D. Frank and Julia B. Frank, *Persuasion and Healing: A Comparative Study of Psychotherapy* (Baltimore: Johns Hopkins University Press, 1993), 35.

9. Albert Ellis, *Reason and Emotion in Psychotherapy* (Secaucus, NJ: Citadel Press, 1977), 19, 22, 104.

10. Søren Kierkegaard, *The Sickness Unto Death,* in *"Fear and Trembling" and "The Sickness Unto Death,"* trans. Walter Lowrie (New York: Doubleday & Company, 1954), 150–54.

11. Frank and Frank, *Persuasion and Healing,* 34–35.

12. Plato, *Symposium,* trans. Michael Joyce, in *Collected Dialogues,* 203d.

13. Plato, *Republic,* trans. Paul Shorey, in *Collected Dialogues,* 403a

14. Jean Baudrillard, *Simulacra and Simulation,* trans. Sheila Faria Glaser (Ann Arbor: University of Michigan Press, 2000), 1.

15. Philip Rieff, *The Triumph of the Therapeutic: Uses of Faith after Freud* (New York: Harper & Row, Publishers, 1966), 13.

16. Jean Baudrillard, *The Intelligence of Evil or the Lucidity Pact,* trans. Chris Turner (Oxford: Berg Publishers, 2005), 19.

17. Sigmund Freud, *The Future of an Illusion,* in *Standard Edition,* vol. 21 (1961); cited in the test as *FI.*

18. Donald P. Spence, *Narrative Truth and Historical Truth: Meaning and Interpretation in Psychoanalysis* (New York: W. W. Norton & Company, 1982), 292–94.

19. Sandor Ferenczi, "Introjection and Transference," in *Sex in Psychoanalysis (Contributions to Psycho-Analysis),* trans. Ernest Jones (New York: Dover Publications, 1956); cited in the text as *IT.*

20. Sigmund Freud, *Analysis Terminable and Interminable,* in *Standard Edition,* vol. 23 (1975); cited in the text as *TI.*

21. Plato, *Laws,* trans. A. E. Taylor, in *Collected Dialogues,* 626d.

22. Details of Newton's impairment were confirmed in James Gleick, *Isaac Newton* (New York: Vintage Books, 2003), 3–19.
23. Camus, *Myth of Sisyphus*, 27, 90.

I

THEMES

1

The Erotization of the Clinic

HAWTHORNE'S WARNING

I had the pleasure recently of rereading Karl Menninger's *Theory of Psychoanalytic Technique,* a didactic text I had not touched since I was an eager undergraduate taking an introductory course in clinical psychology. While reacquainting myself with Menninger's analysis of *erotization resistance*—the erotization of psychoanalysis having been conceived by Menninger as a regressive obstruction of treatment in which the analysand converts the clinical relationship into a physically pleasurable sexual experience—I came upon a peculiar footnote referring to Nathaniel Hawthorne's dismal view of the physician-patient relationship. Evidently, when I was a naïve undergraduate engrossed in early studies of philosophy and psychology, Menninger's reference to Hawthorne's "remarkable comment" failed to draw my attention, for I normally write copious notes in the margins of books, given my tendency to engage in Socratic argument with the authors I happen to be reading; but there were no jottings to indicate that this odd footnote interested me in the least (*TP*, 12).[1] Now, however, in the wake of copious clinical experience, I found the reference intriguing and my curiosity was piqued, so I paused to read *The Scarlet Letter* and soon I was arrested by a psychological fiction that dramatized a deformed doctor's unrelenting quest to identify the paramour of his spouse, the young, beautiful Hester Prynne, whose stern Puritan community forced her to wear the scarlet letter *A* on her breast: a shameful *A* that identified Prynne as a passionate adulteress who had willfully tasted the forbidden fruit of sexual sin. More importantly, I also found Hawthorne warning his readers to avoid intimacy with physicians: not sexual intimacy, but the confessional intimacy that soon would become the pulsating heart of psychoanalysis in the clinical consulting room of Freud (*SL*, 157).[2]

After digesting Hawthorne's moody allegory of sin, shame, and sorrow, I became haunted by his warning, not because he saw the clinical relationship through a dark glass, for this eminent American dramatist saw humankind through a dark glass and he indulged his gloomy vision by framing Hester Prynne's experience of sex, secrecy, and confession in a grim Puritan era in which the act of being human was corrected in the marketplace, in the light of day, by shameful confinement in the pillory, scourging at the whipping post, branding by hot iron, hanging on the gallows, or some other chilling public penance. In truth, I became haunted by Hawthorne's warning because it evidenced the author's astute awareness of the prodigious power and influence of the physician: suggestive power and influence that accrues to dialogical therapists in the clinical confessional. But Hawthorne perceived the clinician's power and influence as daemonic. As a result, this interesting, important, clinically useful "power over the spirits," to use a Faustian reference of the early hypnotic-minded Freud, was treated as a pernicious part of the healer's strategic art of persuasion (*FL*, 21).

In his literary warning, to put a fine point on my reactive reading of Hawthorne, a nineteenth-century author of psychological fiction bequeathed to twentieth-century authors of psychological theory—such as the renowned, shortsighted, morally scrupulous Menninger—a daemonic vision of the power of the clinical confessor and the potential destructiveness of the clinical confession of secrets. During the twentieth century, therefore, it came to pass that an eminent dramatist and an eminent dialogical therapist became enmeshed in a common blindness: an inability to see the erotization of the clinical relationship as a powerful therapeutic tool whose proper use and effective management could facilitate the healing of emotional wounds in symptomatic patients who happen to experience life-affirming enchantments of the clinic.

In the imaginary world of psychological fiction, Hester Prynne's cuckolded husband, the venomous, vengeful, intellectually cultivated healer, Roger Chillingworth, was a skilled physician who "during his Indian captivity, had enlarged his medical attainments by joining in the incantations of . . . savage priests . . . universally acknowledged to be powerful enchanters, often performing seemingly miraculous cures by their skill in the black art" (*SL*, 161). Consistent with the daemonic spirit of this psychological fiction, in the serviceable world of shared experience, where the mental health clinic has a formal role and function, it is widely believed that there is something sinister, suspicious, and potentially evil in the black art of enchantment, as there was "something ugly and evil" in the deformed doctor conceived by Hawthorne as a "diabolical agent [who] had . . . permission . . . to burrow into [a] man's intimacy" (*SL*, 162). As a result of this negative animus toward enchantments that give some people power and influence over others, Hawthorne's dark vision of the clinical confessor who uses the black art of enchantment to pry into the secrets of unsuspecting patients produced a classic fiction that captured a meaningful human conflict of sex, secrecy, and confession in an austere, morally upright Puritan era. Nevertheless, as an ominous warning to people who shelter oppressive secrets—a precise warning to avoid the clinical confession of sexual secrets—Hawthorne's dark vision of the doctor-confessor is a distortion of the enchantments of the clinic, the charms of the clinical confessor, and the potentially helpful effect of clinical confession: a living distortion of clinical experience that survives unmolested in the underworld of the psyche and in the modern world of psychological theory—both worlds of which survive and flourish in a morally vacuous postmodern era.

Having no way of foreseeing that a young, pioneering Dr. Freud would soon conceive psychoanalysis as a clinical intimacy built upon a full confession of secrets, Hawthorne put pen to paper in 1849 and imaged his devilish doctor as a "treasure-seeker in a dark cavern": a kind and friendly appearing healer who descends into a patient's bosom to examine moral principles, to pry into recollections, to probe and to penetrate secrets (*SL*, 157). Given the power and influence of the physician—suggestive power and influence issuing from the physician's seemingly heroic ability to descend into the valley of the beast to combat the fearsome demons, illness and death—Hawthorne warned his readers that even closely guarded secrets would not escape the ear of a clinical confessor who has the opportunity, the license, and the mental skill to undertake a penetrating inquisition. Specifically, if a physician uses his intuitive power of mind to achieve psychological "affinity" with the mind of a patient, receiving each disclosure with some sign of understanding, however mute, the soul of a resisting patient will inevitably dissolve, revealing all the sins, all the shameful secrets, all the mysteries of self hidden beyond the drawn interior (*SL*, 157).

In view of his incisive warning, it seems as if Hawthorne anticipated Freud, for during the halcyon days of psychoanalysis, when Freud was holding court in Vienna, he claimed that confession was "an introduction" to psychoanalysis (*QL*, 189).[3] Not the essence of analysis, of course, because in Freud's inventive mind, the clinical confession of secrets was merely an essential first step in a protracted dig of the psyche undertaken to uncover unconscious roots of psychopathology. Nevertheless, given Hawthorne's daemonic view of the clinical confessor's power and influence, one can imagine how startled he would have been to foresee that approximately thirty-six years after publication of *The Scarlet Letter*, Freud would spend time studying hypnotism with Charcot at the storied Salpêtrière mental hospital in Paris, ultimately adding hypnotic suggestion to the formidable inquisitorial skills of the clinical confessor. Although the dramatic action of *The Scarlet Letter* shows that Hawthorne understood as much as Freud about the reciprocal interaction of sex, secrecy, and confession and the daemonic energy that grows around sexual secrets—*sex leads to secrecy leads to confession*—Hawthorne and Freud were oceans apart in thinking and in vocation. On the American side of the Atlantic, Hawthorne was a solitary soul whose hard-minded realism resulted in a tragic experience of self, life, and world resulting in the view that the great mistakes humans make rarely, if ever, are righted. Consequently the confession of a mistake, particularly a sexual mistake, is bound to result in personal misfortune or disaster. On the European continent, by contrast, Freud's clinical life was motivated by the desire and the will to set aright the dark, distorted world of the human psyche. Accordingly, in Freud's clinical consulting room, the full confession of self, particularly the sexual self, was destined to become an essential first step in the therapeutic process of psychological healing and self-liberation: a clinical process advanced initially by "the miracle of suggestion" (*FL*, 18n2).

In the wake of a fine body of dramatic fiction, Hawthorne died in 1864, eight years after the birth of Freud. Unfortunately, he had no way of knowing the fate of his warning, although one may venture the guess that due to his dark vision of the human estate, he expected his warning to fall on deaf ears or to fall with dire consequences to anyone who happened to hear it. Perhaps Hawthorne would have been surprised to learn that his puritanical warning resonated with Karl Menninger, a modern dialogical therapist who found it reasonable to publish a post-Freudian theory of therapy that taught the students of his day to reject the erotization of the clinic, insofar as erotization is obstructive, immoral, and always harmful to clinic patients.

THE SCARLET CLINIC

Embracing the drama of *The Scarlet Letter* and the spirit of Hawthorne's warning in his seminal text, Menninger conceived psychoanalysis as a "never-ending duel between the analyst and the patient's resistance"; viewing the patient as a person "divided against himself," not only desirous of change and well-being, but also reluctant to change and thus willing to remain ill, Menninger defined resistance as "the trend of forces within the patient which oppose the process of ameliorative change" (*TP*, 102,

104). Although he resolved the duel between therapist and patient in favor of the therapist, as Hawthorne resolved the daemonic struggle between doctor and patient in favor of the misshapen doctor who used "the black art of enchantment" to quest for sexual secrets by prying into the soul of unsuspecting patients, Menninger argued in classic psychoanalytic fashion that the patient is a defensive confessor from the onset of analysis: an emotionally impaired person who "unintentionally but purposively obstructs the very process upon which he counts so heavily" (*TP*, 101).

Menninger clearly championed the image of psychoanalysis as a never-ending duel between clinical confessor and clinical confessant, thereby appearing to convert an engaging literary fiction into modern psychoanalytic theory, but he did not invent the idea of erotization resistance; rather, he was leaning heavily on Freud, whose patients taught him to focus critically on the relationship between physician and patient. Specifically, Freud came to understand that the relationship between physician and patient, analyst and analysand, clinical confessor and clinical confessant, rests precariously on a continuum between two extremes: on the one hand, "passionate, completely sensual love," on the other, "embittered defiance and hatred" (*AS*, 42).[4] Early clinical experience also taught Freud that if a patient's libidinal attachment happened to be "affectionate and moderate" it functioned as an instrument or an important "agent" of his clinical power and "influence"; however, if a patient's erotic tie was "passionate" or suffused with "hostility" it functioned as a resistance to his clinical power and influence: specifically, the patient's interpersonal ability became frozen and the erotization of the clinic became "the principal tool of the resistance" insofar as the libidinal attachment, the erotic tie, effectively "replaces . . . the desire to be cured" (*AS*, 42). While this is enlightening and sometimes true, my experience in the clinical confessional suggests that the therapeutic struggle is not this cut and dried.

If the reader will recall, I previously introduced Sabrina, a demoralized patient whose illuminating letters document an erotization of the clinic from the patient's point of view, not from the vantage point of the therapist as is customarily the case in clinical reportage. Not surprisingly, given her suggestibility—including (a) a history of being controlled by others, (b) an unfulfilled need for intimate communication, (c) receptivity to the therapeutic eros of a clinician, therapeutic eros she conceived as "steadiness, warmth, and deliberation," in conjunction with (d) the seductive intimacy of the clinical confessional and (e) the charming words of a clinical confessor whose therapeutic eros created a psychological "affinity" in the mind of his patient—in one of her outside letters Sabrina commented on her erotic tie to her therapist and the fact that this libidinal attachment became a passionate preoccupation for a time. Not so much a principal tool of resistance that effectively replaced the desire to be cured, as Freud and Menninger maintained, but a compelling passion that consumed her mind and her heart while the principal work of psychological healing proceeded apace. Nevertheless, Sabrina's erotic tie evidenced the fact that the erotization of the clinic is a risky affair that may leave a patient emotionally stuck or suspended if a release from the erotic enchantment is not achieved during the normal course of treatment. To demonstrate the point, I am excerpting a letter that followed the termination of treatment before the erotic tie was properly unraveled. In this confessional letter sent to "someone who has written on my heart," Sabrina confessed:

> Dr. E: Recently, I was thinking that it may have been audacious for me to refer to my mother as a "functional schizophrenic," when I think where my dreams, desires, and fantasies have led me. You stay with me so strongly, or I keep you with me, that I miss your words, that I take consolation you cannot imagine from the fact that you ushered me to the spectacular. I am out here away from you, but I am learning to do it!
>
> But I digress. I wanted to make a point about functional schizophrenia. I spent a lot of time in my transference with you. Group therapy was a good stepping-stone. I see now that in Individual Therapy (which I'd love more of) I was focusing on rapture that all ties in to you. So here is this man—the first man for all the big stuff in life. A therapist whom I am incapable of addressing without an honorific title, yet envision strolling galleries and sharing time with. So much conflicting stuff that seems never ending. But I'm sorting it out. Let's see my ability to "not let the rapture pass me by." Let's see me do life. Deal!
>
> I remember well my intention to be a responsible and "star" patient. I've danced around trying, but also wanting to be more than in your periphery. Why am I doing this? I must think you have a cancellation! I must think your caseload is wanting! I must think you're dying to know these ravings of a woman consumed! ENOUGH! I, I, I, I! Really, I wanted you to know that I'm out here working and that it just feels good to say: I think of you, I miss you, I thank you, and keep you in high esteem.

For the reader's information, when clinical treatment terminated prematurely due to the financial burden of protracted therapy, Sabrina's spouse had commenced treatment with his own therapist in an effort to save his marriage. Noteworthy is the fact that Gerald achieved abstinence from alcohol while undertaking the equally difficult work of making attitudinal changes that would enhance his sensitivity to Sabrina's emotional needs. Moreover, as previously stated, Sabrina's morbid symptoms gradually remitted. By all accounts, her therapeutic gain was remarkable as the following letter written toward the end of our formal clinical relationship suggested: "Dr. E: Last year I thought I'd die. To say I was operating a step away from automatic pilot is optimistic. This summer was a summer of my dreams. In one year I went from feeling like human waste to feeling truly extraordinary. I've settled down now, far away from the former and a proper distance from the latter. So here comes the ride." Sabrina signed this letter "With thanks, respect and admiration." Needless to say, a dedicated dialogical therapist couldn't ask for more following a battle against illness in the clinical trenches.

In spite of her life-affirming forward movement—important elements of which could be symbolized by the fact that she went from being a silent little mouse who could not speak to being the proverbial mouse that roared—given the circus and circumstance of life in the clinical trenches, I realized that the premature termination of treatment was not going to allow me sufficient time to unravel Sabrina's erotic enchantment. Mind you, I had already begun the important process of disenchantment knowing that I would be releasing Sabrina from my care one day in the future. In part, this involved the strategic game of putting Sabrina in the position of making her own decisions and choices—a state of affairs she found frustrating: "The essential point of therapy," she wrote, "not offering comfort, but rather frustration in order to change, well I see this. I feel it. I'm going to have to face things. Choose. Rather than let life unfold as I've done." In another telling letter, Sabrina evidenced her budding disenchantment by suggesting that we see things as we are, rather than seeing things the way they are. Commenting further on her disenchantment, Sabrina expressed the critical insight that her therapist was "imperfect":

> Dr. E: I'm quite preoccupied with today's session and the sessions of the past few weeks. Some kind of "reality" (for lack of a better word) rears its ever-present head in all relations and these sessions marked when I started looking at *you* as other than this perfect therapist. You have helped me along in that regard. Nonetheless you are somehow (and strangely) familiar to me. It's the only word I can come up with. I'm thinking that some separateness, might put one in place for a healthy and grand passion. For rapture. That's what I'm thinking today, as I plot out how I take this leap from my Oceanside cliff. Overlooking not an abyss, as I thought, but rather enticing and sparkling waters.

As a secondary solution to the unfinished business of disenchantment, with Sabrina's consent, I implemented a new treatment plan that included transfer to a cost-effective woman's therapy group I facilitated with my clinical partner, JCG. At the time, I believed that Sabrina would use group therapy to consolidate the considerable gains she already achieved; I also hoped that the dynamics of dialogical engagement with other women, including my female partner, would facilitate the important process of releasing Sabrina from the hypnotic embrace she experienced in the intimate space of the private confessional. Although she remained in the women's group for a reasonable period of time, clearly benefiting from a variety of supportive and challenging peer interactions, by the time of termination, when we bid farewell, the vaunted disenchanting release from the hypnotic embrace of the clinical confessor failed to occur successfully. The following letter received in the aftermath of termination painted a picture of a woman consumed by a passionate remembrance of things past: a painful remembrance indicating unequivocally that this erotization of the clinic—once an agent of clinical power and influence—had been terribly mismanaged:

> Dr. E: I have many long letters piling up, but suffice it to say, simply, thank you. As I look over group and what it has done for me, I marvel again at your work. That you chose to treat me with genuine compassion is deeply felt. That group was, in part, a good "weaning" was . . . well, maybe you are a genius, Did you ever consider that is true? I have much left to do. Much work. But I have an awareness and I am building skills or abilities. That is not to say that I don't literally ache for you. I still wonder at that and time will tell me more about it. A long time ago I felt myself stand taller and feel better to know that I could come across as extraordinary! Not by just anybody, but by someone I hold in the highest esteem. Permit me to presume, for a moment, that it matters in the grand scheme of the world that I feel such for you. What feels like a shearing separation right now, and saying "see you!" to the safety of you, will, I suspect, lead me to a new security. And if not, I'll be back! But as I continue to turn from "safety" at least I know what is true here, in me.

Giving imaginative expression to his personal experience of clinical erotization, Menninger identified erotization resistance as an unintentional obstruction of treatment in which the patient converts the clinical relationship into an illegitimately pleasurable sexual experience. Availing himself of Freudian theory regarding discrete stages of psychosexual development, Menninger continued his exposition by speculating wildly about a deep erotization of the clinical situation, averring that the patient's body experiences an illicit physical pleasure related to the oral, anal, and genital experience of the developing child: a gratification of libidinal desire that issues in an obstructive resistance to psychological treatment and recovery. Reflecting soberly on the patient's erotization of the clinic as if he were delivering a stern religious sermon in the grim Puritan era depicted so ably by Hawthorne, Menninger concluded his commentary on erotization resistance with the following authoritative moral judgment: "The analysand is asking for something improper and—by our standards—immoral. It is immoral in the same sense that giving morphine to an addict would be immoral. The thing wanted is self-destructive, and hence to yield to the importunity, no matter how urgent, is to assist in *hurting*, not helping the patient; and the patient *knows* this. Hence all erotization is an attempted distraction and seduction, a wish to remain ill and to hurt the analyst in revenge (for his alleged seduction of the patient) as well as himself (the analysand) in propitiation" (*TP*, 117).

As a pragmatic existential therapist who has experienced measurable progress with male and female patients who eroticized the clinical relationship, I am convinced that Menninger was misguided in his moralistic judgment of the scarlet clinic. In fact, I am prepared to argue that Menninger inherited two preeminent *dogmas of the therapeutic* that predetermined his stilted argument against random erotizations of the clinic: not only a solemn rule prohibiting harm to patients, but a stern rule forbidding sexual contact with the vulnerable human beings in one's charge. Of course Menninger was not alone in his inheritance of these dogmas, for mental health clinicians uniformly inherit and guide their clinical behavior with reference to uncritically accepted rules of practice and norms of behavior they inherit and may carry unawares. In Menninger's case, he was informed by two dogmas that resulted in the harsh moralistic judgment that any and all erotization of the clinic is a violation of seemingly fixed, inviolable rules of clinical encounter.

In the Greek lexicon, "dogma" means *that which seems* such and so. In view of its *seeming* so, like an oar underwater that seems to be bent, but actually is refracted, a particular opinion or belief may carry the day and after a time it becomes sedimented and self-evident: an authoritative opinion or belief not only widely accepted, but never critically examined because it is experienced as the fixed foundation of a structure of thought or a set of behaviors upon which all other activity in a field of action and reaction rests. I shall say more about dogmas of the therapeutic in chapter 8, "Anarchism and Ethics." For now, suffice it to say, the problem with dogmas is this: whatever their real value or worth in the human community, dogmatic beliefs seem to be an unimpeachable foundation of thinking and behavior. More often than not, large numbers of people are led in the direction dictated by a dogma and they are led uncritically, like children who are enthralled by a parent's godlike power and authority. Putting this sentiment differently, while speaking of rules and their observance in *Remarks on the Foundations of Mathematics*, Wittgenstein observed that we are not so much interested in the fact that human beings have been led in a particular direction by certain rules; rather, "we take it as a matter of course that people—'if they can think correctly'—go *this* way. We have now been given a *road* . . . by means of the footsteps of those who have gone this way. And the traffic now proceeds on this road—to various purposes."[5] Of course the existential purposes may be life-affirming, self-defeating, or worse, collectively destructive.

In view of this danger, the virtue of anarchists is that they question dogmas, thereby placing fellow humans in the Socratic position of determining critically whether a seemingly true or valid, self-evident or unimpeachable, belief has value and is able to carry its weight. For perspective, I shall venture the picturesque notion that humankind is no longer cave-bound because in days of yore, when pre-human creatures huddled in caves around a warm, mysterious fire whose elements were unknown, an anarchistic cave-dweller thought against the visceral sensibility and seemingly self-evident, emotionally charged beliefs of his clan. After bidding farewell to fearful fellows who were convinced that certain death awaited anyone who ventured too far beyond the known world of the cave, the anarchical cave-dweller rose from his fixed place around the warm fire, stretched his hairy legs, grabbed his spear, and never stopped walking until he discovered what seemed to be a promised land, although further discovery revealed the crude fact that the land of milk and honey was also populated by fierce carnivores capable of tearing fragile flesh from bony body parts and appendages.

Menninger was not a cave-dweller; in fact, he was a highly respected member of his clinical clan and his obedience to dogmatic authority is intelligible, considering the risk of mismanaging and harming emotionally disordered patients in the scarlet clinic. But there are times when the erotization of the clinic is not a regressive obstruction of dialogical therapy; rather, by virtue of the power and influence erotization invests in therapists who are practicing the strategic art of psychological healing, an erotization of the clinic may be a useful instrument or tool that assists a therapist in the clinical trenches during difficult dialogical struggles against illness and death. As the reader will shortly see during an anecdotal presentation of the case of Francine, rather than obstructing treatment counter-therapeutically, an erotization of the clinic may be part of a clinical enchantment that facilitates successful treatment, while *obstructing termination* of treatment after symptoms remit and patients are invited to cooperate in a planned farewell enabling them to leave the clinic and get on with the normal business of flourishing in life independently.

In the final analysis, if managed effectively, and often this is easier said than done, a pragmatic therapist can use an erotization of the clinic opportunistically to guide the self-discovery, personal growth, and psychological healing of the emotionally impaired human beings in his care. The pioneering Freud understood this early on when he was inspired to deviate from formal neurological work to give birth to psychological healing as a form of hypnotic influence that used a patient's libidinal attachment to the therapist as a strategic means to life-affirming clinical ends. Given my personal experience in the scarlet clinic, this is a libidinal attachment or an "erotic tie" that issues from unpredictable enchantments of the clinic during which seemingly entranced patients appear to fall under the spell of a dialogical therapist who may be likened to a charming wizard whose suggestive language and ideas have persuasive power and clinical influence.

BASIC INSTINCTS

Many patients find dialogical therapy rich in meaning, particularly when they have been dispossessed of meaning, purpose, and hope in important aspects of their life. For some, the weekly dialogical interaction becomes a style of life; for others, the clinical marriage becomes a surrogate existence, particularly when emotionally needy patients develop a confessional intimacy with a dialogical partner they are paying to be their trusted therapist. Francine demonstrated this beautifully when she resisted my attempt to terminate treatment following cooperative clinical work that resulted in a remission of morbid symptoms and a general recovery of well-being. In this interesting case that set a memorable precedent for others, rather than obstructing clinical treatment in the manner argued by the morally scrupulous Menninger, Francine's erotization of the clinic obstructed the termination of successful treatment, insofar as she demonstrated an unwillingness to separate herself from her therapist and the enticing enchantments she experienced within the clinical confessional.

Following a psychosocial evaluation in the hospital's adult outpatient clinic, Francine received prescriptions for medication to relieve florid symptoms of anxiety and depression. During the introductory phase of our dialogical work she was guarded and reluctant to reveal herself in spite of my best efforts to invite clinical confession during the initial phase of the game of capture and surrender. This made our first few conversations uneasy, but I was still pleased to see her, for she offered me an agreeable break from listening to the extremely disturbed psychotic patients who were the stock and trade of the urban hospital where I became accustomed to treating a full range of psychopathology: everything from simple Adjustment Disorders to Schizophrenia to compulsively pulling-out one's hair. Adding to my pleasure was the undeniable fact that Francine was a stunning woman in her mid-thirties: a petite, fawnlike mortal who caused me grief whenever she came to the clinic, the reason being that my colleagues never tired of ribbing me for being "the one who gets all the beauties."

While working successfully with Francine to help her (a) grieve the death of a beloved surrogate mother, (b) deal more effectively with the continuing stress of a conflicted relationship with a younger man she hoped to marry, and (c) resolve problems of personality that negatively impacted advancement in her professional life, the hospital mandated brief therapy for all but our severely and persistently mentally ill patients. Responding constructively to this administrative mandate that came on the heels of the hospital's involvement in managed healthcare, I developed and subsequently published a time-limited version of pragmatic existential therapy useful in treating less seriously afflicted patients like Francine.[6]

Fortunately, she had been in treatment for almost one year and as a result of medication, grief counseling, and an existential intervention that facilitated decisions, choices, commitments, and actions that moved her out of a variety of self-defeating positions in her personal and professional life, Francine experienced a gradual remission of symptoms and I moved toward a planned termination of treatment consistent with hospital policy—a policy, I should add, that clinical colleagues and I found abhorrent.

When I first addressed the issue of termination, Francine was angry, hurt, and resistant, and she expressed her feelings openly, having learned through our clinical encounter to advocate for herself. Speaking as though I had pulled the proverbial rug from under her feet, she asked how I could do such a thing, after which she barked resoundingly: "This is part of my life!"

This business of therapy becoming part of a person's life should not be underestimated or taken lightly, not the least reason being that it applies to men and women alike. In fact, as I write these thoughts, I am having the intriguing experience of treating men who initially were mandated to treatment by their spouses, as if these women were presiding judges in family court. After successfully engaging in dialogical therapy for treatment of unruly symptoms or some noteworthy aspect of marital dysfunction—often anger or lack of emotional intimacy—these men continued regular office visits as a matter of course, as though they had become enchanted with the clinic, enthused with therapy, or simply accustomed to being embraced by and actively responding to a therapist's fair words. To my dismay, perplexed female spouses have asked their husbands why they remain in treatment: after all, "you're better!" is the common refrain. The gentlemen, who have become productive dialogical partners, often do not know what to say. Embarrassed by the fact that they want to remain in treatment, when clearly there is no apparent need, they customarily lay the issue on the table during the clinical hour, not only reporting the challenging conversation with their perplexed spouses, but also asking my impression, as if they are ashamed of engaging in an unmanly interpersonal relationship and seeking sufficient reason to justify maintaining a clinical relationship that had become an important part of their life. Given replications of this intriguing experience, I recently asked a highly verbal male patient to identify his reason for remaining in treatment when clearly his wife correctly saw and confronted him with the fact that he was better. "Your symptoms are in remission, you are doing very well, so why do you continue coming every other week?" I asked. After careful thought, the gentleman responded by saying: "Therapy is important because it's quiet time; it's dedicated time; it keeps me grounded."

This happens to be a patient's useful formulation of his need to continue dialogical therapy in order to consolidate gains and maintain emotional well-being following agonistic struggles in the clinic. On the other hand, this man's wife wanted her husband to be grounded in her, and to be grounded in her exclusively. Who can blame her? After all, she sent her husband for treatment for this very reason! Threatened by the fact that therapy had become a vital part of her husband's life, she insisted that he was better, not willing to countenance the fact that he was having intimate conversations with another person when there was no apparent need to continue speaking. Commonly at this pass, the clinical relationship is doomed and for some patients, dialogical therapy will no longer remain a vital part of life. But in the case of Francine, things were dramatically different.

At first blush, Francine's testy response to termination suggested a Borderline Personality Disorder: an enduring illness marked by labile emotions, chaotic and unstable interpersonal relationships, fear of abandonment, and a good measure of rage, among other characteristic features that manifest a maladaptive way of interacting with people. Consistent with this diagnostic impression, a patient's resistance to termination could be seen as an effort to avoid the real or imagined rejection or abandonment experienced early on, when the patient was a child. This clinical impression fit Francine perfectly, without the need to stretch clinical impressions on Procrustes' infamous bed; for her biological mother was a cold, emotionally distant woman who failed to bond with her daughter due to serious emotional impairments resulting from the suicide of her own birth mother. Nevertheless, Francine's resistance to termination included other important variables as well. Where else would she find a nonjudgmental partner devoted to hearing and to healing her anguish? Who else could she find to provide a safe confessional intimacy that feeds primary narcissism by promoting unremitting self-reflection and unrelenting self-talk? No wonder demoralized patients cross the threshold of the clinic and find themselves moving ineluctably from an impotent disenchantment with life to an empowering enchantment with the clinic, as disabling symptoms are displaced by fair words, morbidity by hope, the rude whisper of death in mental illness by a newly found pleasure in a promising affirmation of life.

In short, some patients become enthused with dialogical therapy: an enthusiasm evoking the literal meaning of the Greek *entheos*, to be inspired or possessed as if by a god. Additionally, as the early Freud, disciples like Ferenczi, and legions of dialogical therapists discovered since that time, some patients experience "an enthusiasm . . . bordering on adoration" in their intimate confessional relationships with trusted clinical helpers (*IT*, 53).

Adoration can take many forms and it can be expressed in a variety of ways, but the following verbal snippets given to my clinical partner, JCG, by an adult female patient she referred to me for treatment of a Panic Disorder is a representative sample of an enchanted patient's enthusiastic adoration: "Dr. Ellerman has been my savior. I have a connection with him I've never had with anyone else before. He's genuinely caring. He's my rock. He's been such a help throughout this ordeal. I'm in it for the long run with him. I have a lot of issues never put to rest. At the end of the day I'll do anything to stay with him."

In truth, Victoria's experience of therapy was gratifying to hear and her adoration was flattering, but she happened to be a woman who could not afford the handsome fee I charge for clinical services in my private practice. When I attempted to explore the rational option of treatment elsewhere, with a therapist who was a participating provider in her health insurance plan, Victoria insisted that her weekly therapy with me was worth the financial sacrifice she and her family were making. But this was an enthusiasm for therapy, a libidinal connection with a therapist, and a family's financial burden that had a life in a controlling, unread, not yet deciphered drama of childhood.

Specifically, Victoria's father was a critical, rejecting, emotionally unavailable, prickly sort of man. As often happens in cases of this sort, during adolescence and in adulthood, Victoria felt a connection with and was erotically drawn to unavailable males. Predictably, her imaginary therapist was a perfect man: a clinically charming, unavailable man a laser-like libido "chose" to play a part in Victoria's recurring psychodynamic drama of compensating for the past, of becoming liberated from an emotional fixation of childhood, of mastering the felt-experience of failure to secure a father's elusive love. In spite of the financial burden of dialogical therapy, becoming enthused in an eroticized clinic gave Victoria the opportunity to once again try to break down the defense and win the love of an unavailable man whose imaginary charms were chains of illusion. Still, like Sabrina and Francine, Victoria's adoration did not result in an obstruction of treatment, but her enthusiasm confirmed the value of Freud's focus on the intense emotional relationship between clinician and patient, particularly the "hypnotic *rapport*" or as I would say, the clinical enchantment experienced by patients who become enraptured with dialogical therapists while in their care (*AS*, 42).

Regarding this generally unpredictable cognitive-emotional condition, Freud maintained that psychoanalysis, as well as other methods of psychotherapy—dialogical therapy in every form and manifestation— "employs the instrument of suggestion" and when hypnotic rapport is achieved, it "is used . . . to induce the patient to perform . . . mental work" crucial to clinical success (*AS*, 43). In my personal experience, the enthusiasm, the hypnotic rapport, the adoration, the enchantment, is a therapeutic tool that gives an opportunistic therapist the power to influence patients in life-affirming ways, providing the therapist understands the pitfalls and charts his clinical course with a moral compass focused on the patient's best interest. The problem is, these unpredictable enchantments must be well-managed and this is no small task, for the patient's adoration and hypnotic rapport may lead to "incalculable behaviour" as Freud noted, certainly more serious than Francine's resistance to termination (*AS*, 42). Mention of incalculable behavior puts me in mind of Freud's one-time friend and collaborator, Josef Breuer, particularly the result of the counter-transference this respected Viennese physician experienced in the famous founding case of Anna O.

It came to pass that Bertha Pappenheim, a hysteric given the pseudonym "Anna O" by Breuer, was able to successfully induce autohypnotic states. Bertha and Breuer chanced to discover that when she talked while entranced, she experienced a temporary remission of florid symptoms. It is common knowledge in psychoanalytic circles that on some occasions, Bertha referred to this cathartic relief as a "talking cure"; on other occasions she adopted the metaphoric image of "chimney sweeping," giving concrete expression to the idea that talking to Breuer was akin to sweeping a chimney or cleaning her mind. This exploratory work of Breuer and Fraulein Bertha was a crucial part of the novel method of dialogical healing Freud learned from Breuer. But Breuer was overly involved with his patient and Bertha developed a pseudo-pregnancy while in his care. At the culminating moment, while a hysterical Bertha was in the throe of pseudo-childbirth, announcing to the world in a frenzied way that Dr. Breuer's child was fast approaching, poor Breuer was attending Bertha and looking for a way out of the clinical and personal quagmire this unruly erotization of the clinic created. Seeking temporary relief, he managed to hypnotize and calm Bertha, after which he reputedly fled her house in a fearsome sweat and hurriedly left for Venice with his wife the following morning, on a second honeymoon.[7]

Breuer's experience with the erotization of the clinic confirms the wisdom of Shakespeare, particularly his understanding that there are troubling times when even a well-heeled king like Richard III would offer his whole kingdom for a horse or any other fast way out of town. On the other hand, the pleasure of reading Sabrina's bountiful letters, the pleasure of experiencing Francine's enthusiasm for therapy, all the pleasures of the unrelenting struggle in the clinical trenches, put me in mind of the enchantment of the clinical confessor, an oft-unmentioned state of affairs that reminds me of another Elizabethan saying, this one from *King John*, one of Shakespeare's lesser histories: "In sooth, I would you were a little sick, That I might sit all night and watch with you."[8]

In spite of her enthusiasm, Francine was not involved in the type of erotization resistance Menninger viewed as an obstruction of treatment:

an obstruction that precludes the kind of clinical progress measured by a remission of symptoms. Francine's enthusiasm for therapy, her desire to sustain treatment, the pleasure she experienced from confessing, from hearing fair words, from having a confessor's ear, did not obstruct her treatment or her recovery in the least. She was compliant with medication, she worked her treatment plan, and morbid symptoms gradually remitted. Nevertheless, as Hawthorne warned, I had used my power of mind to achieve a psychological affinity with the mind of my patient and this resulted in a hypnotic rapport or a "magnetic passion" for the therapist, to use the descriptive metaphor of the hypnotically minded French clinician Pierre Janet.[9] As a result of Francine's strong emotional attachment to her dialogical therapist, there was an erotization of the clinic, all right, but this was an erotization that obstructed termination due to the fact that Francine had converted a formal confessional intimacy into a meaningful and pleasurable life experience.

When all was said and done, I defied hospital authority; in fact, like an unruly adolescent afflicted with a persistent Conduct Disorder, I snubbed my nose at the directive to terminate treatment with seemingly stable patients who were enthused with dialogical therapy. By cooking the books, to use an apt expression involving some creative storytelling in clinic notes and in formal treatment plans, I managed to sustain clinical relationships with a number of patients who were enchanted with the clinic. In exchange for my defiance of authority I received the gift of understanding that every confession conceals a confession; every secret is a hiding place; each revealing word or phrase also is a mask.[10] The further I pursued secrets within the clinical confessional, the deeper I peered within each hiding place, the more false faces I unmasked, the more haunted I became by Hawthorne's warning, because he understood that the doctor's power and influence is daemonic; however, Hawthorne's dark vision of the human estate, particularly his view that the clinical confession of a sexual secret is bound to result in misfortune or disaster, resulted in a shortsighted vision of the daemonic in human affairs.

Clinical experience suggests that an ineffable daemonic grows dynamically around secrets, moving them ineluctably toward disclosure. But I am inclined to think of the daemonic as energy *in pŏtentĭa*: a volatile latent force that can either affirm *or* destroy human life, in the fashion of atomic energy that has the potential to light *or* destroy a city. Fortunately, in Francine's case, the daemonic that enveloped her secrets finally moved them toward disclosure; as a result, an authentic clinical quest for insight and well-being ensued.

After I defied hospital authority, Francine became an inspired confessant who disclosed a healthy number of life-determining secrets. Apparently, in the mind of this patient and a few others who reaped a clinical benefit, my meager rebellion was seen as an existential act of self-sacrifice within a glorious Wagnerian opera: not only the heroic act of a mere mortal against powerful gods, but a courageous act by virtue of which I placed myself in the position of risking my livelihood and being transported in financial ruin to Valhalla. In reality, in the aftermath of my rebellion, Francine embarked upon a new, self-revealing clinical journey that resulted in the confession and clinical processing of (a) a Female Orgasmic Disorder; (b) frozen rage toward an ambivalently loved father whose divorce and remarriage resulted in Francine's deep feelings of abandonment; (c) shame issuing from a history of promiscuity commencing in adolescence; (d) a maladaptive history of punitive relationships with father surrogates, including an admittedly strong identification with Catherine Tramell, the beautiful, malevolent, knife-wielding female protagonist in the 1992 erotic film *Basic Instinct*. This was a destructive identification that reinforced a style of sexual behavior animated by an obsessive desire to "punish" or "get even with men."

For example, Francine confessed to having seduced a stranger in a sports bar; after a brief two-week affair, she cut him loose by telephoning his wife to report the infidelity in a purposeful attempt to gut the unfaithful man and ruin his family life. She confessed this incident while wearing a smile on her face, a sly smile that bespoke malice aforethought. Given her basic instinct, a thinking person would reasonably expect this arguably malevolent woman to treat her therapist the same way she treated a variety of ill-fated gentlemen she randomly seduced in uptown bars and other social gatherings. In fact, if Menninger's account of the erotization of the clinic were used to inspire a sequel to *Basic Instinct*, Francine would have been scripted to hurt her therapist in the manner of Catherine Tramell. Fortunately, this did not happen, although being on the receiving end of revenge for the emotional damage inflicted by her father was a possibility I entertained at the time.

In the enchanted clinic, things turned out well for Francine and at the end of an aborted termination session that marked the beginning of a new clinical adventure, I told her she did "good work," something I often say at the end of a grueling clinical hour. Hearing these simple words that mean so much to emotionally damaged patients whose healthy sense of self was annihilated early on by discreet forms of parental invalidation, she remarked tearfully: "You do too." As the door closed behind her and I prepared to see my next patient, I recalled Freud's claim that a therapist has "a stronger influence over . . . patients than a Father Confessor over his penitents," in view of the fact that clinical contacts are longer, more intense, and more personal than formal contacts in the religious confessional. Freud also noted that therapists are able to use their greater influence to divert patients from sick thoughts and talk them out of their fears

(*QL*, 189). But I also contemplated the influence confessants have over confessors, understanding that there is an enthusiasm and a suggestive attachment that cuts both ways.

Fortunately, Francine never read Hawthorne's warning. If she had, she might not have given me permission to burrow into her intimacy; I would not have been given the opportunity to use my clinical license to descend into her bosom to examine moral principles, to pry into recollections, to probe and to penetrate dark secrets. As a result, her disorders of mood, anxiety, orgasm, and personality would have remained untreated. If she took her cues from Menninger, chances are good that Francine would not have fallen under a spell and our clinical encounter would not have taught me important lessons about the erotization of the clinic: an agent of power and influence that has an instrumental use in the hands of an opportunistic therapist willing to embrace the enthusiasm and magnetic passion that animates clinical enchantments.

A CLEAR AND PRESENT DANGER

The erotization of the clinic carries a danger for therapists and patients alike. For example, in his *Autobiographical Study* Freud explained that on one occasion, after successfully relieving the suffering of an "acquiescent" patient using the hypnotic method of questioning to carefully trace her painful attacks to origins in the past, the entranced woman awakened and "threw her arms round my neck" in a forceful manner (*AS*, 27–28). In Freud's mind, repeated experience of this sort resulted in "grave doubts" about his use of the clinician's hypnotic power and influence, insofar as "the personal emotional relation between doctor and patient was . . . stronger than the whole cathartic process, and it . . . escaped every effort at control." In the end, according to Freud, one of the reasons he abandoned his early hypnotic method was an effort to "exclude" or at least "isolate" the seemingly uncontrollable libidinal relationship between doctor and patient.

Clearly, Menninger was not the first dialogical therapist to issue a warning about the erotization of the clinic. In fact, Freud reported that many neurologists and professors of psychiatry not only viewed the hypnotic method as "fraudulent" and "dangerous," they also viewed hypnotists with "contempt" (*AS*, 17). Confronting this issue directly in 1909, in "Introjection and Transference," a scholarly paper published in the *Jahrbuch der Psychoanalyse*—now the second chapter of *Sex in Psychoanalysis*—Sandor Ferenczi, a privileged member of Freud's inner circle, as well as an ardent defender of Freud and psychoanalysis, made explicit reference to critical objections to the psychoanalytic movement based upon the clear and present danger of hypnotically effective erotic transferences to psychoanalytic therapists. Addressing this charge as inconsistent, Ferenczi argued cogently that if these libidinal attachments are dangerous, the neurologists opposing Freud should stop treating neurotic patients, as well, insofar as neurologists who use clinical methods that are "non-analytic" or "non-psychotherapeutic" are not only subject to the libidinal attachments of patients, but these attachments often play "the greatest and probably the sole important part" of the clinical treatment of neurosis—clinical treatment whose "curative effect" is mistakenly attributed to "the physical measures" used by specialists in nervous disorders (*IT*, 46).

Enchanted by the psychological theory and the clinical method he imbibed at Freud's knee, particularly the method of hypnosis and suggestion he persisted in using long after Freud abandoned direct hypnosis as a method of questioning patients about the origin of symptoms recollected imperfectly during the waking state of consciousness, Ferenczi continued his defense of psychosexual aspects of psychoanalysis by flatly denying that the clinical transference of a libidinal attachment is harmful to patients. Addressing the opponents of psychoanalysis head on, Ferenczi maintained that those who "scornfully reproach" Freudian analysis for its pansexualism—not only explaining everything, but also seeking to cure everyone, from a psychosexual point of view—"are still far too much influenced by that ascetic-religious view of life, with its depreciation of everything sexual, which for nearly two thousand years has prevented the attainment of insight into the great significance that 'sexual hunger' has for the mental life of the normal and the pathological" (*IT*, 49).

Ferenczi's argument was well-intentioned, if not fully convincing, given the risk of harming emotionally impaired patients who happen to become erotically fixed on their therapists. Nevertheless, I am particularly interested in Ferenczi's defense of erotization because early on, during the 1890s, when Freud was making groundbreaking psychosexual discoveries while laboring to understand the aetiology of hysteria, the ascetic religiosity of Ferenczi's reference made Freud's psychological theorizing and clinical practice a moral problem in Victorian Vienna. In fact, while Freud was inventing psychoanalysis by borrowing Josef Breuer's cathartic method of questioning and eliciting from hypnotically entranced patients, verbal answers cued to (a) current fantasies, (b) oppressive thoughts and imaginings, and (c) historical events that seemed to explain the origin of morbid symptoms, he was struggling against the Victorian sensibility of his time, particularly the argument of seemingly respectable physicians that Freud had a moral responsibility to refrain from sexual inquiry during clinical consultations. Reminiscent of the repressive sensibility informing Hawthorne's warning regarding the confession of sexual secrets, in Freud's Vienna, questioning patients about their sexual lives and, as

Freud put it, "demanding a truthful account from them" in the clinical confessional was conceived as a "danger for the individual and for society"; and in 1898, while defending himself against physicians who believed he was overstepping an ethical boundary by intruding upon his patient's sexual privacy, thereby risking the happiness of family life, offending the modesty of women, and ruining the innocence of younger patients, Freud proclaimed straightforwardly:

> One may well reply that it is the expression of a prudery which is unworthy of a physician and which inadequately conceals its weakness behind bad arguments. . . . Moreover, it is in the interest of us all that a higher degree of honesty about sexual things should become a duty among men and women than has hitherto been expected of them. This cannot be anything but a gain for sexual morality. In matters of sexuality we are at present, every one of us, ill or well, nothing but hypocrites. It will be all to our good if, as a result of such general honesty, a certain amount of tolerance in sexual concerns should be attained.[11]

More than one century has passed since Freud and Ferenczi penned their defense of the erotization of the clinic and much has happened to change the prudish, hypocritical Victorian culture within which they thought and worked. Remarkably, during the second half of the twentieth century, in the aftermath of the inventive work of Freud and dedicated disciples like Ferenczi—pioneering disciples whose clinical work focused on healing the emotional wounds issuing from the punitive Judeo-Christian tribunal of sin, shame, and guilt—ecstatic scholars like Foucault heralded the fact that "a visible explosion of unorthodox sexualities occurred in Western culture."[12] Making the same point in a different way, sedate scholars were satisfied to simply document the success of a historically momentous sexual revolution that validated erotic pleasure by securing "belief in sex as the source of personal meaning."[13]

There is a reasonable argument to support the conclusion that the sexual revolution in the West was begotten by the liberating therapeutic movement initiated by Freud and his disciples. In spite of liberating benefits, clinical experience compels me to state forthrightly that there is an inherent danger in the erotization of the clinic, not the least reason being that these unpredictable erotizations occur naturally, but often in the fashion of a volatile volcano waiting to erupt. During the eruptions, there are times when a patient's erotic tie to the therapist can be used with great success; on other occasions, however, the erotization of the clinic does not easily submit to control, in fact, some erotizations become direct sexual solicitations. In all cases, the erotization of the clinic can be grossly mismanaged in spite of a therapist's best intentions: mismanaged, I should say, with potential damage to the well-being of emotionally impaired patients whose enchantment with the clinic issues from a libidinal attachment, an erotic tie, or hypnotic rapport that may compromise the effectiveness of the clinical work of a psychological healer who is engaged in a dialogical struggle against emotional illness and death.

PYGMY ETHICS

In the scarlet clinic, a dialogical therapist may be blinded by an oath of service that seems to impose an obligation to do anything in one's power to secure the well-being of the men and women who cross the threshold of the clinic and confess their secrets in the confidential confessional. Fortunately, I learned from the respected American philosopher and logician Willard Van Orman Quine that "every" and "any" are not synonymous; rather, these indefinite singular terms have a different scope, with "every" connoting narrow and "any" connoting the widest possible scope.[14] As a result, I make a fine distinction between *everything* and *anything*, and in the enchanted clinic, under the influence of this logical distinction, I am not at liberty to do anything I please or anything a patient wishes. My oath of service may obligate me to do *everything* in my power to secure the well-being of patients, but my oath of service neither obligates nor liberates me to do *anything* I conceive as a means to that end.

Specifically, whenever an erotization of the clinic became a sexual solicitation, succumbing to the entreaty has not been a live option. This firm boundary may appear to be part of Menninger's clinical strategy to counter a patient's obstructive resistance to ameliorative change, but primarily, it is a personal choice: an existential commitment having to do with how I choose to live my life, how I choose to conduct my clinical practice, how I choose to treat and manage men and women who contract to pay me to heal their emotional wounds in the context of a trustworthy interpersonal encounter focused on my reasoned judgment of their best interest. If I commit myself to that contract as a responsible, self-respecting moral agent, I also commit myself to doing everything in my power to guard against taking advantage of a patient's vulnerability in illness. Of course, serious participation in an ethical discussion of this sort hinges on a therapist's desire to become a moral agent. If a person does not care about moral agency, perhaps failing to care about one's fellows at a visceral level of human sensibility, this being the intrapsychic condition of individuals with an Antisocial Personality Disorder, then ethical discussion will sound meaningless and moral distinctions will fall on deaf ears. If this deafness is widespread in a civilization or a culture, history suggests that sooner or later a superorganic structure of this sort will find itself in a protracted state of entropy or internal disintegration.

More to the point, as a pragmatic existential therapist who is intimate with the enchantments of the clinic, I want my patients to heal their emotional wounds, to learn to affirm life, to rage against the dying of the light in all its ugly manifestations: not only biological death, but all manner of self-destructive behavior, not to mention forms of madness Foucault identified felicitously as "the *déjà-là* of death"— the presence of death in life.[15] In my personal attempt to sustain moral agency in the scarlet clinic, I choose to honor a professional contract that obligates me to provide a clinical service, not a sexual service. Although I earn a living by hearing clinical confessions, I am not in the business of taking money to hear sexual confessions, as if these revelations were foreplay, the endgame of which is sexual congress on the clinical sofa. If I had decided to engage in this activity I would have gone into the gigolo business when I was younger and full of promise. Who knows, by now I might have retired to a fine beachfront home in the Caymans! Having made a different pact with Mephisto, it falls to me to say that there are clear enchantments of the clinic and a compelling eroticism animating the relationship of clinical confessor and clinical confessant. But I would argue that the clinical confessional is not the place to engage either in (a) the solicitation of emotionally ill confessants, who clearly are compromised in their capacity for reasoned judgment, rational consent, and constructive choice, or (b) sexual activity with patients remarkably vulnerable to the lure of dialogical intimacy and other clinical enchantments. This is a moral compass, to be sure, the moral compass of a pygmy, thus a meager compass identifying an ethic of sorts.

You see, in the world of analytic philosophy, the academic world of Wittgenstein and Quine, it is reasonable to say that I am unable to justify a moral choice insofar as there is no ultimate foundation or absolute epistemic ground for ethical decisions, choices, or commitments. If seeking a correlation of ethical decisions with moral truths of the universe is a Sisyphean exercise in futility, perhaps all one can say when making an ethical decision is: "This is bedrock for me!" When reason and explanation expire, I take a stand and simply say, "this is where I live and breathe," with no final argument or ultimate justification offered. As Wittgenstein observed when responding to a query regarding obedience to a rule, when justifications for following a rule are exhausted, "I have reached bedrock, and my spade is turned. Then I am inclined to say: 'This is simply what I do.'"[16]

As a philosophically minded existential therapist attempting to manage clinical ethics, I am not delighted with pygmy ethics. In fact, I am particularly dissatisfied with an image of moral agency built upon an absence of epistemic ground for ethical decisions, insofar as another man's spade may be turned in a bedrock composed of entirely different moral minerals—a quick turn of his spade resulting in irrational behavior I abhor. Experience demonstrates that this is frequently true: we appear to be a crazed species whose thinking and behavior demonstrate that distorted needs and irrational behavior often rule. Aristotle may have noted correctly that "reason [is] the best thing in us," but he also argued mistakenly that "reason more than anything else *is* man."[17] From my vantage point in the clinical confessional this is a philosopher's fiction, for clinical confessions reveal that emotional reactivity and irrational behavior are free-floating radicals that often define and control a crazed species of men and women: not only individuals like the malevolent Catherine Tramell, but whole societies like the neurotically religious society that punished the sexual sinner Hester Prynne.

THE CARNIVAL OF CLINICAL PRACTICE

Suffice it to say, confessional intimacy with clinicians has its risks as Hawthorne warned, but not every erotization of the clinic is immoral, obstructive, and harmful as Menninger maintained. In fact, the erotization of the clinic can play a vital role in the therapeutic relationship of dialogical partners who enact the intimate roles of clinical confessor and clinical confessant behind the closed doors of confidential consulting rooms in a variety of respectable and rogue settings, including outpatient hospital clinics, not-for-profit agencies, and a plethora of provincial private practices run by state-licensed, as well as unlicensed and unsupervised sole proprietors. Experience in these settings suggests that in each domain, a carnival of clinical practice is enacted by incompetents, charlatans, mediocrities, and masters, and it is possible for the attributes of each clinical type to inhabit a dialogical therapist simultaneously, although the vices and virtues of each type are not drawn out or active simultaneously. A heavy weight is added to this crude fact of clinical life when one carefully considers the suggestive power and influence of mental health clinicians with reference to Ferenczi's hubristic claim that in the mental health clinic, *"the application of suggestion and hypnosis consists in the deliberate establishment of conditions under which the tendency to blind belief and uncritical obedience present in everyone, . . . may unconsciously be transferred to the person hypnotizing or suggesting"* (*IT*, 78–79).

When the carnival of clinical practice is set in motion, the ferris wheel rotates about its axis, the carousel spins its clinical hobby-horses round and round, and unsuspecting patients pay a fee to hop aboard for a fateful ride. But those in charge of running the show—the clinical show of suggesting and receiving blind belief and uncritical obedience—are the variously educated or uneducated, experienced or inexperienced, incompetents, charlatans, mediocrities, and masters expected to summon the knowledge, patience, and skill to understand and carefully manage the erotic enchantments of clinic patients who come from all walks of life with widely divergent ethnic origins, developmental backgrounds, educational preparations, and elemental understandings of self, world, and others. In truth, Freud identified Ferenczi as "a master of analysis," but he also understood firsthand that dialogical therapists are individuals more or less skilled at practicing "a particular art"; indeed, Freud knew firsthand that dialogical therapists with their own unique personalities are "human beings like anyone else," many of whom, "in their own personalities have not . . . come up to the standard of psychical normality to which they wish to educate their patients" (*TI*, 230, 247).

Freud was well aware of the tendency toward blind belief and uncritical obedience in individuals and in groups. For example, in 1921, while still actively thinking about suggestibility—this time with reference to Le Bon's 1895 *Psychology of the Crowd* and the observation that human beings may regress to primitive levels of thinking, feeling, and behavior in groups—Freud stated boldly:

> From being in love to hypnosis is evidently only a short step. . . . There is the same humble subjection, the same compliance, the same absence of criticism, toward the hypnotist as toward the loved object. There is the same sapping of the subject's own initiative. . . . The hypnotist is the sole object, and no attention is paid to any but him. . . . The ego experiences in a dreamlike way whatever he may request or assert. . . . The hypnotic relation is the unlimited devotion of someone in love, but with sexual satisfaction excluded. . . . We may also say that the hypnotic relation is . . . a group formation with two members. (*GR*, 114)

In chapter 2, we shall see why Freud claimed it is a short step from the hypnotic suggestibility of patients to transference love and why this understanding enabled him to abandon direct hypnosis as a clinical method. But I wish to state at this juncture, when a dialogical therapist is dealing with dreamlike states, unlimited devotion, blind belief, uncritical obedience, humble subjection, compliance, absence of criticism, libidinal attachments, erotic ties, magnetic passions, and illusions of love, the deliberate attempt to solicit these lived experiences may arguably be conceived as a reckless use of clinical power. Call it a daemonic use of power over the spirits: potentially, a pernicious abuse of the psychological healer's strategic art of persuasion, perhaps a misshapen clinician's manipulation of human reason and emotion in a sinless world lacking moral inspiration. For the formal shift from unintentional enchantment to deliberate seduction—the move from discovering that one is a sorcerer to intentionally plotting to become a sorcerer capable of seizing and controlling the reason and the emotion, the adoration and devotion, of vulnerable human beings—is a clinical leap that should raise eyebrows and serious questions about the carnival of clinical practice. This is particularly relevant today, for in our postmodern culture, the erotization of the clinic occurs in an ethical vacuum that is an ironic consequence of Freud's successful struggle to clinically combat the Western world's religious neurosis and its formidable arsenal of sin, shame, and guilt.

To his credit, Freud openly confessed: "There was something positively seductive in working with hypnotism. For the first time there was a sense of having overcome one's helplessness; and it was highly flattering to enjoy the reputation of being a miracle-worker" (*AS*, 17). My experience in the clinical confessional is consistent with Freud's in this regard. But I also know that the reputation of being a miracle worker and enjoying the seductive feeling that accompanies the reputation, as if one really were a worker of miracles, can easily go to a person's head. Unfortunately, this puffed-up condition tends toward human error. For miracles are the stuff of gods, but gods appear to be absent in the human estate, and mortals who aspire to become like gods are sure to stumble, in as much as the wisdom of gods rarely is vouchsafed to mortals.

Summing these things nicely, while warning of the danger of falling under "the spell" of seemingly great human beings, the philosopher of science, Karl Popper, observed: "Our greatest troubles spring from something that is as admirable and sound as it is dangerous—from our impatience to better the lot of our fellows."[18] Popper was writing in 1943 during the Hitlerian apocalypse and he was piqued by Plato because the great philosopher had made a great mistake—great mistakes being the fate of great men and women because they have power and influence over great numbers of people. It came to pass that when Plato was eighty years old and disenchanted with the dream of reason—the hopeful dream that human beings could use the elusive power of reason to temper and control emotional states that led to a war of every man with every man and a war of each man with himself—he used fair words, his noteworthy charm, in a grave attempt to convince his fellow Athenians that a tightly controlled, rigidly structured, authoritarian polis was the best hope of establishing and maintaining social order and civil relations among human beings who could be gentle creatures, but often were savage. This was Plato's blind, zealous attempt to better the lot of his fellows. Blind, because what looks good in theory does not always work smoothly in practice; zealous, because it was a flawed vision that seemed to have the passionate beauty of apodictic truth. Sad to say, as the history of the twentieth century clearly shows, humankind's greatest troubles sprang from the abdication of reason and the human tendency to fall under the spell of seemingly great men who incited to violence by means of evocative language and fictive ideas that had the power to charm the pants off a snake.

In the mental health clinic, where unsuspecting patients may fall under the spell of a seemingly great therapist—the imaginary doctor of Freud's reference—one may find an honorable impatience to better the lot of emotionally ill patients. But zealotry and impatience may lead to mistakes, perhaps not great mistakes, since provincial therapists do not have the power to persuade great masses of people, although Freud was a seemingly great man whose personal influence and power of persuasion altered a whole culture, notwithstanding the fact that his psychoanalytic theory and method are now widely seen as ridden with error. Closer to home, it is not too much to say that a provincial mistake is a grave mistake, particularly when illness and death are wagered in the clinical carnival. In the end, therefore, Popper's warning about falling under the spell of seemingly great humans, particularly those whose myths and fictions have the power to charm, is as important today as it was when he penned his heretical view of Plato. For Popper's warning, like the earlier warning of Hawthorne, consists of fair words that apply with exquisite truth and beauty to postmodern clinicians who ply their seductive trade in a carnival of clinical practice, where unsuspecting patients have a tendency to regress to primitive levels of thinking, feeling, and behavior when they become erotically enchanted with all manner and variety of clinical helpers.

Of course there are unproductive times when the chemistry of clinical enchantment fails to take effect. In these cases, the wizard's spell is ineffective and the therapist is perceived and experienced as ordinary, rather than being perceived and experienced as phantastic. Given this stark reality, the clinic is not eroticized and the battle against emotional illness has a better chance of failing or ending abruptly, either with a vague whimper or in silence. The lack of enthusiasm, the absence of hypnotic rapport, the failure of erotic tie and enchantment, manifested itself in the sad case of Charlene, a young Hawthornean woman who seemed to have a shameful *W* imprinted in her flesh.

THE DEATH OF HESTER PRYNNE

Charlene was an anxious, depressed, thirty-year-old widow who carried indelible scars from deep emotional wounds inflicted by her father. Like her female forebears in a grim Puritan era—humiliated women who carried indelible scars inflicted by a searing hot iron used to burn a telltale *A* onto their flesh, Charlene's father treated her as if she were a malefactress who should be outlawed from a society of goodwives who were spared the grief of committing the unpardonable sin of being human.

Strange as it may seem in the wake of a sexual revolution said to have validated sexual pleasure as a source of personal meaning, deep within Charlene's core psyche, the sins of the slut burned brightly, for Charlene's father was an angry alcoholic who also was a virulent misogynist. Well aware of his daughter's good looks and flowering sensuality, he began calling her a "filthy whore" when she was thirteen years old: the age at which she began dating and in his lively imagination, "screwing and sucking boys." Sitting with Charlene in the clinic, I imagined the effect of her budding charms on her father's desire—sexual desire he attempted to medicate unsuccessfully with alcohol. Perhaps he was simply blind to the gravity of the foul words his daughter was hearing, but I am more inclined to believe he was a tortured man punishing his sensuous daughter for becoming a forbidden "doll of the flesh," to borrow Simone de Beauvoir's trenchant image of female illusion-making produced by cosmetics, provocative dress, and crafty behavior—this common theatrical play-acting being women's collusive response to the inventive erotic objectifications of men.[19]

Hearing herself referred to regularly as a filthy whore produced a deathly metamorphosis: the kind of vulgar transformation of identity that infected Charlene with shame about her sensuous body and guilt regarding her sexual self, all of which conspired to make her feel like the dirty, impaired, gigantic insect Gregor Samsa awakened to in Kafka's surreal existential story, *The Metamorphosis*. In fact, by the time she entered my office, Charlene wondered aloud whether it was "right for me to be a mother!" Clearly, this was a young widow in psychological trouble. Like Hester Prynne, "whose heart had lost its regular and healthy throb," Charlene had long "wandered without a clue in the dark labyrinth of the mind"; now, with some luck and a dialogical therapist able to do some cognitive restructuring, Charlene had a chance to build a healthier self. However, like her Puritan forebear, Charlene was a woman "starting back from a deep chasm" (*SL*, 206).

Unfortunately, Charlene's husband died in a vehicular accident approximately one year before she appeared in the outpatient clinic for a psychosocial evaluation. As a result of his death, Charlene was left to single-parent her precocious twelve-year-old daughter, Pearl. Complicating the struggle with Pearl was the fact that Charlene became sexually intimate with a neighbor after a respectable period of mourning, but Pearl was not happy with this unruly turn of events. Like Charlene's father, the lustful neighbor was a man who had watched Charlene sashaying in short shorts for a number of years, hoping but never believing he would have the opportunity to fulfill his erotic desire. To his surprise, when Charlene surrendered to his advance, he seized the moment, in spite of earlier vows to his wife and the obligations of parenting two children.

Sad to say, Charlene never became enchanted with the clinic or enthused with therapy. Accordingly, she concealed the richest details of her erotic affair; however, during our brief clinical encounter she confessed that her neighbor had awakened her sexually, so much so, that "we did things I never dreamed of doing with my husband." One day, she bowed her head abjectly as if the last vestige of self-respect had gone out the door, and she confessed a skeletal frame of sexual secrets, wondering whether she really was a filthy whore. Given respect for her privacy and diligent care of her fragile soul, I gave the lie to Hawthorne's warning and I made no attempt to creep into her intimacy—no attempt to put flesh on the skeleton by stealing her sexual secrets. But I recalled Hester Prynne and the shameful scarlet letter that flamed on her breast. Rather than descending into Charlene's bosom to probe and to penetrate sexual secrets, thereby doing battle with her resistance to clinical confession during the game of capture and seduction, I descended into myself, wondering what Charlene had done with her neighbor to confirm the shameful *W* her father's searing hot words seemed to have imprinted in her flesh. Things being what they are in my moral conscience, I was soon visited by my old acquaintance, Thomas Aquinas, who caught me in the act of being human. Soon thereafter, I accepted with equanimity the difficult penance of conducting a phenomenological examination of the dialectics of secrecy and openness, of hiding and showing, of concealing and revealing, concluding that we humans often experience a heightened stimulation from the unseen and the unspoken, as the imagination, so rich in creative potential, is allowed free rein to invest with grand fiction whatever mysteries of the cosmos are obscured from feeble finite senses.

Because she never became enchanted with the clinic, Charlene developed a pattern of canceling or "no showing" scheduled appointments, never evidencing a genuine investment in dialogical therapy, a good chemistry with her therapist, or an intention to develop a working clinical relationship. As a result, I closed her active file in conformity with clinic policy before she began to address her emotional problems in earnest. Prior to closing her file, I learned that she had succumbed to something akin to the compulsion to confess sexual secrets by drafting in her diary copious notes about the ongoing steamy relationship with her neighbor: a secret confession about a shared erotic passion her precocious daughter, Pearl, boldly read. From that day forward, as if she were enacting the part of a goodwife in a Puritan drama of sin, shame, and sorrow, Pearl began to call her mother a whore, causing Charlene to feel that her flesh had been branded permanently with a telltale *W*.

When I sat with Charlene and listened to the way she confessed her story, she seemed to be a woman condemned. Recalling the ill-fated Josef K. in Kafka's haunting existentialist tale *The Trial*, it was difficult to determine what she had done to merit the official condemnation, except to say, she was a sensuous woman who enjoyed the pleasures of the flesh, not to mention the esteem she received from being desired and having this desire mirrored in a man's eyes and carnal behavior. But in her mind, the pleasures of the flesh were not simply pleasures, rather, erotic pleasures were also experienced as sins of the flesh. In the end, as with the surrealistic Josef K., Charlene felt as if a knife had been plunged deep into her heart . . . and turned twice. Of course she was in process of dying slowly ever since her father pierced her heart with foul words when she was thirteen, until her daughter, Pearl, finally killed her. Although I have no way of knowing, Charlene's sense of sin, shame, and guilt was so prodigious it was certain to outlive her.

I suppose it was fortunate that Charlene did not live in a grim Puritan era in which the act of being human was redeemed by the pillory or some other chilling penance. In spite of her good fortune, I regret the fact that I was an ordinary therapist who did not have the power or the influence to hold Charlene in therapy, because her suffering was unnecessary and she was unable to use my office to achieve the emotional healing that comes from a clinical struggle that wins the battle of reconciliation with humanness. Still, I am consoled and motivated by the fact that this latter-day Hester Prynne offered a stunning contrast to patients like Francine: the former failing to come under the influence of a clinical enchantment, while remaining emotionally wounded, the latter succumbing to the spell of the "phantastic . . . person" of the therapist, while eroticizing the clinic and having a healing, life-affirming clinical experience.[20]

For the reader's information, the expression "phantastic . . . person of the physician" is from Joan Riviere's early translation of Freud's *Introductory Lectures on Psycho-Analysis*. In the later authorized *Standard Edition* of Freud's *Collected Works*, James Strachey translated this passage as the "imaginary . . . person of the doctor" (*IL*, 454). Although I shall use Strachey's translations from *The Standard Edition* of Freud's works throughout the text, I shall also use Riviere's "phantastic . . . person" as well, not only for the alliteration which is pleasing to the ear. More importantly, by incorporating "phantastic" I am able to focus the reader's attention on the etymological stem, *"pha,"* from which is derived (a) the Greek verb *"phaino,"* the passive sense of which is to come to light, to be seen, to appear, and (b) *"phantasma,"* meaning an appearance, a vision, a dream. Given these connotations, "phantastic" is particularly meaningful in references to enchantments of the clinic and the transformative perception of an ordinary person able to function professionally as a clinical wizard who possesses suggestive power and influence. Plowing similar terrain in *Being and Time*, while explaining the etymology of "phenomenon," Heidegger argued that a particular entity can show or manifest itself in various ways, not the least of which is showing itself as something it is not. On Heidegger's account, the self-showing or self-manifestation that enables an entity to look like or appear to be something it is not, is called "seeming." For example, "φαινόμενον ἀγαθόν [*phainomenon agathon*] means something good which looks like, but 'in actuality' is not, what it gives itself out to be."[21]

NOTES

1. Karl Menninger, *Theory of Psychoanalytic Technique* (New York: Harper Torchbooks, 1958); cited in the text as *TP*.
2. Nathaniel Hawthorne, *The Scarlet Letter* (New York: Dell Publishing, 1972); cited in the text as *SL*.
3. Sigmund Freud, *The Question of Lay Analysis*, in *Standard Edition*, vol. 20 (1959); cited in the text as *QL*.
4. Sigmund Freud, *An Autobiographical Study*, in *Standard Edition*, vol. 20; cited in the text as *AS*.
5. Ludwig Wittgenstein, *Remarks on the Foundations of Mathematics*, trans. G. E. M. Anscombe (Cambridge, MA: MIT Press, 1967), 46–47e.
6. Carl P. Ellerman, "Pragmatic Existential Therapy," *Journal of Contemporary Psychotherapy* 29, no. 1 (1999): 49–64.
7. My brief account of Breuer's ill-fated transaction with Anna O is based on the account of Ernest Jones, *The Life and Work of Sigmund Freud*, vol. 1, *The Formative Years and the Great Discoveries, 1856–1900* (New York: H. Wolff, 1962), 224–25. Freud's account of Breuer's clinical work with Anna O appears in *Studies on Hysteria*, in *Standard Edition*, vol. 2.
8. William Shakespeare, *King John*, in *The Complete Works of William Shakespeare, with Themes of the Plays* (Roslyn, NY: Walter J. Black, 1937), 417.
9. Pierre Janet, *L'État Mental des Hystériques*, 2nd ed. (n.p., 1911), 135, quoted in Peter Gay, *Freud: A Life for Our Time* (New York: W. W. Norton & Company, 1988), 50.
10. In this passage I am recasting the following observation of Nietzsche: "Every philosophy also conceals a philosophy; every opinion is also a hideout, every word also a mask." *Beyond Good and Evil: Prelude to a Philosophy of the Future*, trans. Walter Kaufmann (New York: A Vintage Original, 1966), 229.
11. Sigmund Freud, "Sexuality in the Aetiology of the Neuroses," in *Standard Edition*, vol. 3 (1962), 264, 266.
12. Michel Foucault, *The History of Sexuality: An Introduction*, vol. 1, trans. Robert Hurley (New York: Vintage Books, 1990), 49.
13. John D'Emilio and Estelle B. Freedman, *Intimate Matters: A History of Sexuality in America* (New York: Perennial Library, 1989), 327.
14. W. V. O. Quine, "Logic as a Source of Syntactical Insights," in *The Ways of Paradox and Other Essays* (New York: Random House, 1966), 42–47.
15. Michel Foucault, *Madness and Civilization: A History of Insanity in the Age of Reason*, trans. Richard Howard (New York: A Mentor Book, 1967), 24.

16. Ludwig Wittgenstein, *Philosophical Investigations,* 3rd ed., trans. G. E. M. Anscombe (New York: The Macmillan Company, 1969), #217.

17. Aristotle, *Nicomachean Ethics,* trans. W. D. Ross, in *The Basic Works of Aristotle,* ed. Richard McKeon (New York: Random House, 1941), 1176a, 1178a.

18. Karl R. Popper, *The Open Society and Its Enemies,* vol. 1, *The Spell of Plato* (Princeton, NJ: Princeton University Press, 1971), ix.

19. Simone de Beauvoir, *The Second Sex,* trans. H. M. Parshley (New York: Alfred A. Knopf, 1971). 532.

20. Sigmund Freud, *A General Introduction to Psycho-Analysis,* trans. Joan Riviere (Garden City, NY: Garden City Publishing Company, 1938), 395.

21. Martin Heidegger, *Being and Time,* trans. John Macquarrie and Edward Robinson (New York: Harper & Row, 1962), #29.

2

The Erotization of the Clinician

THE BLACK ART

From 13 October 1885 to 28 February 1886, Freud studied hypnotism with Charcot in the neurological clinic of the Salpêtrière hospital in Paris, where the venerable French neurologist was engaged in the psycho-hypnotic study of hysteria. Initially skeptical of the black art, Freud found himself fascinated, entertained, deeply moved, and disarmed by theatrical demonstrations during which Charcot produced non-organic paralyses in men and women he had placed in a state of hypnotic somnambulism, thereby showing that hysterical symptoms could be produced *and* removed psychologically, by a suggestion presented to the mind of an unwitting patient. Given his enchantment with Charcot and his conviction that the great man was working to replace the religious imagination and its "clerical phantasy" of daemonic possession with the formulations of modern psychological science, Freud planned to add the mysterious black art to the clinical skills he would need when he commenced his private medical practice on 25 April 1886.[1]

Freud's early use of hypnosis was neither a foolhardy lark, nor a misbegotten clinical adventure. In spite of flights of fancy that are the bread and butter of theoretical men and women possessed by creative imagination, Freud was a pragmatic clinician who had learned that electrotherapy, commonly used to treat neurasthenia, was practically useless; he also heard that any success treating nervous patients with electrotherapy was most likely the result of the neurologist's verbal suggestions. Furthermore, he realized that clinical treatment was enhanced when hypnotically entranced patients were questioned about their morbid symptoms, the origin of which they often remembered vaguely or incorrectly during the waking state (*AS*, 16–19). Finally, and not the lesser of these considerations by any means, the black art had cash value: it reduced to dollars and cents in his pocket during lean years in the clinical trenches. Specifically, young Dr. Freud needed to earn a living and patients with nervous disorders were scant even in a large city like Vienna. But in a Darwinian vision cued to the survival of self and kin, Freud noticed that in Vienna, "crowds of neurotics" were coming out of the woodwork as if they were ants: neurotic ants whose "number seemed further multiplied by the manner in which they hurried, with their troubles unsolved, from one physician to another" (*AS*, 16). Seeking to avail himself of the largest pool of patients for his private practice, neurotic patients who might be susceptible to the promise of hypnotic therapy, the opportunistic Freud moved beyond his neurological specialization to openly embrace clinical methods that retrospectively were "haphazard and unsystematic"(*AS*, 17). At the time, however, the inscrutable black art championed by Charcot had clinical utility and pecuniary potential.

After bidding a fond farewell to Charcot, Freud traveled to Berlin with the intention of acquiring a fuller knowledge of children's disorders at the clinic of Adolf Baginsky, an unremarkable figure in Freud's life and clinical legacy. He spent two weeks in Berlin engaged in supplemental medical studies to better prepare himself to assume the duties of director of the neurological department of a new Institute for Children's Diseases opening its doors in Vienna. Departing Berlin, Freud returned to Vienna anticipating an autumn marriage to his beloved fiancée, Martha Bernays. By all accounts, due to the fact that he already was helping to support a large family, he was worried about the added responsibility of becoming a married man. In spite of the fact that he was working diligently to shore-up his dismal finances, by the early summer of 1886, Freud had translated from French into German, Charcot's "New Lectures on the Diseases of the Nervous System, Especially on Hysteria." A few years later, having gained admission to Charcot's inner circle, Freud translated, edited, and wrote a preface to Charcot's *Chacons*—the "Clinical Lectures" of 1887 to 1888. More importantly, demonstrating his enchantment with Charcot and the enigmatic black art conceived by Charcot as working physiological changes in a subject's nervous system, absent the subject's conscious awareness, during his first years of private practice, Freud used hypnotic suggestion as his "principal instrument of work" (*AS*, 17). Regarding this eventful pre-psychoanalytic period when he was flush with the spirit, will, energy, and excitement of scientific discovery, Freud's biographer, Ernest Jones, reported that hypnotic suggestion "often brought gratifying successes and replaced the feeling of helplessness by the satisfaction of being admired as a magician."[2]

Given these reputed successes and the nagging suspicion that intelligible psychological processes were at work beyond the drawn interior of conscious awareness, Freud undertook a clinical adventure that seemed to traffic in magic. But who could fault him, for the mind reels at the possibilities. What if a physician could triumph against illness by means of direct suggestion, using his power of mind and the artificial sleep induced by hypnotic trance to influence patients to suppress the unruly symptoms of an intractable disorder? This is heady stuff! But in a Sisyphean world of gravitational forces and resistances, rolling this clinical boulder to the crest of the mountain of neurasthenia and neurosis was neither as easy, nor as reliable, as Freud hoped or imagined.

He had learned much about the craft of hypnotism from Charcot and he could cast a fine spell, being fairly well versed in the methodical rules of the game. He knew the value of providing a dark, quiet room suitable for sleeping; he could speak with a monotonous, mannered, melodic voice; he could stroke the patient's hair and forehead with a deft hand; he could present an external stimulus to the patient's eye or ear, say a glistening object or a ticking clock respectively. He could use these and other ritualistic measures to induce an artificial sleep that would solicit will-less obedience from entranced patients. But Freud discovered that direct hypnosis is capricious: not only unreliable and impermanent, but he was not always able to induce hypnotic trance in every patient (*IL*, 449). Simply put, direct hypnosis does not work with everyone and even if a clinician successfully suggests a suppression of symptoms, chances are good that the patient will return at some future date reporting either a recurrence of symptoms or a new symptom formation that replaced the original clinical presentation. Besides, while offering the hope of clinical miracles in theory, in practice, direct hypnosis and the repetition of therapeutic suggestions was "*monotonous*" for the hypnotist, insofar as it is a method of entrancement that treats every patient the same formal way. The hypnotic method of Charcot was so boring in practice that on 28 May 1888, Freud literally wrote one of his famous letters to Fliess in his clinical consulting room while a hypnotized patient was fast asleep. "I have at this moment," Freud wrote nonchalantly, "a lady in hypnosis lying in front of me and therefore can go on writing in peace" (*FL*, 21).

In spite of its faults, the impermanence of hypnotic therapy fertilized the thought that clinical success was grounded in the physician-patient relationship, for the apparent remission of morbid symptoms yielded to the recurrence of symptoms upon termination of treatment or some such time when the physician-patient relationship was no longer active. On Freud's account: "Even the most brilliant results were liable to be suddenly wiped away if my personal relation with the patient became disturbed. It was true that they would be re-established if a reconciliation could be effected;

but such an occurrence proved that the personal emotional relation between doctor and patient was after all stronger than the whole cathartic process" (*AS*, 27). In a short time, this pregnant empirical observation resulted in Freud's grand hypothesis that a hypnotized patient's will-less submission to the physician is a result of the transference of affects and erotic ties from earlier sources: the unwitting *transference* to the person of the physician and the *reproduction* in the clinical relationship of libidinal feelings buried in a patient's unconscious parental complex.

At this early stage of his lengthy culture-changing clinical career, before a corrosive disillusionment actively challenged a younger man's fervor with the conviction that humankind is "neurotic" and may be diagnosed with an untreatable "communal neurosis," Freud was a clinician full of hope and dream and promise (*CD*, 144).[3] For a while longer, therefore, he not only sustained his clinical use of hypnosis, but in 1888, he translated and wrote a preface to Hippolyte Bernheim's *Hypnotism, Suggestion, and Therapy*. He also decided that the Paris neurological school of Charcot failed to provide him with the tools required to turn a reliable clinical trick. Seeking a deeper understanding of hypnosis and new experience that would hone his clinical skills, he returned to France in 1889 to undertake additional research on hypnotic suggestion with Bernheim in Nancy. By all accounts, the Nancy school of Bernheim, based in part on the clinical work of the aged Nancy physician Ambroise Liebeault, progressed beyond the somatic theory and formulaic work of Charcot: methodical work that relied on physiological stimulations of the nervous system, thereby wedding the artificial sleep of hypnosis to physical touch and other sleep-inducing optical and auditory stimulations. In retrospect, Freud's brief period of study in Nancy with Bernheim and Liebeault resulted in important new insights that would ground psychoanalytic theory and dialogical therapy forevermore.

Bernheim discovered that suggestibility is the catalytic agent of hypnosis. In fact, Freud learned from Bernheim that "hypnosis itself was already a result of suggestion, a suggested state" (*IL*, 448). As a result of this significant discovery, rather than directly inducing a state of artificial sleep by means of glistening objects, ticking clocks, and other external stimuli that had a hypnogenic effect on a subject's neurological system, Bernheim used suggestion with subjects who were awake and he achieved the same results. In prefatory comments to his translation of Bernheim's book on suggestion, Freud observed:

> The achievement of Bernheim . . . consists precisely in stripping the manifestations of hypnotism of their strangeness. . . . Dr. Bernheim . . . maintains that all the phenomena of hypnotism . . . arise . . . from a suggestion, a conscious idea, which has been introduced into the brain of the hypnotized person by

> an external influence and has been accepted by him as though it had arisen spontaneously. On this view all hypnotic manifestations would be psychical phenomena, effects of suggestions. . . . If the supporters of the suggestion theory are right, all the observations made at the Salpêtrière are worthless; indeed, they become errors in observation.[4]

In a perverse twist of fate, many years later, the empire of psychoanalytic ideas built by Freud would suffer the same devastating critique Freud directed at the Salpêtrière school of Charcot. Clinically and philosophically, Freudian analysis would be accused of being worthless, the result of errors of observation: not empirical observation, but rich observations of a creative imagination given to flights of speculative fancy that invented intrapsychic ghosts with psychodynamic interactions, while neither the ghostly id, ego, or superego and its reciprocal functioning, nor the realm of the unconscious and its repressed sexual wishes, could be proven to exist (see appendix: "Freud's Ghost").

In spite of his gains in Nancy, within Freud's unsettled mind, clinical problems and professional doubts continued to fester. For example, hearkening back to Charcot's warning regarding the danger of hypnosis, Freud considered the possibility that a patient could be robbed of independence by frequent repetitions of suggestion, his concern being that a patient could become addicted to hypnosis as if it were a narcotic necessary for the treatment of morbid symptoms. In addition to the danger of dependency, suggestive therapy was not a clinical method that enabled Freud to understand the etiology or the underlying cause of illness. As a result, suggestive therapy could be likened to a cosmetic treatment of symptoms that had no effect on underlying psychodynamic processes, specifically, the intrapsychic conflicts that in Freud's active imagination were thought to issue in seemingly intractable symptoms. This was particularly bothersome because Freud was a physician who possessed a passion to understand and he sincerely wished to find a reliable clinical method to use in the clinical trenches: a powerful method that would have a lasting curative effect on patients by actively changing the intrapsychic processes thought to lead to the formation of morbid symptoms.

In addition to being haunted by these misgivings, as if he had read Hawthorne's warning and incorporated the daemonic image of the physician-sorcerer, Roger Chillingworth, Freud came to believe that hypnosis "was hackwork and not a scientific activity, and it recalled magic, incantations and hocus-pocus" (*IL*, 449). Disenchanted with the black art and the satisfaction of being admired as a miracle worker and a magician, Freud had come full circle, appearing now to agree with formidable critics who not only saw hypnosis as dangerous, but also viewed hypnotists with contempt. Nevertheless, Freud sustained his belief that psychotherapy of every manner and sort traffics in suggestion, whether a therapist is aware of this or not (*AS*, 42). With this clear vision secured, it is not too much to say that Freud's early interest in and experiments with the black art enabled him to achieve new, groundbreaking insights into the origin, meaning, and power of suggestion as it manifested itself in the special relationship of dialogical therapist and patient: a clinical relationship whose subterranean dynamic happens to be erotic.

Preeminent among these early insights was the novel view that the inscrutable phenomenon Bernheim referred to as suggestibility is "nothing other than the tendency to transference": the transference to the therapist of intense libidinal feelings formed during earlier childhood experience with significant others (*IL*, 446). This was such an important finding that Freud abandoned suggestive therapy as a clinical method, believing that by relinquishing this method he would lose nothing he could not replace, due to the fact that he had rediscovered suggestion as a form of transference. Having collapsed suggestibility into the idea and the idioms of transference, Freud came to understand that the success or failure of dialogical therapy is grounded in transferential aspects of the clinical relationship. If an auto-suggestible patient is able to transfer intense feelings to the person of the therapist—the passionate love of a wife or mistress, the desire to be an affectionate daughter or son, perhaps the longing for Platonic friendship—power, influence, and authority will accrue to the therapist and faith will be invested in his clinical findings. On the other hand, patients who have an insufficient capacity for transference will be indifferent to the therapist, incapable of being influenced, and generally, as Freud commented on patients with a narcissistic disorder, "inaccessible to our efforts and cannot be cured by us" (*IL*, 447). Repeating this recurring theme fifteen years later, Freud simply said: "When there is no . . . transference of emotion . . . there is also no possibility of influencing the patient by psychological means" (*AS*, 42). But there is more here than meets the eye, and when both eyes are opened, they are presented with a panoramic view of an enchanted clinic occupied by a phantastic person preoccupied with the confession of secrets, particularly sexual secrets: the grail of Freud, the curse of Roger Chillingworth, the scourge of Hester Prynne.

SEX AND SUGGESTION

Bernheim's research determined that human beings generally are susceptible to suggestion. In fact Bernheim not only discovered that manifestations of direct hypnosis are the result of suggestion, but in finding that suggestions offered in the waking state achieve the same results as suggestions offered in hypnotic trance, Bernheim handed Freud an enduring foundation on which to construct his psychoanalytic theory and his clinical method. This was especially important in Freud's early clinical years, given his interest in and use of Breuer's method of actively engaging wakened and alert patients in dialogical disclosures of their life history. Equally important, like Charcot, Bernheim failed to determine the cause of suggestibility: a mysterious receptivity for ideas that gives some people unusual power and influence over other seemingly autonomous people who are demonstrably controllable. Filling this vacuum with his psychoanalytic theory and his powerful persona, Freud claimed audaciously that in his clinical consulting room, suggestibility depends on sexuality, specifically, the ability of a patient to invest libido in the person of the analyst. A human being is able to be influenced, even intellectually, if and only if he is able to invest objects with libido; on Freud's account, this is where Bernheim fell short: "He did not know that his '*suggestibilité*' depended on sexuality, on the activity of the libido," particularly libido invested in the person of the physician—the dialogical therapist and trusted clinical confessor (*IL*, 446).

Experiencing his clinical consulting room as a hypnotic milieu capable of eliciting a new species of an older interpersonal attachment activated by a transference of previously formed feelings to the person of the analyst, Freud conceived his pioneering psychoanalytic therapy as a form of suggestion that elicits from analysands a variety of intense feelings during a transference to the analyst of a libidinal attachment that originated in formative experience with significant others. An easy way to clarify the clinical function and utility of these erotic ties is to follow Freud and simply say that a patient's transference provides a therapist with power and influence that can be used not only to "divert" libidinally attached patients "from . . . sick thoughts," but also "to talk [them] out of . . . fears, and so on" (*QL*, 189). On the other hand, the transference of libido can become an obstructive resistance to treatment when it is negative, rather than positive; this often happens when patients transfer feelings of hostility formed in earlier conflicted relationships. Intense sexual desire can become obstructive as well, in as much as a patient strongly affected by a passionate desire for the therapist may focus exclusively on the erotic aspect of the clinical relationship to the detriment of the difficult work of psychological cure. If predominant and prolonged, negative transferences can literally "annul" the constructive work of psychological healing and the dialogical effort to divert a person from sick thoughts may grind to a silent or screeching halt (*TI*, 239).

On Freud's account, in the best possible case, resistance is overcome by providing patients with the insight that current feelings for the therapist originated in and are reproductions of earlier childhood experience having nothing to do with the person of the therapist. In practice, however, the provision of insight is easier said than done because the cognitive-emotional condition of a vulnerable, personality-disordered patient is fragile, often tempestuous, and a therapist's management of this internal state of affairs can make or break the momentum of clinical treatment. Reflecting on his personal experience in the clinical trenches, Freud maintained that libidinal transferences generally are resolved by "convincing" patients that they are reexperiencing repressed remnants of libidinal relationships formed in childhood (*AS*, 43). Given my clinical experience, the stress on "convincing" should not be understated, for the clinical act of convincing erotically attached patients of the transference of libido has the potential for producing in them painful rejection and anger, and when this happens, the insightful encounter, as well as forward momentum, may come to grief.

The strategy of convincing patients of their transference of emotion can be disillusioning. In fact, when the corrective insight is experienced as a personal rejection, particularly in patients diagnosed with a Narcissistic or a Borderline Personality Disorder, provision of insight can literally defeat the motivating enchantment—the clinical spell that increases the power and influence of the beloved therapist and helps to fuel the essential work of cognitive-emotional change. Freud did not speak directly of enchantment but he acknowledged this point in his own way, stating clearly that if a patient experiences a therapist as behaving in an "unfriendly" manner, this would damage "the affectionate attitude" which Freud acknowledged to be "the strongest motive for the patient's taking a share in the joint work of analysis" (*TI*, 233). Unless this sinking ship is cleverly righted, insight regarding transference may become an impediment to the favorable outcome of therapy. Nevertheless, Freud held firm to his dogmatic belief that in every clinical situation one will invariably find "an intense emotional relationship between the patient and the analyst which is not to be accounted for by the actual situation" (*AS*, 42). He also remained convinced that insight regarding meaningful historical relationships provided patients with the golden opportunity to transform a clinical repetition of childhood experience into a potentially curative recollection of an earlier experiential drama, often a drama of a psychosexual sort (*IL*, 444). Suffice it to say, Freud's fixation on transference, setting this in stone as if it were a modern dogma of the therapeutic, precluded him from seeing that a suggestible patient's current intense feelings for the therapist could be a newly formed libidinal attachment to the person of the therapist, rather than a clinical reproduction of childhood experience.

In credible psychological circles, in his own time and after, Freud would be critically challenged on this head, for his exclusive focus on the past and his ensuing failure to focus on the immediate lived experience of therapist and patient was wrongheaded, at least some of the time. Clinical experience suggests that transference may be operative in some cases; in other cases, however, this dynamic is less than clear or it is counter-indicated, given the history of childhood events narrated during clinical confessions. If pressed about this important issue, I am prepared to argue that the intense feelings some patients develop for their therapist originate in the profound intimacy that grows around the full confession and warm acceptance of closely guarded, often shameful, sometimes dark, personal secrets.

The voluntary confession of secrets, conceived by the German sociologist Simmel as an initially tense, ambivalent, existential act of "giving oneself away," may be likened to an irrevocable opening and offering of the inmost self.[5] In a literal sense, the clinical opening and offering of the inmost self fulfills the true meaning or connotation of the word "intimate," for the Latin *intĭmus* was variously used by the orator Cicero, the poet Virgil, the historian Tacitus, and others to convey what is inmost, deepest, most secret. In the clinic, I have had countless male and female patients confide that I know more about them than anyone, including their spouse, lover, and best friend. Indeed, the previously mentioned patient who confided that she had a "connection" with me she never had with anyone else before was expressing the personal experience of giving herself to and experiencing a gratifying intimate relationship with her therapist: a deeply trusting dialogical intimacy that gave her therapist permission to burrow into her inmost self to discover what is hidden, private, concealed, or secret. Everything considered, given the clinical spell that facilitates a full clinical confession—the radical act of giving oneself to a therapeutic confessor—the moral, intellectual, and clinical responsibility of the clinical confessor is profound and thoroughgoing.

Whatever else I might say about clinical spells and dialogical intimacy, one thing is certain: the early Freud was traveling an uncharted road of clinical invention and discovery, having become involved in the modern historical experiment of understanding, managing, and working to resolve intensely emotional, transferential relationships that eroticized the psychoanalytic therapist.

Regarding this intriguing state of affairs, in his postmodern study, *The Birth of the Clinic,* Foucault complained about "the feebly eroticized vocabulary of . . . the 'doctor/patient relationship,'" referring directly to terms like "encounter," an expression I have used quite naturally in this text.[6] Foucault's complaint is justified, for clinical expressions like "significant other" have neither passion nor erotic potential and I am loathe to use them within or outside the mental health clinic. But Freud's vision of the clinical situation and the therapist-patient relationship was loaded with erotic potential and to this day, although his psychoanalytic work has been disvalued and is held in low esteem in reputable empirical quarters, if carefully considered, Freud's early perception of the clinical relationship was illuminating because it was eroticized fully, rather than feebly. But this was not a puerile erotization that wallowed in boorish sexual gratification. Rather, Freud conceived the erotization of the therapist as a useful therapeutic instrument, clinical tool, or agent, involving the illusory attachment of men and women to the person of the therapist: an illusory autohypnotic or auto-suggestive attachment that had a fateful birth and a prior life in a patient's libidinal relationship to significant others.

I value some of Ferenczi's conceptions here because he tried to unravel the causal dynamic of auto-suggestive erotizations while focusing on suggestibility ominously, but correctly, I think, as a vibrant "receptivity for ideas, with the inclination to blind belief and obedience" (*IT*, 60). Having something akin to a blind belief in psychoanalysis until he broke with Freud over the hot issue of the historical truth of childhood sexual experience—Ferenczi continuing to support Freud's original belief in the historical reality of childhood seduction, Freud altering his original seduction theory by embracing the psychodynamics of unconscious wishes—Ferenczi maintained that autohypnosis and auto-suggestion "are states in which unconscious ideas," most notably, the fixations of childhood, "without any intended external influence, bring about all the neuro-psychic phenomena of deliberate suggestion and hypnosis" (*IT*, 71). On Ferenczi's succinct account of Freud's transformative thinking, the eroticized therapist is not the chief actor in the clinical drama of suggestor and medium, rather, the person of the therapist may be likened to a "catalytic ferment" able to elicit an erotic tie or a libidinal transference, while "the unconscious mental forces of the 'medium' appear to be the real active agent" (*IT*, 34, 51).

Perhaps it is not too much to say that a prospective patient's anticipation of the helping therapist, as well as the historical reputation of the mental health clinic as a place of psychological healing, initiate the entrancement of some patients *in advance* of the clinical encounter, as if an imaginary clinic and an imagined clinician were a powerful prelude to a symphony of psychological healing in the minds of auto-suggestible patients. Evidencing this interesting and important preclinical phenomenon, a prospective patient telephoned to determine whether she wanted to pursue clinical treatment with me or not. After confessing a laundry list of serious "mental health issues," to use her language for a mountain of emotional and existential struggles that would have given Sisyphus pause, she confided that she had "Googled me" and thought I had "more depth than the others." I did not ask her to identify the anonymous "others"; rather, I followed the metaphor and guessed that she had gathered evidence of my involvement in psychotherapy *and* philosophy, particularly the latter, insofar as philosophy has a historical reputation for being a "deep" subject for "deep thinkers." She followed this confession by commenting on our current conversation, stating: "You didn't flinch when I told you my mental health issues." Finally, after establishing a date and time for her initial evaluation, she confided: "I like your name, 'Carl Paul' is strong and masculine!"

It may stretch credulity to say that this prospective patient was in the inchoate stage of clinical enchantment prior to crossing the threshold of the clinic and actually meeting her therapist. But I am inclined to entertain this thought, for during the initial telephone conversation when she was "sizing-up" the stranger she would become intimate with clinically, she imagined her future therapist as (a) a strong or powerful individual, (b) a person who had the "depth" or knowledge and mental acuity required to understand her psychological problems, (c) a clinician who was not fearful of descending into Hades and taking on the challenge of her Sisyphean struggles. In advance of treatment, to put it clearly, this prospective patient was involved in the entrancing process of investing libido in an imaginary place and in an imaginary person; and this preclinical investment of libido was an elementary part of the catalytic ferment that elicited an erotic tie that gave an ordinary dialogical therapist the clinical power and influence to effect a psychological healing once thought to be the stuff of miracle workers and magicians.

Mind you, some auto-suggestible patients cross the threshold of clinical adventure as though they were archetypal heroes undertaking the trials and tribulations that will issue in personal revitalization or self-renewal. In these noteworthy cases, therapeutic work occurs in a meaningful context of variables that includes the manifest hope of healing or cure, the intimate, interactive dialogical relationship of patient and therapist, as well as other previously identified features of clinical enchantments, such as an enthrallment with clinical confession, the charming language, ideas, and speech of the therapist and, as we shall now see, the illusional perception of the therapist as a phantastic person. Without this chemistry of nuclear elements, the clinical ferment would be less catalytic and in some cases, dialogical therapy would be as tedious and boring as Freud found the hypnotic method of his phantastic person, Jean Martin Charcot.

THE PHANTASTIC PERSON OF THE THERAPIST

When Freud spoke of libido, he was referring to an unmeasurable quantity of instinctual energy, specifically, energy of the sexual instinct. When he spoke of libidinal attachments, he was referring to an investment of the energy of the sexual instinct. Regarding enchantments of the clinic, with specific reference to a patient's libidinal attachment to a clinician, the single most important thing to know is this: if and when an auto-suggestible patient transfers libido to a clinician, the energy of the sexual instinct is not invested in the actual person of the clinician, rather, it is invested in or attaches to an emanation, an apparition, an imaginary entity, or an illusory person. Since the psychological healer in question is a dialogical therapist, and dialogical therapists come from many different schools that educate them to play many different language games while engaged in the art of clinical persuasion, I shall borrow Freud's insightful notion of the phantastic person, but I shall speak of the *phantastic person of the therapist*, understanding that the phantastic person is a mental health clinician using his power, influence, and charming words to engage in the process of "talking people into or out of things," as Freud suggested in a previously referenced letter to his onetime friend, Fliess.

Demonstrating the virtual existence of the phantastic person with examples drawn from my clinical practice, I can attest to the fact that countless patients have whispered one or another version of the plea, "I trust you, you're the doctor!" not to mention the ominous request, "Just tell me what to do!" One middle-aged male, who had an incestuous relationship with his teenage daughter for approximately five years, begged tearfully: "My father didn't teach me anything, but you're the *wizard*, so tell me what to do!" He was clearly crazed like many patients, but not crazy in the psychotic sense of being afflicted with the kind of hallucinations and delusions that result in a gross separation from shared reality, although he confessed that his twelve-year-old daughter seduced him, repeating the common defense one often hears from sexual perpetrators who hide behind the skirts of their victims. Like a variety of medical doctors, judges, attorneys, teachers, therapists, and other seemingly competent people who present in the clinic as if they are regressed adolescents who do not know how to live their lives, or worse, children who do not know what they are supposed to do, this crazed perpetrator seemed eager to lose himself in his therapist, as if I really were a wizard with Merlin's secret knowledge, magical power, and sorcerer's skill.

In truth, I am embarrassed to say that Merlin seems to exist from time to time in clinical interactions that evolve within the ambiguous, irreal space of the clinical confessional. Of course when I gaze in the mirror, particularly after a long day in the clinical trenches, the wizard never comes into view because I am unable to see what entranced patients are seeing and experiencing during the clinical hour when phantastic things take place beyond my conscious intending. But it would not be a gross exaggeration to say that the imaginary perceptions of auto-suggestible patients are manifestations of certain enchantments of the clinic: an unintended masquerade of artful illusion or a sophisticated masquerade of truth, including complementary roles and functions, theatrical props, and emanations of irreal identity, all of which, when staged and played out in the clinical consulting room, create a true drama begotten by a false manifestation.[7] Often, the true drama gives the lie to Freud's assumption that the intense feelings patients transfer to the therapist are not accounted for by the therapist's behavior, the clinical relationship itself, or the treatment situation (*IL*, 441–42). In fact, the false manifestation suggests a glaring inconsistency in Freud's thinking about the clinical situation. Specifically, in his final assessment of the clinical trenches, as if he had lost sight of his early discovery of the phantastic person, Freud asserted clearly and distinctly that the clinical "relationship is based on a love of truth—that is, on a recognition of reality—and . . . it precludes any kind of sham or deceit" (*TI*, 248). This honorable attitude of mind is unmistakably Socratic, however, I can assure the reader that when a dialogical therapist becomes phantastic in the eyes and ears of a suggestible patient the clinical relationship is not based on a love of truth, rather, the clinical relationship is based on Nietzschean virtues of appearance and illusion—un-Socratic virtues that allowed Freud and phantastic therapists who followed in his wake, to make a fine clinical use of sham and deceit. In the final analysis, the clinical masquerade of truth bestows upon a therapist the power and the influence to do good or ill, depending on discriminating variables of character, clinical skill, conscious intention, and caprice.

I happen to have Dupuytren's Contracture, a fact that was quite evident to a medical doctor I was treating some years ago. Sitting across from me during a clinical encounter in which he informed me that his weekly therapy was a welcome "respite from madness," the astute doctor's medical gaze was drawn to the gross deformity in the little finger of my left hand. "You have Dupuytren's Contracture," he exclaimed correctly, after which he gave me the name of "the best hand man in the city," encouraging me to have this impairment surgically corrected. Now Dupuytren's is a thickening of connective tissue in the hand, in my case, in the knuckle of the little finger of my left hand. This genetic condition, reputedly visited on males who have the blood of Vikings, resulted in a painless bending or contracture of my little finger at the knuckle. Clearly deformed, my finger cannot be straightened or extended; it is fixed in a contracted condition, such that I have difficulty putting on a glove in winter and I am unable to use the finger as I am typing this sentence on the computer keyboard. Surgery will release the contracture so that the finger is straightened, but after surgery the straightened finger cannot be bent or contracted. In fine, I have the choice of a flawed finger that is permanently extended or a flawed finger that is permanently contracted. But that is not the reason I am going on about this disorder. Rather, I was surprised to learn that a patient became fixed on this little finger, in fact, she was so enthralled by the "graceful" appearance of the little finger, silently taking in mental images week after week while my left arm rested atop the arm of the large leather armchair I occupy during the clinical hour, that she literally wrote a brief commentary on the aesthetics of my hand, emphasizing her ongoing fascination with the graceful finger she perceived as beautiful, rather than flawed, ugly, or deformed. Mind you, this was not a case of a man's faults lying gracefully upon him as one might expect in a taut Elizabethan drama. Rather, in this patient's suggestible mind, the natural grace and beauty of the finger resulted in phantastic inferences about the natural poise, elegance, and refinement of the therapist himself. Believing that a man's hands carry mute messages about his personal qualities, as a man might believe that the size and shape of a woman's breasts carry erotic messages about the woman herself, I would venture to say that my patient's libido attached to a therapist, in part, due to a deformity mistakenly perceived as a marker of a therapist's graceful way with women, not to mention refinement in other aspects of his life.

With this in mind, when I speak of the enchantments of entranced patients, I am not only referring to fixations on physical attributes or parts, such as my deformed finger. Rather, I am referring to a more inclusive "dream-like consciousness," to use a comparative expression of the phenomenological philosopher, Merleau-Ponty: a "mythical or dream-like consciousness" which, like "insanity and perception" is not "hermetically sealed," but "open[s] on to a horizon of possible objectifications" (*PP*, 292).[8] Clarifying the point, Merleau-Ponty argued cogently that primitive men and women literally live their myths in the context of a comprehensive assortment of daily activities like hunting and fishing, such that these lived myths "form a world" or, as I would prefer to say, mythical or dream-like consciousness forms a whole world of meaning and intelligibility by virtue of which "appearance is reality" and "real being and appearance are one"; conceived this way, "perceiving is pinning one's faith" or "placing one's belief in a world" of meaning and intelligibility, however veridical or illusory, adequate or inadequate, dream-like perception and mythical belief may be (*PP*, 294, 297).

In this phenomenological context, dialogical therapists of every manner and sort, irrespective of gender, ethnicity, personality type, or professional status, have the potential to become powerful and influential, imaginary or phantastic persons in the eyes of patients, for there are many ways of being seen and imagined, many ways of being enchanting and becoming enchanted, many ways of being experienced or "lived" by a mythical or dream-like consciousness capable of forming a world of meaning and intelligibility and placing belief and expectation in the objectifications that world presents.

For example, my clinical partner, JCG, is a highly skilled female therapist and media personality with a well-deserved reputation for treating victims of trauma. In fact, she specializes in children's therapy down the hall from the consulting room where I generally treat adults. In pre-enchantment days, that is, days preceding my awareness of the enchantments of the clinic, I often thought that children were having a therapeutic experience just being in the presence of my partner. She has a ready smile, a smile so palpable, that I would swear I can literally hear her smiling when I listen to her radio broadcasts. In the clinic, she presents warmly, in an open, inviting way that must feel like a gentle caress, or a life-saving embrace, to emotionally impaired children. She also has a singular capacity to be playful and she is capable of responding to children gleefully in the wink of an eye. In fact, she is a puppeteer who not only learned to make her own marionettes early on during a memorable summer spent working at Pelham Puppets, a puppet factory in Marlborough, near Oxford, England, but she also is responsible for designing and introducing the use of anatomically correct puppets—puppets with a penis—in serious clinical evaluations of sexually abused children.

As I was saying, I formerly thought that children experienced JCG as therapeutic in her person, given her inimitable attributes. But I now believe that she literally enchants and charms many of the emotionally damaged children in her care. In her play therapy room, with its puppets and games, crayons and coloring books, fairy tale pictures and potato heads, clinical seduction and enchantment have a unique form and manner, entirely different from the clinical seduction and enchantment taking place a short distance down the hall where another therapist, who rarely smiles, is intense and highly verbal, has an entirely different way of designing his space and presenting himself in his person, as well as in oracular language, ideas, and speech.

Mind you, in both cases, I am not using the expression "clinical seduction" in the pejorative sense of Dr. X leading patient Y astray, although leading a patient astray in the mental health clinic is not only possible, but also happens from time to time, sad to say. Indeed, I am disposed to believe that leading astray, as well as clinical error, is more likely to happen when a dialogical therapist adopts Ferenczi's application of suggestion and hypnosis, to wit, deliberately establishing conditions under which the tendency to blind belief and uncritical obedience is transferred to a therapist hypnotizing or suggesting. More to the point, when I use the expression "seduction" in the clinical context, I am basing my usage on the Latin *dūcĕre*, from which the verb "seduce" is derived; strictly speaking, *dūcĕre* simply means "to lead" or "guide." What I have in mind, of course, is leading or guiding patients toward emotional well-being or "mental health," as Sabrina wrote in a previously referenced letter when she mentioned her phantastic therapist's "unnerving ability to ask a simple question that leads to a startling realization . . . driving me towards mental health."

When I first brought my conclusion to my partner's attention, the conclusion that she was enchanting and seductively charming her patients, she was understandably startled, more so, when she became an observing ego during the clinical hour and began to raise critical questions about authenticity and theatrical performance, not to mention the truth and falsity of her language, ideas, and speech. After careful consideration and time spent gathering phenomenological evidence, she not only became increasingly aware of her capacity to seductively charm children, she also embraced this gift and now, in a self-conscious way, allows clinical enchantments to manifest themselves and work for the benefit or her patients.

Interestingly, JCG confided that this new awareness "changed her practice" in the trenches of child therapy—changed her practice "for the better." She may be doing the same things she was doing previously, but now, she is doing these things with awareness and a heightened sense of responsibility for the power and influence she possesses and the way she uses it freely. This is why I have invited other dialogical therapists to engage in the adventure of discovering the characteristic ways in which their idiosyncratic gifts, their presentation of self, the clinical milieu they design and inhabit, can put them in possession of the power of the wizard and the enormous responsibility this power and influence bestows upon dialogical therapists, regardless of the style of therapy or the countless language games they play. I would only caution that it is possible to become enchanted with the idea and the reality of being enchanting.

In my own case, I had the pleasure of treating a woman in her early fifties who attended a women's therapy group I facilitated with JCG. At the time, Marilyn was an unmarried foster mother struggling against the odds in the fashion of Sisyphus, a mythic character who awakened one day to find himself struggling with a mammoth boulder in the bowels of Hades. Making her boulder heavier and difficult to move, was a hard to manage, emotionally disturbed adolescent foster child who was in treatment with my partner. Unfortunately, Marilyn had been down on her luck ever since she became a victim of incest, awakening one morning to find herself in her own private Hades when she was nine years old. A hard-working, poorly paid sales clerk, she was neither well educated nor skilled in any special way, except to say, she was a personable woman who had an easy way with people, particularly her peers in the women's therapy group she regularly attended. In fact, her guileless way of seeing, hearing, and speaking was quite charming, although it was off-putting to a few of the women in the group who had a tendency to look down their nose at seemingly simpler folk. In a real sense, Marilyn was an uncut diamond like many of the uneducated criminals I met when I worked in a maximum security prison—uncut, but desirous of being faceted and refined. Offering evidence of her native ability, Marilyn was dedicated to therapy and she processed, participated in, and benefited greatly from the animated dialogue common in the group of better-educated professional women. In retrospect, I can state without reservation that this ingenuous woman benefited more from group therapy than her peers, because she was motivated for treatment, she was involved authentically in the process of confronting her problems, and she never resisted the difficult business of challenging herself, for she harbored the hope of profiting from constructive change in her thinking and behavior. Demonstrating the point, Marilyn had used a good number of illicit drugs during her twenties and thirties, but she achieved an abiding abstinence from chemical substances long before we became acquainted—a result, no doubt, of her true mettle, false appearances of being a dimwit notwithstanding.

While working toward formal treatment goals in the women's group, Marilyn became overwhelmed by some painful remembrances of things past, particularly an emotionally damaging experience of childhood incest and to a lesser extent, the death of a former lover who died unexpectedly from an overdose of chemical substances. Prior to this fateful regression, I had not treated Marilyn individually, however, given the solid clinical relationship that evolved during our weekly group experience, her authentic work, and my sincere desire to turn a therapeutic trick on her behalf, I offered to see her pro bono to help her resolve current emotional struggles. About halfway through our first clinical hour, our first and only clinical hour, to my surprise, Marilyn bemoaned the fact that she had been "stuck in a deep hole" her whole life and was "never able to get out!" This self-generated image of imprisonment, of existential paralysis, of stuckness in life, gave me the magic metaphor I needed to set Marilyn's liberation in motion.

Commonly, during clinical interactions that expose nuclear elements of their personal struggle, patients will offer a colorful image that characterizes and objectifies their existential situation vividly. I always have an ear cocked for these dramatic fictions, for the announcement of a concrete image allows me to empathically enter a patient's experiential world—normally an oppressive world of harsh experience in which a person has been stuck cognitively and emotionally. The image of Sisyphus engaged in endless futile labor on his hellish mountain in Hades is one such image, but there are many others: a deep hole, a sand dune, a hurricane, a locked basement, to name a few memorable fictions. Once inside the patient's experiential world I am able to creatively develop a pragmatic action plan that will liberate a person from the fixed experience of self and world imaged vividly by the dramatic fiction. Accordingly, I loved Marilyn's image of the inescapable deep hole, in fact, I found it delicious because it was a workable existential situation: a phenomenological experience of imprisonment that included a tantalizing upper opening for escape, provided I could help Marilyn find a way to climb up and out of self-imposed imprisonment.

Not given to letting grass grow under my feet during important clinical struggles, this personal animus having found an abiding home in my conception of existential therapy as a dynamic, action-oriented movement of patients toward the future, I seized the moment by embracing the inviting image of the imprisoning hole. Sensing that Marilyn was ripe and ready for liberating movement toward the future; suspecting from previous group encounters that I might have the power and influence of the wizard as a result of Marilyn's investment of libido in her vision and version of a therapist's phantastic person; I looked her squarely in the eyes, held her gaze, and said calmly and authoritatively: "I want you to climb out of the hole, let go of the dead weight of the past, and never look back. It's time. You can do it!" There was no razzle-dazzle here, no hocus-pocus, no sleight of hand, no smoke and mirrors, except to say, I had a notion that when Marilyn was sighing on the sofa in my consulting room she was not seeing a real human person with virtues and vices, including his own flaws of character and agonistic struggles. Rather, I firmly believed that Marilyn was perceiving the powerful phantasm of the seemingly wise, omniscient Dr. E: the emanation an entranced woman experienced during a fateful season of change when she came under the influence of the enchantment of the clinic and allowed a charming wizard with fair words to burrow into her intimacy.

Regarding this instructive clinical interaction and its auto-suggestive elements, I am mindful of the fact that Ferenczi focused on the phantastic appearance of the hypnotist, claiming that auto-suggestion is facilitated by the imposing physical attributes of the suggestor, not only a "black beard," but also "a notable stature, thick eyebrows, a penetrating glance, and a stern expression of countenance," although Ferenczi allowed that an expression that "arouses confidence" will compensate for the absence of the other opulent attributes (*IT*, 58). Clinical experience suggests that Ferenczi was enchanted with theatrical imagery when he authored this paradigmatic description of the Svengalian hypnotist in 1909, for these picturesque physical attributes common in the cathartic world of stage-plays and films are not important in the erotic world of clinical irreality. Yet Ferenczi was on the money when he focused on the patient's erotic disposition toward the phantastic therapist, noting that the success of suggestion is facilitated by the therapist's self-confident attitude and reputation for clinical success, not to mention the esteem that accrues to a respected person of science, whether a doctor or some other clinical type, who has the good fortune to occupy a seemingly sacred, honored station in life. Furthermore, Ferenczi's clinical experience, particularly his considerable experience with auto-suggestive patients, taught him that hypnotic "commands . . . must be given with such decision and sureness that contradiction should appear to the patient as quite impossible. . . . A preliminary condition of every successful suggestion . . . *is that the hypnotist . . . must be able to arouse in the [subject] the same feelings of love or fear, the same conviction of infallibility, as those with which his parents inspired him as a child*" (*IT*, 58, 60).

In retrospect, the critical element of self-confidence; the reputation for success; the esteem attached to being a clinician; the decisive command impervious to contradiction; the appearance of infallibility bespeaking the authoritative relationship of powerful parent to obedient child; the arousal of love or some other libidinal feeling; this mélange of potential enchantment applied with uncanny success to my single, fateful encounter with a woman who convinced herself erroneously that she had been imprisoned in a deep hole her whole life, in the fashion of Sisyphus, who was condemned to life in Tartarus: a dreary place of punishment deep within the bowels of the underworld, much lower than Hades, the realm of the dead.

I am still astonished to think that Marilyn followed my authoritative command to climb out of her hole; for climb out she did, posthaste. Indeed, she returned to the women's group a few days later like a reborn analogue of Frankenstein quickened into life by an electrical charge that compelled her to gleefully shout: "I'm alive, I'm alive!" Specifically, Marilyn advised her peers that she had climbed out of her hole and as a result of our single therapy session, experienced significant emotional relief, now feeling a renewed sense of self and a new determination to do everything in her power to change her life. Naturally, she received considerable support from her peers and soon thereafter, she commenced the search for a new, better paying, more elevating job. She purchased a new navy blue suit for job interviews and in short order, she found a better paying, more prestigious job as a flight attendant, of all things—an interesting find, in view of the fact that she climbed out of her hole running and then seemed to take wing, as if she were flying. Soon thereafter, in order to travel south for in-flight training, she left the women's group and bid farewell to the enchanted clinic because her new life required relocation out of state.

For a time, Marilyn reported by phone intermittently, expressing gratitude to everyone who helped change her life. During one call taken by JCG, she reported a budding new romance, but she also confided: "He's not Dr. E!" Auto-suggestibility, libidinal attachment, power and influence, talking people into and out of things, overcoming resistance: clinical experience with this enchanted patient seemed to offer unequivocal evidence of these Freudian variables. But clinical situations of this sort are loaded with daemonic potential and they may become dangerously seductive, both for the enchanted patient and the enterprising phantastic therapist who, by virtue of his charms—fair words and various other visible and imagined illusions of his station—comes into possession of an intoxicating power to heal and to do great harm.

I recall one gentleman I was treating in the adult outpatient clinic of the urban hospital where I labored and learned from my patients in the fashion of Freud in Charcot's neurological clinic. Halfway through the clinical hour, he suddenly rose from the sofa, knelt at my feet submissively, and embraced my legs with both arms, in mute adoration. When I reacted in startled disbelief, gently pushing him away from my body, he ran from my office and cowered in a corner of the waiting room, utterly rejected and emotionally decomposed. After a vain attempt to bring him to his senses, security was called to transport this poor man to the inpatient wing due to his unmanageable decompensation. Less severe, but equally telling, at the end of a tearful, emotionally cathartic clinical hour, as she rose to leave the consulting room of my private practice, a married, bright, college-educated woman asked nonchalantly if she could have a hug. Given her painful clinical confession, I complied with her request naïvely, hoping to console her before she left the office and drove away discomposed in traffic. She went limp in my arms as if she were ecstatically transported, like Teresa of Avila, experiencing the delectable torment, distress, and death described so vividly by the ecstatic saint of Jesus.[9] As I secured her dead weight to protect her from falling to the floor she whispered in my ear: "I've fantasized about this; I'm taking you in by your smell." In another case, finding herself emotionally relieved by the noteworthy progress I managed to achieve with her delinquent daughter, a grateful mother put it baldly: "Dr. Ellerman is God!" Like everything else in the human estate, this cuts both ways. I shall never forget the self-absorbed woman who commented grossly during one memorable clinical confession: "You're my toilet; it's nice to come in here every week and dump on you!"

Needless to say, comparison to a toilet is a draining of esteem; identification with God is heady stuff, the kind of power and influence capable of intoxicating a person who is not in command of his own narcissistic drama. Please understand: if I had crossed the path of these enthralled individuals outside the clinic, without benefit of my title and the trappings of a seemingly elevated station, not to mention other variables capable of creating a phantasmal appearance, they would not have given me a second look. I am neither a man of notable stature, nor a Svengali-like figure with a lengthy black beard, thick eyebrows, a penetrating glance, or stern countenance. Within the clinic, however, the advanced degrees on the wall, the glorified title "doctor," impressive books luxuriating on glass-encased shelves, abundant fair words, the grand expectation of healing life's emotional wounds, the aura of secret knowledge that promises power over mental illness, as if a clinical demigod had the power, courage, and will to descend into the valley of death to battle the beast of eternal darkness—all the illusions of an elevated station give phantastic dialogical therapists daemonic power and influence over large numbers of suggestible people.

On the other hand, the patient who appeared in the clinic regularly to "dump on" Dr. E, as if he were a living receptacle for linguistic feces, was never going to become enchanted with her dialogical therapist. Human beings do not become enchanted with toilets or with fecal matter unless they are sexually disordered fetishists in the throe of coprophilia or happen to use the toilet and fecal matter sadistically, to humiliate and degrade others during erotic contact. Given the urgency of another pressing disorder, I did not pursue the possibility of a paraphilia with the "toilet lady"; but I can confirm the fact that this particular patient never enveloped herself in her therapist, as if she were mindful of the fact that if she were enveloped, she risked being flushed away with the transfer of her problems, as if she were foul feces.

It is one thing to believe that psychological healing is achieved by the use of charms: fair words spoken to an enthused patient in an enchanted clinic. It is quite another thing to elaborate on Plato's dark saying with reference to auto-suggestive erotizations, libidinal attachments, infallibility, blind belief and obedience, in short, unyielding devotion to an illusory person who happens to be quite human. Still, these conceptual formulations have the ring of truth, in fact, these inflammatory ideas are remarkably consistent with my clinical experience of Marilyn and other seemingly entranced patients who became enchanted with the clinic and effectively charmed by and sometimes blindly devoted to a dialogical therapist's phantastic person.

The erotic attachment of patients to the phantastic person of the therapist is an important clinical tool whose use may be interesting, even exciting. In practice, however, the clinical journey down this dusty back road is replete with danger. There are bumps in the road at every turn and no one is wise enough to see all the potholes ahead, because human motive and emotional reactivity can be irrational, ambivalent, unpredictable, and sometimes as inscrutable as enigmatic dark matter hiding surreally and surreptitiously in intergalactic space. In fine, the ease with which I manage and use these words about enchantments, auto-suggestion, enthrallments, and erotic attachments to phantastic persons fails to accurately convey the intense emotional experience of the enchanted patient, the interpersonal difficulties that arise in the attempt to manage and use these enchantments constructively, and the problems that occur when the enchantment is grossly mismanaged, not to mention the possibility that an unscrupulous therapist might abuse the power and influence, the blind obedience, and the will-less submission issuing from an erotization of the clinical relationship. This latter possibility, I suspect, was one of Menninger's apprehensions when he offered his analysis of erotization resistance, thereby condemning the erotization of the clinic as immoral and harmful to patients. Given a modern psychological reading of Hawthorne and a realistic hunch that underneath the pretense, the illusions, the false appearance of things, clinicians are confessors of a lesser god, this was a prudent fear that the deformed character of a learned doctor like Roger Chillingworth would give him the "faculty of transforming himself into a devil": a fiendish man capable of becoming "not a spectator only, but a chief actor, in the poor [patient's] interior world," enabling the devilish doctor to "play upon him as he chose . . . as at the waving of a magician's wand" (*SL*, 211, 176).

A SPELL THAT DOES NOT CURE

I am acutely aware of the fact that my remarks concerning a therapist's phantastic person fail to clean clinical windows, for once he trips the light phantastic in the eyes and ears of a patient, a therapist must do something productive with the phantasmagoria his phenomenal presence catalyzed and cocreated. By all accounts, this is where Freud's clinical work came a cropper. In spite of his dedication, his insights, his powerful persona, the reputed miracle of suggestion, and the transferences of libido, in short, the instrumental enchantments begotten in his eroticized clinic, Freud's phantastic person failed to produce the clinical results he desired and worked hard to achieve. This is a stunning turn of events given the fact that in his clinical consulting room at 19 Berggasse in Vienna, Freud was not seeking the moon! Comparing my own desire for lunar orbit with Freud's penchant for keeping his feet on the ground, Freud's clinical goals seem humble, realistic, and achievable. For example, regarding patients with maladaptive character disorders—fixed patterns of thinking and behavior that have a deleterious effect on personal and interpersonal functioning—Freud stated that his aim was not to "rub off every peculiarity of human character for the sake of a schematic 'normality,' nor yet to demand that the person . . . shall . . . develop no internal conflicts. The business of the analysis is to secure the best possible psychological conditions for the functions of the ego; with that it has discharged its task" (*TI*, 250).

Needless to say, the clinical goal of securing the "best possible" functioning of the ego is not only modest, but realistic, showing that Freud had come to understand that intrapsychic change was elusive when dealing with disorders that identify a person's essential nature. Similarly, in today's crazy world of managed healthcare, third-party insurers will not reimburse clinical work targeting personality disorders, although in many cases these maladaptive disorders of self are not only prominent, but oftentimes, the central agent of personal unhappiness and professional dysfunction. Nevertheless, Freud's clinical goal seems modest and achievable, not the least reason being that "best possible" functioning of the ego is ill-defined, indiscriminate, and unmeasurable: as open-ended and ambiguous, as Socrates' antique quest for best possible state of the soul. As a result, we are left to wonder why enduring therapeutic results were not achieved in the clinical trenches within Freud's consulting room where psychoanalytic war was waged against the idiosyncratic emotional illnesses and communal pathology of psychological man.

Early on in his clinical career, Freud was a man who harbored serious reservations about his medical training and his clinical skills; writing forthrightly to Fliess in 1888, during the interval between his studies of hypnotism with Charcot and his work on suggestion with Bernheim, Freud confessed: "I have not learned enough to be a medical practitioner. . . . So it seems I must remain what I am; but I have no illusions about the inadequacy of this state of affairs" (*FL*, 23–24). In spite of these personal reservations, for a brief time, as we have seen, due to the miracle of suggestion, Freud's feeling of clinical helplessness was replaced by the satisfaction of being admired as a magician. But he became a clinical magician whose psychoanalytic method failed to produce psychological healing, as if a wizard's charming words were falling on deaf ears. In the mind of Freud, this was no minor matter, for when this clinical failure is experienced as a deafness or a deficit in the patient it can produce the "tyranny of suggestion," by force of which a jilted hypnotist may wish to visit verbal violence on patients who fail to become enchanted, spellbound, influenced, or controlled by therapeutic suggestion (*GR*, 27–28). Whatever the case may have been with the tyranny of suggestion in Freud's early clinical experience, much later, in 1937, in a final assessment of his struggles in the clinical trenches, while focusing on psychoanalysis as a therapeutic technique, Freud compared the business of dialogical therapy to other "'impossible' professions in which one can be sure beforehand of achieving unsatisfactory results" (*TI*, 248). Cancer-ridden, Freud died two years later, leaving both admirers and detractors with this concluding remark, widely seen as overly pessimistic or soberly realistic.

A quarter century later, at the onset of the turbulent 1960s, while reflecting realistically on the unproductive nature of Freudian analysis, a former president of the American Psychological Association alluded to Freud as a wizard without clothes, proclaiming critically: "From testimony now available from both the friends and the foes of analysis, it is clear that, at best, analysis casts a spell but does not cure."[10] In his own time at the end of an extraordinary culture-changing career, Freud was poignantly aware of this state of affairs. In his final assessment of the future prospects of his flawed brainchild, psychoanalysis, he maintained that positive therapeutic results hinge on "the power" of psychoanalytic therapy to strengthen a patient's ego; he also stated clearly in a telling reminiscence of hopeful things past that "no substitute for hypnosis has yet to be found. From this point of view we can understand how such a master as Ferenczi came to devote the last years of his life to therapeutic experiments, which unhappily, proved to be vain" (*TI*, 230).

A puzzled person may reasonably ask why Freud's clinical interventions were unproductive. Specifically, if I grant that Freud had the ability to cast a clinical spell, why did his particular spell fail to result in some sort of enduring psychological healing or emotional cure? If it is true that a clinical spell gives a therapist the power and the influence to talk people into and out of things, in fact, to talk people out of fears, and so on, to use Freud's felicitous formulation, a reasonable person might find himself baffled when considering the notorious failure of Freudian enchantments. Evaluation of my own clinical experience suggests five simple answers that shed some light on spells that do not cure.

In the mental health clinic: (1) it is not the enchanting spell that cures, rather, the clinical spell is a useful instrument or a valuable tool that facilitates the difficult work of using language and ideas to persuade patients to move toward the future in a way that enables them to realize petrified potentials; (2) in order to initiate and control the process of psychological healing it is not sufficient to cast a clinical spell that results solely in protracted dialogue and interminable analysis of the past, absent a pragmatic treatment plan that compels remedial action on the part of symptomatic patients whose maladaptive attitudes and behavior require targeted change; (3) the seemingly banal task of talking people into things translates into the critically important life-changing task of talking people into cognitive attitudes and concrete historical action that enables them to move toward the future by addressing the real problems of life head on—unending, Sisyphean problems, the avoidance of which usually results in clinical symptoms of depression and anxiety; (4) the seemingly commonplace task of talking people out of things translates into the life-affirming task of using charming words to talk people out of attitudes and behavior that are self-defeating or worse, self-destructive; (5) if remedial action in the physical environment or in the lifeworld of persons, places, and things is blocked and a person cannot move toward the future by escaping the field of action, an adaptive change of attitude is required to achieve a Sisyphean reconciliation with the distressing situation. I have witnessed this reconciliatory move firsthand in the cognitive attitudes and alterable moods of inmates imprisoned in the tightly controlled maximum security prison where I once taught philosophy. To a greater degree, the inability to alter the contour and context of life also obtained in Nazi death camps, where inmates engaged in a daily Darwinian struggle for physical and emotional survival at the extremes of human experience. Culling wisdom from his early experience in Dachau and Buchenwald, concentration camps in use before Hitler's infamous death camps were constructed, child psychologist Bruno Bettelheim concluded that no matter how bad the treatment and whatever the conditions of life, each person had one remaining human freedom, to wit, the freedom to choose an attitude toward one's existential situation.[11]

Trite as it may seem, one essential difference between a spell that does not cure and a spell that has a chance of achieving measurable results is the use of clinical dialogue to persuade struggling patients to find workable solutions to the real problems of life, the avoidance or neglect of which often results in sedimented symptoms. Given this pragmatic spirit, an opportunistic existential therapist uses charming words and other instrumental agents of change to engage patients in concrete historical action that resembles the unappealing image of Sisyphus straining under the weight of his boulder in the lower underworld of Hades. By comparison, Freud's clinical work may have been a spellbinding exercise of dialogical persuasion, of talking people into and out of things, as young Dr. Freud averred. But talk is cheap, even in an enchanted clinic, unless talk has cash value that issues in concrete action that works to generate constructive change in the internal environment of cognition and belief or the external environment of persons, places, and things that identifies a person's existential situation.

Thematizing this clearly in 1959, while reporting on his struggle for survival in Theresienstadt, Auschwitz, and Dachau, after losing his father, mother, brother, and wife to the horrors of a living nightmare, pioneering existential therapist Viktor Frankl observed pragmatically: "Our answer must consist, not in talk . . . but in right action. . . . Life ultimately means taking the responsibility to find the right answer to its problems and to fulfill the tasks which it constantly sets for each individual."[12] Earlier, in 1946, after fighting in the French Resistance against occupying Nazi forces, the existential philosopher Jean-Paul Sartre offered a defense of existentialism premised on the optimistic thesis that human beings are able to create themselves, that the destiny of humankind is within each of us, but life hinges on deeds, in fact, there is hope only in action.[13]

The clinical application of this hard-won existentialist wisdom is this: the ability to elicit an auto-suggestive spell gives dialogical therapists increased power and influence, but power and influence must be put to good use and not misspent on analytic chatter that often identifies protracted or interminable dialogical therapy. Spent wisely, a clinician's power and influence midwifes pragmatic action that addresses, in some concrete way, the agonistic struggles patients bring to the clinic. Successful resolution of these struggles does not occur in every case, to be sure, and in the trenches, the struggle against illness and death is never unfailing or certain, even with use of psychotropic medication as a weapon. Nevertheless, clinical experience suggests that when a patient becomes (a) enchanted with the clinic, (b) libidinally attached or erotically tied to the phantastic person of the therapist, and (c) effectively charmed by the fair words and therapeutic eros of a dialogical therapist, psychological healing—the hard work of measurable change—has a better chance of taking place.

FOOTNOTE TO A REVOLUTION

Enchantments of the clinic were not featured in my earlier revival of existential therapy and certainly not mentioned in my commentary on existential therapy as I conceived it when reflecting soberly on the attitudes and behavior of survivors in extremity.[14] But some years have passed since my original conceptions were put to print and I have come to understand that this erotic substrate of dialogical therapy is an important aspect of clinical interventions that facilitate in patients life-affirming decisions, choices, commitments, and actions, the goal of which is movement toward the future and fulfillment of patients' latent potentials. Because I am the author of this pragmatic vision of the enchanted clinic, it seems quite rational to me. But not everyone would agree, particularly Nathaniel Hawthorne, a nineteenth-century author of psychological fiction, who warned against the dangers of confessional intimacy with clinicians, and Karl Menninger, a twentieth-century author of psychological theory, who believed the erotization of the clinic was obstructive, immoral, and harmful in every case.

Weighing their prohibitive ideas on a scale that balances the potential for harming and healing patients, I find some comfort in the illumination that what is rational at a certain time in human history is neither natural nor self-evident.[15] Like common sense, what is rational appears to be historical. I say this with some assurance because what is rational during a particular historical era is recorded in the discourse of the time. Given the historical evidence of this evolving discourse, it is demonstrably certain that what seemed rational in days of yore may seem meaningless or absurd today. I have in mind an earlier time when the diagnosis of daemonic possession was all the rage and use of a circular saw to bore a hole in a person's skull to allow evil spirits to escape was rational treatment. This seems absurd today because we dwell in a hyper-enlightened postmodern era whose neuroscientists are scanning and mapping electrochemical traffic in the Amygdala, the Medial and Dorsolateral Prefrontal Cortex, and the Anterior Cingulate Cortex, thereby lighting up the brain in a sophisticated effort to replace formerly self-evident beliefs about demons in the *milieu intérieur*—evil demons whose certain existence warranted cranial trephining—with statistical truths that are the empirical darlings of scientific method. Who can argue with a scanner? And who in their right mind would request tea and a crumpet to be followed by a skull trepanation?

Still, until such time when scanners help us discover more rational methods of treating morbid symptoms that are ineludible aspects of the agonistic life of humans, crowds of crazed people will continue coming out of the woodwork like ants: a crazed species of ants whose number seems to multiply by the manner in which they hurry with their troubles from one clinician to another. Imprisoned temporarily in this existential situation, a rational person might find it reasonable to applaud Freud's early imaginative attempt to make clinical use of the erotization of the clinician, as Freud applauded Charcot for working in a disarming way to replace the religious imagination and its idea of daemonic possession with the formulations of modern psychological science. Taken at its flood, it was this sort of work, if I understand the early postmodern discourse of Foucault correctly, that gave birth to (a) the modern clinic, (b) medical conceptions of unreason, and (c) psychology as a science of the individual. Indeed, given humankind's loathing of and "obstinate relation to death," the communal work of separating disease from "the metaphysic of evil" by using "the anatomo-clinical method" to study disease, with reference to the illness and death of the individual, gave the universal experience of death an individual face and "each individual the power of being heard forever."[16]

As a minor footnote to the Freudian revolution and a grateful acknowledgment of Freud's founding role in the invention of the modern clinical confessional, I am simply suggesting that from time to time, the clinical act of confessing and being heard, as well as the clinical struggle against illness and death, is better served when enchanted patients are listening to the charming words of a phantastic person to whom they are suggestively related and erotically tied.

NOTES

1. Sigmund Freud, "Charcot," in *Standard Edition*, vol. 3, 22.
2. Ernest Jones, *The Life and Work of Sigmund Freud*, vol. 1, *The Formative Years and the Great Discoveries, 1856–1900* (New York: H. Wolff, 1962), 235.
3. Sigmund Freud, *Civilization and Its Discontents*, in *Standard Edition*, vol. 21; cited in the text as *CD*.
4. Sigmund Freud, "Preface to the Translation of Bernheim's *Suggestion*," in *Standard Edition*, vol. 1 (1966), 75, 77.

5. Georg Simmel, *The Secret and the Secret Society*, part 4, *The Sociology of Georg Simmel*, ed. and trans. Kurt H. Wolff (New York: The Free Press, 1950), 334.

6. Michel Foucault, *The Birth of the Clinic: An Archaeology of Medical Perception*, trans. A. M. Sheridan Smith (New York: Vintage Books, 1975), xiv.

7. In this passage I am using a playwright's intriguing view that when erotic fantasies are enacted in a brothel, we are dealing with "a true image, born of a false spectacle." Jean Genet, *The Balcony*, trans. Bernard Frechtman (New York: Grove Press, 1966), 75.

8. M. Merleau-Ponty, *Phenomenology of Perception*, trans. Colin Smith (New York: Humanities Press, 1970); cited in the text as *PP*.

9. Saint Teresa, *The Life of Teresa of Jesus: The Autobiography of St. Teresa of Avila*, ed. and trans. E. Allison Peers (New York: Image Books, 1960), 195–96.

10. O. Hobart Mowrer, *The Crisis in Psychiatry and Religion* (Princeton, NJ: D. Van Nostrand Company, 1961), 121.

11. Bruno Bettelheim, *The Informed Heart: Autonomy in a Mass Age* (New York: Avon Books, 1979), 158.

12. Viktor E. Frankl, *Man's Search for Meaning: An Introduction to Logotherapy* (New York: Washington Square Press, 1965), 122.

13. Jean-Paul Sartre, "Existentialism Is a Humanism," trans. Philip Mairet, in *Existentialism from Dostoevsky to Sartre*, ed. Walter Kaufmann (New York: Meridian Books, 1960), 291, 302.

14. Carl P. Ellerman, "The Absurd Sensibility of Existential Psychotherapy: Clinical Application of Survivors' Experience of Treblinka and Other Death Camps," *Journal of Contemporary Psychotherapy* 27, no. 2 (1997): 119–30.

15. For remarks on the historicity of what is natural or self-evident see Martin Heidegger, *What Is a Thing?* trans. W. B. Barton Jr. and Vera Deutsch (Chicago: Henry Regnery Company, 1967), 39; for similar remarks on the historicity of common sense see Jacob Bronowski, *The Common Sense of Science* (Cambridge, MA: Harvard University Press, 1966), 19, 26.

16. Foucault, *Birth of the Clinic*, 196–97.

3

The Erotization of Confession

THE COMPULSION TO CONFESS

During the early 1920s a devoted disciple of Freud gave an intriguing series of lectures at the Teaching Institute of the famed Vienna Psychoanalytic Society. In his enlightening presentation, published in 1925 with the provocative title *The Compulsion to Confess*, Theodor Reik openly acknowledged that he had learned an important lesson from the venerable Freud, who earlier wrote: "He that has eyes to see and ears to hear may convince himself that no mortal can keep a secret. If his lips are silent, he chatters with his finger-tips; betrayal oozes out of him at every pore."[1] Not satisfied with this snippet of wisdom, like a penniless pauper who had been given a miserly nugget from an unexplored gold mine, Reik went underground to excavate the mine and find the motherlode himself.

Shortly after descending into this psychodynamic gold mine, Reik fell into the belief that human beings are driven by a collective unconscious compulsion to betray themselves by confessing secrets to some other person, particularly a substitute for parents who provided a formative experience with secrecy and confession (*CC*, 251).[2] Encouraged by this finding, Reik dug deeper until he discovered an elementary drama of human resistance that works to inhibit the confession of guilty secrets. Specifically, in the underworld of human experience, a person's conscious will to defend against the disclosure of secrets engages in a fierce struggle with an unconscious "counter-will," whose "dark intentions" are the emotional driver of self-betrayal during formal and informal confessions (*CC*, 49). Excavating further, until he discovered the dark intentions that made intelligible the self-betraying denouement of this compelling human drama, Reik mined a stunning rejoinder to Freud, while also unwittingly illuminating the logic of Hawthorne's warning, striking gold with the glistening idea that in the subterranean sewers of the human estate, self-condemnation and a perverse need for punishment are stronger than conscious will and have the power to defeat all rational resistance to the confession of criminal, sexual, and other closely guarded secrets (*CC*, 50).

These are seductive ideas whose merit readers can partially judge for themselves by means of scrupulous self-examination. Depending on the severity of the crime, the nature of the infraction, or the quality of the indiscretion, not to mention the inestimable deflation of self-esteem that promises to issue from a denuding self-revelation, some readers will undoubtedly confirm Freud's observation that medieval confessions extracted by torture are very much like the clinical communications of his troubled patients (*FL*, 224). Given Reik's adoration of Freud and a habit of anchoring his theoretical work in the acquired wisdom and psychoanalytic themes of his respected master, it is not surprising to find that Freud's medieval analogy of resistance, torture, surrender, and self-betrayal was borrowed and developed by Reik, who speculated that the external compulsion to confess inflicted on individuals during the medieval era by means of barbaric torture was transferred to the internal psyche and now, in modernity, exists as an unconscious compulsion to confess crimes, sexual secrets, and petty misdemeanors of every manner and sort (*CC*, 276, 349).

This train of thought may be farfetched, perhaps as improbable as the existence of a universal unconscious compulsion to confess. In fact, the glistening gold Reik thought he discovered may have been fool's gold in the final analysis. But Freud and Reik were experienced clinicians trying to understand their personal experience in the clinical trenches; and what they experienced while sitting with and listening to the confessions of guilt-ridden patients behind the closed door of their respective therapeutic confessionals was a compelling human drama of emotional turmoil, including willful resistance, internal surrender, and self-betrayal following a clinical command or a polite invitation that teased out an irresistible temptation to confess closely guarded secrets believed to be the harbinger and hiding place of mental illness.

In spite of Reik's grand claim regarding a universal compulsion to confess, willful resistance to the confession of closely guarded secrets may be likened to a powerful sentinel or a rational guardian protecting the integrity of the psychological self. From time to time, willful resistance is the dominant warrior in the internal struggle: so powerful in defense against its nemesis, counter-will, that it successfully defends against the temptation to confess secrets during an internal struggle that is self-evidently real and compelling. In an interesting way, Freud evidenced the success of his rational sentinel when he resisted the temptation to confess a closely guarded secret of his own.

Specifically, during the summer of 1899, Freud put pen to paper and wrote *The Interpretation of Dreams*, a psychoanalytic work of dream analysis that also contained a drama in the making: the drama of Freud's internal struggle to resist the public confession of a closely guarded secret. In the preface to the first edition, Freud honestly confessed that this new book contained interpretations of his own dreams; nine years later, in the preface to the second edition, Freud further confessed that the book contained self-analytic work regarding the death of his father. Making sure that his readers understood the importance of the personal secrets he was surrendering by publicly disclosing his emotional reactions to his father's death, Freud began by confessing that the death of a father is "the most important event, the most poignant loss, of a man's life" (*ID*, xxvi).[3]

Whether readers agree with Freud or not regarding the singular importance of a father's death, it is important to understand that Freud was not merely confessing personal secrets in his seminal psychoanalytic work; he was also confessing his emotional reaction to his public confessions, as if self-betrayal were oozing from every pore. Furthermore, Freud's meta-confessions—personal confessions about the personal confession of secrets—revealed that Freud's ostensible compulsion to confess carried a tormenting emotional resistance. Revealing his resistance to public confession, as well as an intense anticipatory anxiety, Freud confided: "If I . . . report my own dreams, it inevitably followed that I should have to reveal to the public gaze more of the intimacies of my mental life than I liked. . . . Such was the painful but unavoidable necessity; and I have submitted to it rather than totally abandon the possibility of giving the evidence for my psychological findings" (*ID*, xxiii–xxiv). Demonstrating the fact that his temptation to confess did not overwhelm his conscious will's rational resistance to self-betrayal, Freud continued his personal confession by offering another revealing meta-confession. "I have been unable to resist the temptation of taking the edge off some of my indiscretions by omissions and substitutions. But whenever this has happened, the value of my instances has been very definitely diminished. I can only express a hope that readers of this book will put themselves in my difficult situation and treat me with indulgence" (*ID*, xxiv). Later on, deeper in the text, while revealing his expectation that readers would doubt the trustworthiness of his self-analysis, Freud continued to demonstrate a tortured internal struggle with his rational resistance to public confession: "I have . . . difficulties to overcome," he openly confessed, difficulties "which lie within myself. There is some natural hesitation about revealing so many intimate facts about one's mental life. . . . But it must be possible to overcome such hesitations" (*ID*, 105).

Pursuing the surrender of personal secrets for the sake of psychoanalytic science, and writing as if a victorious counter-will had finally succeeded in toppling the rational resistance of the conscious will that defends the integrity of the psychological self, Freud made a vainglorious gesture toward a full and honest confession by inviting readers "to plunge along with me, into the minutest details of my life" (*ID*, 106).

Suddenly, as he approached the abyss of self-betrayal, ready to overcome resistance and give himself away, Freud withdrew, revealing an inability to fully disclose a frank interpretation of an important dream of his own. In the end, when push came to shove, taking a voluntary leap into the abyss of full and irretrievable self-disclosure repulsed him, as if he were revolted by watching a serpent coiled back upon itself while swallowing its tail. Accordingly, Freud found himself entangled self-consciously in the struggle of countless clinical confessants who, while reclining on the sofa in his consulting room, experienced their own anxious struggle with the recurring acts of self-betrayal Freud demanded in his pioneering psychoanalytic confessional.

Interestingly, in the same text, Freud outlined a preparatory method of free association for his patients, including suppression of critical self-observation while lying on his sofa in a restful attitude with their eyes shut. As if he were experiencing the full weight of corrosive hypocrisy, given his unwillingness to betray himself in the voluntary manner demanded of his patients, Freud commented rather testily on his resistance to confessing the minutest details of his life: "I will not pretend that I have completely uncovered the meaning of this dream or that its interpretation is without a gap. . . . I myself know the points from which further trains of thought could be followed. But considerations which arise in the case of every dream of my own restrain me from pursuing my interpretive work. If anyone should feel tempted to express a hasty condemnation of my reticence, I would advise him to make the experiment of being franker than I am" (*ID*, 120–21).

Freud believed that human beings are unable to keep secrets; but he clearly had a personal understanding of the struggle between the conscious will to resist and the counter-will Reik envisioned as driving the confession of intimate secrets. This may have figured prominently in Freud's strategic conclusion that in his clinical consulting room, the avoidance of eye contact would facilitate the confession of secrets in the free associations of his patients. On the other hand, referring to the placement of therapist and patient as a "ceremonial," Freud acknowledged that the arrangement of the patient reclining on a sofa with the therapist sitting to the side out of the patient's field of vision was a historical "remnant of the hypnotic method out of which psychoanalysis was evolved"; additionally, Freud confessed that this formal arrangement was motivated by the fact that he could not countenance being stared at by patients for eight or more hours each workday.[4] This quirk of Freud notwithstanding, clinical experience suggests that useful information is lost when therapist-confessors are not positioned to see and interpret the facial expressions and other idiosyncratic quirks of clinical confessants, in spite of the fact that the avoidance of eye contact enables some confessants to overcome the intense shame of confessing secrets to a confessor who studiously avoids a complementary betrayal of self. This later point will soon be demonstrated when I present the peculiar circumstances resulting in the clinical confessions of "The Rabbit Lady."

Regarding Freud's clinical conclusion that self-betrayal oozes from every pore and Reik's subsequent hypothesis of a universal unconscious compulsion to confess, there is no denying the fact that some confessants experience an incisive invasion of self when confessing secrets, particularly secrets regarding the forbidden thoughts, feelings, desires, and lived experiences that identify and expose the erotic self. From a phenomenological point of view, within these vulnerable confessants, the opening of self is a critical act of surrendering the preeminent defense of privacy in favor of a risky public exposure of self; surrender is thus a threat to the safety offered by self-possession: safety and security reinforced by defensively shielding the secrets of some unacceptable behavior or reproachable identity. As a result of the threat to the integrity of the psychological self, there is a natural resistance to opening oneself to view when receiving a subtle or a direct invitation to break out of the penetrable chrysalis in which true thoughts, wishes, impulses, anxieties, and dreams are safely enveloped and concealed.

Alternately put, in some confessants, there is a natural resistance to the zealous attempt by others to access the psychological self by probing secrets sequestered in the dark cavern of Hawthorne's reference. For the formal attempt to penetrate the inner sanctum by inviting, subtly pressuring, or demanding that an autonomous confessant surrender guilty or shameful secrets—and with these secrets, the naked truths of self held fast in private possession—may tickle the limits of vulnerability to the extent that the invasion of self is experienced as deathly and, as Freud showed in his willful resistance to exposing the secrets of a dream, exposure of this sort may simply be too much to bear, notwithstanding a powerful temptation to confess, to betray oneself, to give oneself away.

But Freud was a public figure and he can be treated with indulgence as he wished, for in his day and age, unlike our own, few wanted to expose intimacies in the public arena, especially when the arena happened to be international. On the other hand, in clinical confessionals across the globe, Freud's temptation to confess, his resistance and his shame, has been shared by countless clinical confessants: nameless, faceless self-betraying individuals whose temptation to confess was more powerful than willful resistance. As the reader will see when looking into the clinical confessional through the eyes of Erica, I have been privileged to put names and faces to the overwhelming shame that sometimes comes with a healthy inability to resist a painful exposure of the erotic self.

EYES OF SHAME

At the time of our first clinical encounter, Erica was a sixteen-year-old female referred for treatment following a rash attempt to take her life due to a failed relationship with a rejecting boyfriend. She was a soft-spoken adolescent whose graceful countenance reminded me of the young Renaissance women appearing in Botticelli's ethereal *Graces*. Erica's parents were bitterly divorced and Erica was sadly estranged from her rejecting father. Given my attunement to enchantments of the clinic, I was not surprised when she developed a strong attachment to her older male therapist. In short order, to be more precise, I became a phantastic person in Erica's eyes: an imaginary, idealized father whose therapeutic eros filled the vacuum left by a critical, unloving biological father who never became a warm, affirming dad in the heart and mind of his daughter. In due course, given antidepressant medication, a solid clinical relationship informed by Erica's enchantment, and a healthy number of fair words spoken sincerely week after week, attempted suicide became a distant memory. Following a lengthy period of emotional stability supported by Erica's productive participation in adolescent group therapy, early admission to college during her senior year of high school, and other significant gains in self-development, including the healthy esteem she derived from my successful effort to have one of her lyrical poems published in a mental health quarterly, we terminated clinical treatment successfully and Erica went her merry way, as if the world had been set aright.

Unmanageable things being what they are in the distorted world of mental illness, self-destructive features of Erica's Borderline-Narcissistic Disorder resurfaced several years later, resulting in a series of misadventures with illicit drugs and sex, an unwanted pregnancy, and a guilt-inducing abortion. As a result of these momentous events, Erica spiraled out of control and she attempted to take her life once again. Following inpatient hospitalization, she was referred to me for a second round of outpatient treatment; this time, however, the loveliest of Botticelli's delicate *Graces* reminded me of the impeccably wounded poet Sylvia Plath. Like the anguished Plath, whose confessional poetry of pain is a powerful tribute to the crazed coalition of insight and madness, Erica seemed horrified by a dark malignancy lurking within her; and by virtue of a long overdue clinical confession, a shameful self-betrayal demonstrating defensive resistance, painful fore-anxiety, and final surrender at the end of a serious game of clinical capture and surrender, I discovered that Erica experienced her darksome thing in the fashion of Plath, whose stunning metaphors bore witness to the fatal fact that she could not bear the equation of human love and cancer.

Erica committed herself to a second round of therapy and I redoubled my effort to dress her emotional wounds with persuasive words, hoping that somewhere, somehow, a merciful god would undertake the difficult work of healing her wounds and gluing together her fractured psyche. Fortunately, we became reacquainted rather quickly, in fact, it seemed as if Erica never lost her enchantment with the clinic or her attachment to her confessor. Accordingly, one afternoon, Erica began her confession with an ambiguous smile that had ambition: the kind of anxious ambition that tells a therapist his patient is struggling with the confession of a sexual secret. Erica's ambiguous smile also reinforced my observation that every sexual confession conceals a confession, every sexual secret is a hiding place, each revealing word or phrase is also a mask.

Beginning the shameful process of unmasking herself by surrendering the dark thing lurking malignantly within her, Erica whispered: "I've done something very naughty!" Looking down shamefacedly, but finally coming clean in the presence of her curious confessor, she openly stated: "I've been lying to you." Then a fuller confession followed as Hawthorne warned and Freud and Reik predicted, with Erica's soul finally dissolving, allowing into the light all the sins, all the shameful secrets, all the mysteries of self formerly hidden beyond the drawn interior.

Referring to a previous therapy session with a former boyfriend, Erica asked: "Do you remember when I came with Richard and told you we had a problem with sex. I said that I was able to have an orgasm when I masturbated, but I couldn't have an orgasm with him." I acknowledged my remembrance of this particular confession and stole a moment to remind Erica that I became confused after inquiring about the possibility of an orgasmic disorder. In fact I remained confused because Erica never fully answered my question and in a concerted effort to respect her privacy, I did not actively pursue this line of inquiry, not wanting to invade her privacy, once again giving the lie to Hawthorne's warning that clinical confessors were diabolical agents who would invariably exercise their license to descend into a patient's bosom to pry into each and every secret.

Consistent with Reik's observations about the confessional struggles of criminals, clinic patients, and other formal confessants, Erica was clearly involved in an emotional struggle and she continued to resist further self-betrayal, thereby sustaining her suffering of the painful anxiety of confession. On this particular afternoon, however, she also seemed driven by something akin to a compulsion to confess; as a result, she did not succumb to Freud's temptation to take the edge off confession by certain omissions and substitutions. With ambivalence waging a fierce war within her, Erica studiously avoided eye contact by glancing down at her lap. Then, looking up, as if she were a shy maiden ready to surrender to the temptation to unveil, thereby, as Reik put it, "showing . . . [her] own ugliness naked before all," she tried in vain to speak the truth by gazing at my eyes (*CC*, 309). Unable to confess face to face in customary clinical fashion, she averted my glance once again, this time by covering her face with both hands, repeatedly reporting: "I'm so ashamed! I'm so ashamed!" Given the extent of her emotional turmoil and her willful resistance, I secretly wished I were sitting adjacent to the leather sofa where Erica was struggling with the endgame of capture and surrender, such that my voice was the primary contact and I was out of sight. I had little doubt that Freud's ceremonial placement would have made it easier for Erica to give herself away by confessing the dark thing she experienced as a malignant secret.

Suddenly, at the climax of an epic struggle between rational will and the counter-will whose victory offers the end-pleasure that occurs in the overcoming of anxiety, Erica leaped into the abyss of self-betrayal as if taken by an impulse to release herself from the agitated tension that exists in the pulsating psyche of a person who has labored long with a shameful secret. Plunging headlong into a full confession of the minutest details of her life, Erica finally gave herself away by surrendering the secret that when she had sex with Richard she had fantasies of women: fantasies of forbidden erotic acts that enabled her to achieve an orgasm while in the arms of a man whose erotic skill seemed insufficient to bring her from the initial arousal of foreplay to the end-pleasure figured symbolically in romantic literature as the little death (*La petite mort*).

Continuing her sexual confession by disclosing her desire to partake of forbidden fruit, Erica confided that she often looks at women in public places, invariably fantasizes about women when she is sexually intimate with guys, and generally imagines women when masturbating and pleasuring herself. Sometimes she imagines one woman, sometimes two, frequently one woman with a dildo whose penetrating thrust enables her to achieve a wonderful orgasm. Adding a footnote to a sexual text that was a shame-filled surrender of privacy and the protection offered by secrets, Erica confided that she had "trouble imagining women below the waist." Intrigued by this unexpected disclosure, I interrupted the confessional flow with a question aimed at uncovering the reason for this particular problem. Although many years have passed, I remember being surprised when Erica answered as if she were Tertullian in modern dress: "I wouldn't want to lick a woman," she blurted-out, with a facial grimace that expressed a gynophobic revulsion for the gamy secretions emanating from the genitalia of the second sex.[5] In an effort to relieve some of Erica's shame by focusing on our lengthy therapeutic process, I asked pointedly: "What precipitated your confession today after all this time has passed?" Erica looked directly into my eyes and stated forthrightly: "I never told anyone about this, but I talked to myself this morning after doing it with a vibrator and fantasizing about a woman with a dildo; and I want to know if you think I'm a lesbian."

The reader should understand that during her tortured confession, Erica covered her eyes intermittently with both hands as she slowly unmasked herself and came out of hiding, thereby still trying to hide from the gaze of her confessor. Erica's act of shielding her eyes is an interesting repetition of Adam and Eve's storied use of fig leaves to shield their naked bodies after eating forbidden fruit in the paradisiacal garden of pleasure. This need to cover-up one's nakedness during exposure; the impulse to shield the mirrors of the soul while denuding the self during a particularly intimate confession; the attempt to avoid seeing the eyes of the person who is gazing into the private nooks and crannies of the soul; is a manifestation of the uniquely human experience of shame, a word whose root, *skam*, means to cover. Shame and its cohorts, humiliation and disgrace, are irascible demons that may be roused from light sleep during a painful, anxiety-laden confession of secrets that not only undermines a person's idealized image of self, but also unmasks the theatrical persona crazed human beings commonly present to others during seemingly authentic or illusory interpersonal encounters. Make no mistake: this denuding of self is no minor mortification, no delicate defeat, no puny punishment or puerile penance. For a biological organism that gives birth to a psychological self, the imaginative idealization of self may be likened to an agent of psychological survival by means of which people from all walks of life are able to dress the self with assets and attributes, faculties and powers, meaning and significance, creative of an acceptable, supportive, affirming identity that reinforces the emotional lifeblood of self-esteem. But art and artifice of this sort is not as uncomplicated as it seems, like everything else in the human estate.

For example, in her estimable reflections on self-glorification, neo-Freudian psychoanalyst Karen Horney conceived self-glorification as a neurotic process, noting that in human beings, the imagination unconsciously creates an idealized image of self by means of which a person may endow the self with "unlimited powers and with exalted faculties," such as "a hero, a genius, a supreme lover, a saint, a god"; Horney referred to this imaginative process as a "*comprehensive neurotic solution*" to the problems of life, a solution that a crazed person clings to compulsively.[6] Horney's point of view is not only intelligible, but on the clinical mark when one considers the fact that the art and artifice of self-glorification can become part of an overcompensatory narcissistic process involving an attempt to actualize a perfect self—an impossible task that takes a pathological toll on self and others.

On the other hand, there are times when an idealized image of self feeds a healthy narcissism that enables a person to construct and affirm a useful identity, create a viable way of existing, even a way of suppressing the terrifying prospect of death. In his stunningly realistic Pulitzer Prize–winning *The Denial of Death*, Ernest Becker argued cogently: "Our central calling, our main task on this planet, is the heroic" (*DD*, 1).[7] What Becker was suggesting by means of a flamboyant concept that seemed to stand Horney's selective clinical thinking on its head, is the demonstrable fact that human beings are narcissistic creatures hell-bent on protecting organismic integrity: physiochemical identity, as well as the symbolic identity constructed by language, ideas, images, and dreams. In part, the ability to construct a symbolic identity—whether hero, genius, supreme lover, saint, or demigod—enabled a biological organism to transcend its baser animal nature, while developing, nourishing, and expanding the psychological self in a way that endowed this reflexively self-conscious creature with meaning, value, and significance. On Becker's account, this "working level of narcissism is inseparable from self esteem," in fact, "it expresses the heart of the creature: the desire to stand out, to be *the* one in creation. When you combine natural narcissism with the basic need for self-esteem you create a creature who has to feel himself an object of primary value. . . . An animal who gets his feeling of worth symbolically has to minutely compare himself to those around him, to make sure he doesn't come off second-best" (*DD*, 3–4).

With reference to the clinical confessional and daily repetitions of the compulsion to confess, the point of these remarks is that the idealized self and the self-esteem issuing from it are vitally important aspects of a psychological self. Indeed, the favorable presentation of self appears to be a daily drama undertaken by Everyman: a theatrical performance by means of which crazed human beings create a meaningful, empowering presentation of self that not only supports self-worth, but also guides, controls, and directs favorable impressions reflected in the mind and the mirroring of others. When this comes to grief in the clinic during a confession that issues in an honest revelation of seemingly base, dishonorable, or ignoble secrets, the drama of self-presentation encounters a deflating reversal, the idealized image of self is undermined, the dramatistic persona is unmasked, and shame may rear its ugly head as the handmaid of self-betrayal. The deflation of esteem that issues from a self-betraying clinical confession is compounded by the fact that clinical confessors involved in their own image-making and theatrical performance may be experienced as phantastic persons who, by comparison with the unmasked patient who has shown her ugliness, appear to have their own lives and selves well ordered. In this clinical context, to develop the thinking of Reik, the stripping bare or denuding of self by the patient is unintelligible unless the self-betraying act of confession is a means to some other important end. In the mind of Reik, the unspoken erotic end is "an eloquent plea for absolution" that "serves the wooing for love, the urge to receive renewed love through the very punishment [of confession] itself" (*CC*, 208).

This psychoanalytic speculation may stretch credulity beyond a tolerable limit. In fact, throughout *The Compulsion to Confess*, Reik's argument is diffuse and packed with psychoanalytic myth: Oedipus looms large in the unconscious and the landscape of repression is dotted with fictive drives and needs that seem like sturdy oak trees implanted in the firmament of heaven. But when one abstracts from psychoanalytic myth, there is some gold in Reik's gold mine and more than a little wisdom about the human condition.

One week or so after confessing her shameful secret Erica returned to the clinic confessing: "I've kissed my first woman!" She described this experience in terms that left little doubt that the forbidden kiss was erotically inspiring. There was something unspoken in her words, something bright but unspoken in her eyes—a mute confession of the fact that Erica would continue exploring the enthrallments of the forbidden. But I was mindful of the fact that I had diagnosed Erica with a serious personality disorder whose dominant features are chronically unstable affects and interpersonal relationships, as well as a persistent identity disturbance, the clinical marker of which is a profound uncertainty about self-image, sexual orientation, and types of lovers to pursue. Needless to say, this did not bode well for the future and when we terminated treatment a second time, after I managed to dress her emotional wounds with fair words that seemed to glue her fractured psyche together, I was reasonably certain that at some future date I would once again hear Erica's confession in an enchanted clinic where self-betrayal and self-exposure would be experienced as a painful pleasure.

PAINFUL PLEASURE

Experienced clinicians will undoubtedly agree that Erica's drama of rational will and counter-will, of resistance and surrender, of self-defense and self-betrayal, is a common experience in the clinical trenches. Some fellow therapists may also agree with my view that the pleasure patients derive from clinical intimacy, specifically, the pleasure derived from sharing one's innermost thoughts and feelings, fantasies and desires, gross problems and petty frustrations, may be likened to an enthrallment of clinical confession or an enchantment that acts as an inducement to self-betrayal, particularly if a clinical confessor is able to manifest the life-affirming therapeutic eros emotionally needy patients experience as steadiness, warmth, and deliberation. But Reik advanced psychoanalytic theory beyond this manifest level of healthy eroticism when he presented self-betrayal as a painful pleasure: not only a masochistic erotization of confession that seemed dark and Dionysian, rather than sunny and Apollonian, but an erotization of confession that placed the therapist-confessor in an ethically and clinically compromising existential situation.

Reik did not openly frame his hypothesis of the compulsion to confess with reference to an erotics of self-betrayal or an erotization of confession, and he never used the expressions "Apollonian" or "Dionysian," although he did speak of the "dark intentions" of self-betraying confessants. But some years ago, when I began to critically reflect on the subterranean dynamics of clinical confession, wondering why so many people were sighing on the sofa and showing their ugliness before a clinical confessor, I was mindful of the psychoanalytic notion that when a harsh moral conscience is at work in the sewers of the psyche—a "sadistic super-ego" generating a masochistic "need for punishment," to use a felicitous formulation of Freud—self-condemnation and the need for punishment have the power to defeat all rational resistance to the confession of secrets (*CD*, 136). What also focused my mind at the time was Reik's psychodynamic postulate that confession itself is a painful part of the pleasure of self-punishment in the sense that "the work of confession itself affords a partial gratification of that masochistic need for punishment" (*CC*, 268).

This may sound surpassing strange to readers not accustomed to thinking about the dynamics of confession with reference to the underworld of pleasurable punishment or the Dionysian world of painful pleasure. But if a dialogical therapist struggles long in the clinical trenches, while also becoming curious about the widespread success of the Freudian revolution—specifically, wondering why "parading one's own weaknesses" became fashionable with so many self-betraying individuals who, during the twentieth century, unwittingly colluded with clinical confessors in generating a triumph of the therapeutic—the eroticism of confession gathers intelligibility (*CC*, 208). But the parade and the triumph, the self-betrayal and the collusion, are best seen, perhaps only seen clearly, in the historical context of confession and its perverse adjuvant, punishment.

More precisely, during the second half of the twentieth century, in the rich postmodern mind of Foucault, it was clear that "Western man has become a confessing animal," a reputedly wise or sapient animal who routinely confesses crimes, sins, intimate thoughts and desires, illnesses and countless life problems—publicly and privately, voluntarily and involuntarily—to priests, police, doctors and psychiatrists, parents, teachers, and lovers; but in the life and time and collective mind of *Homo confessus*, if I may speak this way following Foucault's observation, punishment of all sorts, even "torture," has followed confession like a "dark twin" or "shadow."[8] Preceding Foucault by more than fifty years and delivering his illuminating lectures on the compulsion to confess in the wake of Nietzsche's inflammatory proclamation of the death of God in 1883, Reik's modern mind was not only focused on the intimate relationship of religion and confession, but also seized by the understanding that "wherever religion still exerts its great power over souls . . . it inflicts heavy and oppressive punishments upon the sinner after confession" (*CC*, 300–301). Adding psychoanalytic substance to the demonstrable historical relationship of confession and punishment, while offering a thinly veiled adumbration of the erotics of confession, as if a self-betraying confessant were in the throe of sexual arousal and release with a punitive lover, Reik advanced the fertile idea that with some guilt-ridden patients the need for punishment effectively shifts from the suffering of physical punishment to suffering painfully pleasurable aspects of confession itself, such as the anticipatory anxiety or "fore-anxiety" that precedes the gratifying release or "end-pleasure" of a guilt-ridden, self-betraying, cathartic clinical confession (*CC*, 203).

A student of religion and culture; a disciple of Freud who understood that "religion intuitively preceded psychoanalysis"; a psychological man who undoubtedly heard of the cultural death of God, but also believed that "in religion, mankind professes, in the form of penitence and atonement . . . the eternal wishes by which it is stirred"; Reik correctly noted that in human cultures dating to ancient Babylonia, a confession of bad deeds generally resulted in some sort of punishment (*CC*, 250, 299). But in the clinical trenches, while wearing psychoanalytic fatigues and combating mental illness and death, Reik reasoned that in the emotional life of a confessant, if the anticipation of punishment happens to be intensely anxious or tension-filled, the anticipation of punishment may be experienced as punishment itself—intrapsychic punishment that results in emotional, rather than physical pain and suffering. Accordingly, Reik concluded: "To suffer the anxiety of . . . the act of confession, which itself is felt to be painful, is, therefore, that partial gratification of the need for punishment which we claim, for the confession. . . . Therefore I'll by no means deny that there is pleasure in the unpleasurable overcoming of anxiety in the confession" (*CC*, 204). But Reik didn't stop here in adumbrating an erotics of clinical confession.

As we have seen, while trying to make self-betrayal intelligible as punishment, Reik speculated that the act of parading one's weaknesses in a clinical confession could be likened to an appeal to parents or parent surrogates for punishment and forgiveness, for absolution and love. For example, considering Francine's identification with the base instincts of Catherine Trammel and her confession of maliciously ruining the life of a man she purposefully seduced in a bar, her clinical confession amounts to saying: "Look how mean and malicious I have become. Punish me, forgive me, but love me again, in spite of who I truly am." As an emotional appeal to a confessor, according to Reik, a self-betraying clinical confession of this sort partially fulfills the need for punishment and simultaneously functions as a "wooing for love," the goal of which is accomplished by means of the punitive confession itself (*CC*, 208).

It doesn't take a genius to understand that in the Dionysian underworld of human experience, if a guilt-ridden patient's need for punishment is being partially satisfied by the painful pleasure of clinical confession, not to mention the painful pleasure of morbid symptoms, there is a gain, in fact a Pyrrhic victory, in remaining sick. Indeed, a patient crazed in this way may harbor the wish to remain ill while in treatment, for remaining emotionally ill, thereby resisting a therapist's Apollonian struggle to secure psychological healing or emotional well-being, enables a person to continue enjoying painfully pleasurable acts of confession. Consistent with this reasoning, Reik speculated further that the gratification of the need for punishment was the secret driver of neurotic illness: "The neurotic disturbance serves to a significant extent the need for punishment; the suffering from it clearly exhibits the character of punishment" (*CC*, 280). Now Reik did not arrive at this understanding of crazed motives in the clinical trenches independently; in fact, Freud evidenced the unconscious need for punishment and its satisfaction on phenomenological grounds by referencing his clinical experience with seemingly hopeless patients who: (a) remain ill, (b) recover but relapse into illness, (c) recover but have an accident that results in renewed pain and suffering, or (d) somatize and experience acute, unrelenting physical illness. Given phenomenological evidence of this sort, Freud viewed his patients' need for punishment as resistance—a major impediment to the success of dialogical therapy. Conceiving the need for punishment as a powerful masochistic wish, Freud observed: "The need for punishment is the worst enemy of our therapeutic efforts. It is satisfied by the suffering which is linked to the neurosis, and for that reason [a guilt-ridden patient] holds fast to being ill"—holds fast to being ill, I would add, while experiencing the painful pleasure of morbid symptoms *and* protracted clinical confession (*NI*, 108).[9]

Reflecting on the complementary roles of clinical confessor and clinical confessant and the seemingly healthy therapeutic relationship of listening, hearing, and speaking, the experience of painful pleasure is an ethically and clinically compromising element of eroticism in the clinical relationship. Specifically, if the subterranean thinking of Freud and Reik has merit it follows that on occasion, while actively hearing, interpreting, and responding to the clinical confessions of guilt-ridden patients, dialogical therapists are placed in the dilemmatic position of colluding in the fulfillment of their patients' need or desire for punishment. This is a can of worms Reik opened and never adequately cleaned up, except to counsel rather impotently: "To promote the gratification of the need for punishment is . . . wrong, as it permits the patient the enjoyment of his masochistic impulses, namely revelry in self-torment or in torture by others engineered by him" (*CC*, 238). Baldly put, some guilt-ridden patients are likely to experience painful pleasure in the clinical confessional by virtue of the act of confession itself; and there is little that a therapist can do about this perverse state of affairs while struggling diligently against symptoms formed around a guilt-ridden moral conscience, except to guard against promoting the painfully pleasurable gratification. In the end, given the fixed confessional nature of dialogical therapy, while hearing confessions in the clinical trenches, "the patient must be allowed a certain measure of gratification of his urges, even of the need for punishment. . . . Analysis can do little more perhaps than protect the patient from the crudest self-inflictions" (*CC*, 238–39).

Readers sensitive to clinical ethics may wish to focus on Reik's language here, specifically, the difference between *promoting* and *allowing* the gratification of a patient's need for punishment. The unstated premise of Reik's moralistic argument that it is wrong for a therapist to promote the gratification of the need for punishment seems to be that during a clinical confession of secrets, any verbal or nonverbal communication on the part of the therapist-confessor that promotes the gratification of a patient's need for punishment violates a seemingly sacred dogma of the therapeutic: the dogma that prohibits a therapist from harming patients in his care.

With philosophic tongue in cheek, I shall confess that when I first entertained this argument after studying *The Compulsion to Confess*, it seemed to me that Reik had read the *Summa Theologiae* and was having a heated argument with the eminent scholastic philosopher Thomas Aquinas, who was fully capable of splitting hairs over the most minute, seemingly indivisible aspects of the distinction between mortal and venial sins. For Reik was suggesting that if a therapist knows there is an "inner connection of the compulsion to confess and the need for punishment," while engaged in the formal act of hearing a clinical confession, he is not actively promoting, but passively allowing a patient to experience the painfully pleasurable erotic gratification of a masochistic need (*CC*, 300). To actively promote the gratification of the need for punishment, thereby reinforcing masochism, is a grievous offense, something akin to a mortal sin in the scrupulous theocentric world of Aquinas, for it violates a clinical commandment, a sacred dogma of the therapeutic that prohibits harming patients in one's care. But to passively allow the gratification of a need for punishment and the perverse pleasure therein is a lesser offense, like a venial sin, since passively allowing the gratification of a masochistic need in one's patients is the ineludible result of the noble Apollonian effort to battle mental illness and death by hearing and responding remedially to confessions in the clinical confessional.

Now Aquinas was referred to as a "dumb ox" by his Dominican peers due to the fact that he was a corpulent good man at the table. But he wasn't a fool, in fact, he was a skilled logician—a logical nitpicker who could drive a person nuts! For example, when considering sins of the sensual appetite in *Summa Theologiae*, Aquinas observed: "An impulse of the sensual appetites is a venial sin before reasoned consent, but mortal after the consent. The impulse of the sensual appetite that is antecedent to reasoned consent never itself becomes a mortal sin; the mortal sin is rather the act of the reason consenting."[10] In the case at hand, if Reik were arguing with Aquinas in a clash of the medieval and modern imagination, Aquinas might have responded to Reik in similar fashion, saying: "If a therapist actively solicits the confession of secrets in the clinical confessional, and he suspects or actually knows in advance that the act of confession will allow some patients to pleasurably gratify their need for punishment, the therapist would have promoted the gratification of the patient's need for punishment, not only by agreeing to hear the confession, in which case reason is consenting to the patient's punishment, but also by actually listening to the secrets, this being a clinical act of reason consenting to the patient's pleasurable punishment, notwithstanding the fact that the solicitation of guilt-ridden secrets is a means to the noble Apollonian end of psychological healing."

The sainted Aquinas was a God-fearing man, but I imagine he would have experienced something akin to daemonic delight by hoisting Reik on his own petard. For Freud's devoted disciple had argued skillfully that with guilt-ridden confessants, clinical confession is something akin to penance, in fact, a painful pleasure; yet he continued hearing clinical confessions for years on end, not only accepting payment for participating in this compromised endeavor, but also consenting to a dilemmatic erotization of clinical confession, insofar as he was reinforcing in self-betraying clinic patients the masochistic drama of painful pleasure he seemed to detest.

My amusing imaginary argument of Aquinas and Reik aside, I would like to cash out Reik's unpaid claim that religion preceded psychoanalysis intuitively, by briefly elucidating historical aspects of the intriguing relationship of confession and punishment, with hope of making intelligible latent aspects of the erotics of clinical confession in the consulting rooms of Freud and Reik and in contemporary clinical confessionals, as well.

A BRIEF HISTORY OF CONFESSION AND PUNISHMENT

Although he did not clarify the interesting details, leaving curious readers wondering what he was talking about when he made much of the intuitive connection of religion and psychoanalysis and the significance of this connection for his provocative hypothesis of the compulsion to confess, Reik cast some light on his thinking when he advanced the idea that the masochistic need for punishment had shifted from the suffering of physical punishment to suffering painfully pleasurable aspects of confession itself. On my reading of the cultural life and salvific drama of *Homo religiosus,* the relationship of religion and confession may be conceived as a tale of confession and punishment: a nasty tale not only ripe for picking, but also an interesting story that offers an instructive introduction to the eroticism haunting Reik's hypothesis of a collective unconscious compulsion to confess. In fact, if it is historically true to say with Foucault that confession and punishment are "dark twins," it is equally true to say, in Western culture there has been a clear historical shift in what I would conceive retrospectively as the theory and practice, the logic and science, the art and craft of punishment, as if the neuronal wiring of adolescent dark twins had been pruned and rewired and now was able to function in the clinical confessional, like a seemingly mature post-adolescent brain that has fewer, faster neuronal connections.

Once upon a time, prior to this fanciful rewiring, early church fathers conceived sin, particularly sexual sin, as a disease of the soul. Complementing the conception of sin as disease, priests were conceived as healers who had the power to cure the soul of disease, with spiritual health as a goal. But how was this cure of soul achieved: by what manner, means, or method? With this question, the interesting, sometimes sordid history of confession and penance, of self-betrayal and punishment, begins. As Andreas Snoeck observed in *Confession and Psychoanalysis* and Hawthorne dramatized so well in *The Scarlet Letter*, the confessional cure of souls was premised on a rigorous philosophy of punishment aimed at restoring a moral world order disrupted by the dirty doings of mortal sin. In this hard, uncompromising worldview, as Hester Prynne discovered, the pride of sin was opposed by shame and humiliation, abuse of others by self-abnegation, forbidden pleasure by compensatory suffering (*CP*, 8).[11]

For example, "exomologesis" was a term used in the early Catholic Church to identify a prolonged, ritualized process of public confession of sins and public punishment, consisting of shameful humiliations and painful mortifications of the flesh. Established during the second century A.D., the exomologesis of conscience was prescribed for the satisfaction of the most serious sins of homicide, sexual impurity, and apostasy. Conceived as a severe discipline tailored to achieve satisfaction of sins and reconciliation of the sinner with God, church, and community, the harsh penitential exercises could be performed only once during a sinner's lifetime.

The word itself sounds chilling, but the Greek term *exomologeomai* used by Plutarch and other ancient authors, simply means "to confess in full." Despite the benign meaning, enactment of the exomologesis justifies the chill, in as much as these severe penitential exercises reinforce the perception that some human beings will go to extreme lengths to purify others, while other human beings will go to extreme lengths to achieve a healing purification of body, mind, and soul. In fact, as the history of torture shows, human beings have an infinite capacity to inflict excruciating torment on the sensitive nerve endings circumagitating the fragile bodies of fellow humans, not to mention the sensitive psychological nerve endings connected to self-worth within the *milieu intérieur*. Regarding this history, Tertullian, a Christian apologist born in Carthage circa 150 A.D., is responsible for writing two of the most influential ancient Christian treatises on the forgiveness of sins: *De paenĭtentĭa* (On Penitence) and *De pŭdīctĭa* (On Purity). In *De paenĭtentĭa,* Tertullian described exomologesis as "a discipline which leads a man to prostrate and humble himself. It prescribes a way of life which, even in the matter of food and clothing, appeals to pity. It bids him to lie in sackcloth and ashes, to cover his body with filthy rags, to plunge his soul into sorrow, to exchange sin for suffering. Moreover, it demands that you know only such food and drink as is plain. . . . It requires that you . . . sigh and weep and groan day and night . . . that you prostrate yourself . . . and kneel before the beloved of God, making all the brethren commissioned ambassadors of your . . . pardon" (*OP*, 31–32).[12]

Tertullian proceeded to document the fact that the shameful public exposure of a pitiful sinner was followed by a rigorous daily and nightly ritual of harsh self-abuse thought to issue in purification of the humiliated penitent, restoration of the well-being of the community, and reintegration of the sinner with fellow believers. Although the sinner was given the opportunity to engage in a purificatory exomologesis of conscience only once during his lifetime, the severe disciplinary penance could last a lifetime: a protracted state of self-abuse which, on Tertullian's account, "requires that, unwashed and filthy, they live without joy, in rough sackcloth and frightful ashes, their faces wasted from fasting" (*OP*, 34).

In the religious confessional, long before Catholicism's private black box was invented, penitential punishment was not only administered to self-betraying sinners, it also was invited and accepted, in as much as mortifications of the flesh were linked to purification, forgiveness, atonement, redemption, and otherworldly salvation in the mind of penitent confessants. In some instances, as extant records of the Spanish Inquisition show, a penitent's masochistic acceptance of painful punishment fulfilled the complementary erotic identity and sadistic desire of priestly prescribers of penance who, while allegedly fulfilling their duty to an omnipotent, omniscient, omnipresent deity, were vested with the extraordinary power of eliciting and examining the finest points of the flesh in order to uncover the slightest nuance of thought, fantasy, wish, desire, impulse, dream, and behavior to be confessed as sin and redeemed by painful physical penance. Crazed as it may seem to a hyper-enlightened postmodern sensibility, the dark twin that shadowed religious confession yields a sordid story of very human interactions, including the desire of some humans to mercilessly punish other humans and the need and desire of the others to confess, to be forgiven, to atone and be saved by means of harsh physical punishment during psycho-religious dramas of penitential correction.

With reference to the historical drama of the cure of souls that unfolded in the Judeo-Christian tradition, there is no escaping the fact that sadomasochism was a live germ: not only a live germ of sacramental confession and punishment, but a revealing manifestation of the significant role of painful pleasure in the complementary erotic drama of religious confessor and religious confessant. Speaking to this issue, as if he were elucidating psychosexual aspects of sacramental confession, while taking a retrospective look inside the Western world's religious matrix, historian Stephen Haliczer wrote suggestively about the wide acceptance of physical abuse and the erotization of physical abuse in medieval and early modern time:

> Medieval and early modern ascetics slept on the ground in the coldest weather and wore hair shirts and corselets filled with iron studs that bit into their flesh. Flagellation and other forms of physical mortification were also practiced. . . . The acceptance of extreme forms of mortification and physical abuse . . . tended to legitimize the expression of the sadomasochistic urges that provide carnal gratification for certain individuals. These tendencies . . . were given unprecedented scope by the link between mortification and holiness.[13]

Parenthetically, although Reik was silent about the confessor's erotic pull, the possibility of collusive sadomasochism complicating the clinical situation may explain why he took pains to note that it is wrong for clinicians to promote the gratification of the confessor's need for punishment; for this would allow an enthralled patient the enjoyment of masochistic impulses, while also allowing an enthralled confessor the complementary enjoyment of sadistic impulses, namely, pleasure in the pain of the confessant, whether directly promoted or passively allowed by him.

Regarding pleasure in self-torment and the potential for pleasure in the torment of others, while sadomasochism remained an integral component of the religious matrix, the early exomologesis of conscience was gradually replaced by commerce with shame in the religious confessional. This was certainly good news for future generations condemned to birth within a powerful religious matrix that manufactured the correlation of confession, corporal punishment, cure of soul, and spiritual health. With the gradual superannuation of the flesh as a focus of compensatory punishment, pragmatic religious confessors forged a new link between confession, the experience of shame, purifying penance, cure of soul, and spiritual health. Given its ability to produce shame, speaking into the ear of a confessor replaced the public mortification of the flesh. Conceived and used as a shaming humiliation, private auricular confession was ultimately accepted as the penitential exercise that shifted sinners from confession to atonement: the healthy felt experience of being at home with oneself and at one with a merciful God.

In fine, by the thirteenth century, dramatic changes had taken place in the psychology of confession and in the practice of punishment. In the mordant mind of *Homo religiosus*, where punishment is valid as the correction or satisfaction of sin, compensatory penances first prescribed as harsh mortifications of the flesh became subtler, discrete emotional penances involving shaming punishments I shall identify as *mortifications of the soul* or *penances of the psyche*. Consistent with this change, religious confessors began to use shame purposefully as a pragmatic instrument of penance that generated the corrective satisfaction of sin, particularly the sexual sins of women solicited and heard by reputedly celibate male priests in private confessionals. Documenting this historical change, Thomas Tentler observed that by the ninth century theologians began to understand that "the chief virtue of confession derived from the shame it engendered when the penitent was forced to tell his sins to another man. . . . Shame made confession itself a work of satisfaction. . . . We see [here] the affirmation, even the exaltation, of a personal sense of shame. . . . It . . . occupies a prominent position in the history of penance."[14]

Reik did not have much to say about shame in *The Compulsion to Confess*; like Freud, he was focused primarily on the moralistic superego and the human experience of guilt. But shame is a different concept, a vastly different order of experience when compared to the experience of guilt that may be a consequence of some perceived behavioral wrongdoing, such as Erica's abortion. Self-loathing may accompany both guilt and shame, but with shame, the kind of shame experienced by Erica, there is intense self-loathing: a prodigious self-loathing that occurs when a person feels *ontologically defective*. To experience oneself as ontologically defective is to have the visceral sense that there is a profound flaw in the core self: an incorrigible defect or irreparable fault in the inalterable person one happens to be.[15] The experience of being defective—of being wrong, rather than having done something wrong, of being an incarnate mistake, rather than having made a mistake—is reminiscent of the archaic Christian notion of birth with original sin, although in the world of *Homo religiosus*, original sin was conceived as a stain on the ghost in the machine—the separable soul inhabiting the body—while in the world of psychological man, an ontological defect is experienced as an immutable contamination of one's intrinsic being or self. Unfortunately, in severe cases of patients who experience an ontological defect, atonement seems impossible, for the attempt to atone for the human person one happens to be is often experienced as a futile Sisyphean struggle, unless a shamed person discovers how not to be the person one is, without falling prey to schizophrenia or some other disorganizing illness.

In the history of religious confession, the experience of shame was conceived as an essential part of the penance that issued in a healing cure of soul, for the experience of shame—the painful shame generated by the act of confession itself—was an integral part of the psycho-religious drama that shifted *Homo religiosus* from confession to atonement to spiritual health. Alternately put, as a critical feature of the art of listening to sexual secrets in the religious confessional, the gradual evolution of a universal injunction to avoid eye contact had little to do with an enlightened desire to decrease the shame of penitent confessants, for shame was conceived as a vital part of the healing purification of soul thought to be achieved in a corrective sacramental confession. In fact, shame was conceived as a tool whose penitential use encouraged the self-control of sick, sexually sinful religious confessants.

Whatever else one might say about the promotion and purposeful use of shame in the religious confessional, one thing seems clear: medieval theologians possessed a pragmatic state of mind informed by a good eye and ear for the practical consequences of action. In this case, they were eyeing and listening to what might work for confessors in the religious confessional: religious confessors who believed they were waging a fateful struggle for the immortal souls of men and women taught to experience themselves as ontologically defective, having been born into a theocentric world presumably stained, corrupted, and deformed by original sin.

Interestingly, the modern history of torture includes documentary evidence of a decline in barbaric punishment within the European penal system, not to mention its counterpart in the New World. But the gradual decline of corporal punishment occurred much later in the European penal system than in the Judeo-Christian matrix. Having researched the evolution of non-corporal punishments conceived poetically as "penalties of the soul," Foucault found that by the end of the eighteenth century, certainly by the beginning of the nineteenth, barbaric corporal punishment was dying out: "One no longer touched the body, or at least as little as possible, and then only to reach something other than the body itself.

. . . Since it is no longer the body, it must be the soul. The expiation that once rained down upon the body [was] replaced by a punishment that acts in depth on the heart, the thoughts, the will, the inclinations."[16] A student of crime and punishment, a scholar of the confessional, and an experienced clinical confessor, Theodor Reik was well versed in the historical evolution of punishment. Acknowledging the historical shift from the flesh to the soul, from the body to the psyche, Reik confirmed that the noteworthy reduction in the severity of punishments prescribed for religious confessants since the Middle Ages was followed by an evolutionary development in criminal law. In both the criminal and religious domains, Reik averred: "The psychic agent shifts from punishment to admission," from physical punishment to confession itself (*CC*, 302). Of course confession still had a dark twin or a stealthy shadow, but the modern shadow had a life in subtler penalties designed and experienced as mortifications of the soul, that is, penances or penalties of the psyche.

In the rich, imaginative, error-ridden world of psychoanalytic speculation, given a clear understanding of the historical shift from physical punishment to admission, from mortifications of the flesh to penalties of the psyche, it was not a sudden inferential leap or a crazy twist of logic that resulted in the giddy view that a self-betraying clinical confession could be a subtle punishment of the soul, a painfully pleasurable penalty of the psyche, an erotic agent of absolution and penitence. Accordingly, in the educated imagination of Theodor Reik—not only an adventurous theoretician who descended into the underworld of human experience to mine the secrets of confession, but also a notorious lay analyst who became intimate with the tormented mentation of a cultural character type caricatured as psychological man—clinical confession was conceived as a modern evolution of an ancient and medieval religious antecedent, while the modern clinical confessional was exposed as eroticized space where archaic desires for penitence and atonement, as well as masochistic needs for punishment and love, were at once dialogically challenged, passively allowed, and perversely fulfilled.

When Laura crossed the threshold of the clinic on what was shaping-up to be an eventful day, she walked into this historical context of meaning and intelligibility. During the instructive period that led to her confession of murder, her gravest sin, she not only eroticized the clinical confessional, but she confirmed my hypothesis that at the onset of the twenty-first century, some patients appear to be walking the seam between the religious and the psychological worlds. In ambiguous cases of this sort, I feel as if I am hearing the clinical confession of a religious individual who is paying a fee for a psychological cure of soul, while I am a psychological man accepting a fee for a cure of the psyche that should have been a cure of soul. In short, some clinical confessants still think and feel and behave like guilt-ridden sinners and their idiosyncratic behavior in the eroticized confessional adds a dramatic subtext to the dry text comprising the American Psychiatric Association's *Diagnostic and Statistical Manual of Mental Disorders*. "The Rabbit Lady," to use a nickname I have given this unforgettable patient, added human drama to confession, as well as evidence of the fierce struggle of will and counter-will, of self-betrayal and dark intentions, of a wooing for love, and other noteworthy aspects of the erotics of confession.

THE RABBIT LADY

Laura was a twenty-five-year-old divorced female who surprised me with a strange request following her intake in the hospital's adult outpatient clinic. Speaking as though she wished to replicate the religious experience of confessing sins within the dark box of sacramental confession, she asked permission to enter and speak to me from the closet in my consulting room. Clearly, Laura was experiencing something akin to the intense shame and "fore-anxiety" of Reik's reference: the anticipatory anxiety that is wed to the compulsion to confess one's secrets and the expectation of punishment as a way of atoning for having been a sinner. Mind you, Laura was not fearful of receiving corporal punishment in the mental health clinic—a penalty of the flesh that once followed the confession of secrets as a dark twin; rather, as Reik observed when speaking of guilt-ridden confessants, fear of physical punishment has been transformed into fear of confession, such that the terrifying anticipation and ultimate confession of bad deeds is experienced as punishment itself. In cases of this sort, clinical confession may be likened to a clinical penance that partially gratifies a guilt-ridden patient's quest for punishment—penance or punishment, I should add, in pursuit of redemption.

Having become an opportunistic clinician who keeps clinical options open, while also wishing to help this patient quell her anxiety so that productive therapeutic work could proceed apace, I granted Laura's request with some hesitation, given its unorthodox nature. As I watched her enter the dark closet and listened to her speaking through a crack in the door, completely out of my range of vision, I began the fruitful process of reflecting on (a) dialogical therapy as religio-clinical confession, (b) dialogical therapists as religio-clinical confessors, and (c) emotionally ill patients as religio-clinical confessants—not every patient, of course, but some, like Laura, who walk the seam between worlds.

The confessional ceremony of entering and speaking from the closet functioned nicely for a month or so: Laura and I adapted rather easily to this novel religio-clinical situation and I was growing accustomed to hearing her confess her thoughts, feelings, and distorted life experience from the dark closet with the door ajar, all the while testing in myself the hasty conclusion of the Jesuit scholar Snoeck, that "psychoanalysis knows no sin. . . . It stands outside of good and evil" (*CP*, 64). Then one day unexpectedly, in the throe of self-betrayal during the confession of bad deeds, Laura walked out of the closet voluntarily and she remained in the consulting room proper; although now she requested permission to speak while reclining behind the sofa that was stationed opposite the armchair where I normally hear clinical confessions while dialoguing with patients face to face.

"Why not," I thought pragmatically, "this game of capture and surrender seems to be working." Granted, I was not crazy in love with the resistance or the hiding and I felt I was missing much by not seeing eyes of shame. But I was documenting the struggle of conscious will and counterwill in clinic notes and Laura's confidence seemed to be growing with each passing week. Her resistance to self-betrayal was gradually breaking down, no apparent harm was being done, and final surrender seemed imminent, insofar as she was conditioning herself to sit openly, face to face, with her confessor. Accordingly, I granted her request, this time with less hesitation. In this fashion, with Laura speaking from a reclining position on the carpeted floor behind the traditional Freudian sofa, we began the second stage of religio-clinical confession from a defensive, but less protective hiding-place, where my disturbed patient neither saw nor was seen by me.

I cannot deny that these clinical interactions were a bit weird, but in time the conditioning was effective: the anxiety of disclosing guilty secrets to an opaque stranger decreased, willful resistance to self-betrayal was defeated, and Laura finally surrendered and came out of hiding, more comfortable with the perverse experience of sitting on the sofa and confessing her secrets eye to eye, in full view of her therapist-confessor.

I say "perverse" because I am referring to the erotics of confession, thereby playing the game of speculating with Reik that this self-betraying patient was experiencing a guilt-ridden need for penance and atonement, for punishment and redemption, that not only (a) gradually defeated her willful resistance to the confession of a gravely experienced bad deed, but also (b) prolonged her experience of the foreplay, the intense anxiety, that delivers the gratifying punishment residing in painfully pleasurable confession itself. Aware of the erotics of confession, I also was mindful of the fact that I was an accomplice in the gratification of my patient's need for punishment by accepting her strange request for prolonged confession in hiding. Perhaps it is cavalier to say this so many years later, but I have no regrets, for this instructive experience focused my attention on the subtle and manifest, overt and covert, ways in which therapist-confessors unwittingly collude in granting the penance of guilt-ridden patients who, as Reik proclaimed, "must be allowed a certain measure of gratification of their urges, even of the need for punishment" (*CC*, 238).

On the sofa in full view, in a memorable act of surrender and self-betrayal, Laura finally came clean and confessed her grave sin. As she made the move from experiencing the gratifying pain of anticipatory anxiety to experiencing the gratifying release that identifies the painful end-pleasure of a shameful, cathartic clinical confession, Laura averted her eyes to avoid my gaze, then she confessed to killing her pet rabbit by placing him in a plastic bag inside her freezer.

Why had she done such a horrible thing to her beloved pet? Such a slow, awful, painful freezing to death! In truth, my rabbit lady was severely and persistently mentally ill: a "SPMI," as we stated characteristically during treatment reviews with an interdisciplinary team in the hospital clinic. Prescinding from critical examination of her particular psychosis, this troubled young woman had become unemployed and she could no longer afford to feed her pet. As a result, she attempted to dispose of the rabbit by putting him in a ziplock freezer bag and placing the bag in her refrigerator. After waiting a few hours she pulled the bag out of the refrigerator, placed it on the floor, opened it, and removed the rabbit to see if the creature had died. Not surprisingly, the ice-cold bunny bit Laura on the hand, less than gleeful about the experience of being forced to find that mystical lost lane to heaven before his time.

Unable to tolerate this assault and now seeing Bugs Bunny as an aggressive beast, all hell broke loose deep within the rabbit lady's paranoid interior. With fierce wrath doubling her determination to have the furry beast off the planet, she returned the rabbit to the ziplock bag, but this time, she placed the bag in the freezer, until the poor rabbit died.

Convinced that Laura would become haunted by the dead rabbit, who would accuse her of being a murderess deserving punishment—severe punishment undoubtedly self-inflicted—I guided her away from her initial idea of burying the rabbit in the yard behind her apartment. Although things settled down for a while following interment of the rabbit in a suitable burial plot miles away from her apartment, the chief of psychiatry decided that it was dangerous for me to continue seeing this enchanted patient, for she became fixated on me in the throe of a confessional wooing for love and absolution, the same way Anna O became erotically fixed on Breuer. As a result, Laura began to call my residence in the wee hours of the morning with invitations to engage erotically. When I confronted her appropriately during a therapy session that happened to be our final clinical hour, she gave every sign of becoming enthralled with the idea of putting me in a sealed bag in her freezer, as if I were a clinical cannibal who had taken a bite out of her heart.

Needless to say, this was an interesting case of a clinic patient whose behavior suggests that she experienced a compulsion to confess a grave, guilty secret. But this religio-clinical confession confirmed Freud's educated claim that in the clinical trenches, the most serious problem a therapist will confront is the management of eroticism. Experienced clinicians understand that management and control may have comical aspects, as we saw in Breuer's flight from Anna O; but management also has potentially serious ramifications as I discovered with a female confessant whose erotic disposition resulted in the wish that I were dead like her rabbit. In both comical and serious cases, in the clinical confessional, Freud's wisdom remains sound: the erotic tie is often "unavoidable," "complicated," and "difficult to clear up"; from time to time, even the most skilled therapist will draw down the "full enmity" of a patient scorned, in which case, the best interests of clinical treatment can no longer be protected and the therapist must withdraw unsuccessfully.[17]

THE CONFESSING ANIMAL

While steadfastly involved in developing the hypothesis of the compulsion to confess, Reik corrected Freud's shortsighted view that confession was merely an introduction to psychoanalysis. Conceiving confession as "an essential part of psychoanalysis" Reik supported this revision of the reputed master with evidence from his own clinical practice—phenomenological evidence enabling him to say that by virtue of clinical confession, patients not only become better "acquainted" with themselves, but also have "the best possibility for self-understanding and self-acceptance," these critical aspects of dialogical therapy resulting in "a better kind of adjustment to reality" (*CC*, 204–5). In spite of this direct challenge to the patriarch of psychoanalysis, the aging Freud thought that the future of psychoanalysis was invested in younger disciples like Reik and he strongly approved of Reik's critical focus on the central role of the moralistic superego in shaping a guilt-ridden confessant's unconscious quest for punishment. In the final analysis, however, unlike Freud, Reik's eyes were focused intensely on "the therapy of confession" itself: his right eye on the pleasure that issues from the self-betraying confession of guilty secrets, his left eye on the partial gratification of the need for punishment secured in painfully pleasurable clinical confessions (*CC*, 201). This set Reik apart. In fact, Reik's left eye earned him a rightful place in a pantheon of seers, such as Hawthorne, who had a penetrating vision of the erotic underworld of self-betrayal—the subterranean sewer of confession.

In spite of his noteworthy insights and Freud's approval of his work, Reik placed himself on a theoretical limb that could not bear the heavy weight of his root metaphor, "compulsion," insofar as the compulsion to confess applied universally to humankind. Realizing he was out on a limb with the idea of a universal compulsion, Reik hedged his bet, claiming that the "universal significance" of the compulsion presupposed certain "cultural conditions"; but Reik never identified the conditions, rather, he stated vacuously that in the phrase "the compulsion to confess," it is not the term "compulsion" that is prominent, rather, the term "*confession* is to be given prominence" (CC, 180). Adding additional difficulty to the acceptance of his grand hypothesis, Reik also claimed thoughtlessly that the "compulsive character" of confession can be "deduced" from the fact that "all inner and outer resistances" are overcome in confession; yet this hasty conclusion is gainsaid by the demonstrable fact that some human beings will not confess secrets to save their own skin. As I reported elsewhere, Julius Fuchik, a respected Czech journalist, was such a man.[18] In his smuggled *Notes from the Gallows,* written on scraps of paper under the nose of the Gestapo while he was imprisoned at Pankrats, Prague, Fuchik described his state of mind while waiting his turn to confess. Waiting and listening to the shrieks and moans of fellow inmates, all the while wondering about the savaging he soon would experience, Fuchik made the following mental note and later, half broken, scribbled it on a torn shred of paper: "You see people go in strong and healthy; they return two or three hours later broken and crippled in the grilling. . . . You see a person go in with clear direct eyes; but when he returns he dares not look you in the face. He met a moment of weakness . . . in the inquisition room . . . an overpowering wish to save himself. . . . The sight of someone who has lost his courage and his conscience is worse than the sight of one whose body has been crippled. . . . Those who weaken are pitiful."[19]

Sadly, while playing a part in the history of confession and punishment, Fuchik was brutally tortured and murdered by the Gestapo, after which he became a national hero in honor of the fact that he had not betrayed his fellows by surrendering his resistance to confession, notwithstanding the ghastly experience of medieval torture: an external compulsion that failed to dominate one man's indomitable will to remain courageous and in his conscience, honorable.

Arguably most damaging to Reik's hypothesis of a universal unconscious compulsion to confess is the fact that the hypothesis rested on psychoanalysis itself; in fact the hypothesis lived and died with the mythologems of Freud. According to Reik, the "assumption" of a universal unconscious compulsion to confess is as "irrefutable as a scientific postulate because of the theoretical points of view of psychoanalysis" (CC, 180). This was a big mistake! In fact, by the 1950s, Freud's psychoanalytic work was critiqued in significant ways that eroded his power and influence. But neither Freud nor Reik could have foreseen that during the second half of the twentieth century, Freud and his beloved brainchild would be deconstructed ad nauseum in a hyper-enlightened tour de force in which psychiatrists were compared to witchdoctors, mental illness was conceived as myth, and the madman construed as a socially constructed scapegoat of the Age of Reason.[20]

Hammering another nail into the coffin of the Freudian mystique in 1990, in "New Notes from Underground," I embraced the sardonic thesis that *Homo sapiens* is an evolutionary error, such that a second genesis of humankind is in the making. Identifying the second genesis as a shift from natural selection to the artificial selection of the human genotype, I argued that the Freudian character type, *Homo psychologicus*, is currently being displaced by *Homo biologicus*: a novel cultural character type I parsed as "the experimental darling of advanced research in biochemistry and the neurosciences, the soulless, genetically manipulable, organismically curable phenotype of the twenty-first century."[21] Fourteen years later, in the first French edition of *Le Pacte de lucidité ou l'intelligence du Mal*, Baudrillard offered a similar appraisal at the onset of the twenty-first century, arguing boldly that in postmodern time, humankind is "eliminating the natural world in all its forms," in favor of "an increasingly artificial reality," that is, a "hyperrealization of all its possibilities," including its "genetic perfection."[22]

In spite of the assault on Freud and collateral damage to Reik's grand hypothesis, Reik was a lay analyst giving clinical voice to earlier literary views that the human soul dissolves when subjected to inquisition. Like Hawthorne, an American author whose Puritan novel about sex, secrecy, and confession focused on the daemonic struggle of self-betrayal and atonement, Reik's work involving secrecy and confession demonstrated that he had clinical experience with the erotics of resistance and surrender, punishment and pleasure, penance and atonement, within the human animal. Reik also understood that he was not a lone voice crying in this wilderness. In fact, he was very familiar with Dostoevsky, a great Russian litterateur who possessed similar psycho-religious interests. Writing as if his thesis were torn from the pages of *Crime and Punishment*, Dostoevsky's critically acclaimed fiction of 1886, a psychological fiction devoted to drawing out in excruciating detail a protagonist's struggle with guilt and the internal struggle of self-betrayal, Reik subtitled his work *On the Psychoanalysis of Crime and Punishment*. In a clear, compelling way, Dostoevsky's penetrating analysis of the criminal mind, particularly his rich psychological insights concerning the criminal's indirect confessions and moral need, demand, and quest for punishment, leaves no doubt that the great Russian author would have agreed with Reik's bold argument that secrets beg to be revealed, that "compulsion" is the correct term for the dynamic counter-will that defeats the conscious intention to hide, that the compulsion to betray oneself in direct and indirect confessions results from an unconscious desire for redemptive punishment in guilt-ridden human beings (*CC*, 49–50).

In the aftermath of Reik's intriguing lectures and the subsequent publication of his book, religious confessors and scholarly academics followed suit by conceiving human beings as inveterate confessants. For example, while comparing sacramental confession to secular psychoanalysis in 1964, the Jesuit scholar Snoeck drew upon his experience in Catholicism's dark box and used the literary idioms of Hawthorne and Dostoevsky to expose the ambiguous human urge to confess "stirrings of [the] soul and . . . hesitations of [the] will," as well as "sinfulness" and "moral evil" (*CP*, 58, 60). In 1976, Foucault argued boldly that "Western man has become a confessing animal" for whom sex is a "privileged theme": from the Christian penance of the Middle Ages to the psychiatric couch of the perverse modern era, Foucault declared with characteristic lucidity, "truth and sex are joined, through the obligatory and exhaustive expression of an individual secret."[23] Finally, while addressing the ethics of confession in the early 1980s, moral philosopher Sissela Bok noted carefully that Theodor Reik would be surprised at the immense number of professionals who are tasked with facilitating the compulsion to confess in contemporary culture; referring to the seemingly unlimited modalities of dialogical therapy available to clinical confessants, Bok also warned rather ominously: "The therapeutic value of any of these techniques is far from established; and the need for caution in choosing persons best qualified to listen to personal revelation is increasingly clear. . . . One cannot trust all who listen to confessions to be either discrete or especially capable of bringing solace or help."[24]

Against this background and with Hawthorne's warning in mind, I would add the thought that in the clinical confessional, during dialogical interactions with a trusted confessor, the attempt to defend against self-betrayal often is defeated by a healthy desire for well-being. Occasionally, there is an impulsive surrender to the enthrallments of confession: the lure of intimacy, a guilt-ridden need for punishment, an ambiguous pleasure that comes from undressing, from baring the soul, from breaking out of the chrysalis, exposing one's ugliness, and giving oneself away. For the clinical confessor, these charms of confessing are paralleled by the desire to provide some sort of psychological healing, but also, on occasion, the charms of confessing are paralleled by the fascination of listening and the pleasure of hearing secrets disclosed during an invasion of and descent into a patient's psyche. From time to time, in spite of every good intention, the fascination of hearing secrets may lead to a confessor's *mōrōsē dēlectātĭon*: a lingering pleasure derived from imagining enactments of the secrets confessed. In view of these enthrallments of confession, there is an acquired art of listening. This is the fine art of clinical confessors who understand the pleasures and the pains of breaking out of, and the frailty and the finesse involved in breaking into, the chrysalistic self of *Homo confessus*: the uniquely secretive, reflexively conscious, ambivalently disclosive, confessing animal.

UNRULY FACTS

Freud published *The Question of Lay Analysis* in 1926, the year following publication of *The Compulsion to Confess*. The reason I mention this polemical essay in which Freud referred to confession as an introductory aspect of psychoanalysis is that it was written in part as a defense of Theodor Reik, a dedicated disciple who had neither medical training nor a medical degree. Reik received a PhD in psychology from the University of Vienna in 1912. Following conferral of his doctorate, he studied psychoanalysis with Freud for several years and during this time, given his professional promise, Reik and his family were supported financially by Freud who, by all accounts, discouraged Reik from pursuing his choice of a medical education in favor of acquiring the theoretical mind-set and clinical skills of a Freudian analyst.

A favored member of Freud's inner circle, Reik also became a nonmedical member of the Vienna Psychoanalytic Society, often giving thought-provoking presentations such as his intriguing lectures on the compulsion to confess. In spite of his affiliation with Freud, in 1925, municipal authorities in Vienna formally charged Reik with engaging in an unauthorized medical practice. Complicating the matter and making Reik's future look as bleak as wind-driven snow in Siberia, during the spring of 1925, Dr. Newton Murphy, an American analysand of Reik who became dissatisfied with the results of his clinical experience, accused Reik of being a quack and he advanced a formal lawsuit to that effect.

Things being what they are in the criminal justice system, Reik was ordered to stop his nonmedical practice of psychoanalysis by the Viennese court. Naturally, he resisted and he prudently enlisted Freud's help in his defense. Although the atmosphere was charged and a heated debate was underway among members of the Vienna Psychoanalytic Society regarding the sobering question of nonmedical or lay analysis, Freud sprang to his protégé's defense and in short order he wrote an instructive polemical dialogue entitled *The Question of Lay Analysis*. Elaborating on his personal view that psychoanalysis is independent of medicine and should be considered a foundational part of psychology, Freud argued in favor of lay analysts like Reik, claiming that the practice of psychoanalysis does not require a formal medical education and that analysts without a medical education are perfectly able to effect psychological healing in a responsible way. Granting that an ideal curriculum for training aspiring psychoanalysts had not yet been created, Freud maintained that an ideal curriculum would certainly include "elements from the mental sciences, from psychology, the history of civilization and sociology, as well as anatomy, biology, and the study of evolution" (*QL*, 680).

In my clinical work with patients, to add a personal footnote to Freud's outline of an ideal curriculum, studies of evolutionary theory, particularly recensions of Darwinian theory in evolutionary biology and evolutionary psychology, have benefited me greatly while using language, ideas, and speech to help patients achieve an understanding of the human condition and a recognition of their active role in the evolutionary experiment of testing whether a neotenous, emotionally driven learning animal with a rational intellect and ethical scruples is equipped to survive and pass on its genes while flourishing beyond the reactive impulse-driven lives of other species. Most of all, these studies have been influential in the work of talking patients into a healing reconciliation with humanness—their own humanness, as well as the humanness of their kin and other fellows. Sad to say, the degree to which we are justifiably characterized as a crazed species, in spite of our magnificent technological accomplishments and efforts to become an ethical species, evidences the fact that the human experiment is an evolutionary experiment that runs the risk of failing in the fashion of many other evolutionary experiments that over time, proved to be maladaptive.

Ultimately, all charges against Reik were dropped by the Viennese court. Lay analysis was legitimized in Europe and in America in spite of many dissenting voices; Reik continued to explore the underworld of human perversion, publishing *Masochism in Modern Man* in 1941; and during the twentieth century, the carnival of clinical practice flourished across the globe in the consulting rooms of medical and lay analysts alike. But not as Freud intended! For all too often, dialogical therapists do not have educational preparation in many aspects of the ideal curriculum identified by Freud when he defended his favored disciple. What follows from this distortion of Freud's eager defense of Theodor Reik is the unruly fact that in the eroticized clinic, the persuasive art of using fair words to talk people into and out of things is practiced erratically by incompetents, charlatans, mediocrities, and masters, all of whom may be imaginatively perceived as phantastic persons who hear the clinical confessions of crazed patients while engaging in the experiment of using idiosyncratic language, ideas, and speech to effect one or another sort of psychological healing, whatever "psychological healing" is believed to be or taken to mean.

I realize that this formulation of unruly facts may sound like an echo of Hawthorne's warning to avoid confessional intimacy with clinicians, insofar as some therapists might be deformed in wisdom, belief, judgment, or understanding. This is certainly not my intention, although I am mindful of the fact that enchanted patients have a diminished ability to referee the distinction between reality and its arch rival, illusion, particularly the imperceptible distinction between the true identity and the phantastic appearance of the implicitly trusted, fascinating, seemingly powerful, wizardly, godlike therapist who is sometimes perceived ingloriously as a toilet in the eyes of patients who are not clinically enchanted.

Regarding the distinction between reality and illusion—a distinction that has faded in postmodern time, according to Baudrillard, due to the fact that we dwell increasingly in a media-saturated virtual reality that amounts to a "deregulation of the very reality principle"—it occurs to me that clinical confessors are pleased to advertise the availability of therapeutic eros: sensitivity and respect, empathic understanding, warm regard and acceptance, trustworthiness and dependability, and unyielding devotion to the well-being of patients.[25] But there is another side of the mental health clinic that rarely shows its ugliness naked before all. My experience of this darker underside supports previous suggestions that in the mental health clinic: (a) confession and punishment are "dark twins," (b) shame and other punishments play an interesting, sometimes unexpected role, (c) from time to time, there is a legitimization of sadistic urges that may gratify some therapist-confessors—a distinct pleasure sometimes directly promoted, other times passively allowed.

For example, when I was an inexperienced intern acquiring basic training in an outpatient clinic, like a lowly private under the foot of barking sergeants in boot camp, I was assigned the instructive task of co-facilitating therapy groups for sexual perpetrators of children. All the groups were populated by men mandated to treatment by the criminal justice system and my co-facilitators happened to be female therapists reputedly armed with therapeutic eros and experienced in the art of talking adult males out of the crime of abusing children. From time to time, hearing the lurid details of child sexual abuse did not sit well with my co-facilitators, some of whom seemed to naturally fall into the hardwired role of protective mothers rearing children. Sometimes the association of male perpetrators and female therapists was toxic, other times it seemed lethal! I often felt that this formal clinical setting was the perfect arena for a demonstration of the antisocially disordered male perpetrator's gross indifference to the sexual victimization of innocent children. Given the triumph of the therapeutic and concomitant illusion that the mental health clinic must be therapeutic, the formal clinical setting also seemed to be a judicially sanctioned arena for shaming and humiliating sexual perpetrators, given the emotional reactivity of a handful of state-licensed lay clinicians.

When I stepped into the fray armed with my version of therapeutic eros, including devotion to the well-being of sexual perpetrators, I was pulled aside and advised in no uncertain terms that I was not the lead therapist. And this was true, to say the least. Nevertheless, this so-called clinical experience—a judicially sanctioned therapeutic experience that unwittingly promoted penalties of the psyche for court-mandated patients, not to mention unknowingly allowing release of the questionable practices and pleasures of lay therapist-confessors—raised serious questions about the identity, training, and oath of service of mental health clinicians. Unfortunately, Freud is long gone and no masters have risen to offer guidance regarding unruly questions relating to medical and nonmedical therapists alike. Perhaps Kafka put this best in an enigmatic parable regarding the absence of kings and the prevalence of couriers: "They were offered the choice between becoming kings or the couriers of kings. The way children would, they all wanted to be couriers. Therefore, there are only couriers who hurry about the world, shouting to each other—since there are no kings—messages that have become meaningless. They would like to put an end to this miserable life of theirs but they dare not because of their oaths of service."[26]

NOTES

1. Sigmund Freud, *Fragment of an Analysis of a Case of Hysteria*, in *Standard Edition*, vol. 7 (1953), 77–78.

2. Theodor Reik, *The Compulsion to Confess: On the Psychoanalysis of Crime and Punishment*, trans. Norbert Rie (New York: Grove Press, 1961); cited in the text as CC.

3. Sigmund Freud, *The Interpretation of Dreams*, in *Standard Edition*, vol. 4 (1975); cited in the text as *ID*.

4. Sigmund Freud, "On Beginning the Treatment (Further Recommendations on the Techniques of Psycho-Analysis I)," in *Standard Edition*, vol. 12 (1975), 133.

5. Tertullian's gynophobic image of woman as "a temple built over a sewer" is quoted without details of attribution in Simone de Beauvoir, *The Second Sex*, trans. H. M. Parshley (New York: Alfred A. Knopf, 1971), 167. Tertullian also referred to women as "nymphs of the sewers" in *On the Pallium*, trans. Rev. S. Thelwall, *The Ante-Nicene Fathers: Translations of the Fathers down to A.D. 325*, vol. 4, ed. Rev. Alexander Roberts, D.D., and James Donaldson, LL.D. (Grand Rapids: Wm. B. Erdmans, 1994), 10. Interested readers are referred to Thelwall's sixth footnote on p. 10 for an explication of Tertullian's suggestive use of the Latin *Clŏāca* (sewer).

6. Karen Horney, *Neurosis and Human Growth* (New York: The Norton Library, 1950), 22–23.

7. Ernest Becker, *The Denial of Death* (New York: The Free Press, 1975); cited in the text as *DD*.

8. Michel Foucault, *The History of Sexuality: An Introduction,* vol. 1, trans. Robert Hurley (New York: Vintage Books, 1990), 59.

9. Sigmund Freud, *New Introductory Lectures on Psycho-Analysis,* in *Standard Edition,* vol. 22 (1964); cited in the text as *NI.*

10. St. Thomas Aquinas, *Effects of Sin, Stain and Guilt,* in *Summa Theologiae,* vol. 27, trans. T. C. O'Brien (New York: McGraw-Hill, 1974), 59.

11. Andreas Snoeck, *Confession and Psychoanalysis,* trans. Theodore Zuydwijk (Westminster, MD: Newman Press, 1964); cited in the text as *CP.*

12. Tertullian, *On Penitence,* trans. William P. LeSaint, in *Tertullian: Treatises on Penance* in *Ancient Christian Writers,* ed. Johannes Quasten and Walter J. Burghardt (Westminster, MD: Newman Press, 1959); cited in the text as *OP.*

13. Stephen Haliczer, *Sexuality in the Confessional* (New York: Oxford University Press, 1996), 176–77.

14. Thomas N. Tentler, *Sin and Confession on the Eve of the Reformation* (Princeton, NJ: Princeton University Press, 1977), 20, 128.

15. While developing my concept of ontological defectiveness, I benefited from the popular work of John Bradshaw, *Healing the Shame That Binds You* (Deerfield Beach, FL: Health Communications, 1988).

16. Michel Foucault, *Discipline and Punish: The Birth of the Prison,* 2nd ed., trans. Alan Sheridan (New York: Vintage Books, 1995), 11, 16.

17. Sigmund Freud, "Observations on Transference-Love (Further Recommendations on the Technique of Psycho-Analysis III)," in *Standard Edition,* vol. 12, 159, 167.

18. I previously reported on Fuchik in the moral philosophical essay "A Talent for Life," *The Journal of Value Inquiry* 32 (1998): 191–204.

19. Julius Fuchik, *Notes from the Gallows* (Salt Lake City: Peregrine Smith Books, 1995), 32–33.

20. E. Fuller Torrey, *Witchdoctors and Psychiatrists: The Common Roots of Psychotherapy and Its Future* (New York: Perennial Library, 1986); Thomas S. Szasz, *The Myth of Mental Illness: Foundations of a Theory of Personal Conduct* (New York: A Delta Book, 1967); Michel Foucault, *Madness and Civilization: A History of Insanity in the Age of Reason,* trans. Richard Howard (New York: A Mentor Book, 1967).

21. Carl Paul Ellerman, "New Notes from Underground," *Inquiry: An Interdisciplinary Journal of Philosophy* 33, no. 1 (1990): 8.

22. Jean Baudrillard, *The Intelligence of Evil or the Lucidity Pact,* trans. Chris Turner (Oxford: Berg Publishers, 2005), 33–34.

23. Foucault, *History of Sexuality,* 58, 61.

24. Sissela Bok, *Secrets: On the Ethics of Concealment and Revelation* (New York: Vintage Books, 1984), 80.

25. Baudrillard, *Intelligence of Evil,* 17.

26. Franz Kafka, "Couriers," in *Parables and Paradoxes,* trans. Clement Greenberg (New York: Schocken Books, 1966), 175.

II

VARIATIONS

4

The Therapy of Confession

IN THE SHADOWS

Franklin was not a fictitious character created by a fine author like Dostoevsky, but his struggle with crime, confession, and repentance was reminiscent of the tormenting intrapsychic struggle infecting Raskolnikov, Dostoevsky's guilt-ridden protagonist in *Crime and Punishment.* Given the nature of his transgressions, including the gross betrayal of his family, Franklin's sexual confession may not elicit the reader's sympathy. Yet in his own way and time, like the admittedly sick underground man in Dostoevsky's groundbreaking existentialist fiction, *Notes from Underground,* Franklin was a tormented man of conflicting elements who developed a subterranean existence that kept him attached to life in a deathly way. Existing in the shadows of life, within a chrysalis of his own creating, his experience of the therapy of confession is a powerful summation of the clinical liberation of countless patients whose lives are insular and self-cannibalizing. But it all started many years ago when he crossed the threshold of the clinic blind to the fact that he was about to embark upon a life-changing therapeutic adventure.

When I first laid eyes on Franklin, he was humiliated, confused, and depressed. In his sixties, he was referred for treatment following the unexpected disclosure that he had sexually abused the eighteen-year-old nephew of his anguished wife, Angelina. The sudden exposure of an aberrant sexual identity, coupled with clinical confessions exposing a sordid history of sexual encounters with a number of young males, was ruinous to Franklin's marriage and to virtually every other aspect of a middle-class existence that once offered the false appearance and safe cover of respectability.

Before he retired, Franklin was a college professor who had spent his entire adult life watching, desiring, and fantasizing about adolescent males, some of whom he was responsible for educating. As a result of his sexual identity and experience of perverse desires, he was a thoroughly shamed, guilt-ridden gentleman who had neither self-esteem nor self-respect. As long as he could remember, within the closed chamber of condemnatory self-awareness, he experienced a virulent self-loathing due to his irrepressible ego-dystonic desire for boys.

Disgraced in the aftermath of exposure, Franklin wanted desperately to save his marriage, to regain the respect of his son, and to achieve self-mastery. This would be a tall order even for a phantastic therapist with a dictionary of fair words. A lesser therapist, I agreed to work with Franklin to achieve his stated goals, although I expressed serious reservations about the wisdom of his firm decision to suppress the dominant part of his bisexual nature: a struggle he vowed to undertake while attempting to live within his broken marriage as a heterosexual male. Given my reservations, I urged Franklin to seize the moment to use our therapeutic encounter to carefully think about his life, not only the past, but his future course, hoping that the clarity he achieved through thoughtful self-examination would beget a healthy process of reconciliation with the inescapable realities of sex, self, and humanness. Yet, silently and secretly in my Sisyphean gut, where visceral illuminations are governed by the height of mountains, the weight of boulders, and Newton's law of gravity, I had come to believe rather nihilistically, that we often perish by the identity we choose, such that claiming a name, any name, is to blindly lay claim to an unforeseen existence that contains a precise calculus of thinking, feeling, interpersonal relations, and events, the existential equations of which predict a precise mode of collapse.[1]

Given his wishes and the tentative support of Angelina, Franklin and I coauthored a clinical treatment plan that included abstinence from sex outside his marriage, particularly sexual contact with males, especially sensitive fair-haired boys whose adolescent charms enticed him. In fact, in a formal treatment plan that identified specific persons, places, and things he would strictly avoid in order to prevent a sexual relapse, Franklin committed himself to the self-estranging work of suppressing the dominant part of his bisexual self. During many clinical encounters that included painful confessions of sexual conduct that admittedly repulsed him immediately after the act, Franklin disclosed a shadowy erotic life that included: (a) a twenty-year intimate relationship with Angelina's brother, Anthony, a man whose incestuous desire for Angelina was temporarily fulfilled on occasion when Franklin fellated Anthony as Anthony watched his sister sunbathing by the pool in her backyard; (b) brief sexual relationships with a variety of consenting young men; (c) engaging in the act of fellating several male students, the most noteworthy being one who successfully blackmailed Franklin during a predator to predator confrontation; (d) the seduction of the young nephew responsible for exposing Franklin's subterranean existence.

One morning, after a particularly cathartic clinical hour that brought into relief the painfully pleasurable emotional cleansing that comes from disclosing guilty secrets to an empathic confessor—shameful sexual secrets whose inescapable truth is capable of instilling an annihilative self-renunciation—Franklin rose from the sofa and extended his open hand. Squeezing my hand firmly, while sustaining eye contact to reinforce the sincerity of his soul-searching message, he dissected his insular life and his liberating experience in the clinical confessional: "I always wanted to tell someone and I trust you implicitly. Now I feel like I'm out of the shadows. I've been cocooned-up my whole life. I always wanted to be liked for who I am, but it's been too dangerous. A person needs to claim himself . . . I mean have an identity and expose it!"

Neither Dostoevsky nor Hawthorne could have written a better, more succinct literary confession in spite of the fact that they mastered the modern art of writing psychological fiction. If they had been flies on the wall in the mental health clinic that morning, listening to the fluctuating interplay of dialogical partners, they would have admired Franklin's clear, insightful expression of the human need to possess, to claim, to expose, an authentic identity. Given Freud's experience of self-betrayal oozing from the pores of his patients and Reik's comprehensive work on the compulsion to confess, I imagined Freud and Reik smiling knowingly at Franklin's claim that a person needs to expose his identity. Unless I am mistaken, Dostoevsky and Hawthorne would have understood in their own case, the human need to be accepted for being the flawed person one becomes. Whether this imaginary inference is valid or not, I am more certain of my suspicion that in his simple, elegant, meaningful confession, Franklin disclosed an intimate understanding of the tormenting experience of Dostoevsky's underground man: the experience of never feeling fully alive, of having lost touch with real life, of having subsisted in the gray shadows of being and time, as if he were an insect that had spun a silky case around itself and lived within this chrysalis from which it never broke out.

Stillborn, petrified, and immobile in this pupal stage of psychological development, Franklin became a cocooned, self-cannibalizing ego who failed to fashion an identity he felt comfortable claiming as his own. Within the chrysalis, unable to exist in the interpersonal world openly and authentically, he managed to feed, excrete, mate, and avoid exposure for the longest time. Like Dostoevsky's sick, self-consumed underground man, Franklin did not know what life was or where to find it. Forced out of the chrysalis by circumstances beyond his control, he crossed the threshold of the clinic where he confronted himself honestly and openly in the presence of another person for the first time. Happily, after venturing into the clinical confessional and embracing the agonistic struggle to claim an identity by searching, exposing, and reconciling with identifiable aspects of his authentic self, Franklin put away the things of a sexual perpetrator. In time, by virtue of his enchantment with the clinic, our mutual commitment to the difficult work of dialogical therapy, and the painfully pleasurable therapy of confession, Franklin became a more thoughtful, responsible adult, still haunted by powerful sexual demons, but no longer a criminal, stillborn, crippled, and cocooned in the shadows of life.

THE WORM OF CONSCIENCE

Franklin's self-exposure demonstrated that he was not a garden-variety sexual perpetrator: a man with an Antisocial Personality Disorder whose clinical marker is a total lack of remorse for having ruthlessly victimized innocent children. Contrary to this typical antisocial presentation, Franklin neither justified his behavior, nor manifested indifference to his victims. In fact, clinical experience with Franklin evidenced Reik's pregnant claim that "confession is conscience speaking up" (*CC*, 205).

One of the more intriguing things about Franklin's confession of conscience is the fact that he was an educated man who knew a good deal about the interdependent genetic and environmental shaping of biological organisms. When he finally came to the clinic for treatment of his disorder, I supplemented his scientific knowledge by teaching him about the emotional load of family of origin dynamics. For example, Franklin's older brother had been a powerful, dominating, physically aggressive, athletic adolescent esteemed highly by his parents and pursued by many girls. He was a classic alpha male, to put it bluntly. By comparison, as a youth, Franklin was a sensitive, shy, withdrawn bean-pole. A bookworm who had no experience with girls, he was admittedly controlled, disesteemed, and invalidated by his parents. In fact, his father was physically and emotionally unavailable and early on, strange as it may seem, Franklin's mother dressed him like a girl for a Halloween party at school. One can only imagine the emotional beating inflicted by his peers. Everything considered, Franklin envied his brother; for he was Franklin's earliest and best model of who and how to be, although Franklin knew in his gut that he never would achieve his brother's alpha male status.

In the clinic, Franklin discovered that each of the teenage boys who attracted him had one or another of the masculine attributes shared by his brother: a strong will, a fine physique, independence, defiance, all of which resulted in fearless risk-taking behavior. In short, each of the adolescent boys whom he fellated possessed qualities of the alpha "males who I am not." After processing many clinical confessions, Franklin learned that the act of incorporating the penis and swallowing the semen of alpha males—an act that actually repulsed him—was a compensatory strategy for incorporating alpha male attributes he did not possess. From a psychodynamic point of view, an act that seemed to be intrinsically sexual had more to do with trying to become the powerful alpha male he admired, envied, and never could become.

In spite of his intelligence, his scientific knowledge, and the supplemental education he received from his trusted clinical confessor, Franklin had difficulty accepting his sexual identity, although he had no doubt that if a bisexual student came to him for advice, the student would receive knowledgeable information to facilitate a healing reconciliation with self. This is irrational, but deep within the limbic brain where humans live crazed lives of self-cannibalization, Franklin felt like a repulsive sinner. As a result, he was unable to apply his knowledge and rational understanding to himself. He had eaten forbidden fruit and acquired knowledge of good and evil; soon thereafter, he condemned himself to die the death that follows forbidden desire and the repeated commission of sexual sins. He knew that he would always have a desire to fellate fair-haired boys and this fatal flaw convinced him that he was a perverted sinner, with little hope of atonement, nor prayer of redemption.

While living in the shadows, Franklin's confrontation with self never was an affair of rational intellect, for his long night of the soul turned upon the crucible of conscience: an uncritical forging of cruciform terms of existence that encoded how a loathsome worm should see and think and feel. Like Teresa of Avila, Franklin believed he was a "loathsome . . . worm . . . befouled . . . by all the offences it has committed"; like St. Teresa, Franklin also took pleasure in the punishment of the penitent, believing that "by this distress the soul was purified . . . like gold in the crucible."[2] In the shadows of life, where pain and pleasure are committed partners, Franklin experienced his chronic mood disorder as a refined calculus of retributive justice that did the unending work of purifying a soul fouled by vices of the flesh. From time to time, therefore, in a perverse manner, he delighted in the pleasures of self-punishment, although he never confessed to experiencing Teresa's infamous ecstasy, flight of spirit, or rapture.

Sad to say, while lending an ear in the clinical confessional, I often hear the voice of the loathsome worm that has violated the authoritative demands of a harsh moral conscience. Although I have joined with Freud, his disciples, and their successors, in the clinical struggle to oppose and lower the demands of the tyrannical superego, it falls to me to say that the lesson of the worm and the reason for Reik's clinical view that the need for punishment is a psychological necessity in some guilt-ridden patients, is that moral conscience is deep and inviolable, not actually subject to much change or alteration. Once a person has a moral conscience, whatever the encoding, it may be in that person's best interest not to violate it, for he will surely pay the heavy price of feeling as if a worm is in his heart, gnawing slowly, millimeter by millimeter, until the worm of conscience consumes the heart and then moves toward the soul to begin a graver symposium and banquet.

A DEVIL'S BARGAIN

Dostoevsky and Hawthorne prowled the underworld of confession in their psychological fictions, but what these masterful authors did not know firsthand is that dialogical therapists quickly learn not to be surprised at any turn of events in the clinical confessional, not the least reason being that a patient's healthy care of self may yield to self-defeating behavior and other phenomenological evidence of guilt and penitential pleasure. Focused on this underworld of human experience in the clinical confessional, Reik came to understand that "the reduction of the need for punishment" is one of the most "difficult therapeutic problems" a clinician will encounter. Of course Reik was not speaking in a vacuum, for he had learned from Freud that when a tyrannical superego is introjected or turned against the self aggressively, the worm of conscience can inflict devastating self-punishment, leaving little room in life for happiness or well-being. In a later formulation, Freud observed: "The sense of guilt, the harshness of the super-ego, is . . . the same thing as the severity of conscience. . . . The need for punishment . . . become[s] masochistic under the influence of a sadistic super-ego; it is a portion . . . of the instinct towards internal destruction. Consequently, we are very often obliged, for therapeutic purposes, to oppose the super-ego, and we endeavour to lower its demands" (*CD*, 136, 143).

Reik found the problem of lowering the demands of the super-ego so difficult that he bemoaned the inability of Freudian analysis to reduce the need for punishment in guilt-ridden patients (*CC*, 238). According to Reik, a psychoanalyst must not only uncover repressed causes of the patient's need for punishment, but then he must make the unconscious conscious by transforming unconscious guilt into conscious awareness. Acknowledging the fact that this Freudian strategy is an incredibly slow process requiring years of confession and intensive analysis, Reik was openly disheartened by his inability to cope with guilt-ridden patients' apparent need for punishment. Confronting his clinical impotence head on, he pulled no punches:

> The answer to this question gives little comfort—almost nothing can be done about it. . . . The patient must be allowed a certain measure of gratification of . . . the need for punishment. . . . An active therapy . . . of prohibition or command does more to damage than to help. Prohibition of a certain instinctual gratification makes the patient strive for the forbidden just because of his need for punishment. . . . The moral of this is: new harm has resulted. . . . Until the unconscious causes of the feeling of guilt are uncovered . . . analysis can do little more than perhaps protect the patient from the crudest self-inflictions. (*CC*, 238–39)

From time to time in the clinical trenches I feel comfortable saying that Reik's conclusion was not a counsel of despair; rather, it was an honest assessment of clinical experience accompanied by a seasoned confessor's frank admission that self-defeat and other perverse punishments appear to be a psychological necessity in some hopelessly guilt-ridden confessants. To a certain extent, Reik's clinical experience is consistent with mine, except to say, I strongly disagree with his conclusion that actively prohibiting self-punishment or commanding restraint results in more damage than help. On better days, when the phantastic person of the therapist has power and influence; on the best days, when the dictionary is opened and common words become fair words that seem magically charmed; prohibition and command can be quite effective.

Confirming this discovery in *The Psychology of Confession*, while commenting on suggestibility with reference to the personal influence and authority of confessors, Erik Berggren noted that self-interest—a person's investment in self-preservation—is what produces suggestibility and makes it an invaluable tool in religious, clinical, and other formal confessional contexts (*PC*, 162).[3] Alternately put, self-interest is the principal reason why demoralized patients invest ordinary men and women with phantastic qualities and attributes; self-interest also accounts for the fact that help-seeking patients develop emotional ties with confessors, then fall under the influence of these seemingly powerful authorities who are quite mortal, imaginary views of the clinic and dream-like perceptions of the therapist notwithstanding. Digging deeper to ferret out the working principles of suggestibility, Berggren found that confessants subject themselves to the influence and seemingly infallible authority of religious and clinical confessors by accepting the "whole context" of language, value, and belief within which confessors lend their ears to secrets:

> A characteristic thing about the confessant is his acceptance of the whole background which the authority represents. . . . In making his confession, he wants to surrender himself completely and become part of this context, to make its values his own. He is more inclined to do so because of his perplexed and helpless state, and because he does not see any possibility of ex-

> tricating himself from his difficulties. He is in a condition that renders him specially disposed to accept without criticism what the confessor conveys to him. (*PC*, 162–63)

With suggestibility, personal power and influence, and fair words increasingly in mind during formative years when I began to focus on the self-defeating attitudes and punitive behaviors of guilt-ridden patients, I initiated the peculiar strategy of speaking to some patients about the convicted criminals I encountered during my experience teaching philosophy in a maximum security prison. I used vigorous prose to inform self-punishing patients that the convicted criminals I worked with committed atrocious crimes—murder, sodomy, armed robbery, and selling drugs to children—serious felonies for which they received a determinate sentence in a tightly controlled state correctional facility. Prescinding from consideration of the most vicious inmates who were serving double life sentences for heinous crimes, in my recitative, I always focused on the crucial fact that after guilty inmates served their time—ten, twenty, or thirty years—the criminal justice system released them from captivity and formal punishment came to an end. I purposefully compared the penitential experience of the convicted criminals with the penitential experience of the guilt-ridden patient, whose self-punishment never ends, being sure to stress the fact that the patient is serving a self-imposed life sentence of his own devising with neither hint of parole nor promise of pardon. Focusing patients' attention on the stark reality of the unspoken, unrecorded, unpardonable life sentence they were serving, I made it quite clear, by direct comparison, that after serving their allotted time, even cold-blooded murderers were released from the correctional facility.

Often, the artful analogy was heard as the voice of reason, as if guilt-ridden patients had found the lost lane to Aristotle's golden mean between excess and deficiency in thinking and behavior. But a crazed human being is not a rational animal as Aristotle imagined when he dreamed up the absurd notion that "reason more than anything else *is* man." Accordingly, in the clinical trenches, at the very edge of therapy, I have offered some guilt-ridden patients the option of remaining in their penitentiary and continuing self-punishment for past crimes, but for a specific period of time, perhaps three months, six months, or nine months, as if the self-condemned patient were a convicted criminal who finally had a formal sentence of record—this time, however, a sentence that was time-limited, rather than a sentence that was indeterminate or open-ended. With a hopeful eye on an end of self-punishment and release from the correctional facility the worm of conscience had constructed, the offer of a specific sentence was premised on the mutual understanding that time served would be a complete reparation for past crimes. Furthermore, the devil's bargain was premised on my patients' promise to begin the therapeutic process of replacing self-defeating behavior with self-care, as if self-care were a formal obligation of parole, a parole the patient must begin to prepare for when voluntarily accepting the offer.

I struggled with this clinical strategy as I have struggled with a variety of strategies that have a life at the edge of therapy. Depending on the absurdity of the idea, particularly ideas that posed the most risk to patient care, I struggled in the fashion of Kafka, a self-cannibalizing author who remarked tormentingly: "I have not produced a single line that I am able to endorse, and I have effaced everything. . . . My whole body cries out against every word; before allowing itself to be written down by me, every word scans the horizon; the sentences literally crumble in my hands, I see inside them and have to stop at once."[4] In spite of these Kafkaesque struggles, I still use the artful analogy of criminal and patient for a variety of reasons, not the least being that discerning patients find the whole thing quite amusing and frequently we laugh uproariously at the absurdity: the absurdity of the endless penitential life the patient is living, as well as the absurdity of a devil's bargain in a respectable mental health clinic whose raison d'être is emotional healing, not the kind of retributive justice that is the logic of life in a maximum security prison, the pretense of rehabilitation notwithstanding.

In retrospect, I have never had a patient literally accept the offer, but sometimes it had the most profound effect on a patient's self-defeating behavior, as if a moment of sanity had insinuated itself in the synapses of self-discovery. In fact, I am relatively certain that some patients who listened and laughed, but did not take me up on the devilish offer, internalized the bargain and maintained it as an existential therapist's crazy jest. I can honestly say, in some of these cases, the artful analogy seemed to provide a clinical benefit as if it were charmed. Specifically, some patients who are stung by the analogy, particularly those who are severely pricked by the comparative severity of their life sentence in the light of a brutal murderer's eventual release from a penal institution with time off for good behavior, begin to exercise a degree of self-restraint, while remaining imprisoned in an intrapsychic penitentiary that continues to extract a painfully pleasurable penance.

Interestingly, in his allegorical short story "In the Penal Colony," Kafka focused on the fact that a condemned soldier about to be executed did not know his sentence; in fact, the condemned man did not know that he had been sentenced. Exploring the internal logic of this intriguing state of affairs, Kafka stressed the salient point that a man who does not know he has been sentenced cannot know whether his defense has been effective or not. But in the absurd, naturalistic world of Kafka, this detail is beside the point, the crucial point that the condemned prisoner is never given the opportunity either to formulate or to mount a defense, for his "guilt is never to be doubted"; besides, there really is no point in advising the condemned prisoner of his sentence, for he will ultimately learn his sentence "on his body."[5]

Bizarre as it may seem, the existential situation of Kafka's condemned soldier resembles the existential situation of many guilt-ridden clinic patients whose worm of conscience is gnawing away continually. Specifically, in the intrapsychic penal colony of their devising, guilt is never doubted, there is no defense, and the lifelong sentence manifests itself in self-defeating behavior, as well as in morbid symptoms that inflict punishment on the body and the mind. Confronted with this incorrigible situation, Reik confessed his impotence, but in my mind, a devil's bargain may be a better choice for the laughs alone.

In the throe of clinical symptoms, emotional suffering, and self-defeating behavior, the mutual laughter of confessor and confessant can be a healing experience in itself: a temporary expedient, to be sure, but a healing experience like the therapy of confession. Of course a healing belly-laugh does not betoken the kind of passionate attachment that leaves a suggestible patient swooning and falling to the floor in erotic transport. But it would be a mistake to minimize the strength or the clinical utility of the temperate emotional bonds reinforced by laughter. Mutual laughter is a great benefactor in the clinical trenches and less intense emotional bonds suggest a comfortable intimacy that may be used to influence guilt-ridden patients, some of whom will respond to their therapist-confessor in a state of heightened suggestibility. When a patient is in this mental state, as we shall see, an opportunistic dialogical therapist has a unique opportunity to use language and ideas to convey a world of meaning and intelligibility. This is consistent with the notion that when an unsuspecting confessant falls under the spell of a confessor, he unwittingly begins to accept the whole context of language, value, and belief within which a confessor is lending an ear to secrets.

A LESSER LOVE

While elucidating essential features of the psychology of confession, Berggren identified the trusting relationship of confessor and confessant, confidence in the confessor's guidance, hope of redemption or cure, scrupulous self-examination, the confession of secrets to an authoritative confessor, and the cathartic discharge of morbid affects through self-disclosive speech. Unwittingly, Berggren also confirmed important aspects of my personal clinical experience when he noted correctly: "The development of suggestion does not necessarily demand the intense manifestations of emotion which psychoanalysts have been able to note on the part of their patients"; nevertheless, even a lesser "affective devotion" is a useful tool in producing psychological healing and other admirable features of the therapy of confession (*PC*, 161).

For example, when I first shook his hand and invited him to take a seat on the comfortable leather sofa in my consulting room, Ben was a chronically depressed, guilt-ridden businessman in his mid-fifties—a man who owned and operated a retail business that has a widespread reputation for being unscrupulous. Although Ben claimed that he ran a "clean shop" in comparison to his competitors, the public has the perception that the order of the day in this notorious business is "conning" customers, rather than giving them an honest deal. At first, Ben's involvement in this enterprise made sense; later, however, as clinical confession became enchantingly addictive and I had the opportunity to take a closer look, I came to understand that underneath the rough exterior, he was a sensitive man with fellow-feeling—in short, the kind of man who might clean up a dirty business.

According to Ben, his father was "a beast of a human being" who belittled him constantly when he was a boy, conditioning him to believe he was not only "stupid," "fat," and "crippled," but a "bastard" who was not his son. Given these daily assaults that instilled a toxic invalidation, Ben learned to defend himself by identifying with his aggressor. Mastering this defense, he became a rage-filled youngster who developed a "nervous tick," a habit of torturing frogs, and a passion for fistfights among other clinical markers of a conduct disorder that rivaled the childhood impairment of Isaac Newton.

Later, evidencing the development of antisocial traits, Ben described sexual experimentation during adolescence as "angry sex," something akin to "rape in my head," but rape with "no boundaries"; he also drew no boundaries around the abuse of alcohol and more serious drugs, including cocaine and hallucinogens. Equally important, a veritable warehouse of unresolved guilt resulted from the suicide of a beloved brother characterized by Ben as his "first love." Although an unsuccessful suicide attempt was a defining moment that should have alerted Ben and other family members to be on guard, Ben confessed that he was entirely self-involved at the time and he failed to "save" his brother. As a result, his brother's death left Ben feeling indelibly responsible for "not doing enough" to stem the predictable tide of self-destruction. During the ensuing years, this tormenting experience resulted in a punitive, guilt-ridden codependency: an unhealthy addiction to rescuing and solving the problems of others, often, at the expense of Ben's own needs and desires.

After remaining faithfully married for thirty years, during which time he built a successful business, attended church regularly, and discharged the responsibilities of a family man without complaint, all the while keeping his nose to the grindstone of rescuing others, Ben found himself in an extramarital relationship that fulfilled his own emotional needs and prodigious erotic desires. It came to pass that Ben separated from his wife with the idea of pursuing this fulfilling relationship; but his chronically anxious spouse somatized her fear of losing her life-supporting husband. Deeply struck by the intense fear that his spouse would become morbidly ill like his deceased brother, thus compelled to save his wife from an imagined disaster, Ben returned home to rescue her. During this time, according to his spouse, Ben became "depressed," "unhappy," "confused," "remote," and "withdrawn." In this emotional condition, he crossed the threshold of the clinic hoping to gain "perspective" on his marriage, his "sensuous" extramarital affair, and his direction in life. This was particularly important because he admittedly was aging, anticipating the end of time, and he wished to find a way to "enjoy the next ten years."

In the clinical confessional, Ben proved to be a highly verbal confessant. Guilt-ridden, he also felt ontologically defective to the nth degree. One morning, after achieving a number of illuminating insights, including an understanding of his recently developed erectile disorder, Ben stopped in his tracks as he was leaving my office. Turning to face me, then gazing directly into my eyes, he stated earnestly, as if he were experiencing euphoric recall: "This is like cocaine! Now I know why people say they love their therapists." Needless to say, Ben had become enchanted.

By comparing and contrasting use of the common expression, "I love you," with the passionate expression, "I'm *in love* with you," readers will undoubtedly confirm my observation that use of the former expression is triggered by an emotion of lesser magnitude and intensity, while use of the latter is reserved for relationships of emotional depth and passionate intensity. Considering the psychology of confession, particularly the important finding that the development of suggestion does not demand the intense emotion experienced by patients who experience the erotic transport of Teresa of Avila, Ben was confessing a lesser love or a less intense affective devotion for his therapist, as well as an addiction to dialogical therapy or an enchantment that was clinically useful.

On another memorable occasion, knowing that Ben harbored an affective devotion I could use in a therapeutic effort to persuade him to identify and renounce self-punishment that mitigated guilt in a painfully pleasurable way, I summoned the devil's bargain and expressed my willingness to play a judicial role in his penitential life. Ben laughed uproariously at my suggestion that he serve a final six-month sentence, given the fact that he was not a murderer and he already had served a punitive sentence of fifty years. When the belly laugh subsided and a relaxed contentment set in, he stated in a heartfelt way: "That's a good one . . . I really like that." Ben did not refuse the devil's bargain, but he did not openly accept it either. This left me with the impression that self-punishment would continue unabated, such that like Freud and Reik, I would remain in the impotent position of allowing my patient to gratify his masochistic tendency.

As I stated earlier, Reik continued his exploration of pleasurable punishment long after publishing *The Compulsion to Confess* and being accused of clinical quackery. For some inscrutable reason, the human striving for physical and psychic punishment, essentially the quest for pleasurable pain, was a life-long obsession, as well as a problem Reik attempted to solve since writing his doctoral dissertation, *Flaubert and His Temptations of Saint Anthony*. Reik's comprehensive account of masochism appeared in 1941, when he published *Masochism in Modern Man*. This was not only an assault on the naïve speculations of philosophers who assumed that *Homo sapiens* is a pleasure seeking animal motivated to avoid pain, it also was an attempt to conceive masochism in a way that transcended the pansexual theories of Freud.

On Reik's account, "pain, ordinarily avoided, is the very aim of masochism. Not only is masochism not 'escape from pain and discomfort' but it is the exact opposite, a desire for them, an actual 'pull' towards them" (*MS*, 4).[6] Attempting to move beyond Freud's sexualized analysis of masochism, while remaining focused on the subterranean enthrallments that actually motivate human behavior, Reik decided that he would not restrict himself to viewing masochism as a sexual aberration. Advancing a desexualized form of masochism, Reik claimed that masochism was an attitude toward life whose satisfaction is the enjoyment of one's own pain and suffering. Viewing the human predicament in this broad social context, Reik wondered why many people consciously avoid pain, while striving unconsciously for pain and humiliation: not only strive for pain and humiliation, but unconsciously stage their own misery and life disasters. Elucidating a desexualized social masochism, Reik observed:

> Unconsciously . . . people inflict punishments on themselves to which an inner court has sentenced them. . . . These individuals act as if they were controlled by stringent moral laws and prohibitions . . . as if they were forced to punish themselves for disobeying them. . . . But in such an attitude, where is the hidden pleasure? The answer is that it lies in the satisfaction of an unconscious desire for punishment, which is a reaction to the forbidden wishes of the ego. . . . Although the masochists complain bitterly about the blows from fate, unconsciously they receive them joyfully. (*MS*, 10–11)

Interestingly, in an appendix to the third revised edition of its *Diagnostic and Statistical Manual of Mental Disorders* (1987), the American Psychiatric Association offered the Self-Defeating Personality Disorder as a proposed diagnostic category requiring further study. Divorcing itself carefully from association with the term "masochism," as well as from association with the psychoanalytic notion that unconscious pleasure is derived from suffering, the American Psychiatric Association was considering a new personality disorder identifying individuals who (a) avoid or undermine pleasurable experiences, (b) are drawn to situations or relationships sure to promote suffering or painful consequences, (c) prevent other people from actually helping them either by sabotage or refusal of help. Other variables of the proposed Self-Defeating Personality Disorder are depression or guilt in response to positive life events; failure to complete tasks crucial for success; sexual disinterest in or boredom with nurturing or caring persons; frequent, excessive self-sacrifice while doing things for others.[7] Unfortunately, in the fourth edition of the *Diagnostic and Statistical Manual* published in 1994, the Self-Defeating Personality Disorder disappeared without mention, the behavioral variables of this unique diagnostic entity having collapsed within the black hole of Borderline and other commonly accepted psychiatric disorders.

As I was about to say before introducing Reik's account of masochism, several months after I offered Ben a devil's bargain, chronic symptoms of his Dysthymic Disorder remitted. In truth, I was not only surprised by this favorable turn of events, but also surprised to receive the following email I have edited for length. Addressing me informally, by using my given name, "Carl," Ben expressed his current emotional state and his temperate love in the following personal confession:

> I feel no sense of loss. I feel no guilt! I feel potentials, I feel full of unfulfilled possibility. I do not feel old! I do not feel tired. I do not feel depressed. I feel peace within myself for possibly the first time in my life. I feel communicative, open, honest, alive. I have forgiven myself. I am resisting worrying about the approval of others. I feel unburdened. I feel strong. I want to live, really live. I choose eros. Thank you, Carl. I believe in sharing not fixing. Fixing is controlling and I have to let it go. I want to share my deepest thoughts, dreams, songs, and love without fear or embarrassment. I see clearer now. I see beauty where I didn't. I am no longer weighing and measuring: is it the right thing, the selfish thing. It's just the thing itself. Is it fulfilling my needs? Is it positive, reaffirming, or will it create negativity? Remember you told me you could see someone at the grocery store and tell that they were depressed, and I was one of them? How do I look now? Thank you, Carl, you have helped me with perspective. You have helped me see and change my life. I never forget. I will always be grateful.

Ben's written confession demonstrated clearly that during the period of his clinical addiction, while in an enchanted state, he heard, accepted, and was behaving with reference to the transforming language, values, and beliefs informing his therapist's existentialist thinking. This self-interested acceptance of, surrender to, and lived experience of the cognitive world of his therapist-confessor was manifest in Ben's hope-filled references to potentials, unfulfilled possibility, and choice of eros. For the reader's information, "potentiality," "possibility," and "choice" are prominent existentialist concepts I often use while performing the clinical task of conditioning suggestible patients to embrace their freedom and ability to make decisions: commitments issuing in concrete action that will get them unstuck and moving toward the future in life-affirming ways. "Eros," a concept I often use in references to self-creative and self-validating affirmations of life, is contrasted with "thanatos," a concept I use to refer to a deathly stuckness—a morbid, penitential, dreary death in life.

When I speak of possibility and choice I am acknowledging intellectual debts to a number of existential philosophers, particularly Heidegger and to a lesser degree, Sartre; but both existential philosophers were leaning hard on earlier thinking. For example, in 1844, in his insightful preclinical analysis of anxiety, the disquieting dread or anxiety awakened during the process of becoming a self and confronting the uncertain risks of existence, one of the founding fathers of existentialism referred to "possibility" as the "heaviest of all categories," in as much as "possibility means *I can*." Clarifying this important existentialist insight, Kierkegaard referred to "the alarming possibility of being able" to do such and so or to become such and so, likening this dreadful experience to a "dizziness of freedom," a dizziness during which it often happens that "freedom succumbs." With a hint of eroticism that may be undetectable unless erotic sensibilities have been finely tuned in the crucible of personal experiment, Kierkegaard observed that when a person confronts a dreadful possibility, specifically, the temptation to risk oneself by actually making a concrete choice, there is an experience that fascinates and startles with "sweet anxiety."[8]

Clinical experience with Ben suggested that the artful analogy between the life of the penitential patient and the felon's penitential life worked its charm indirectly, rather than directly. Whether direct or indirect, when the analogy does its job, suggestible patients are more likely to exercise self-restraint while remaining imprisoned in an intrapsychic penitentiary that extracts an endless penance on the body and the mind. In fact, at critical moments of decision, choice, and commitment, patients like Ben are poised for constructive change and considerable progress can be made in the clinical trenches contrary to Reik's complaint regarding the impotence of psychoanalytic therapists. On the other hand, with some guilt-ridden patients who seem to be serving life sentences in the kind of penal colony that had a life in Kafka's rich literary imagination, the artful analogy doesn't have a chance of working. These are incorrigible cases that may leave a dialogical therapist disheartened and thinking forlornly: "Almost nothing can be done about it."

NOTES

1. I have taken the liberty of putting flesh on the bones of the following original idea of the expatriate Romanian philosopher E. M. Cioran: "One always perishes by the self one assumes: to bear a name is to claim an exact mode of collapse." *The Temptation to Exist*, trans. Richard Howard (Chicago: University of Chicago Press, 1998), 34.

2. Saint Teresa, *The Life of Teresa of Jesus: The Autobiography of St. Teresa of Avila*, ed. and trans. E. Allison Peers (New York: Image Books, 1960), 192, 196.

3. Erik Berggren, *The Psychology of Confession* (Leiden, Netherlands: E. J. Brill, 1975); cited in the text as *PC*.

4. Franz Kafka, *I Am a Memory Come Alive: Autobiographical Writings by Franz Kafka*, ed. Nahum N. Glatzer (New York: Schocken Books, 1974), 21.

5. Franz Kafka, "In the Penal Colony," in *The Penal Colony: Stories and Short Pieces*, trans. Willa Muir and Edwin Muir (New York: Schocken Books, 1976), 197.

6. Theodor Reik, *Masochism in Sex and Society*, trans. Margaret H. Beigel and Gertrud M. Kurth (New York: Grove Press, 1962); cited in the text as *MS*.

7. American Psychiatric Association, *Diagnostic and Statistical Manual of Mental Disorders*, 3rd. ed.-rev. (Washington, DC: American Psychiatric Association, 1987), 371–74.

8. Søren Kierkegaard, *The Concept of Dread*, trans. Walter Lowrie (Princeton, NJ: Princeton University Press, 1970), 40, 44, 55, 140.

5

The Edge of Therapy

THE HERESY OF DR. Z.

If I place myself inside the crazed, surrealistic world of Kafka, where no one gets what everyone expects, while everyone gets the unexpected absurdities no one wants to live with, I can imagine a functional role for a fictitious character I shall refer to simply as Dr. Z. Unlike Josef K., the besieged protagonist in Kafka's unfinished novel, *The Trial,* in fact, a fictitious bank clerk who was arrested, tried, and executed, but never informed of the nature of his crime, Dr. Z. happens to be a fictitious character who harbors heretical ideas: peculiar notions of clinical practice at variance with the orthodox ideas of his peers. In the "clinical trenches," a combative image he dreamed up to keep himself attuned to his experience of clinical work as a strategic war against a relentless opponent who has a better than even chance of winning every battle, Dr. Z. engages in a fierce struggle against illness and death at the edge of commonly accepted clinical practice. From time to time, he goes over the edge! In fact, unlike Kafka's modern antihero, Josef K., my postmodern protagonist, Dr. Z., does not appear to be a completely innocent man, although he has not received a formal summons to appear before the law, like the bemused, nondescript chief bank clerk, K.

Whatever else I might say about the man and his methods, Dr. Z. is a dedicated dialogical therapist who committed himself to securing the well-being of his patients at the onset of his clinical career when he was an eager intern full of every good thing a devotion to human service promised. In this ingenuous state of mind, he bamboozled himself into thinking that he was doing god's work—the noble work of bringing a bit of good into a god-forsaken world. But everyone has a tragic flaw and Dr. Z. happened to be a defiant sort of man who would never pass a formal test designed to measure obedience to authority or frustration tolerance. Unlike Sisyphus, a deeply internal character imprisoned in a deathly underworld of mythopoeic imagining, Dr. Z. is fully in the world and he is a decisive man of action who has trouble accepting "no" for an answer, whether "no" comes from the mouth of gods, lesser mortals, or the fateful furies of archaic imagining. Given this obstinate predisposition, a characterological pathos that tends toward excess in the interpersonal world of action and reaction, Dr. Z. awakened one morning to find himself unwilling to accept the conclusion that nothing can be done about the self-defeating behavior of severely guilt-ridden patients who are being devoured from within by the worm of conscience.

Although there were no external signs of the heresy brewing within him, in the days and weeks following that besotted awakening, Z. reasoned that strategic advantage would accrue to a clinical warrior who accepted the view that guilt is real, not a figment of a sick person's imagination. Mind you, there was nothing untoward or heretical about his thinking at this incipient stage of development. In fact, his reasoning was remarkably consistent with a commendatory interpretation of Freud that viewed him as a dedicated doctor who gave birth to an "ethical . . . conception of human sickness"; in the mind of Freud, according to this forsaken point of view, clinic patients are "moral agents" and neurosis is not merely a sample of symptoms, but always "an element of character," such that "moral character" became the central focus of psychoanalytic treatment.[1]

To his credit, Z. realized that many of the problems that challenged Freud at the end of the nineteenth century and into twentieth, were no longer his own. After all, he was tweaking the art of dialogical therapy in the twenty-first century, not in a false-faced Victorian era when prudery and repression were all the rage. A liberating sexual revolution was long past and in his decadent postmodern era, when the moral conscience of many men and women had been eviscerated, guilt and shame had trouble finding a place to call home. Still, in the clinical trenches, Z. discovered that a shrinking number of patients still had a moral conscience. In some it was weak, to be sure, but others were consumed by guilt: the kind of guilt I found in Franklin—a sexual perpetrator who created victims in the shadows of existence.

As I was about to say, there was nothing heretical about Z.'s thinking until he began to extend the implications of Freud's ethical conception of emotional illness. Specifically, Z. reasoned that in the moral conscience of some guilt-ridden patients, in a suspicious synapse where an ugly worm with a ravenous appetite is eating away, there exists an expectation of penance or retribution, even punishment! Unable to shake these nagging thoughts, Z. began to entertain the outrageous notion that in the mental health clinic, where irony and intrigue are never strangers, if he provided a slight penance to some guilt-ridden patients, he might countermand their tendency toward harsher self-inflictions: scalding showers, cutting of arms and legs, burning of genitalia, pulling out fingernails or toenails, or both, to name a few penitential practices confessed by self-crucifying patients.

Z. is not a stupid man, so he understands that his heretical thinking is hopelessly reactionary, insofar as it belongs to a superannuated world-view in which sin, shame, and guilt, as well as penance, atonement, and redemption, had a logical home. Furthermore, Z. has scoured the Freudian canon, so he also realized that his heretical strategy for dealing with the moral character of clinic patients conflicts with inherited conceptions of mental illness and clinical care that supplanted the penitential imperatives governing the lengthy life and time of *Homo religiosus*: a cultural character type whose sins are destined to be judged by a tyrannical "old Nobodaddy," to use the satirical expression of the visionary poet, William Blake—"old Nobodaddy aloft" who "Farted & belchd & coughd / And said, I love hanging & drawing & quartering / Every bit as well as war & slaughtering."[2]

Undaunted by his conflict with the clinical orthodoxy of his peers, yet frustrated by the fitful experience of being impotent with a number of incorrigible cases, a defiant Dr. Z. charted an independent course of pragmatic action that enabled him to become a decisive actor in the penitential life of guilt-ridden men and women who happened to become his patients. Forging ahead silently, secretly, and self-consciously at the edge of therapy, he was captured by the hope that if he prescribed a redemptive penance to some guilt-ridden patients, he would become a moderating influence in the lives of tormented human beings who live as if they committed a heinous crime, were summoned before the law in the fashion of Josef K., and now are condemned to serve a wretched life sentence in a punitive penal colony with no possibility of time off for good behavior. But there were odd twists and turns in Z.'s thinking, as well; and in a clear, compelling way that seemed made in heaven, Dr. Z. and his guilt-ridden patients were a perfect fit, like a lock and its unique key or a hand and a fine-fitting lambskin glove.

You see, when he extended the implications of the Freudian view that patients are moral agents, thereby entertaining the notion that guilt is authentic and justifiable, Dr. Z. was mindful of the fact that some of the tormented individuals he treated in the mental health clinic had literally committed crimes or unredeemed bad deeds similar to or more serious than the bad deeds confessed by Franklin: a sexual perpetrator who created victims in the world at large, while also destroying his family, not in a surreal world of unfinished fiction, but in the real world where human conduct has historical consequences that can be plotted on a continuum that measures destructiveness in graduated steps from minor to disastrous. And in the mind of Dr. Z., a fictitious therapist trapped in a clinical drama of Kafkaesque proportion, if crimes or unredeemed bad deeds have been committed, and the consequences are moderately to fully disastrous, then condemnation, self-loathing, and penance may be completely justified. In a meager sort of way, Z.'s thinking was evident in my treatment of Franklin: a guilt-ridden gentleman who achieved a good measure of psychological healing by accepting his therapist's suggestion to perform a continuing community service that would benefit disadvantaged individuals who were irrelievable victims of life itself.

Strange as it may seem to enlightened men and women who have been educated to think and feel and see and believe with reference to the clinical world of psychological man—a shared world of diagnosable mental illnesses and dialogical treatments, coupled with the inalienable right to be embraced by empathic understanding and other elements of therapeutic eros—a human being's need for redeeming penance has been likened to a "sensible and healthy striving toward wholeness": a quest for well-being, I would rather say, achieved by a hard-won reconciliation with one's god, self, world, and others.[3] In the event that this striving sounds like spiritual nonsense to readers who have no ultimate concern beyond self-interest, I can offer every assurance that Z. was not a religious man, strictly speaking, in spite of his inane idea of doing god's work in the embattled trenches. Still, in the pragmatic mind of Dr. Z., if moral character is at stake in the clinic, such that authentic guilt and unredeemed bad deeds are implicated in an anguished life of self-defeating symptoms, it followed that something akin to a moral solution to the problem of guilt, including the clinical prescription of penance, may temporarily resolve the underlying moral problem inflaming the moral conscience of incorrigibly sick, self-crucifying patients.[4]

Having premised the clinical saga of Dr. Z. on an imaginary connection with the surrealistic world of Kafka, a paradoxical world, according to Camus, in which "the more extraordinary the character's adventures are, the more noticeable will be the naturalness of the story," I should confess that I am unable to say what motivated Kafka to bring Josef K. to the attention of the reading public during the war weary winter of 1916–1917, when he was hard at work on *The Trial* and seventy million human beings were embroiled in the world's first global war.[5] Stepping out on a limb, I have a hunch that Kafka was consumed by the gnawing belief that being born is a crime in itself, while being human is an incurable illness that even the best doctor on the planet can't cure. If backed against a wall, I would also say that in the disturbed mind of Kafka, the crime of being born is simply the crime of being born with human genes. In effect, being human is a crime par excellence. I think Kafka made this clear in *The Metamorphosis*, an allegorical tale in which a fictitious salesman awakens one morning from uneasy sleep to discover that he has become a grotesque insect. Evidently, Kafka was not only thinking ugly things about the human estate, but also repulsive things about himself, while dreaming up surrealistic stories and staring into a looking glass that returned a malignant image.

Kafka's motivation aside, I am bringing the heresy of Dr. Z. to the reader's attention in this postmodern era for a few simple reasons that may be connected peripherally with the crime of being human. Specifically, I wish to expose the idea that *some* severely guilt-ridden patients may be likened to displaced moral agents who happen to cross the threshold of the mental health clinic seeking a clinical cure for a moral problem that cannot be addressed successfully by Prozac or cognitive-behavioral therapy, however potent these clinical emollients may be. When guilt is authentic and the root problem is moral, self-loathing may be justified and condemnation by self and others is not a serial mistake. In cases of this sort, an unredeemed moral agent can't be tricked into thinking, or medicated into feeling, that what he thinks and feels isn't so, even if an individual wears the label "clinic patient" and his medical insurer is footing the bill for treatment.

Having embraced this point of view, Dr. Z. reasoned that neither contemporary psychiatry with its psychotropic medications, nor dialogical therapy with its fair words and reputed enchantments, has an effective method for dealing with authentic guilt. In fact, it sometimes seemed to Z. that almost nothing could be done about real guilt except to "protect the patient from the crudest self-inflictions" as a disgruntled disciple of Freud once confessed. But clinical impotence of this sort was anathema to Dr. Z.: a defiant dialogical therapist who arrived at the heretical conclusion that a quasi-clinical strategy of confession, penance, and atonement may equip him to deal more effectively with guilt-ridden patients whose main task in life is self-crucifixion. Therefore, at the very edge of therapy, in the enchanted consulting room of Dr. Z., the psychology of atonement became a live option for dealing with the real guilt of morally compromised patients who learn that an authentic reformation of character may also involve a dramatically changed style of life, including elements of confession, penance, restitution, self-mastery, and personal sacrifice sufficient to restore moral character and psychological well-being.

In the real world of clinical practice, the result of Z.'s heretical strategizing is predictable: it might work for a while, but the moral solution is nothing more than a temporary expedient until guilt worms its way into reflexive consciousness and a new round of scalding, banging, burning, pulling, and cutting begins. Nevertheless, I am bringing the clinical heresy of Dr. Z. to the reader's attention because in a former time, when Freud was being assaulted on all fronts and psychoanalysis was properly accused of degenerating into years of unproductive talk, Freudian analysis was credited with being an enchantment that cast a spell; but the praise was disingenuous, for the real message behind the praise was that Freudian analysis was a clinical enchantment that did not cure because it failed to shift analysands from confession to atonement.[6] This is the shift that Dr. Z. sought to set in motion when he made the decision to advance his heretical thinking from the safe realm of quasi-clinical theory to the risky realm of clinical practice.

In the final analysis, if Z.'s heretical thinking has merit, it follows that Theodor Reik asked a superficial question when wondering whether a therapist should *allow* guilt-ridden confessants some gratification of their need for punishment, while every effort to continue the therapeutic program of purging guilt proceeded apace. In the Kafkaesque mind of Dr. Z., the cutting question is whether therapeutic benefit would accrue if a therapist *prescribed* some sort of penance to satisfy a morally compromised patient's need for redemptive punishment: a psychological need destined to result in the painful pleasure of morbid symptoms, self-defeating life choices, or grotesque self-mutilative behavior.

I have no doubt that Freud would have scoffed at Z.'s heresy as he scoffed at the heretical thinking of Alfred Adler, Otto Rank, and C. G. Jung, not to mention other disciples who betrayed orthodox psychoanalysis. Specifically, in the context of his ethical conception of human sickness, when treating the moral character of moral agents who happened to be clinic patients, Freud was principally engaged in the struggle to lower the demands of the sadistic super-ego; and this was an agonistic struggle that did not include the heretical strategy of purposefully satisfying the demands of a harsh moralistic conscience in any way or form. I am equally certain that Reik would have objected to Z.'s thinking, although in the real world of clinical practice, Reik's dedicated work on masochism and the pleasurably painful underworld of confession demonstrated a clear understanding of the strategic fact that there are times when a dedicated dialogical therapist may find it reasonable "to obey . . . absurd laws," while at the same time resolving "not to tire in fighting against them" (*CC*, 239). When all is said and done, this guidance is consistent with the thinking and the clinical conduct of Dr. Z.: a fictitious therapist who happened to live in a crazed world where no one gets what everyone expects, while everyone gets the unexpected absurdities no one wants to live with.

What stands fast in this crazed world of obedience to absurd laws and concomitant struggle against them is the sound advice a prison chaplain gave to the accused, Josef K., while trying to disabuse K. of certain delusions about the inscrutable court of law to which he sought admittance and the elusive door of salvation apparently closed to him. "Don't be too hasty," the priest admonished, "don't take over someone else's opinion without testing it."[7] So it came to pass that in a concerted effort to stop a terribly guilt-ridden patient from beating herself to death over a trifling sexual act she experienced as seriously sinful, I embraced Freud's ethical conception of human illness when I asked Eileen to identify her favorite television program. When she offered the name of a well-known soap opera after giving my impertinent question careful thought, I prescribed the penance of not watching the next few episodes, advising her that this sacrifice was a suitable compensation for her grievous offense: a trifle light as air, as Shakespeare might have said in a taut Elizabethan drama, but to a moral conscience inflamed by a gnawing worm, Eileen's sexual act was an unpardonable sin permanently etched in clay tablets that carried the title "holy writ."

Although she was enchanted with the clinic, devoted to her clinician, and enthralled with clinical confession, Eileen was taken aback and she responded by admitting that not watching this particular TV program would be a terrible loss, since she was virtually addicted to viewing it and thoroughly enjoyed the daily twists and turns of fate her favorite characters enacted for years on end. In view of the fact that she had a ripe moral conscience pressing for punishment, while I possessed the power and influence of a charming therapist with a thesaurus of fair words, Eileen accepted the seemingly harmless penance I prescribed as an act of contrition that promised to issue in the satisfaction of her sexual sin.

At the end of this peculiar clinical hour, during which time I seemed to be playing the ambiguous part of a clinical cleric, while Eileen enacted the complex role of a clinic patient who experienced herself as a guilty sinner seeking atonement, she left the clinic with every intention of performing the prescribed penance on two successive afternoons. As if we dwelled in the best of all Kafkaesque worlds, Eileen returned to the clinic the following week with a faint smile on her face, a noticeable sense of relief, and a noteworthy absence of self-condemnation. She was in the dark regarding the dramatic situation of her beloved TV characters, all right, but her darkness at noon was experienced as a decisive way of atoning for a niggardly sin, the nightly repetition of which Eileen experienced as grievous.

At the end of the day, perhaps it was the following morning when I gazed into the mirror I use to guarantee a close shave, I was reminded of Ferenczi's claim that "*the application of suggestion and hypnosis consists in the deliberate establishment of conditions under which the tendency to blind belief and uncritical obedience present in everyone . . . may unconsciously be transferred to the person hypnotizing or suggesting.*" This now seemed very true, horribly true in a real sort of way, and I began to wonder how far Eileen would have gone if I urged her on and used my clinical power and influence to guide her in this or that direction. In other words, what are the limits of blind belief and uncritical obedience in members of a crazed species susceptible to enchantments? For some, no doubt, the Aristotelian midpoint between excess and deficiency would be a reasonable limit that facilitates moderation in thinking and behavior; for others, however, there is an outer limit that tends toward excess—the kind of excess in thinking and behavior whose control can be transferred to someone hypnotizing or suggesting, no matter how mindless or thoughtful, uneducated or educated, compassionate or predatory, that individual might be.

Perhaps a person shouldn't have the kind of power and influence that elicits the blind belief and uncritical obedience of his fellows; however, if a person discovers that he has daemonic power, the heart of virtue might lie in not exercising it, unless, like Dr. Z., he is playing a leading role in a psychological fiction in which the delusion of doing god's work has no real historical consequences. Failing virtue, a sure bet in parlous times, the better part of wisdom might be to engage in a serious search for wisdom in order to better understand the use and abuse of enchantments, all the while reminding oneself of Socrates' critical conclusion that "wise" is an "epithet . . . proper only to a god."[8] Although the search for wisdom may be inconclusive, this paradoxical state of affairs having been the experience of Socrates and his dialogical partners, clinical experience suggests that the Socratic quest for wisdom, truth, and best possible state of the soul is a particularly important undertaking for a dialogical therapist who risks the danger of moving back to the future by walking the seam between the religious and the psychological worlds.

ACTS OF REALISM AND IRREALISM

If the reader is wondering why I made such a fuss about the heresy of my postmodern protagonist, Dr. Z., the answer is, I used this fictional therapist to make a point about the clinical relevance of radical relativism or irrealism: a postmodern point of view that eschews the commonsense view that we live in a single, fixed, serviceable world already made and discovered. By contrast, the hyper-enlightened postmodern view finds human beings thinking and feeling, working and playing, eating and sleeping, living and dying, and I should also add engaging in dialogical therapy, in a multiplicity of diverse, possibly conflicting versions of world as we traffic through our lives willy-nilly, unmindful of the variety or versional differences of our disparate worlds. If insightful—and I use "insightful" rather than "true," because "true" becomes problematic in this vision of world-versions—this postmodern vision of world-versions profoundly impacts the identification, diagnosis, and treatment of individuals seen and heard in the mental health clinic. This insight is particularly important when the individual being treated has been educated in a version of world whose meaningful symbols, cognitions, and emotional sensibility will not translate seamlessly into the meaningful symbols, cognitions, and emotional sensibility identifying the world of the hapless therapist: a dialogical therapist trying to keep his feet planted securely on clinical ground, while talking people into and out of things that are distressful or dreadful in the patient's version of world.

When I speak of radical relativism in this way, I am referring to the epistemology of Nelson Goodman, a highly respected early postmodern philosopher who made a strong case for irrealism: a hyper-enlightened shift from the ancient, medieval, and modern paradigm of a single, fixed, discovered world with unique, discoverable absolute truth, to diverse, right, conflicting versions of worlds in the making—conflicting versions with different truths. This postmodern aestheticism is light-years away from alluring relativisms that offer one familiar serviceable world, within which are countenanced conflicting individual experiences and divergent cultural views. This is the classical "man is the measure of all things" relativism that drove Socrates nuts, insofar as it is premised on the troubling notion that things are not what they are in themselves. Rather, the chill of the wind, good and evil, that which is beautiful, and every other human experience, is to me what it appears to be, and to you, what it appears to be, although our respective experiences may be profoundly different, even conflicting. Socrates referred to the Protagorean doctrine that man is the measure of all things as a "dark saying" for the important reason that if no given thing has being in itself or an intrinsic nature of its own, but is what it is perceived to be due to its intercourse with human sensation, no person is wiser or a better judge of things than anyone else, including the madman whose thinking is disordered and mistaken, or dreamers, who believe the wildest things. In fact, infallibility reigns in the human estate, such that false perceptions and other potential mistakes of thinking, hearing, and seeing would not be countenanced as false, for things are what they are experienced as being to every individual, whatever the individual's mental state may be.[9]

With irrealism, by contrast, the single, fixed world that is measured by me and measured differently by you is lost and replaced by the idea of multiple actual worlds: a state of affairs that makes a clean understanding of what is true and false, real and unreal, fiction and history, not only plastic, but elastic, thus highly questionable. To be precise, while giving the constructionalist philosopher, Goodman, his due, in the postmodern context of radical relativism, in which men and women are conceived as dwelling in "multiple actual worlds," not only is "reality in a world . . . largely a matter of habit," but "even reality is relative," such that "truth cannot be defined or tested by agreement with 'the world'; for not only do truths differ for different worlds but the nature of agreement between a version [of world] and a world apart from it is notoriously nebulous" (*WW*, 2, 20, 17).[10]

In spite of the foul appearance of his quasi-clinical work, in the postmodern context of radical relativism, Dr. Z.'s prescription of penance is not properly seen as a queer clinical strategy involving a regressive return to the past or a reactionary retrieval of a superannuated religious worldview that is worlds apart from the legacy of Freud, the promise of psychological science, and accepted paradigms of clinical practice. Granted, a progressive clinician worthy of the name would have no part of Z.'s seemingly regressive strategy, for it appears to be an antediluvian action plan outside the integral boundary of the mental health clinic. But a reactionary clinician and a more progressive colleague may dwell on the same planet, in fact, they may have offices in the same building, share the same restroom, and refer sick patients to one another for years on end. Yet, they inhabit vastly different worlds. It might be more accurate to say, they have incompatible, perhaps incommensurable, versions of worlds in the making, understanding that a different mythology, human quest, and emotional sensibility, informs each version.

More to the point, in the separate cases of Franklin and Eileen, there is an interesting argument to be made that (a) clinical treatment was enriched, and (b) the prospect of well-being was enhanced, by a therapist's passing acquaintance with irrealism, a postmodern point of view in which "a diversity of right and even conflicting versions of the world in the making" replaces the commonsense paradigm of a single, fixed, discovered world allowing for absolute truth (*WW*, x).

Mindful that this peculiar point of view results in a perversion of the perennial quest for truth—the classical Socratic quest to find the unvarnished truth of the one, shared, intersubjectively verifiable world people with a modicum of common sense firmly believe they inhabit—radical relativism gave me the lens to see that my patients and I may dwell in (a) multiple worlds with divergent truths or (b) many different right versions of world, such as the versions of *Homo religiosus* and *Homo psychologicus*, if I can use these pretentious constructions of scholarly academicians. These and other conflicting versions of world are informed by different mythologies and divergent human quests which, when programmed by inheritance and education, beget unique, profoundly different, cognitive-emotional sensibilities. For example, the worlds of *Homo religiosus* and *Homo psychologicus* differ in a variety of significant ways. Living and dying in the former, one thinks, talks, and has feelings about, while behaving with reference to, the integral components of a spiritual life, such as (a) God, (b) faith, (c) clergy, (d) sin, (e) church, and (f) otherworldly salvation. Living and dying in the latter, one thinks, talks, and has feelings about, while behaving with reference to, the integral components of a therapeutic life, such as (a) self, (b) insight, (c) dialogical therapists, (d) sickness, (e) clinic, (f) psychological salvation or secular healing.[11] While there may be correlations between these versions of world, the cognitive-emotional sensibility acquired in one world differs from the cognitive-emotional sensibility acquired in the other, although the world of psychological man may be conceived as a remaking of the world of religious man: a slow transitional reformulation, resulting in an ambiguous intersection of these two separate ways of living and dying in a world.

Missing in postmodern relativism is the conception of a seam between worlds and the possibility of walking a seam for various reasons, purposes or ends. In retrospect, it seems to me that Freud may have recognized something akin to a seam of this sort when adumbrating his ethical conception of emotional illness: the complex view that clinic patients are moral agents and neurosis is an element of moral character, as well as a diagnostic sample of clinical symptoms. Stretching the point, when I imagine different versions of world, I also envision an imaginary seam separating one version from its predecessor and its successor, something like an imaginary equator drawn on a terrestrial globe to distinguish the northern from the southern hemisphere. The imaginary seam between worlds stretches along its axis, because it is malleable like a rubber band, whose unique property is the inherent capacity to be flexible. The seam also leaks and leaches its life-blood of language, ideas, and immutable truths, from one world to the next, as if it were an elastic sieve perforated with a thousand holes.

With this in mind, I can honestly say that in an interesting, meaningful, and useful way, during protracted dialogical encounters with Franklin and Eileen, I found myself walking the seam between conflicting versions of world: the world of religious myth and sacerdotal fiction in process of etiolating and the world of psychological myth and clinical fiction having remade the former by transforming its dying body and feeding off its carcass. As I suggested previously, when throwing clinical orthodoxy to the wind and moving back to the future by walking the seam between the religious and the psychological worlds, while treating Franklin and Eileen, I felt as if I were hearing the clinical confession of religious individuals who were paying a fee for a psychological cure of soul, while I am a psychological man accepting a fee for a cure of psyche that should be a cure of soul. But walking the seam between worlds is nothing I would recommend to contemporary clinicians who have no taste for radical relativism or postmodern irrealism.

On the other hand, although Kafka died in 1924, his lungs ridden with tuberculosis, I think he would have understood the irreal adventure of the heretic, Dr. Z. For Kafka was a modern existential author who constructed literary-philosophic fiction that was both natural and surreal. As a result, in his own way and time, Kafka demonstrated that he was skilled at walking an imaginary seam between worlds: the natural world of a man who fishes in his bathtub and the surreal world of a man who chooses to continue fishing, all the while knowing that he will never catch a fish or even get a bite.[12] But Kafka's fiction leached language, ideas, and absurd truths few humans could tolerate in any version of world, even if they had a dialogical therapist willing to walk the seam hand in hand in a struggle to protect them from the crudest self-inflictions.

NOTES

1. Philip Rieff, *Freud: The Mind of the Moralist* (Garden City, NY: Anchor Books, 1961), 11, 12.
2. William Blake, "Let the Brothels of Paris Be Opened," in *The Complete Poetry and Prose of William Blake*, ed. David V. Erdman (New York: Anchor Books, 1988), 499.
3. O. Hobart Mowrer, *The Crisis in Psychiatry and Religion* (Princeton, NJ: D. Van Nostrand Company, 1961), 199.
4. The clinical proposal of a moral solution to the problem of guilt, as well as therapeutic elements of redemption, was originally offered by Mowrer in *The Crisis in Psychiatry*; however, the heretical idea of prescribing penance at the edge of therapy is entirely mine.
5. Albert Camus, "Hope and the Absurd in the Work of Franz Kafka," in *The Myth of Sisyphus and Other Essays*, trans. Justin O'Brien (New York: Vintage Books, 1961), 93.
6. Mowrer, *Crisis in Psychiatry*, 101.
7. Franz Kafka, *The Trial*, trans. Willa Muir and Edwin Muir (New York: The Modern Library, 1956), 269.
8. Plato, *Phaedrus*, trans. R. Hackforth, in *Collected Dialogues*, 278d.
9. Plato, *Theatetus*, trans. F. M. Cornford, in *Collected Dialogues*, 151e–58a.
10. Nelson Goodman, *Ways of Worldmaking* (Indianapolis: Hackett Publishing Company, 1978); cited in the text as *WW*.
11. For a comprehensive analysis of the succession of *Homo religiosus* by psychological man, including elucidation of the comparative variables I have identified, see Philip Rieff, *The Triumph of the Therapeutic: Uses of Faith after Freud* (New York: Harper & Row, 1966).
12. While exploring the art of Kafka in "Hope and the Absurd," Camus used the example of a testy encounter between a seemingly crazy man fishing in a bathtub and a doctor who, having ideas of psychiatric cure, thought to disabuse the crazy fisherman of his strange habit.

6

Trail of the Human Serpent

FATE AND FURY

When Diane was twelve years old, her father put a pistol to her head and forced her to fellate him. Although she learned to cower in a corner in reaction to his drunken fury when she was three years old, this was her first real taste of his power: a raw, primitive power that turned her life to grief. On this fateful morning, while kneeling submissively on trembling knees with a pistol to her head and a penis shooting gametes toward her gullet, her heart beat fiercely, causing pert young breasts to heave as her slender body sweat from head to foot. But for one brief immutable moment—a transcendental epoch encoded in brain and body memory—she experienced a beatific union of stark terror and reverence. She once confessed that she was so awestruck, she felt as if her father were God!

When it was over, no words broke the silence between them, no Greek chorus interpreted the signs or announced that this forbidden union of father and daughter would have a tragic end. As if the Fates and Furies were teasing out a twisted version of an ancient drama, Diane put away the things of a child and surrendered to a distortion of a daughter's desire for her father's love and attention. In the months following this violent epiphanic event, she grew as his lover, he ripened as a criminal. By the time she was seventeen, the year their incest was finally discovered, she was regularly stoned on marijuana. In this altered state of mind, Diane was unmindful of the fact that she had become the female lead in a provincial American drama heading toward a classic Sophoclean reversal and denouement.

Following discovery of the incestuous affair by an angry mother who accused Diane of destroying the woman who gave her life, the family fell apart, giving every sign that it was broken and ruined forever. In the fashion of Electra, a fictional sister trapped in an ancient matricidal drama, Diane had no answer to the hopeless question: "Where could you find a cure . . . for my troubles which know no cure?"[1] Absent a clear answer to the important question of cure, Diane decided to escape the madding drama by moving north, from Florida to New York. Consistent with the complications of a convoluted drama, she did not have enough money to start life anew, so she telephoned her father and invited him to meet her in a motel, where she would voluntarily sell herself for cash. As if he were playing his part in a masterfully crafted drama aching for an unexpected reversal and denouement, this father accepted his daughter's offer, for Diane was well advanced in the *ars erotica* and she promised to do whatever he wanted during this final afternoon of pleasure.

As part of their last liaison, with malice aforethought, Diane's father insisted on taking erotic pictures of his daughter as a fond remembrance of things past. After all, she promised anything, he had a pocketful of cash, she needed the money, and they would never see one another again. Less a benevolent deity offering a helping hand than a manipulative serpent who developed a devious strategy to reconcile with his spouse by pointing an accusing finger in his daughter's direction, he cast a bright spotlight on Diane by taking a series of salacious pictures that illuminated the full range of her sexual secrets, leaving little doubt about Diane's leading role in the family's tragic drama. Fresh from his daughter's bed, he gave these humiliating photos to Diane's mother, who viewed the erotic images as irrefutable proof that her evildoing daughter was not the gateway to the devil, but the devil herself.

After being accused of stealing her mother's husband and denounced for being a sick pervert who seduced her father, as if she were a sleazy incarnation of Electra, Diane took the money she earned from selling herself, she bought a ticket on the first Greyhound headed north, and skipped town, hoping to put the whole affair out of her mind and never again lay eyes on her mother or her father. Given the unexpected twists and turns of fate and fury, she returned to Miami several years later to testify for the prosecution in a separate sex abuse trial that condemned her father to a maximum security prison where powerful men force less powerful men to fellate them, when they are not forcing disempowered perpetrators to turn their backside for a penetrating review.

I never mentioned this to Diane after first hearing her sexual confession, but when I thought of her distorted experience and the availability of intentional evil in a crazed world of freaks, follies, and fables, I recalled the lurid sights, the shrieking sounds, and the putrid smells of the filthy prison where I labored Socratically for many years. Lost in these fugitive elements, with vivid recollections of the agonistic life endured by caged humans who had corrupted a small corner of the world while trafficking in evil, I had an image of the goddess of retribution and her righteous anger; and I thought of Nemesis with a faint smile, imagining the depth and intensity of an evil father's newly found pain, against the background of his earlier pleasure. On other occasions, when my mood was more or less temperate, particularly on weekends when I was away from the clinic and not responsible for the lives of patients, I thought of the argument Socrates offered in his defense during his ill-fated trial for corrupting the young: the logical argument that a thinking man like Socrates, or a criminal like Diane's father, would not become an evildoer intentionally, given his understanding that the perfidious evil he visited on others would eventually rear its ugly head and bite him. Unconvinced by Socrates' self-serving defense, like the Athenian jury who found his prudential argument naïve and silly, I embraced the autumn argument of the American psychologist and pragmatic philosopher William James, who offered his astute vision of the morbid mind in 1902, when he was sixty years old.

Demoralized as Diane, who had forsaken a cure for her depression; disillusioned as Freud, who claimed that humankind was suffering from an incurable communal neurosis; James wrote clearly and distinctly, as if he were a juror in ancient Athens responding to Socrates' shaky defense: "Healthy-mindedness is inadequate as a philosophical doctrine, because the evil facts which it refuses . . . to account for are a genuine portion of reality; and they may after all be the best key to life's significance, and possibly the only openers of our eyes to the deepest levels of truth. The normal process of life contains moments as bad as any of those which insane melancholy is filled with, moments in which radical evil gets its innings and takes its solid turn" (*VR*, 140).[2] Contrasting the healthy mind with the morbid mind, as if he were drafting a memoir or a personal confession, James claimed that the healthy mind is constitutionally optimistic and focused generally on the good, both in people and in the world. Not able to tolerate perpetual suffering, the healthy-minded person either ignores the evil aspects of things, or does not take these evil aspects of life to heart, perhaps denying them in whole or in part, or defensively minimizing by not making too much of them. By comparison, the morbid mind is the constitutional sensibility of a sick soul who maximizes evil. Experiencing evil as the essence of life, this typically anhedonic person is not only burdened by an unrelenting consciousness of life's evils, but he is destined to suffer from this predisposition, while struggling to find some lasting solution to the problems that evil invariably presents throughout the life cycle (*VR*, 114–16).

Given his realism, his naturalism, and his morbid disposition, James conceived religion as a crying plea for help. Perhaps that is why in the prison where I engaged in Socratic dialogue with captive inmates, many of the convicted felons carried a religious tome of one sort or another, as if paradise could be regained and salvation were sure to follow. Like Diane's father and Socrates, none admitted evildoing or guilt; yet virtually all the condemned gentlemen I spied during my tenure availed themselves of a heavenly consolation that enabled them to bear their brutal lives. But Diane was different! She didn't buy religion or any other healthy-minded fable. Rather, given a few new twists of fate and fury, she finally brought her sick soul to the mental health clinic, where she began the long quest to answer Electra's seemingly hopeless question regarding emotional healing or cure. It does not take an imaginative genius like Freud to guess that an impaired incest victim would eroticize her attempt to answer Electra's question. But this is exactly what happened in the clinical trenches during appointments with Electra, while I struggled to heal the emotional wounds of a seemingly cursed, contemporary woman whose tragic life was eminently Sophoclean.

UNHOLY TRUTH

Fourteen years after selling herself to her father in a cheap motel in Miami, as if she were a down-and-out actress auditioning for a leading role in a seedy film noire drama, a tearful, intelligent, highly verbal, cannabis-dependent mother of two children brought her lurid story of protracted incest to the clinic. Complaining of anxiety and depression, chronic impairments whose intensity was increased by her husband's recent discovery of her extramarital affair, Diane confessed that she had betrayed her spouse and her children. As a result, she believed she had destroyed her best chance of having a decent life. Compelled by her honesty and her painful story, I began to treat Diane regularly in the hospital's adult outpatient clinic, where dialogical therapy and psychotropic medications are routinely offered as a cure for every trouble, whether the trouble is a mental illness or not. After she received medication for symptom relief, I learned that Diane suffered from a Female Orgasmic Disorder, as well as other gross impairments that reflected traits of several maladaptive personality disorders, whose interwoven dynamics compromised her ability to maintain a stable emotional relationship with self and others. In short, she was emotionally besieged in all quarters and easily given to tears or savage weeping.

During the first years of our lengthy clinical encounter, a contentious legal divorce, a series of failed relationships, an unexpected pregnancy, and a daughter born out of wedlock impeded my effort to help my patient reconcile with her past and achieve emotional stability. In spite of these obdurate obstacles, Diane worked diligently to set her world aright and she progressed in many important ways: she achieved a gradual reduction in the use of cannabis, she secured gainful employment as a nurse, and she acquired liberal visitation rights and overnight stays with her children. In time, she made significant progress co-parenting her children, although there were ongoing problems with a hostile ex-husband who had sole custody of the children by decree of family court. Additionally, Diane craved intimate relationships with men and at one time during the early stage of our clinical encounter, she was managing sexual affairs with three men simultaneously. Given formative experience in her father's bed and painful memories of a pistol pressed hard against her head, these erotic intimacies were driven by a distorted need to please and to punish her sexual partners: a regressive need to give men some pain mixed with pleasure.

Given the haunting awareness of her complicity in protracted incest, Diane had an appetite for self-punishment. On one memorable occasion, she arrived at our weekly therapy session crying hysterically, sporting a few nasty bruises on her face. After collecting herself, she recounted the early morning experience of gazing into a mirror, while performing the falsifying ritual of painting her face by applying cosmetics to her eyes, cheeks, and lips. Stuffed with self-loathing, repulsed by the masquerade of truth and the true character of the caricature she spied in the mirror, she used her hairbrush to smash the looking glass that reflected the painted face that mocked the unholy truth hidden within her. Then she punched herself wildly about the head and face until her rage was exhausted.

Predictably, Diane had difficulty reconciling herself to who she thought she was and to what she believed she had done: a combination of shit and sin as putrid and vile as any abomination found in the tragedic literature of Sophocles, Euripides, and Aeschylus. In her distorted mind, she was not a victim and there never was a moment's doubt about her active role in the perverted drama that coupled her foul body and soiled soul with the forbidden body and serpent's soul of her father. No matter how much make-up she applied, she could not become false enough to stem an ever-present engulfing tidal wave of self-condemnation. As hard as she tried, she could never hide from herself or lose condemning self-awareness, particularly when putting on a transparently false face that looked back knowingly in a mirror: gazed back with omniscient precision into eyes that once observed obscene lips surrounding and embracing a father's forbidden penis. This daily furtive glance in the mirror, while washing her face, cleaning her teeth, brushing her hair, or applying lipstick, blush, and mascara, never failed to return the shameful vision of an ontologically defective woman whose tormented conscience was ruled by a virulent remembrance of unforgivable things past, yet indelibly present.

Although he taught psychology at Harvard, wrote a voluminous treatise entitled *The Principles of Psychology,* and held fast to the morbid-minded belief that radical evil occurred normally in daily life, I am not convinced that William James would have understood Diane's lengthy incestuous affair, particularly the grave act of choosing to sell herself to her father. When all is said and done, this is the sensational stuff of great Greek tragedy, the startling stuff Freud might have used to embellish a psychoanalytic theory, or the steamy stuff a pedigreed scholar would teach students in English 101 at a fine Ivy League college. This was not the sordid stuff a privileged gentleman-scholar would have personally encountered during his daily trek through Harvard Square. As a result, James might have experienced an emotional kinship with the reproachful, pietistic moral philosopher Immanuel Kant, who had a rigid deontological frame of mind focused inflexibly on duty, particularly the solemn duty a human person has to himself. If James had a Kantian experience when thinking about an electrifying woman like Diane, he would have entertained the notion that she was a human being with a free will who used her freedom to sell her most precious possession, her *person,* thereby allowing herself to become a disposable *thing* to be used by others as they please. Having degraded herself by selling herself and becoming a means to another person's pleasurable ends, Kant would have accused Diane of failing to reverence both her own person and humanity. Becoming an object of contempt for these reasons alone, Kant would have experienced Diane as a woe-begotten woman who lost her self-respect and her moral worth as a person.[3]

These are the harsh thoughts of a moral philosopher one would not expect to hear in the mental health clinic, where innocent victims of sexual trauma are introduced to dignity and respect, the virtuous handmaidens of empathic understanding and other elements of therapeutic eros. Granted, Freud may have experienced human beings as animals born between urine and feces, but he was old, in ill health, burned out, and disillusioned (*CD,* 53n3). Besides, in this case of protracted incest that had the look and taste and smell of a forbidden erotic experience, Diane blamed the victim, while having a deep Kantian experience of herself. In fact, by the time she crossed the threshold of the clinic she had spent a lifetime brushing her hair and averting her eyes from the freakish reflection in her mirror. As a result, while gazing in her cracked mirror, she experienced self-contempt rather than self-respect and she could not escape the fixed feeling that she was foul and impure. More worthy of degradation than reverence, she was a woman whose distorted duty to self was self-destruction.

APPOINTMENTS WITH ELECTRA

Due to an arresting experience with her father and the hypnotic milieu of the clinic, Diane developed an intense emotional attachment to a pragmatic existential therapist who was eighteen years her senior. This was a libidinal attachment to a phantastic person that was sexualized and repeatedly expressed. In retrospect, I am certain that if I had accepted her sexual entreaty—the entrapment of a black widow spider who spins a web of illusion that facilitates the capture and consumption of her man—a woman so impaired would have pleased and punished me for succumbing to the seduction. But this was not in the stars, even in my opportunistic galaxy, where a scrupulous pragmatism may conflict with precious dogmas of the therapeutic.

Conceiving Diane's erotization of the clinical relationship as a classic example of the transference of a libidinal attachment that originated in distorted experience with her father, I began to process Diane's feelings in typical Freudian fashion, not only advising her of the transference of sexual energy from her father to me, but also attempting to transform this alleged repetition of an earlier emotionally charged experience into recollective insight that would facilitate the abreaction of unresolved intrapsychic conflicts—as if she needed recollection! In retrospect, this might have been a coward's way of dealing with a patient's genuine feelings and the patient might have been more insightful and courageous than her therapist when she flatly denied that her feelings had anything to do with her father or with the transference of feelings for him to me.

Contrary to classical psychoanalytic theory, Diane maintained steadfastly that she was experiencing genuine emotional feelings begotten by the intense relationship of a woman and a man sitting opposite each other in the present moment, engaged in honest, open, trusting, caring, mutually respectful conversation. These are not her words exactly, but this is the gist of her response to my Freudian strategy for dealing with a complicating clinical problem. Whether Diane's interpretation of her feelings was true or not, I honestly do not know, but I can attest to the fact that Diane was not alone in rejecting the idea of transference love: a "peculiar" and "compulsive" love, according to Freud, that generally "disregards . . . every variation in personal attraction, age, sex, or class" (*QL*, 225).

Clinical experience suggests that the rejection of the Freudian view is common when patients become clinically enchanted and eroticize their therapist, for the idea of transference seems to invalidate the intense emotional pull some patients experience toward male and female therapists alike, making this strong and valued emotional bond seem false and unreal. What's worse, interpreting the patient's feelings of love as a manifestation of transference may result in counter-therapeutic feelings of rejection, as if the patient's true love were unrequited and the dialogical therapist's fair words are hot air. Without question, this can disturb the future course of dialogical therapy. Still, on Freud's account, psychoanalytic technique hinges on generating the transference, while the successful outcome of therapy depends on handling transference love skillfully; however, dealing with it involves "the gravest mistakes," as well as "the greatest successes," not the least reason being that a responsible therapist is not a person who has "conjured up spirits and run away from them" after these erotic spirits suddenly appear in the clinical situation (*QL*, 227).

Strictly speaking, on moral and clinical grounds—the former having to do with a dogma of the therapeutic prohibiting sexual contact with patients, the latter having to do with correct and appropriate clinical method to achieve the psychological healing that is the presumptive goal of dialogical therapy—the beloved therapist should not and cannot surrender to the demand for physical intimacy arising from the transference. Rather, in the Freudian clinic: "The only possible way out of the transference situation is to trace it back to the patient's past, as he really experienced it or as he pictured it through the wish-fulfilling activity of his imagination. And this demands from the analyst much skill, patience, calm, and self-abnegation" (*QL*, 227). Although Freud did not say it, the way out also requires a good dose of therapeutic eros.

Whether it is a theatrical performance that is part of a clinical charade, or genuine attitude and behavior governed by Rogersian authenticity, a clinician's therapeutic eros—sensitivity and respect, empathic understanding, warm regard and acceptance, trustworthiness and dependability, devotion to the patient's well-being—demonstrates a remarkable capacity for the kind of intimate holding and personal care emotionally ill patients desire and desperately need.[4] I realize that dialogical therapists are paid a fee for professional services—a hard, cold fact of life that identifies a business relationship that under normal circumstances would preclude or logically limit the emotional involvement of the payee with the professional person receiving the fee—but therapeutic eros is a set of attitudes and behaviors apart from all others: a tough act to follow, and anyone who tells you differently is out of touch with the realities of clinical experience. For example, Diane once confided that while she was luxuriating in a Jacuzzi with Dave, her significant other at the time, he questioned the origin of the black and blue mark on her leg. The bruise was the result of an injection given by an inept nurse employed by her primary care physician. But Diane was a wary incest victim skilled in self-punishment and she decided to test Dave's capacity for understanding and acceptance by telling him the bruise was self-inflicted. "Don't tell me that, it's whacko-psycho shit, I don't want to hear it," Dave retorted.

This smack in the face taught Diane a crucial lesson: she never could be truly intimate with her intimate partner! She never would be able to undress and really expose herself; never be able to confess her darkest secrets; never be comfortable dropping her guard and sharing her complicity in incest, her pleasure, her shame, her distorted need to punish and to receive punishment.

Unfortunately, Dave was not sensitive, understanding, or accepting; on the other hand, in the fashion of countless legions of sisters in incest, Diane had already confessed her awful Sophoclean secret to a warm, steady, nonjudgmental clinician who accepted her fully. In a human world where emotional pull, rather than reason, determines the dimension of the day, why wouldn't she become disenchanted with her lover, attached to her therapist, and enchanted with a gratifying dialogical intimacy? Although protracted clinical relationships are staged as one-way intimacies in which the therapist tells little or nothing, while the patient pays a fee to safely tell all, Diane's encounter with her primary partner was a noteworthy experience of estrangement that left her feeling as if Dave had put a gun to her head and pulled the trigger. Disenchanted at home, like other patients who report the emotional unavailability of significant others, Diane embraced a relationship within the clinical confessional, where, by contrast, she experienced a warm, sensitive, respectful, empathic, accepting, trustworthy, dependable dialogical therapist: another forbidden erotic union, all right, but the kind of forbidden, loving union she never had.

As a result of therapeutic eros and years of difficult self-work on her part, Diane found a few answers to Electra's hopeless question of cure. With therapy functioning as dialogical anti-venom, Diane became enchanted with the clinic and she enveloped herself in her version of a therapist's phantastic person. But this was sexualized to a lesser extent as time wore on, illusion wore off naturally, and the authentic work of generating health and well-being gained overriding importance. In due course, her father succumbed to cancer in prison and Diane managed to reconcile with her mother, after this woebegone woman finally realized that she had been to bed with a poisonous snake and like her damaged daughter, she was also severely bitten.

I realize that Sophoclean dramas do not have happy endings, but in this case, miraculously, Diane went on to lead a fairly normal life: a major achievement for a tragic woman who colluded in protracted incest, then sold her flesh to her father for cash. To my surprise, prior to formal termination, Diane conceded that her therapist represented the benevolent father she never had. By this time, of course, I was older and beginning to gray at the temples—a twist and turn of fate and fury that added Svengalean weight to hypnotic suggestion.

Truth may be stranger than fiction, as the saying goes, but in this case, fiction may have been the truth—the psychoanalytic fiction of transference love, not Diane's romantic fiction of unrequited love. The problem is, no one actually knows, for psychoanalytic theories are unverifiable in principle and in fact. Nevertheless, as a pragmatic existential therapist who has had the humbling opportunity to hear the struggles of heroes and villains from all walks of life, I can confirm the unvarnished wisdom of William James, who noted: "The trail of the human serpent is . . . over everything," particularly everything that carries the venerable name of truth: seemingly incorrigible truth that "also has its paleontology, and its 'prescription,' and may grow stiff with years of veteran service and petrified in men's regard by sheer antiquity."[5] Due to the trail of the human serpent, whenever I am involved in a clinical relationship with an enchanted patient who eroticizes the clinic and perceives an ordinary therapist as phantastic, I follow James in thinking pragmatically about the *utility* of seductive ideas like transference love, focusing always on the success with which speculative ideas work to benefit my patients during the committed struggle against illness and death.

CONFESSORS OF A LESSER GOD

There is a vast literature on transference and the clinical twists and turns of the erotic tie are well documented therein. But Diane was not privy to conflictive opinion on the subject; accordingly, she stood alone as she held her ground during our electrifying clinical encounter, remaining unaware of the fact that her rejection of Freud's theory of transference love reflected the formal instruction offered many years earlier by Frieda Fromm-Reichmann: an honest, introspective student of Freud and Harry Stack Sullivan, an American psychiatrist who advanced the social psychological theory that personality consists of interpersonal, rather than intrapsychic, processes and events, such that personality can neither be understood nor studied in isolation from interpersonal relationships. Leaning on Sullivan in her *Principles of Intensive Psychotherapy*, a didactic text that preceded Menninger's *Theory of Psychoanalytic Technique* by eight years, Fromm-Reichmann credited Freud with being the first analyst to understand and describe the process of dialogical therapy with reference to the interpersonal experience between analyst and analysand; but she also faulted Freud for treating this clinical intimacy as the transference of unresolved conflicts with parents or surrogates who played a significant role in a patient's childhood.

As if she were thinking and writing in concert with the raw sentiments of Diane, Fromm-Reichmann began her text by referring to the "danger in carrying this insight too far," explaining that the danger lies in a failure to focus on the moment and the actual lived experience of therapist and patient, thereby failing to gain important insight into the mutable dynamics of the actual therapist-patient relationship (*PI*, 4).[6] Drawing on insight from her personal experience in the clinical confessional, Fromm-Reichmann claimed there is not only "a fluctuating interplay between doctor and patient" flowing from the interpersonal nature of the dialogical process, but the therapist's inner reactions to the patient's emotional and behavioral manifestations can be a useful instrument in the clinical process of learning about the patient's maladaptive interpersonal communications (*PI*, 5–6).

By all accounts, Fromm-Reichmann was an experienced therapist who learned invaluable lessons from trial and error in the clinical trenches. Longtime supervisor of psychotherapy at the reputable Chestnut Lodge Sanitarium in Rockville, Maryland, she was neither blind to clinical reality, nor naïve about the inevitable complications of dialogical intimacies in the clinical confessional. Accordingly, after making serious comments about the emotional aspect of the relationship between therapist and patient in the first chapter of her text, she took a page out of Hawthorne's book by drafting her own warning about the danger of intimacy in the clinical confessional. As if she were speaking to confessors of a lesser god, while making direct reference to problems that may arise during the fluctuating interplay between clinical confessors and clinical confessants, Fromm-Reichmann openly declared: "It is . . . common knowledge that the professional relationship . . . precludes any sort of nonprofessional mutual intimacy," in view of the fact that nonprofessional intimacy may result in "undesirable therapeutic consequences" (*PI*, 8).

Expressing critical acceptance of this widely held dogma, in lockstep with the clinical community, Fromm-Reichmann fleshed out her version of Hawthorne's warning by identifying listening as an art, while also noting that mastery of the art of listening is the prerequisite of successful dialogical therapy. Focused on the difficulties encountered by the listener, particularly when hearing sexual confessions that may titillate the imagination, Fromm-Reichmann not only warned clinical confessors about the possibility of bodily satisfactions, she literally instructed them to have other sources of satisfaction in their personal life, in order to avoid using clinic patients for their own sexual satisfaction.

Although she never used the expression "morose delectation," Fromm-Reichmann focused her reader's attention on techniques and problems of listening by arguing forthrightly that if a therapist uses a patient's sexual confession as a stimulating means to engage his own erotic fantasies, say projecting himself into the patient's role or the role of the patient's partner, this will interfere with the ability to listen in a way that benefits the patient clinically. If therapists are unable to listen in an artful manner without the interference of erotic fantasy, they are expected to use their awareness of the problem to protect patients from undesirable consequences. Writing as if she were a scholastic theologian in modern dress, Fromm-Reichmann observed: "The therapist has to safeguard strictly against using the patient, actually or in fantasy, for the pursuit of lust, so that sexual fantasies regarding the patient or the partners whom the patient mentions, or identifications with the patient or his partners regarding their sexual experiences, do not interfere with the . . . ability to listen" and function therapeutically (*PI*, 9–10).

An authentically honest teacher and reporter, clearly disturbed by the potential danger of using patients' sexual confessions for personal satisfaction, rather than using confessions of sexual secrets as a source of helpful information about patients' emotional illnesses, Fromm-Reichmann offered the startling confession that mental health clinicians "will only rarely be able . . . to fulfill this ideal" of the venerable Hippocratic oath (*PI*, 8).

This purposeful attempt to speak about and develop an art of listening is astonishing, to say the least. In fact, it is a public display of honesty that rivals the scrupulous introspection of Augustine, arguably the founding father of literary confession. Fromm-Reichmann's confession also rivals the honesty of Nietzsche, who openly confessed during Freud's lifetime, that a person's philosophy is autobiographical in nature, that is, an "involuntary . . . memoir," or a "personal confession."[7] Whatever else I might say about the interactive erotizations of the clinic, the clinician, and clinical confession, given Freud's account of erotic ties and transference love, the published warnings of Fromm-Reichmann and Menninger, and Fromm-Reichmann's role in focusing dialogical therapists on the need to master the art of listening, the latent reality of erotization appears to have been a sharp thorn in the side of Freud and post-Freudian therapists tasked with suppressing erotic satisfaction in favor of a refined, clinically useful, erotics of the clinic.

Readers should understand that Fromm-Reichmann was not shooting in the dark when she drafted her warning. She never mentioned the deplorable history of the sexual solicitation of women in the Catholic confessional, the intriguing literature of morose delectation on the part of Catholic priests, or the historical attempt of medieval and modern theologians to develop an art of listening to sexual confessions in the sacramental confessional. But the fact is, while recent disclosures of widespread sexual abuse of young boys by priests are appalling, these scandalous reports of pedophilia pale in comparison to the historical abuse of women by the sexual solicitations of father confessors. Having researched the history of auricular confession in the Latin Church, the nineteenth-century American historian Henry Charles Lea remarked: "The seduction of female penitents by their confessors . . . has been a perennial source of trouble to the Church since the introduction of confession. . . . It was an evil of which repression was impossible, notwithstanding penalties freely threatened" (*HI*, 95).[8]

The historical record evidences the dismal failure of religious confessors who not only wallowed in illicit pleasure while hearing sexual confessions, but also engaged rather freely in the sexual solicitation of female confessants. During the sixteenth century, sexual solicitation was so extensive that the Spanish Inquisition used its terrifying power of trial and punishment to repress the shameful conduct of a clergy whose scruples were shallow, whose flaws ran deep. In spite of its power, the Inquisition was uniformly unsuccessful in repressing an allegedly celibate clergy and in suppressing the eroticism haunting the religious confessional: a phenomenon of the pre- and post-Reformation eras conceived by Lea as a "corroding cancer" (*HI*, 99). Evidence gathered during Lea's formidable research convinced him that the erotization of the religious confessional was such an unyielding problem that he commented forlornly on the uncommon virtue required to resist temptations of the flesh arising from listening to sexual secrets: "The strain of the confessional is too great for average human nature" (*HI*, 137).

Readers should bear in mind that the private confessional box was not developed until the middle of the sixteenth century and its use was not actually imposed until 1850 or soon thereafter, close to 1856, the year of Freud's auspicious birth. Prior to this mutation of the Catholic confessional, it was common practice for religious confessants, most of whom were women, to sit at the side of the authoritative male confessor or to kneel submissively at his feet, in his residence perhaps, or in some other private, opportunistic place, where sexual confessions were extracted, the organs of hearing were stimulated, and sexual solicitation proceeded undetected. But development of the dark, partitioned box with grill through which the confession of sexual sins occurred did not deter the erotic enthrallments of religious confession. The historical record is replete with accounts of sexual activity both in and out of the box, including kissing (even insertion of the tongue through the grill), fondling of breasts, genitalia, and other body parts, masturbation by the confessor while listening to sexual confessions, mutual masturbation, as well as self-stimulation on the part of the confessant. There are numerous accounts of sexual intercourse prior to use of the closed box, but even after its inception, the closed box became an electrically charged erotic space: a private, provocative, intimate place where confessor and confessant planned sexual assignations.

Mortification of the flesh, including prescribed penances of spanking, flagellation, and wearing pain-producing garments, such as a girdle with sharp spikes, spread far and wide under the arc of religious confession; but Haliczer's research of sexuality in the sacramental confessional unearthed the surprising fact that "the largest single category of offense was verbal," specifically, confessional transgressions relating to speaking and hearing, to telling and listening.[9] The reader is invited to use the richest possible imagination here, for the list of erotic intrigue seems as long and as various as the range of human desire: not only scatologia—the satisfaction of the need to hear obscene sexual language spoken either by confessors or confessants—but provocative verbal exchanges regarding the confessant's erotic dreams and fantasies; suggestive remarks designed to stimulate lascivious thoughts, fantasies, desires, or actions, even demands by the confessor to hear the intimate details of a confessant's erotic play with her husband or lover. Lea is precious here, as clinical confessors will quickly understand, for he acknowledged shrewdly that for Spanish inquisitors, "the question of lewd and filthy talk was an especially puzzling one, for the confidences of the confessional presuppose a license to hear subjects usually forbidden between the sexes, which may readily be abused by a brutal, foul-minded priest, and it is impossible to frame a definition which in practice shall rigidly differentiate moral instruction from heedless pruriency or deliberate corruption" (*HI*, 110).

In view of her warning, I believe Fromm-Reichmann would have agreed that the question of verbal offense may be equally puzzling in the clinical confessional, for the confession of illness and impairment in clinical space presupposes a license to listen to many sensitive subjects. For example, on any given day, clinical confessors may find themselves listening to details of the Sexual Desire Disorder of male or female confessants; this may result in probing questions about sexual fantasies and desires for sexual activity. Confession of a problem with sexual arousal may result in a brief clinical query regarding a woman's inability to maintain an adequate lubrication-swelling response during intercourse or a man's inability to achieve and maintain an erection. Some female confessants like Diane confess to having an Orgasmic Disorder, whose clinical challenge includes the confessor's judgment that orgasmic capacity is deficient given age, sexual experience, and sexual stimulation. In the final analysis, Hawthorne was right: confidences in the clinical confessional presuppose a license to inquire about many subjects normally forbidden in polite conversation, including exhibitionism, fetishism, frotteurism, sexual masochism and sexual sadism, voyeurism, and paraphilia not otherwise specified—a broad category of human desire that fails to meet the American Psychiatric Association's criteria for one of the aforementioned disorders.

This is heady stuff that may tickle the perimeter of moral choice and clinical ethics, but I certainly would not agree with Lea, who stated preposterously, "the strain of the confessional is too great for average human nature"; nor would I agree with the strangely extravagant conclusion of Fromm-Reichmann that the lofty ideal of not using patients' sexual confessions for personal gratification is achieved "rarely" in clinical practice.

The fact is, dialogical therapy is not fun and games. Some clinic patients come from families trapped in chronic intergenerational crisis; a number of these sad men and women have simply given up on themselves and on life. For all these suffering patients, dialogical therapy remains the difficult work of establishing a clinical alliance with a knowledgeable, trustworthy, skilled, ethical clinician capable of inspiring a psychic turn that facilitates a functional reconciliation with seemingly futile Sisyphean terms of existence. Without mincing words, trench warfare of this sort is much ado about inspiring in beleaguered patients a fierce determination to live, despite the reality of hopeless conditions that go to Electra's question of finding a cure for troubles which know no cure. Besides, given decent training and development of a clinical mind-set, sexual confessions are typically experienced as a routine gathering of facts that is neither stimulating nor pleasurable; in fact, many erotic narratives are uninspired, some are downright boring, others are anguished and these are painful to hear. From time to time, however, even anguished confessions have the power to elicit a lingering pleasure after vibrating sympathetically within the middle ear: a lingering pleasure that blurs the medieval theologian's scrupulous boundary between a momentary impulse antecedent to and a protracted impulse conditioned by willful, reasoned consent. As Sade discovered during sodomistic days in Durcet's chateau of Silling: "The sensations communicated by the organs of hearing" are not only "the liveliest," but these auditory sensations are capable of producing a pure "voluptuousness" within a confessor—a discovery Sade made while anticipating the intense pleasure he would receive from simply hearing the details of debauchery (*DS*, 218).[10]

Readers undoubtedly have heard that Sade was an infamous pleasure seeker and chronicler of sexual aberrations. Less well known is the fact that he had interesting things to say about sexual confession and the organs of hearing. Sade was not only an avid storyteller, he also was a sexual perpetrator who forced debauchees to confess discrete details of carnal pleasure outside the moral boundary of the clinic. Few like to admit it, for Sade is a despised literary confessor, but his literary legacy includes stunning insights acquired through forced confessions and other criminal practices, not the least being that the organs of hearing produce a voluptuous pleasure capable of inflaming the dullest imagination. Sade also was an eighteenth-century trickster who, in his published account of the sexual confessions of debauchees, included a scientific-sounding researcher's hope of identifying and illuminating specific details of the effects of erotic transgression on "human personality," as well as on "human manners, and man's character," providing confessants demonstrate a "willingness to disguise no circumstance" (*DS*, 271).

With similar goals in mind, while deconstructing confession in a culturally respectable manner, Foucault addressed the curious fact that Western men and women routinely confess their crimes, sins, intimate thoughts and desires, illnesses and life problems—publicly and privately, voluntarily and involuntarily—to priests, police, doctors and psychiatrists, parents, teachers, and lovers. Seeking to expose the spiral of power and pleasure underlying a variety of confessional relationships—parent and child, educator and student, doctor and patient, psychiatrist and pervert, criminal and penal system—Foucault focused critically on the element of power in the binary spiral of power and pleasure, failing to adequately examine the erotic pleasure derived from confessing and from hearing sexual secrets.

Foucault's polished elucidation of the thesis that formal confession takes place within the context of power relationships begotten by discourses that create and exclude madmen, criminals, perverts and other deviant types from the broader society of human beings perceived and accepted as normal is certainly an illuminating chapter in the history of confession, not to mention being the author's revealing personal confession. I am referring here to Foucault's personal stake in the cultural and political disqualification of homosexuality. Despite his considerable achievement in drafting a provocative history of sexuality, Foucault failed to flesh-out the enthrallments of religious, clinical, and other culturally sanctioned confessions, not the least of these enthrallments being the pleasure of listening. Consequently, in "The Confession of the Flesh," a stimulating chapter in Foucault's *Power/Knowledge*, astute critic Alain Grosrichard challenged Foucault on this head, noting that the emphasis on techniques of confession ignored techniques of listening. Pressing the point against Foucault with knowledgeable precision, Grosrichard observed that in most manuals for religious confessors there are clear references to morose delectation: the sin of taking a lingering pleasure in imagining the confessant in sexual scenes confessed.[11]

Cutting to the heart of the matter, an accursed matter that drove nitpicking scholastic philosophers nuts, the Latin *mōrōsā* is unrelated to the common meaning of the English "morose": a sullen, sad, or gloomy person or mood. The Latin *mōrōsā* is derived from *mŏra,* meaning delay. The point is, pleasure is conceived as lingering or delayed when deliberative reason delays and the will fails to repel a sudden impulse of the sensual appetite. When a person fails to repel a sensual impulse, there occurs a deliberative, willful, reasoned consent to some forbidden pleasure; and when this happens, sin was thought to stain the soul. Plowing this terrain in his great *Summa Theologiae,* the sainted scholastic philosopher Thomas Aquinas observed:

> Venial sin is contingent upon the incompleteness of the act, namely that it is just a sudden impulse of the sensual appetite. But if the [impulse] is protracted, then reasoned consent comes in and the [impulse] takes on its own specific nature. . . . Should the delight in such matters not be long-lasting, the sin is venial by reason of the incompleteness of the act. . . . . For [an impulse] is said to be protracted and delight prolonged by reason of the consent of deliberative reason. . . . Venial and mortal sin differ as the incomplete and the complete in the category of sin.[12]

For confessors of all stripes—religious, criminal, medical, psychiatric, pedagogical, and parental—the sensitive subject of listening to secrets raises the critical question of how to hear sexual confessions while not committing Sade's sin of debauching the confessant by finding a lingering pleasure in extracting and listening to secrets. The difficulty of this undertaking is evidenced by countless pages of practical instruction offered in the confessional manuals of Grosrichard's reference. These early *Summa confessorum* and later manuals of confession written by Catholic theologians dating from the thirteenth century critically addressed a variety of problems encountered by penitent confessants: not only the nature of sin and the proper manner of sin's confession, but also the nature of absolution and cure of the soul. The summas and manuals provided religious confessors with specific guidelines for conducting private auricular confession; given the erotic tension pervading the confessional, due to the reputed celibacy of male confessors tasked with listening to women's confessions of the flesh, the manuals also included many references to the moral requirements of listening, not the least being the scrupulous suppression of morose delectation.

The historical record shows that the confessional manuals were a popular genre of literature in a bygone era: a wildly popular genre of literature read by priests and penitents alike. The *Confessionale-Defecerunt* of the Dominican Archbishop Antoninus of Florence was one of the fifteenth century's most frequently printed books; and Jean Charlier de Gerson, a distinguished voice in the pastoral cure of souls, wrote the *Opus Tripartitum* containing a treatise on confession, as well as another treatise, *On the Art of Hearing Confessions*, both of which were widely translated, published, and reprinted throughout the European continent. But even later, during the sixteenth and seventeenth centuries, as Haliczer reported in his illuminating study of ways in which the religious confessional was profaned by sexual solicitation in early modern Spain: "Confessors' manuals proliferated. An entire ancillary literature aimed at instructing and informing confessors was created by the Catholic press."[13]

The existence, wide dissemination, and general popularity of these confessional manuals is a fascinating testament to the eroticism haunting the religious confessional. By all accounts, this was an underworld of impulse and desire, of power and manipulation, of seduction and forbidden pleasure, where confessors of a lesser god traversed the trail of the human serpent while hearing sexual confessions. Following the trail of the human serpent, a reasonable person could infer that the history of religious confession is the revelation of an erotic underworld that haunts the clinical confessional as well, although the human serpent, unlike an evil biblical forbear, is a learning animal capable of ethical understanding and scrupulous nitpicking that may issue in mastery of the delicate art of listening.

THE DREAM OF REASON

Several years passed following a planned termination of Diane's treatment due to the fact that I resigned my clinical position at the hospital in favor of full-time private practice. One day, out of the blue, I received a telephone call from Diane informing me that she had a steady job in nursing and finally was financially stable. She reported improved co-parenting with her ex-husband, a solid relationship with her children, and enduring reconciliation with her mother. She also mentioned her ability to identify and avoid men who would treat her like a thing by using her as a means to selfish ends. Kant would have been pleased, to say the least. Diane went on to say that she continued to work on making life-affirming choices and decisions, after which she expressed gratitude for the work we had undertaken during the eventful years of our clinical relationship. She ended the conversation by confiding: "I think of you often"; she also expressed gratitude "for always being there for me."

Diane did not identify our clinical work in specific terms, but I can report that some of it was very concrete and deceptively simple. For example, rudimentary work on pragmatic decision-making was cued to the process of learning to contain emotional reactivity in favor of a rational approach to the nuts and bolts of daily living. This involved teaching my patient to ask some very basic, deceptively simple questions: "Is this choice going to help me or hurt me?" "Will this decision affirm my life or somehow destroy my life?" If Diane's answer to these simple questions happened to be "help me" and "affirm my life," then the choice became a candidate for serious consideration. On the other hand, if the answer to the simple questions was "hurt me" or "destroy my life," then these choices were ruled out automatically. Trite as it may seem, regular use of these simple questions enables arrested patients to begin the difficult process of replacing emotionally reactive decisions with critical thinking and rational choice. Within the context of pragmatic existential therapy, the hope is, when thoughtful decisions generate positive results in the real world of interpersonal relationships, the benefits will slowly reinforce rational decision-making to the extent that eventually, patients whose development is arrested can take over the therapeutic function of the pragmatic therapist, rather than being wedded to him for life. Of course the painstaking work of talking severely damaged victims of incest into and out of things is grounded in the difficult work of helping them achieve an abiding reconciliation with inalterable humanness. Everything depends on that.

I have stated that my concrete questions are "deceptively simple" because a person rarely can predict with certainty the outcome of choices that involve the unknown twists and turns of fate and fury. Unfortunately, this blind venturing of self toward the future makes what seems simple, quite risky and complex. This is why Kierkegaard spoke of "the alarming possibility of being able" and "the dizziness of freedom," not to mention the startling response of "sweet anxiety" that occurs when an individual takes the risk of making one or another concrete choice. The crude fact is, the most a person can hope for when asking my simple questions is some purchase on the probability that a particular decision, choice, and commitment will result in some sort of benefit, rather than harm to self and others. This existentialist thinking may seem melodramatic, but there is an important complication to consider. Specifically, if a person's thinking is distorted, and this commonly is the case in emotionally arrested victims of incest and sexual abuse, particularly victims like Diane who are caught in the trap of blindly fulfilling distorted needs in self-defeating ways that seem rewarding, there is a good likelihood that what is experienced as helpful and life-affirming actually is harmful and life-destructive. One pertinent example of this is the compulsive use of drugs to alter a mood that is chronically disordered due to victims' common shame-inducing belief that they are accomplices in forbidden acts.

For clarity, allow me to state the obvious: human beings have a variety of physical and psychological needs, some of which are healthy, life-affirming needs that facilitate survival and well-being; I am thinking of basic Maslovian needs for safety, food, shelter from harsh elements, and supportive emotional relationships. Human beings also have a healthy need to self-actualize by fulfilling latent potentials, creative work being a manifestation of this healthy need to grow and develop an authentic self. Less commonly known, but manifest in the crazed world of the clinical confessional, is the displacement of rational behavior that fulfills healthy needs by irrational behavior fulfilling self-defeating or self-destructive needs I refer to as "distorted." Hearing confessions of the fulfillment of distorted needs is one of the more common experiences I have had in the mental health clinic, not only with incest victims like Diane, but with other seemingly normal men and women who hold positions of power, responsibility, and respect in their respective communities.

When I explain distorted needs to patients, I usually offer the concrete example of the distorted needs of victims of sexual abuse, since this makes the concept of distorted needs clear and compelling. For example, it is common knowledge in the clinical community that the body of a child who is sexually abused may naturally respond to being touched by a perpetrator. Frequently, these victims will come of age experiencing shame and guilt due to the undeniable fact that during sexual contact they experienced a pleasurable physiological response that results in the mistaken belief that they were accomplices in the bad act. Not only that, some victims, such as Thomas, an eleven-year-old child I am currently treating, have experienced a desire to remain in an incestuous relationship in order to sustain the pleasurable feeling of sexual arousal and release. Consistent with this state of affairs, patients like Thomas often develop a guilt-ridden need for punishment to atone for their participation in forbidden behavior. Accordingly, during adolescence, a positive, life-affirming need for human relationship—for love, affection, affirmation, and support—may be displaced by a distorted need for relationships that will be punitive, self-defeating, or more harmfully destructive. Frequently, once on the trail of the human serpent, guilt-ridden victims of sexual abuse will be drawn into relationships with people who punish them physically and emotionally. In fact, some victims are drawn to punitive relationships irresistibly because the inner voice of conscience has educated them to believe that they are loathsome worms who need to be punished to compensate for childhood sins: not only the sin of receiving the pleasure of sexual contact, but the sin of not stopping sexual abuse by informing on their perpetrator. Remaining faithful to the distorted need for punishment until they cross the threshold of the mental health clinic, these tormented victims are trapped in a self-perpetuating cycle of distorted thinking, self-defeating behavior, and manifold forms of punishment resulting in a pleasurably painful death in life.

As I stated early on, clinical confessions suggest it is a mistake to believe that reason guides human motivation and desire; it is more likely the case that emotional needs, oftentimes distorted emotional needs, are the driver of human conduct, with reason used as a tool to develop strategies to fulfill these needs. My clinical experience of widespread irrationality in the human estate, particularly the secondary role of reason and the primacy of emotional reactivity, is consistent with the empirical research of contemporary neurologists who are focused on evolutionary biology in a collective effort to understand the irrationality underlying humankind's crazed condition. One neurologist, who specializes in the treatment of neurodegenerative disorders, thematized his findings as follows: "Reason is a biological product, a tool whose power is inherently and substantially restricted. It has improved *how* we do things; it has not changed *why* we do things. . . . To deny that reason has a role in setting our goals seems . . . odd. . . . But reason is only contributing to the 'how' portion of these decisions; the more fundamental 'why' element . . . is driven by instinctive self-preservation, emotional needs, and cultural attitudes."[14] What the good neurologist failed to say, because he did not have the privilege of hearing confessions in the mental health clinic, is that frequently, the fundamental "why" element of behavior seems to be driven by an emotional need for punishment and when this distortion of primary human needs runs deep, the gratification derived from self-negation may carry with it a uniquely human, perverse pleasure.

In the case of Diane, the glue of erotization kept her solidly attached to her therapist and to the therapeutic work of affirming life, not the least reason being that while she was fixed on her therapist, he was able to help her make regular adjustments in the stream of attitude and behavior. As a result, deceptively simple yeoman's work in the clinical trenches proceeded apace with a view toward realizing the elusive dream of reason shared by Socrates, Plato, Aristotle, and other like-minded philosophers. On the other hand, following Diane's phone call, after spending a few moments dwelling on her remarkable achievement, I began to wonder about the paleontology of Electra and reasons why this matricidal drama was steadfast in the human psyche: steadfast, I thought, considering indelible clinical experience, as well as the different ancient dramas authored by Sophocles (*Electra*), Euripides (*Electra*), and Aeschylus (*Oresteia*), the modern stage plays written by Giraudoux (*Electra*), Sartre (*The Flies*), and O'Neill (*Mourning Becomes Electra*), the opera of Strauss (*Elektra*), and films, such as *Electra* by Cacoyannis. Failing to develop a definitive answer to adequately explain the enduring emotional pull of this tragedic drama of mothers, fathers, and daughters, I drafted a few notes to myself, focusing on my conclusion that Diane's erotic attachment to her therapist helped rather than harmed her, insofar as her powerful libidinal attachment functioned as the hypnotic glue that kept her connected to the therapeutic work she needed to sustain in order to gain a measure of well-being by virtue of a working reconciliation with humanness.

In retrospect, my notes were consistent with the thinking and clinical experience of Freud, who recorded his impression that "personal influence is our most powerful dynamic weapon. . . . The neurotic sets to work because he has faith in the analyst, and he believes him because he acquires a special emotional attitude towards the figure of the analyst. . . . The emotional relation which the patient adopts . . . is, to put it bluntly, in the nature of falling in love"; but Freud mistakenly concluded that this "unexpected complication" is noteworthy, insofar as "the analyst does nothing to provoke it" (*QL*, 53–54). From a phenomenological point of view, dialogical therapists are practicing and mastering the art of listening and a therapist committed to psychological healing tries to respond constructively to the intimate confessions he hears, thereby actively and regularly offering the benefits of therapeutic eros, while treating emotionally wounded patients, some of whom are autosuggestible. Coupled with the aforementioned illusions of the clinical station, enchanting illusions that contribute to an ordinary mortal's ability to cast an unintentional spell, dialogical therapists may be countenanced as pragmatic agents of change who draw emotionally needy patients into an emotionally embracing clinical intimacy, rather than "keep[ing] at a distance from the patient" and "surrounding himself with some degree of reserve," as Freud claimed myopically (*QL*, 225).

Given their experience in the clinical confessional, perhaps Fromm-Reichmann and Menninger were well aware of the dialogical therapist's complicity in constructing and maintaining the erotics of the clinical relationship; and in the case of Menninger, this explains why he was not only seduced by Hawthorne's warning, but found it reasonable to publish a puritanical argument against the erotization of the clinic in all its forms and manifestations. Given the evidence of their respective texts, Fromm-Reichmann and Menninger might have vehemently disagreed with my pragmatic perspective, in fact, these renowned dialogical therapists might have argued vociferously that I was an accomplice in the erotization of the clinic, such that my use of Diane's erotization of the clinician was morally wrong and fraught with clinical danger. Nevertheless, clinic notes recorded my steadfast belief that Diane's erotic attachment to an opportunistic existential therapist gave him the power to hold her in treatment so that he could influence her decisions, choices, commitments, and behavior in a way that enabled her to release her potential to begin the difficult process of creating a healthier self, new life-affirming terms of existence, and a healing reconciliation with humanness.

On the other hand, these notes did not include my aesthetic view that in her choice of life, after experiencing the promise of a bullet from a pistol pressed hard against her head, Diane went to the end of a forbidden experience that made her life look like a work of art, at least from the outside looking in. Sophocles, Euripides, and Aeschylus would have understood this; so would other litterateurs, composers, and filmmakers given to recording in different ways, the forbidden experience of fellow humans.

Not all art is beautiful, of course, in fact some works of art attempt to find beauty in evil, like Baudelaire's transgressive *Flowers of Evil*, one incisive poem of which explores the ambiguities and the ambivalence of being a human being who is at once a cut or gash and the knife that produced the gash, a slap and the face slapped, a leg and the instrument that breaks the leg, a person who tortures and the tortured person whose skin is stripped or flayed.[15] But in my clinical life, finding beauty in evil is neither my job nor my ambition, although I always ask patients who have been victimized to discover something learned or gained as a result of their annihilative experience. The discovery may count as beauty when it initiates or is otherwise implicated in the process of psychological healing. Sometimes, there is neither beauty, nor healing, nor discovery. Still, as a pragmatic existential therapist tasked with drawing out of myself an empathic understanding of murder, incest, and other lived experiences whose lineaments are not lived lines in my psyche, I am forced to come to terms with humankind's enthrallment with the forbidden as Freud did in *Totem and Taboo,* where he identified incest as one of "the most powerful longings to which human beings are subject" (*TT*, 35).[16]

NOTES

1. Sophocles, *Electra,* trans. David Grene, in *Greek Tragedies,* vol. 2, ed. David Grene and Richmond Lattimore (Chicago: University of Chicago Press, 1964), #876–77.
2. William James, *The Varieties of Religious Experience: A Study in Human Nature* (New York: Collier Books, 1967); cited in the text as *VR*.
3. Immanuel Kant, *Lectures on Ethics,* trans. Louis Infield (New York: Harper Torchbooks, 1963), 120–24.
4. For an illuminating account of the clinical relationship that includes authentic aspects of therapists and the therapeutic process, see Carl R. Rogers, *On Becoming a Person* (Boston: Houghton Mifflin Company, 1961).
5. William James, "What Pragmatism Means," in *Essays in Pragmatism,* ed. Alburey Castell (New York: The Hafner Library of Classics, 1966), 150–51.
6. Frieda Fromm-Reichmann, *Principles of Intensive Psychotherapy* (Chicago: Phoenix Books, 1960); cited in the text as *PI*.
7. Friedrich Nietzsche, *Beyond Good and Evil: Prelude to a Philosophy of the Future,* trans. Walter Kaufmann (New York: A Vintage Original, 1966), 13.
8. Henry Charles Lea, *A History of the Inquisition of Spain,* vol. 4 (New York: Macmillan Company, 1907); cited in the text as *HI*.
9. Stephen Haliczer, *Sexuality in the Confessional* (New York: Oxford University Press, 1996), 156.
10. Marquis de Sade, *The 120 Days of Sodom,* in *The 120 Days of Sodom and Other Writings,* trans. and comp. Austryn Wainhouse and Richard Seaver (New York: Grove/Weidenfeld, 1987); cited in the text as *DS*.
11. Michel Foucault, *Power/Knowledge: Selected Interviews & Other Writings, 1972–1977,* trans. Colin Gordon, Leo Marshall, John Nepham, and Kate Soper (New York: Pantheon Books, 1980), 214.
12. Saint Thomas Aquinas, *Summa Theologiae,* trans. T. C. O'Brien (New York: McGraw-Hill, 1974), 67, 69.
13. Haliczer, *Sexuality in the Confessional,* 5.
14. Donald B. Calne, *Within Reason: Rationality and Human Behavior* (New York: Vintage Books, 2000), 8.

15. Charles Baudelaire, "Heautontimoroumenos," trans. Roy Campbell, in *The Flowers of Evil* (New York: A New Directions Paperbook, 1958), 67.

16. Sigmund Freud, *Totem and Taboo*, in *Standard Edition*, vol. 13 (1955); cited in the text as *TT*.

7

The Hysterization of Incest

ENTHRALLMENT WITH THE FORBIDDEN

His father was a sexual tyrant and the only person Allen ever loved. In spite of the cruel incest and shameful memories of being an obedient child who serviced his father's diverse desires for ten long years, Allen confessed to missing the sin and the secrecy, the taboos and the transgressions—all the enthrallments with the forbidden that identify an erotic existence. Distorted by childhood experience that left him searching for lost treasure in comfortable underworlds of adult experience, Allen succumbed to a dissolute life of sex, drugs, and crime until he became a convicted felon when he was twenty-nine. Following incarceration for selling cocaine and a failed attempt to fulfill his wish for a "normal life" in the wake of his parole, Allen came to the mental health clinic seeking relief from morbid symptoms.

Although he was chronically depressed, Allen's physical appearance showed that he was favored by the gods. By all accounts, Socrates would have found him as desirable as Charmides, once considered "the great beauty of the day" in and around Athens; but Socrates would not have succumbed to Allen's physical charms, for Allen did not possess a noble soul and in the discriminating mind of Socrates, even if his loins "took the flame" and he was "overcome by a sort of wild-beast appetite," a noble soul was the driver of irresistible desire regardless of a man's physical charms.[1] Still, like Charmides, Allen had a handsome face, as well as a magnificently sculpted body produced by a daily diet of pumping iron with fellow inmates who discovered that lifting dead weight is a useful way to build esteem and pass the time—endless time in a penal colony where each convict knew his sentence and vowed to go to any length to avoid the horror of relearning the sentence on his body.

Given his physical attributes, women found Allen irresistible and I include my female colleagues among his admirers. Loins aflame, as if they were indulging a wild-beast appetite without thought of the soul's noble or ignoble state, they loitered in the waiting room of the outpatient clinic week after week to catch a glimpse of the great beauty of the day, who was waiting in the reception area expectantly, given his enchantment with talk therapy. A high-testosterone male whose biological inheritance was buttressed by a hefty dose of self-adoration, Allen took advantage of his physical charms by bedding every woman who caught his eye. But he was never satisfied, in fact, it seemed as if his soul were possessed, for he confessed to having a strange desire to recapture the exquisite pleasure he received from the forbidden life of sin and secrecy, of taboo and transgression, that animated his distorted universe until his father released him from sexual bondage when he was shy of sixteen and showing the promise of being a full-bodied man.

During one unflinching confession, Allen expressed wistful feelings of love and longing for his estranged father. Suddenly, his eyes glazed over and he stared off into space as if he had fallen under a spell and had been whisked away to a peculiar place that combined the pains of heaven with the pleasures of hell. Entranced and speaking in a whisper, he recollected being a little boy who heard his father commanding him to "turn around!" Fearing the painful invasion of his backside by a monstrous penis, Allen beseeched his father to relent, pleading ingenuously, "No daddy, let's just do it the normal way," as if fellating a father were normal behavior for a six-year-old child. But Allen's father was a sexual tyrant and at that precise moment, or sometime earlier—I am uncertain of the exact time, for no mortal can achieve precision in these prodigious matters—it came to pass that this obedient child was destined to carry the visceral sensibility that good and evil are kin. So near of kin that regardless of my clinical charms, particularly the fair words I used to combat the breach of Aristotelian logic, in Allen's distorted universe, the incestuous coupling of opposites—of good and evil, of pleasure and pain, of love and excrement—would resonate deeply, variously, and meaningfully in his incarcerated experience of space-time.

Whatever the reader may think of Allen's criminal behavior and subsequent incarceration, his candid clinical confessions were an illuminating disclosure of the inner torment inhabiting a man who embraced a shared silence with an ambivalently loved father: a contemptible man who taught his son stubborn lessons about the fittingness of fair and foul. As a result of indelible learning in the bed of his father, Allen's clinical confessions offered an unforgettable lesson about the uncanny power wielded by the pull of eroticism and enthrallments with the forbidden. Freud took a measure of this uniquely human experience in *Totem and Taboo,* while comparing the mental lives of primeval savages and the neurotics of his day. Although he never used the expression "enthrallment," a term that conveys the tension of being enslaved or held spellbound by a person, a place, a process, or a thing, Freud's commentary on ancient prohibitions, powerful and persistent human longings, forbidden objects of love, and the conflictive experience of ambivalence, leaves little doubt that he would have recognized an enthrallment with the forbidden in Allen's psychical predisposition. But in his clinical consulting room, while viewing Allen through a psychoanalytic lens—a fixed lens instructing him to believe that a child's first object choice is incestuous—Freud would have seen Allen as an obsessional neurotic not yet liberated from "psychical infantilism," insofar as he was an adult not freed from the forbidden wishes of childhood (*TT*, 17).

In view of the fact that language, ideas, and speech issue in clinical action that impacts the lives of patients directly, I am obligated to clearly state my view that when he spoke of the incestuous wishes of children, Freud was involved in a hysterization of incest not likely to have helped victims of childhood incest in their recovery, but more than likely to have resulted in an experience of revictimization—a novel experience of clinical abuse cued to the failure to have one's life experience validated, confirmed, or believed. This important clinical issue having been stated, the reader should understand that "the hysterization of discourse" is an imaginative expression invented by the early postmodern philosopher and psychoanalyst Jacques Lacan to refer to "the structural introduction, under artificial conditions, of the hysteric's discourse."[2] Departing from this Lacanian convention introduced in *The Other Side of Psychoanalysis,* where Lacan unpacked the psychoanalytic act by means of which an analyst grounds himself in clinical work, my reference to the hysterization of incest is incited by the perception that certain discourses carrying the pretense of truth traffic in violent or violating metaphors and images that seem to obscure or pervert the epistemic function of discursive prose, as if the courier of a king or the messenger of a queen were using the frenzied discourse of the hysteric to deliver an important message that promised to clarify the human condition, while speaking in a convulsive state a rational person would experience as cognitively deranged and emotionally disordered.

For example, Augustine of Hippo (A.D. 354–430), a classical misogynist with a chronic case of gynophobia, demonized the pleasures of the flesh: the flesh of women and the sexual pleasure a man received by entering a woman's unclean body. A convulsive confessor who experienced the pleasures of the flesh during his profligate youth, Augustine used the discourse of the hysteric in *Soliloquies* to record "how vile, how detestable, how shameful, how dreadful . . . [is] the embrace of a woman."[3] Believing he had found a cure for his revulsion with the unclean genitals of women, St. Augustine renounced the vile embrace of women in a variety of violating passages in his classic *Confessions,* all of which used hystericizing discourse to deliver the irrational message that when a man is "sunk in death," due to "wallowing in filth and scratching the itching sore of lust," he will surely experience a "disease of . . . soul" requiring the cure of purification.[4] Similarly, as if they were responding to the sainted Augustine during the last quarter of the twentieth century, a coterie of influential women experienced themselves as collaborators in their violation by men: an excruciating violation issuing from the experience of being born with a body that can be penetrated, entered, and occupied by men who have social, political, economic, and physical power and without fail, use their power to dominate, control, and violate women. Delivering this message in her feminist classic, *Intercourse,* in the second part entitled "The Female Condition," Andrea Dworkin used the frenzied discourse of the hysteric in the following convulsive confession:

> There is the outline of a body, distinct, separate, its integrity an illusion, a tragic deception, because unseen there is a slit between the legs, and he has to push into it. There is never a real privacy of the body that can coexist with intercourse: with being entered. The vagina itself is muscled and the muscles have to be pushed apart. The thrusting is persistent invasion. She is opened up, split down the center. She is occupied—physically, internally, in her privacy. . . . Intercourse is a particular reality for women as an inferior class; and it has in it, as part of it, violation of boundaries, taking over, occupation, destruction of privacy, all of which are construed to be normal and also fundamental to continuing human existence. (*IN*, 122–23)[5]

With these interesting examples in mind, I shall suggest that Freud hystericized the incest of some, perhaps many, of his patients, when he referred to incest as the wish of children; I shall also suggest that the protracted incestuous experience of some of my patients, particularly patients like Allen and Diane, is not only a forbidden experience a parent may initiate in violence, but also an erotic experience that violates a victim's inner self: a noisily conscious violation during which a person exists in a enduring state of erotic annihilation. Upright clinicians may feel that any reference to eroticism in the context of a patient's incestuous experience is heretical at best, clinically irresponsible and contemptible at worst. These judgments are intelligible and accepted at face, for disquieting things of this sort rarely are spoken, like a dangling modifier written but unsaid. But in the underworld of clinical experience, where things are dark, yet sometimes clearer; on the clinical sofa, where dangling modifiers are treated as precious gems, rather than unwanted discourse left to dangle; on the other side of psychoanalysis, where clinical speech has been felicitously conceived as "the hysterization of discourse"; incest may be treated as a forbidden experience that possesses nuclear elements of eroticism, not in every case, of course, but in certain select cases that may never have been reported, but appear out of nowhere like a mirage in the desert or some other phantastic vision out of the blue.

Revolting as it may be to an imagination not inured to the hysterization of discourse that arises in psychoanalytic, religious, literary critical, and other human quests that use the instrument of language to understand and communicate the disordered meanings of forbidden experience, the historical experience of Allen and Diane in their father's respective beds evidenced discrete elements of eroticism, some of which were disclosed in the convulsive discourse of Georges Bataille, whose early postmodern study of erotism, death, and sensuality not only referred to death as "vertiginous" and "hypnotizing," but also exposed eroticism as the uniquely human psychological quest of "assenting to life up to the point of death"(*ER*, 11, 13).[6] Not surprisingly, in the paroxysmal discourse of the hysteric, this is no ordinary assent to life and no commonplace death; rather, in the hystericizing discourse of Bataille, at the peak of erotic experience, when blood is pulsing with intense fury and a madding pleasure takes hold of rational consent, "there is a minor rupture suggestive of death"—a deathlike rupture that "adds up to a sense of transgression" during which "we are admitted to the knowledge of a pleasure in which the notion of pleasure is . . . suggestive of the taboo that fashions the pleasure at the same time as it condemns it" (*ER*, 106–7).

When fashioning this spastic discourse, Bataille was not thinking of historical victims like Allen or Diane: incest victims being treated for sexual abuse in a mental health clinic experienced as enchanted. Rather, Bataille was focused on the ecstatic eroticism of hysterical exemplars like St. Teresa of Avila. A discalced Carmelite, Teresa identified her erotic rapture as "a death so delectable that my soul's desire was never to escape from it"; explaining her erotic experience in terms of an arresting enthrallment with the forbidden, Teresa referred to her concurrent feeling of "distress" and "bliss"; illuminating her distressing bliss with violent images of burning in a fire or having an arrow driven deep into her entrails by an embodied angel of God, this eroticized lover of Jesus exclaimed hysterically, as if she were maddened: "So delectable is this distress that life holds no delight which can give greater satisfaction" (*LT*, 272–73).[7]

Unfortunately, scholarly analyses of the forbidden often focus on some aspect of sadomasochism as the consummate forbidden experience, but the forbidden consists of finer boundaries, the penetration of which is capable of producing an exquisite pleasure that may tickle, rather than violently assault, multiple senses. Bear in mind, in the human estate, anything can be sexualized, anything can be countenanced as forbidden, anything can be experienced as sinful or transgressive behavior. From a clinical point of view this includes commerce with inanimate objects (fetishism); corpses (necrophilia); animals (zoophilia); urine (urophilia); feces (coprophilia); enemas (klismaphilia); self-exposure (exhibitionism); touching or rubbing against a stranger (frotteurism); the psychological or physical suffering of self (masochism), the psychological or physical suffering of others (sadism); cross-dressing (transvestic fetishism); watching unsuspecting people (voyeurism); and sexual contact with prepubescent children (pedophilia).

Speaking of the latter paraphilia, I shall never forget treating a sexual perpetrator who penetrated the mouth of an infant with his penis, offering his sexual organ to be sucked as if it were the mother's breast. This was neither an impulsive act, nor accidental behavior. Rather, the infant's need for milk and its sucking response, the analogy between a substance-emitting penis and a substance-emitting breast, including the material kinship of sperm and milk, all were contemplated in advance by an intelligent perpetrator who had a predatory knack for spotting the most vulnerable victims and moving in like a stealthy lion for the kill. On the lighter side of foul things all too human, I once facilitated a men's therapy group that included a dedicated pedophile and a man who had sexual congress with a farm animal. Not surprisingly, during one memorable therapy session, it came to pass that the pedophile and the zoophile engaged in a heated debate focused on who was the worst transgressor: the man who had sexual congress with children or the man who had sexual congress with an animal. When I managed to regain control of the clinic and restrain the hostility that had erupted, there was no clear winner, although each man held his ground and remained convinced that the other fellow was the worst offender.

More to the point, enthrallments with the forbidden may include an ambivalent union of yes and no that tests a person's devotion to the erotic self and its secrets. Generally, the ambivalent experience of yes and no is "an alteration of fascination and horror, of affirmation and denial," as Bataille maintained astutely when processing the enigma of incest (*ER*, 211). Whether affirmation or denial possesses the power to determine attitude and behavior at a particular moment in time, anything is possible and everything has a day, either in the warmth of the sun or during the still of night. Accordingly, if the forbidden is interpreted broadly and inclusively, incorporating a vast array of individual proclivities, the enthrallment with the forbidden encompasses an illimitable array of manifest and subtle practices, all of which may elicit contradictory cognitions and conflicting emotions begetting a transgressive experience during which a person feels fully alive, while experiencing intrapsychic annihilation.

In the clinic, I have frequently encountered the discourse of the hysteric in the eyes, in the voice, and in the mutilated body parts of adolescents—so many adolescent females who are cutting their bodies and sometimes licking, even quaffing their own blood. Strange as it may seem outside the literary context of Sade's fancies, from time to time, this vampiric practice is performed with another person, the boundary of the forbidden breached being a finer subtlety of erotic pleasure involving the mutual cutting and licking of the body of the other. Given the compulsion to confess these contemporary secrets during the clinical hour, a sixteen-year-old female I treated briefly for depression offered a picturesque recitation of her self-mutilating vampirism in a voice that delivered the discourse of the hysteric: "The blood flows so quickly," she said as I scribbled feverishly on my trusty yellow pad, "twisting freely in rivers on my skin, dancing down the slopes as I pick up my feet. I can feel the rip of the soft tissue once pink—tints of purple, now deep scarlet. My heart jumps to my throat, settling when no one comes in. At first the red is bright and after, almost black. Slits in my skin open up, whispering praise—a quiet comfort. I can't even feel them anymore. My finger fits in one of the openings and offers a familiar taste. The faintly bitter, slightly metallic warm liquid at once goes cold. The evidence destroyed as I swallow."

In the final analysis, it is true, but trivially true, to say that humankind has a fascination with the forbidden; and I am not speaking in a vacuum when I offer this impression: a clinical impression consistent with the literary confessions of Sade, the clinical conclusions of Freud and Reik, the psychological reflections of the scholarly academic William James, and the cultural criticism of Simone de Beauvoir, all of whom commented perceptively on the enthrallment with the forbidden that informs the secret desires and transgressive behavior of humans.

Specifically, on 22 October 1785, while imprisoned in the Bastille, Sade began to draft the final revision of his once-scandalous masterpiece, *The 120 Days of Sodom*. Completed one month later, on 28 November 1785, *Sodom* is a shocking collection of erotic encounters exploring the libertine's proposition that "through vice alone is man capable of experiencing [a] moral and physical vibration which is the source of the most delicious voluptuousness"(*DS*, 198). Unruly and distasteful as it may be to rational intellects not accustomed to the violating discourse of the hysteric, the moral and physical vibration of Sade's reference may be seen as a novelist's way of capturing the experience of sin and secrecy, as well as the awareness of taboo and transgression, informing the incestuous experience of clinic patients like Allen, the inveterate charmer, and Diane, who appeared to her therapist as a postmodern Electra.

Refining Sade's experiential observation during the twentieth century, Reik focused on the underworld of human experience in *The Compulsion to Confess*, noting: "The wisdom of all peoples proclaims that the forbidden incites to transgression" (*CC*, 250). Similarly, in the late 1940s, in her groundbreaking feminist manifesto, *The Second Sex*, Beauvoir proclaimed: "Many neuroses have their source in a madness for the forbidden that can appear only if taboos have been previously established. . . . Temptation is born of the forbidden" (*SS*, 195–96).[8] Earlier, in the 1890s, in *The Principles of Psychology*, writing as if he were intimate with Sade's personal enthrallment with the forbidden, James offered the following penetrating insight into humankind's fascination with and temptation to embrace the horror of forbidden experience: "It is the very badness of the act that gives it . . . vertiginous fascination. Remove the prohibition, and the attraction stops. In my university days a student threw himself from an upper entry window of one of the college buildings. . . . Another student . . . had to pass the window daily in coming and going from his room, and experienced a dreadful temptation to imitate the deed. . . . He told his director, who said, 'All right! If you must, you must,' and added, 'go ahead and do it,' thereby instantly quenching his desire."[9]

Whether we call it a moral and physical vibration, an incitement to transgression, a vertiginous fascination, a madness for the forbidden, or an enthrallment with the forbidden, the shared temptation to violate a boundary of the forbidden can be heard in the disparate clinical confessions of young and old, religious and irreligious, enlightened and unenlightened, courageous and timid, male and female patients alike. But these are not strangers in our midst, like the protagonist in Camus' existentialist classic *The Stranger*: a man without a soul, who possessed no moral qualities, lacked decency, and regretted nothing.[10] Rather, like Adam and Eve, mythological ancestors who breached a boundary of the forbidden by violating the prohibitive commandment of their creator, these are agonistic men and women whose clinical stories suggest that human desire may tempt a person to build a mansion in tempting places where pleasure promises to follow. Often, however, what follows in this mansion of love is an enthrallment with the forbidden that may be likened to a disease of the soul requiring a psychological healing or some other purification.

DISCOURSE OF THE GENIUS

Like a number of Freud's patients who confessed to having traumatic childhood experience—real sexual experience Freud conceived as wish-fulfilling fantasy—the protracted incest of Allen and Diane was all-too-human and very real. In spite of his controversial decision to retract an original seduction theory that not only authenticated the reality of childhood incest, but also had the inflammatory effect of indicting fathers who were perpetrators of sexual abuse in a repressive Victorian culture often identified as decadent fin de siècle Vienna, Freud showed that he fully grasped the human capacity for incest in *Totem and Taboo,* the first two essays of which were published in 1912, approximately fifteen years after he first expressed skepticism about the sexual confessions of his patients in a letter to Fliess dated 21 September 1897. This is a fascinating letter in which Freud confided his nagging suspicion that "widespread perversions against children are not very probable" in view of the fact that "in all cases, the *father,* not excluding my own, had to be accused of being perverse"; adding weight to the suspicion that confessions of widespread incest were not true was Freud's "certain insight that there are no indications of reality in the unconscious, so that one cannot distinguish between truth and fiction that has been cathected with affect" (*FL,* 264).

I shall not draft a lengthy formal argument to critique this ill-conceived point of view because it is beyond the scope of this work. Suffice it to say, when read with a cold, critical eye, the sentiments expressed in Freud's letter to Fliess enable one to understand why twentieth-century philosophers were justified in referring to Freud as a speculative genius whose allegorical work was "damagingly popular," insofar as he spent his days examining the mythical (see appendix). Specifically, with incest, the devil lurks in the details and an experienced clinician has a good chance of accurately distinguishing truth from fiction in a fair number of cases, one pertinent example being a child of tender age who has details about the body and its functioning unknown to innocent children unless some sort of sexual contact has taken place. For example, during an initial clinical evaluation, a four-year-old child used crayons to draw a penis that appeared to have a nondescript substance coming out of its tip. When Peggy was asked what she was drawing, she said: "Daddy's private with the white stuff coming out." After making this startling statement and referring to daddy's ejaculate as "white puke," Peggy began to suck on the crayon, drawing it in and out of her mouth nonchalantly. Adding the weight of truth to a telling confession of this sort, is a child's voluntary inclusion of sensory detail; for example, does the allegedly abused child offer discriminating judgments about the taste, smell, and feel of the white puke? The more accurate the detail volunteered, the more the devil can be suspected of incest, unless a clinician is wed to the mythical structures and dynamics of the unconscious, thereby finding himself unable to distinguish between truth and fiction, or historical reality and intrapsychic wishes, allegedly cathected with affect.

In fairness to Freud, when he confessed his inability to distinguish truth from fiction, historical reality from psychic reality, factual incest from an unconscious wish for incest, he was referring to the sexual confessions of adults whose free associations delivered painful recollections of traumatic events that allegedly occurred many years earlier during the impressionable era of childhood. Obviously, when hearing the clinical confession of an emotionally impaired adult, Freud was not able to judge either the knowledge base of an innocent child or the accuracy of a child's sexual confession. But when I think about the hysterization of incest and Freud's unwitting participation in this violating use of language and ideas, I am intrigued by the fact that on 1 May 1883 when he was twenty-seven years old, Freud was appointed junior resident in the psychiatric clinic of Theodor Meynert, a renowned physician young Dr. Freud regarded as a "great man" (*AS*, 11). During his six-month tenure, Freud acquired some basic psychiatric experience, while also learning a good deal about Meynert's Amentia, otherwise known as acute hallucinatory psychosis. You see, Meynert believed that wish fulfillment was related etiologically to hallucinatory psychoses and in an interesting way, as if he were enthralled with Meynert, Freud recast his psychoanalytic theory by conceiving wish fulfillment as the subterranean dynamic of psychopathology, including pathology ostensibly induced by traumatizing incest. Much later, when his native curiosity and intellectual vision were focused beyond the clinic to much larger cultural concerns affecting humankind, Freud conceived religious ideas as "illusions . . . derived from human wishes"; in Freud's active imagination a religious belief was an illusion because "wish-fulfillment is a prominent factor in its motivation" (*FI*, 31). Principally, Freud was thinking about (a) the feeling of helplessness in children, (b) a vulnerable child's need and consequent wish for protection against powerful external forces, (c) the subsistence of this dynamic in the emotional life of adults, and (d) the analogical translation of the child's protective father into humankind's wish for and images of powerful, protective deities.

Freud may have considered Meynert a genius, but he had dramatic differences of clinical opinion with him, not the least being a public dispute concerning Freud's experience with Charcot. You see, Charcot discovered that he could use hypnotic suggestion to produce hysterical paralyses in women *and* men; given the incontrovertible evidence presented by Charcot during his enlightening psycho-hypnotic presentations at the Salpêtrière, Freud accepted this novel finding whole cloth and he returned to Vienna prepared to support a radical departure from current thinking. Inane as it may seem in our hyper-enlightened era, the Greek *hustera* means womb and in Freud's patriarchal culture, where hysteria was conceived as a gross dysfunction of the uterus, Freud's report of male hysteria was destined to be met with scorn by Meynert and other authoritative physicians who were members of the Viennese Society of Medicine: literalists of the imagination who could not understand how a human being without a uterus could be hysterical. In the end, Meynert's public disagreement with Freud resulted in a rift in their relationship that was never mended. Nevertheless, aspects of Freud's psychoanalytic theory, particularly the resolution of his inability to distinguish between truth and fiction during adult confessions of incest as well as his sober reflections on the psychodynamics of religion evidence his intellectual indebtedness to Meynert: a reputed genius who believed that wish fulfillment was the root of hallucinatory psychoses.

But Freud argued against himself like a tormented genius who gazed long into a distorted mirror that returned the misshapen image of a mad scientist in the throe of self-doubt: unyielding self-doubt that admittedly "caused . . . many distressing hours" (*NI*, 120). Although he clearly harbored doubts about the historical reality of the sexual confessions of his patients, Freud elucidated the paleontology of incest admirably in *Totem and Taboo*, where he compared the mental lives of primeval savages and the mental lives and behavior of contemporary neurotics. Contending that taboos are primitive prohibitions involving activities toward which human beings have the strongest inclination, Freud argued cogently that the persistence of a powerful prohibition indicates that the desire to commit a forbidden act endures as well. Identifying incest as one of humankind's "most powerful longings" Freud also claimed that the combination of a powerful longing, an awareness of prohibition, and a temptation to transgress, underlies the experience of emotional ambivalence that accompanies human commerce with the forbidden (*TT*, 35). In the psychomythic imagination of Freud, to tally the cash value of this analysis, the experience of emotional ambivalence involves a powerful longing for some forbidden experience in a person who is "noisily conscious" of an externally imposed prohibition such that the temptation to breach a boundary of the forbidden, thereby embracing incest or some other tabooed behavior, is opposed by horror—the kind of horror that often functions as a deterring detestation (*TT*, 29–30).

Freud's lucid account of the emotional ambivalence that often accompanies the temptation to violate a taboo was evidenced in the case of Phillipe and Juliette, a father and daughter who crossed the threshold of the clinic in the grip of a transgressive wish that was swimming in a surfeit of erotic ambivalence. In spite of the justified furor regarding Freud's retraction of his original seduction theory in favor of a hystericized view that presented incest as psychically real wish fulfillment, this case of an enthrallment with the forbidden clearly showed that there are times when the historical reality of wishing figures prominently in clinical presentations. In this noteworthy case that documented a madness for the forbidden, the temptation to build a mansion in a forbidden place brought a tormented father and daughter together, while also forcing them apart, as if they were noisily conscious of a primeval taboo, the experience of which resulted in a moral and physical vibration and an incitement to transgress, as well as a deterring horror in the face of a nagging temptation.

LOVE'S LABOR LOST

In 1994, *Reviving Ophelia* focused critical attention on the traumatized condition of adolescent females who come of age in a media-saturated culture whose music, advertising, TV, and films have a tendency to poison the emerging self. Although Pipher painted a compelling image of young women imprisoned in a "junk culture," whose media create enormous pressure to achieve sophistication and beauty—premature sophistication and beauty that translates into early sexual behavior and a destructive use of chemical substances—clinical confessions suggest that the author fell short in her analysis of the complex relationship of fathers and daughters.[11] There is much truth in Pipher's pages and her use of Ophelia as a literary analogue is effective, insofar as adolescent females may be likened to the Shakespearean character who drowned after surrendering to a fine Renaissance madness, the initial dramatic action of which found Polonius forbidding his daughter, Ophelia, to have further romantic involvement with Hamlet, whose true love Polonius doubted. In spite of the book's popular success, evidenced by the fact that it became a *New York Times* bestseller, clinical confessions suggest that in postmodern time the Renaissance madness may have become a madness for the forbidden not captured in *Ophelia,* where well-meaning, inept fathers are depicted as having failed to become emotionally involved with their daughters, while distant fathers are conceived as working busily outside the home, enacting boyhood training in misogyny, or disvaluing nurturing relationships due to having received a maladaptive socialization to the male role. Other fathers, like the fathers of Allen and Diane, were correctly conceived as sexual perpetrators who betray their parental responsibility by incesting their innocent children.

Clinical confessions confirm the ugly truth that many adolescent females are emotionally annihilated by the experience of developing an acceptable self in a decadent postmodern culture in which a constant barrage of media-manufactured images not only provide models by means of which gender and sexual identity, morality, and other aspects of self are formed, but also blur the boundary between reality and unreality, often rendering meaningless the ancient and modern distinction between reality and unreality. For young women coming of age in this existential situation, the psychological problem lies in the inevitable failure to become the unreality that media-manufactured images of beauty and sophistication dictate. As a result of this drama of defeat, deflated self-esteem, mood and anxiety disorders, suicide attempts, eating disorders, and self-mutilation are flourishing in a vulnerable female population plagued by a confusing onslaught of unrealizable demands at a time in which a young woman is adjusting to the development of a pubescent body that has a new, alluring appearance and an alarming reproductive function. Equally important, clinical confessions offer phenomenological evidence to support the conclusion that many fathers leave their defeated, distraught daughters around the time when daddy's little girl begins to develop physical attributes that manifest budding aspects of a sexual self. In *The Second Sex,* Beauvoir paid lip service to this dynamic, while offering a feminist's erudite observations on ways in which men have not only demonized women historically, but have established women as the "the Other"; according to Beauvoir: "The little girl, not yet in puberty, carries no menace, she is under no taboo. . . . In many primitive societies her very sex seems innocent. . . . But on the day she can reproduce, woman becomes impure; and rigorous taboos surround the menstruating female. Leviticus gives elaborate regulations, and many primitive societies have similar rules regarding isolation and purification. . . . Since patriarchal times only evil powers have been attributed to the feminine flow" (*SS,* 139, 148–49).

Largely unexplored in Pipher and in Beauvoir is the fact that in some cases, when the sex of daddy's little girl no longer seems innocent, there is an underworld of temptation and a prodigious silence about the incestuous implications, as some fathers experience an enthrallment with the forbidden too shameful to be faced, too sinful to be spoken, too madding to be embraced. On the part of some fathers who exist in full retreat from developing daughters, there is confusion, fear, anger, shame, silence, self-reproach, and long-distance running. On the part of bewildered daughters, who once occupied the esteemed position of being daddy's little girl, there is a mood-disordering experience of love's labor lost and a wounded fury that finds release through self-defeating, or worse, self-destructive behavior. In the mental health clinic, where "to be enchanted, or not to be enchanted" is a controlling question, the silence of the forbidden is sometimes broken during clinical confessions that offer compelling insight into an eroticism that is the tormenting destiny of some fathers and some beleaguered daughters.

Regarding this supremely delicate affair, an *affaire de coeur* Freud conceived as a daughter's wish-fulfilling fantasy, a latter-day Ophelia first entered my office following a suicide attempt precipitated by a decision to terminate an intimate relationship with her Hamlet: an angry, abusive boyfriend who figured prominently in this young woman's crazed decision to kill herself in order to end the disordered life she no longer could bear. Separating Elizabethan fiction from contemporary truth, I have a vivid recollection of an anguished set of parents bringing their sixteen-year-old daughter to the clinic literally begging me to do something to save her life. Juliette was a learning-disabled young woman who presented with a history of academic failure, abuse of alcohol and marijuana, and premature sexual activity. She was demonstrably depressed and a lethality assessment revealed suicidal ideation coupled with a well-defined method, but no current intent to take her life. As a result of her initial psychiatric evaluation, Juliette was prescribed an antidepressant medication and I withdrew her from school temporarily, insofar as the social cruelty endemic in peer relationships had become a severe psychosocial stressor.

Psychosocial history revealed that Juliette lost her virginity when she was fourteen years old. An unwanted pregnancy and miscarriage followed, as well as a pattern of sexual intimacies with a number of teenage boys, the last of whom sounded like a crazed chimpanzee who undermined Juliette's confidence and esteem by ridiculing her horribly. Apparently, Juliette tolerated this emotional and physical abuse until she finally decided to end it all by taking her life. To make matters worse, Juliette had been raped five months prior to her suicide attempt. Because she had placed herself in harm's way, while under the influence of alcohol and marijuana, Juliette and her mother, Celeste, put their heads together and decided they would not report the rape to the authorities. They also agreed to not reveal the rape to Juliette's father, Phillipe, due to the fact that "he would have a fit," notwithstanding the fact that Juliette and Phillipe became estranged following Juliette's pregnancy and miscarriage. This father and daughter lived in the same house, all right, but they rarely spoke, and if they spoke at all, angry words were exchanged. You see, when Phillipe learned about Juliette's first sexual experience he was shaken, so profoundly shaken, that he had an explosive fit and told his daughter repeatedly: "You're a fucking slut!" This sudden transition from daddy's little girl to fucking slut was another deadly metamorphosis: the same vulgar transformation that infected Charlene with guilt and shame about her sexual self, this time leaving Juliette feeling like a dirty insect in a Kafkaesque metamorphosis.

Juliette had been daddy's little girl since childhood, a memorable mode of being that included nightly bedtime stories while tucked safely in Phillipe's warm bed. Juliette had no intention of ever losing her father's trust, respect, or adoration; still, every mode of being carries existential implications that include a precise mode of collapse and being daddy's little girl is no exception. Consequently, a beloved daughter became sexually intimate with a stranger and a devoted father reacted like a horribly wounded animal who could not bear the thought of his little girl in the passionate embrace of a stranger: a mindless chimpanzee whose love Phillipe had good reason to doubt. In fact, Phillipe's imagination ran riot and his temper flared whenever he envisioned this witless teenage nincompoop delighting in the pleasures of his daughter's flesh: soft white flesh that overlay a young, shapely body he watched develop in artful silence for many years. Obsessed with images of Juliette's venereal concupiscence, to borrow the discourse of patristic fathers like Augustine, he imagined his beautiful little girl removing the clothes he worked so hard to put on her back. Did she actually strip, take to her back, and spread her legs to allow that stupid chimp entry into the vestibule of pleasure he had not seen since the last time he bathed her? In his mind's eye, making Dworkin's images as real as they can be, he pictured him pushing into the slit between her legs with a persistent thrusting invasion, not only occupying Juliette internally, but robbing him of his daughter's sexual secrets. How could she do this to him? And how would he ever countenance this tragic deception?

Unable to salve the gaping wound generated by Juliette's betrayal of his devotion, incapable of ever finding the magic potion that would return Juliette to a prior state of innocent attendance, Phillipe ran as far and as fast as he could, leaving Juliette devastated by his invalidation. Believing she would never again be reflected adoringly in her father's eyes, Juliette began to despise and to disrespect Phillipe, although her thoughts and feelings were consistent with Beauvoir's view of a daughter's need for a father's love and positive mirroring:

> What Freud calls the Electra complex is not, as he supposes, a sexual desire; it is full of abdication of the subject, consenting to become object in submission and adoration. If her father shows affection for his daughter, she feels that her existence is magnificently justified; . . . she is fulfilled and deified. All her life she may longingly seek that lost state of plenitude and peace. If the father's love is withheld, she may ever after feel herself guilty and condemned; or she may look elsewhere for a valuation of herself and become indifferent to her father or even hostile. (*SS*, 287)

Given Phillipe's volatility and intermittent explosions, Juliette colluded with her mother to conceal the traumatizing rape, the physical abuse, and self-destructive, emotionally reactive behavior that virtually ruined her life. In spite of this deceitful intrigue and their two-year estrangement, when this troubled family finally came to the clinic begging for salvation, Juliette and Phillipe sat side by side on the sofa, while Celeste took a position in a comfortable armchair removed from the intimate working circle of father, daughter, and therapist.

At the time, I had an art print hanging on the wall over the armchair where Celeste was seated; it was a print of Picasso's *Family of Saltimbanques*. This is a curious painting of a circus family consisting of a harlequin, two young acrobats, a very young ballerina, and a rotund jester standing together in a nondescript landscape. Strangely removed from the family and facing away, as if she were totally unrelated to the circus family that seems to be the center of artistic focus, an adult female sits alone as the acrobats and the harlequin gaze vapidly in her direction. I sometimes use this ambiguous work of art as a handy thematic apperception test to elicit patients' unique experience of the family constellation, but I never had members of a family voluntarily configure themselves as though a meaningful imitation of Picasso's artwork were taking place in my presence. When I brought the picture to Celeste's attention, carefully comparing her distance from the field of clinical action to the placement of the woman in Picasso's beautiful work of art, she did not respond, in fact she appeared to be as stoic as the vacant women Picasso had painted. Several weeks later, however, Celeste voluntarily confessed that she had always felt displaced by Juliette: displaced, more precisely, by her husband's love for his little girl.

As time wore on and Juliette's therapy proceeded apace, Phillipe became accustomed to sitting close to his daughter on the clinical sofa, although he became demonstrably angry when each new family secret was revealed. One memorable afternoon, while struggling to understand why Juliette's rape was not reported to the police and prosecuted formally, Phillipe turned to Juliette and confessed: "I love you!" Looking long into her eyes, as if he were trying to capture her attention, hold her in his gaze, and draw her into his linguistic embrace, Phillipe offered an unambiguous confession of an enthrallment with the forbidden that defied primitive taboos and moral conventions. "You left me for him," he whispered candidly, referring to the adolescent competitor who stole the secrets of a daughter's sex fatherhood denied him. Strange as it may seem, after hearing her father's expression of love and incorporating the inference that she belonged to him and he wished to possess her, Juliette experienced a psychic turn for the better, for she now had hope of recovering that lost state of peace and plenitude that follows a father's deep abiding affection.

A few weeks later during an individual psychotherapy session, Juliette volunteered a bold comment on the interminable conflict that defined her parent's marriage. Sliding forward on the sofa to achieve the kind of confessional intimacy that accompanies the revelation of shameful secrets, she expressed disdain for her mother and the fervent hope that her parents would separate. When I asked why she desired her parents' separation, she looked squarely in my eyes and stated without reservation: "If they separate, I could have him!"

I reflected on this meaningful transaction between a father and a daughter while recalling Freud's commentary on the persistence of the incest taboo and the logical connection he made between the persistence of a taboo and abiding human desire. With this in mind, I began to suspect that some horrified fathers flee from budding daughters in an attempt to permanently suppress a transgressive eroticism that results in a madness for the forbidden more common than civilized humans would like to imagine. In spite of our collective illusions, many of which issue from suppressions of the shadow side of the human animal, the shamed withdrawal of some fathers explains beyond commonly accepted cant, the agonistic struggles of fathers that drive Ophelia mad. Hystericizing incest further, I realized that the real madness may be that devastated daughters have no understanding of the fact that a father's abandonment may be governed more by eros than by thanatos, more by forbidden love than by obstinate hatred. While tracking the elementary particles of eroticism and using the discourse of the hysteric to record his findings, Bataille illuminated this madness when he commented straightforwardly: "For the man in love . . . the fervour of love may be felt more violently than physical desire. . . . In spite of the bliss love promises, its first effect is one of turmoil and distress. . . . If the lover cannot possess the beloved he will sometimes think of killing her; often he would rather kill her than lose her. Or else he may wish to die himself" (*ER*, 19–20).

Perhaps it is not too much to say that when death has dominion in a father who is noisily conscious of a taboo that expresses one of humankind's most powerful longings, the wish to die may manifest itself in subtle and in overt behavior whose self-defeating blows are received with acceptance. On the face of it, these self-inflictions are emotionally reactive responses to the pull of eroticism and the enthrallment with the forbidden: irrational reactions prescribed to satisfy the stringent demands of a harsh superego. In fact, when the marriage of fair and foul reveals itself in the clinical confessional in the communication between fathers and daughters, an artful listener may hear a sigh of pleasure when self-punishment works to satisfy the sin of wishing to embrace the forbidden. Occasionally, painful pleasure may be welcomed with open arms by agonistic fathers, notwithstanding the fact that their forbidden love will never be consummated, save for wishing, and the fulfillment of wishing in erotic fantasy, where love is a labor, but a labor rarely lost.

Having confessed their enthrallment with the forbidden, Phillipe and Juliette were reviving their relationship when I last saw them. Juliette's depression had lifted, suicide was no longer a threat, and she achieved abstinence from chemical substances. Although Phillipe did not like it, he accepted the fact that Juliette had a new boyfriend with whom she was sexually intimate. Regarding Celeste, who remained distempered and withdrawn in an infernal Elizabethan drama of her own, all I can say is that the strained relationship of mother and daughter remained constant, although Phillipe was considering a formal separation from Celeste and a move out of state. My best guess is that he never packed his bags, for during his last confession he admitted to having a strong reluctance to leave his daughter, claiming: "Juliette is all I really have!"

Many human dramas confessed in the clinic involve an elemental conflict of love that has a life in forbidden desire and impossible dream. Often, the symptom-producing conflict is aggravated by the disparity between desire and reality: a profound discrepancy between the gratuitous wishes of imagination and the hard wall of reality against which the world of wishing inevitably collides. Seen this way, many human dramas are reenactments of archetypal conflicts in which tragicomic characters tease and torment, seduce and reject, pleasure and punish, nurture and destroy, the unobtainable other they are fused with in fatefully daemonic ways. No less true is the observation that when wish and reality collide, these ill-fated humans must achieve some compromise with the forbidden and the impossible, as Joyce McDougall concluded in *Theaters of the Mind,* a psychoanalytic study of the world as a Shakespearean stage where human players enact dramatic parts that are metaphors for psychic realities (*TM,* 7–8).[12] While we busily occupy ourselves constructing an identity based upon a compromise with the forbidden and the impossible, there is bound to be some mourning, as McDougall suggested—a symptomatic mourning for whatever is lost or suppressed in a sullen concession to reality; but I think this author mistakenly concluded that out of mourning there will be some "recompense" for the forbidden desire and the impossible dream each person must relinquish (*TM,* 12). Clinical experience suggests that out of mourning, rather than some compensatory reward, there will be quiet resignation if a person is lucky and a reconciliation with self, world, and other, if a person is favored by the gods and somehow enchanted with the clinical situation. This existentialist view is not a counsel of despair, but it is consistent with Freud's late claim that discontented humans pay a price for becoming civilized, the cash value of which is a loss of happiness due to a renunciation of the instinctual aims of eros and thanatos—the daemonic idiots of sex and aggression.

DISCOURSE OF THE HYSTERIC

Some years ago I had the good fortune of visiting Santa Maria della Vittoria in Rome, where I viewed Gian Lorenzo Bernini's beautiful life-sized marble sculpture, *The Ecstasy of St. Teresa.* This is not only a breathtaking baroque sculpture of a woman's erotic rapture, but an artistic genius's vivid depiction of an enthralling, euphoric, destabilization of self referred to in religious circles as "transverberation": an altered conscious state of religious ecstasy. There is an abiding controversy about the nature of Teresa's ecstasy, in fact, in spite of his sensitivity to the vertiginous fascination of the bad act, in *The Varieties of Religious Experience*, William James viewed Teresa through a harsh critical lens that returned the image of a superficial, egotistic, exploitative bride of Jesus whose idea of religion reduced to "amatory flirtation . . . between the devotee and the deity" (*VR*, 276). But during the seventeenth century, in a visionary attempt to communicate a perfect vision of Teresa's transverberation, Bernini used his magnificent gift to carve the likeness of a sainted woman who appears to be experiencing an exquisite orgasm as an angel is poised to strike her with a spear that symbolizes God's phallus.

Like Charlene, a patient who appeared to me in a vision of Hester Prynne—the same enthralled woman who recorded in her diary every nuance of forbidden pleasure experienced during erotic encounters with a predatory neighbor—Teresa recorded her erotic experience in a diary published later as an autobiographical memoir. Regarding the erotic act in question, after identifying an embodied angel standing beside her, Teresa confessed that she observed a long golden spear in his hands at the end of which was a fiery point. With this iron spear, she wrote, giving expression to her intimate thoughts and desires: "He seemed to pierce my heart several times so that it penetrated to my entrails. When he drew it out I thought he was drawing them out with it and he left me completely afire with a great love for God. The pain was so sharp that it made me utter several moans; and so excessive was the sweetness caused me by this intense pain that one can never wish to lose it. . . . It is not bodily pain, but spiritual, though the body has a share in it—indeed a great share" (*LT*, 274–75).

I realize that I am communicating inflammatory ideas that are useless, perhaps violating, to innocent victims of incest who cross the threshold of the clinic seeking symptom relief. But I am referencing this noteworthy example of the discourse of the hysteric because it helps to illuminate important aspects of the inner life of individuals who dwell by force, wish, or acquiescence on the underside of human experience, particularly the violent erotic underside identified by the sainted Teresa in her wish-fulfilling encounter with her God's piercing penis. In fact, in his influential post-Freudian study of eroticism, in addition to claiming that a person who violates a taboo remains fully aware of transgression while breaching a boundary of forbidden behavior, Bataille offered the complementary thesis that eroticism is much ado about violence or violation (*ER*, 17). But he was not thinking of the kind of violence promised by the pistol pressed hard against Diane's head, although there are intriguing parallels between Diane's historical experience of fellating a godlike father who threatened to kill her with a pistol and St. Teresa's hysterical experience of having an angel of God drive a phallic spear through her heart and into her entrails, thereby producing "a death so delectable that my soul's desire was never to escape from it." Strictly speaking, when Bataille spoke of violence, with reference to the ecstatic eroticism of his hysterical exemplar, Teresa, he hystericized the discourse of eroticism and added an early postmodern voice to the repertoire of convulsive learning that illuminates interesting aspects of incest and other experiences forbidden in the human estate.

On Bataille's account, erotic violence is a profoundly disordering inner experience conceived as a partial annihilation of the person: an inner violation I would liken to a deranging of the psychological self or a disordering of being itself. In this translation of eroticism, the most violent or violating experience is death, a crude encounter with which literally "jerks us out of a tenacious obsession with the lastingness of our . . . being" and presents us with the possibility of "suddenly be[ing] snuffed out"; unpacking experiential aspects of this being-disordering experience, Bataille asked his readers: "What does physical eroticism signify if not a violation of the very being of its practitioners?—a violation bordering on death, bordering on murder? The whole business of eroticism is to strike to the inmost core of the living being, so that the heart stands still. The transition from the normal state to that of erotic desire presupposes a partial dissolution of the person. . . destroy[ing] the self-contained character of the participators as they are in their normal lives" (*ER*, 17).

Tempering Bataille's convulsive discourse for clinical purposes, I shall offer the suggestion that an erotically induced *ontological violation* of a person is a destabilization of well-being, including a deranging loss of self-control and a profound suspension of self-possession, resulting in a violent, seemingly real dissolution of being itself. In short, an ontological violation is a fragmentation of self that is a harbinger of death—a death in life itself. While evidencing this ontological condition, the clinical confessions of patients like Allen and Diane suggest that incest victims may experience contradictory cognitions and conflicting emotions capable of producing an ambivalent erotic experience during which they feel vitally alive, while existing in the tormenting throe of self-annihilation. Fear and horror may grip a person poised to experience an erotic dissolution of self, but fear and horror also have a life in the temptation to breach restrictive boundaries of identity and behavior due to the pull of eroticism and an enthrallment with the forbidden. Supporting this observation, Bataille joined Sade, James, Freud, Reik, and Beauvoir in claiming that when human beings become conscious of restrictive, self-defining boundaries that identify a zone of the forbidden, they also experience an inner desire to overstep these personal limitations: "We want to overstep them, and the horror we feel shows to what excesses we shall be brought" (*ER*, 144). But overstepping a self-defining boundary is easier said than done. Mathematicians may compare life to a game while engaged in cognitive games themselves. Yet the game of life has real players, rules and prohibitions, as well as mortal winners and losers. Baldly put, life is a terminal game as anyone tempted to go to the end of finite experience will attest. Imagine standing at a window with your feet on the sill and contemplating a leap and free fall to the ground. The mind reels in vertiginous fascination, the body sways outward and back from the abyss, while the epicenter of being quakes with the awareness of how it feels to be at once fully alive, while being tempted and recoiling from, yet for another millisecond, being compelled to choose and recoiling from, the horrifying promise of the end of life, an end of experience, the end of self itself.

For all its merit, Bataille's analysis of erotic violence did not withstand critical scrutiny. Referred to earlier as an erudite feminist who used the discourse of the hysteric to depict the violation of women by men, Dworkin imaged Bataille facetiously as "a philosopher of the erotic and therefore a classy guy"; revealing what she really meant by "classy guy," Dworkin used an acrid pen to conceive Bataille's "conflation of sex and death" as a "convergence of sadism and sex on the woman's body" (*IN*, 190–91).

For my part, Bataille's analysis went awry when he stated unequivocally that eroticism is not only a violating transgression of taboos, but a transgression of humanity (*ER*, 145). In full confession, I am always piqued to hear that some all too human behavior is outside the human estate. In the underworld of erotic experience, where the finer subtleties of a madding pleasure are weighed and measured, it may be true that eroticism traffics in despoilment and beauty may be desired in order to experience the pleasure of befouling or profaning it (*ER*, 145). But rhesus macaques, baboons, chimpanzees, and other intelligent primates offer little evidence of appreciating or purposefully profaning beauty. Appreciating and profaning beauty is the meaningful experience of intellective human beings and all forms of degradation and debauch are all too human as well. This points to the internal contradiction in Bataille's discourse on eroticism, particularly as it relates to incest. On the one hand, he spoke as if eroticism necessitates an inner life, an inner life of reflexive self-awareness that separates human beings from lesser beasts. On the other hand, he spoke as if some erotic practices reduce human beings to animals who exist outside the boundary of humanness. This tortured logic demonstrates unequivocally that the eminent scholar lost sight of the fact that his argument is premised on the irrevocable claim that the finer subtleties of eroticism involve the kind of inner life that is irreducibly human: the kind of inner life that may find pleasure in the pain of others and pain in the tormenting pleasures of self.

In full retreat from this subterranean aspect of the *condition humaine*, rational philosophers have advanced simple-minded conceptions of pleasure, or absence of pain, as the motivating driver of human behavior. The great English philosopher John Stuart Mill was no exception; and in 1863, sandwiched in time between the publication of Hawthorne's *Scarlet Letter* (1849) and the inauguration of Freud's clinical practice in Vienna (1886), Mill published *Utilitarianism*, an important essay in moral philosophy. As if he were totally blind to the forbidden desires and temptations that informed the literary world of Hawthorne—sexual secrets that soon would be confessed in the consulting room of Freud—Mill constructed a teleological ethic on the *Greatest Happiness Principle*, otherwise known as the Principle of Utility: "Actions are right in proportion as they tend to promote happiness, wrong as they tend to produce the reverse of happiness. By happiness is intended pleasure, and the absence of pain; by unhappiness, pain, and the privation of pleasure" (*UT*, 7).[13]

Mill understood the way things work in the best of all possible worlds, a fictional Aristotelian world where rational intellect has sovereign power; but in the human world of ambivalence and ambiguity, a crazed intrapsychic world where human beings are enthralled with the forbidden and the union of fair and foul reigns, this rarely is the way things work. As it turned out, Mill's Principle of Utility rested on a theory of life that became hopelessly naïve after Freud began to publish his findings, thereby inviting humankind to become a fly on the wall of his clinical confessional. Specifically, Mill's moral philosophy is grounded in a simple-minded theory of life whose principal tenet is: "Pleasure, and freedom from pain, are the only things desirable as ends; and that all desirable things . . . are desirable either for the pleasure inherent in themselves, or as means to the promotion of pleasure and the prevention of pain"; answering the counter charge that the pursuit of pleasure is a goal worthy of swine—mindless beasts whose life is devoted to satisfying the crude appetite for pleasure—Mill elevated his conception of human pleasure to include gratifications of the intellect, imagination, and moral sensibility (*UT*, 7–8).

Mill was a distinguished moral philosopher, but his theory of life suggests that he was a lesser student of the erotic enthrallments motivating fellow humans. This was a fatal flaw that lent credibility to Nietzsche's prophecy of 1887 that psychology was destined to become the discipline that addresses humankind's "fundamental problems," while "philosophers of the future" would be experimenters who gain insight into humankind's fundamental problems by daring to descend to the depths of human experience.[14] Unbeknown to Nietzsche, Freud began this experimental descent one year earlier on 25 April 1886 at Rathausstrasse 7 in Vienna, when he opened the door to his private practice and commenced clinical experiments with hypnosis and suggestion. Having later made the descent to fanciful depths with Freud, Theodor Reik detected the flaw in Mill's theory of life and in 1941, while an apocalyptic struggle was savaging the European continent, Reik mounted a direct assault on the rational philosophers' ivory tower. With his clinical canon sighting moral philosophers from Herbert Spencer to Bertrand Russell, Reik expressed serious reservations about the philosophers' dubious notion that *Homo sapiens* is an animal who seeks pleasure while attempting to avoid pain. Firing a contrary salvo in his published account of masochism, Reik argued unequivocally that human beings may seek pleasure consciously, but in the underworld of human experience, many people not only strive for pain, but also stage their own misery, self-defeat, and personal disaster.

Whatever the predicates of eroticism may be, in the aftermath of Freud, the psychoanalytic revolution, and the ensuing modern psychiatrization of human experience, when human beings are divided against themselves in the fashion of Allen, Diane, Phillipe, and Juliette, they cross the threshold of the mental health clinic and rent some space in the consulting room of a dialogical therapist, as if the clinical consulting room were a sacred place to confess enthrallments with the forbidden, petty misdemeanors, and greater crimes against self and others. In this palace of clinical enchantment, as in religious mansions of old, the Latin *săcer* carries the sense of something sacred, holy, or set apart and *sacrārĭum* refers to a sanctuary where human beings are not only reverenced, but protected from violation.

Often, while offering this protection, dialogical therapists play the part of skilled rhetoricians who effectively translate a patient's sexual experience into a discourse of victimization, the clinical goal of which is to produce a psychological healing that will assuage the guilt and shame arising from an enthrallment with or an involvement in forbidden experience. When I speak of rhetoric in this context, I have in mind Plato's distinction between the art of rhetoric practiced by the person who masters persuasive speech and the art of dialectic practiced by Socrates and other philosophers whose life involved a dedicated quest for truth. Commenting on this important distinction in *Phaedrus*, Socrates maintained that the art of rhetoric has to do with influencing the mind of others by means of words. Socrates also referred to the rhetorician who masters persuasive speech as "the devil's advocate," the critical point of this disparaging reference being that skilled rhetoricians who use words to instill one or another conviction neither know nor search for truth; rather, political orators, officers of the court, and other rhetoricians, present "what will be thought so," since persuasion depends not on truth, but on what is seemingly true and convincing.[15]

By all accounts, rhetorical persuasion is commonly practiced and refined in the mental health clinic; in fact, rhetorical persuasion—"talking people into or out of things," as Freud put it—figured prominently in my treatment of Diane, for she was disturbed by her active role in protracted incest and deeply conflicted about the madding pleasure she received while involved in forbidden experience with her father for many years. In a clinical mind-set when treating incest survivors like Allen and Diane, I am prepared to argue against Plato, insofar as there are times when the art of persuasion has a right employment, particularly in the mental health clinic, where rhetoric is used to do God's work of bringing some good into a god-forsaken world. And who would argue that psychological healing is not one of humankind's greater goods?

NOTES

1. Plato, *Charmides*, trans. Benjamin Jowett, in *Collected Dialogues*, 154a, 155d–e.
2. Jacques Lacan, *The Other Side of Psychoanalysis*, trans. Russell Grigg (New York: W. W. Norton & Company, 2007), 33.
3. Saint Augustine, *The Soliloquies of Saint Augustine*, trans. Thomas F. Gilligan (New York: Cosmopolitan Science & Art Service Co., 1943), 57.
4. Saint Augustine, *Confessions*, trans. R. S. Pine-Coffin (Baltimore: Penguin Books, 1966), 181, 131.
5. Andrea Dworkin, *Intercourse* (New York: Free Press Paperbacks, 1997); cited in the text as *IN*.
6. Georges Bataille, *Erotism, Death and Sensuality*, trans. Mary Dalwood (San Francisco: City Lights Books, 1986); cited in the text as *ER*.
7. Saint Teresa, *The Life of Teresa of Jesus: The Autobiography of St. Teresa of Avila*, ed. and trans. E. Allison Peers (New York: Image Books, 1960); cited in the text as *LT*.
8. Simone de Beauvoir, *The Second Sex*, trans. H. M. Parshley (New York: Alfred A. Knopf, 1971); cited in the text as *SS*.
9. William James, *The Principles of Psychology*, vol. 2 (Cambridge, MA: Harvard University Press, 1981), 1159.
10. Albert Camus, *The Stranger*, trans. Stuart Gilbert (New York: Vintage Books, 1946), 127.
11. Mary Pipher, *Reviving Ophelia* (New York: Ballantine Books, 1995), 13.
12. Joyce McDougall, *Theaters of the Mind: Illusion and Truth on the Psychoanalytic Stage* (New York: Brunner/Mazel Publishers, 1991); cited in the text as *TM*.
13. John Stuart Mill, *Utilitarianism*, ed. George Sher (Indianapolis: Hackett Publishing Company, 1979); cited in the text as *UT*.
14. Friedrich Nietzsche, *Beyond Good and Evil: Prelude to a Philosophy of the Future*, trans. Walter Kaufmann (New York: A Vintage Original, 1966), 31–32, 52.
15. Plato, *Phaedrus*, trans. R. Hackforth, in *Collected Dialogues*, 260a–61a, 271a–72e.

III

ABERRATIONS

8

Anarchism and Ethics

DOGMAS AND DEATH CAMPS

I still have a vivid image of Jacob Bronowski squatting in a pond outside a crematorium at the Auschwitz death camp. Thirty years had passed since the place closed down and Bronowski had not traveled east of Krakow to loiter mindlessly in a pool of putrid water. In fact, he was dressed impeccably in a crisp white shirt and tie and a white handkerchief was folded elegantly in the breast pocket of his finely tailored suit. Suddenly the camera panned back, slowly revealing this eminent scientist crouched low in a pool of sludge that was meandering meaningfully over a shiny pair of shoes that seemed to be spit and polished. As I continued viewing the BBC's masterfully crafted thirteen-part TV series *The Ascent of Man*, this particular episode being the eleventh weekly segment entitled "Knowledge or Certainty," I overheard Bronowski speaking softly, but pointedly: "This is the concentration camp and crematorium at Auschwitz. This is where people were turned into numbers. Into this pond were flushed the ashes of some four million people. And that was not done by gas. It was done by arrogance. It was done by dogma. It was done by ignorance."[1]

This was the articulate voice of an agonistic Socratic man in modern dress, speaking to an estimated two million viewers about the arrogance of ignorance, telling his audience that in modernity, the arrogance of ignorance found a home in the acceptance of seemingly true, widely held, uncritically accepted beliefs that resulted in the premeditated mass murder of millions of undesirables, most notably, Jews, East European Slavs, and homosexuals. But something was amiss! Having become an inveterate nitpicker while growing a philosophic persona during years of scholarly labor, I was unable to accept a few of Bronowski's formulations. After all, the systematic slaughter of millions was done by gas and by ovens in factories of thanatos. Tesch and Stabenow of Hamburg, as well as Degesch of Dessau, having acquired the patent from chemical giant I. G. Farben, supplied lethal Zyklon B crystals to the Auschwitz death camp; while I. A. Topf and Sons, a respected manufacturer of heating equipment in Erfurt, looking to make a nifty profit in mass murder, won the highly competitive bidding to build four crematoria in Oświecim. Clearly, by that pond east of Krakow, not only arrogance and ignorance, but technology, bureaucracy, and human greed went hand in hand with genocide.

Another aspect of Bronowski's presentation that gave me pause was his view that the Auschwitz death camp issued from dogma, for I concluded independently that racial and romantic myth produced the concentration camps and the death camps that dotted the map of Eastern and Western Europe during the late 1930s and 1940s; and I later published this finding in a philosophic essay focused on the blindness of intellectuals who forsook the perennial quest for truth in favor of a celebration of myth.[2] In retrospect, I now realize that Bronowski and I used different concepts to make a fine point about mass murder, but I do not think we had a significant disagreement, for we both were saying that a system of fictive beliefs had not only been accepted by a ruling elite, but seemed to be true in the minds of large numbers of people in the ruling elite's sphere of power and influence. Regarding this daemonic state of affairs, Plato used "dogma" (δόγμα) in references to that which *seems* such and so to someone, or that which *seems* to be the case to certain people. And it may have seemed that Jews were inhuman rats to Hitler and his Nazi thugs. Perhaps it seemed to a society of card-carrying National Socialists that they were surrounded by the sacrificial *Untermenschen* of Nietzsche's daemonic solicitation, the pre-psychotic Nietzsche of 1886, who found it reasonable to write: "A good and healthy aristocracy . . . accepts with a good conscience the sacrifice of untold human beings who, *for its sake*, must be reduced and lowered to incomplete human beings, to slaves, to instruments. . . . Society must *not* exist for society's sake but only as the foundation and scaffolding on which a choice type of being is able to raise itself to its higher task and to a higher state of *being*."[3] But its seeming so did not make it so, even if the powerful proponents of racial hatred were seemingly wise.

Unfortunately, the phantastic business of *seeming*, in conjunction with the profitable businesses of heating equipment and industrial chemicals, coalesced with terrible consequences at the death camp by that pond at Auschwitz. To the SS manning the camp, prisoners seemed to be "shit," in fact, "shit" and its adjuvant, "asshole," were the dehumanizing metaphors used to make the condemned seem like disposable excrement. Foul waste to be disposed of not only with good conscience, but with a sense of decency and honor, if one happened to read Himmler's address to his SS officers at Posen: a confidential address of 1943, in which the chief of the infamous black shirts, a seemingly mild-mannered chicken farmer, identified members of his terrifying police apparatus as "decent fellows" writing "a page of glory in our history" by undertaking the systematic "extermination of the Jewish race."[4] But its seeming that human beings are undesirable shit, or its seeming that cold-blooded murderers are decent fellows, after being conditioned to see and think and feel this way, did not make it so, even if a whole society happened to be inhabited by the kind of rabid certainty that is the lifeblood of bloodthirsty myth, particularly dehumanizing racial myth, as native American Indians or African slaves pirated to colonial America would attest.

I realize that Hitler and the Nazis are a cheap target, in fact, the Fuehrer and Nazi culture have been critically examined, reviled, and exploited ad nauseum, to make a million salient points about one thing or another. But sometimes a cheap target is the best target because it can't hide: it is clear and visible for everyone to see, even if a person happens to be blind. In this case, to some, the Fuehrer seemed to be a great man, to many, he was a phantastic person and he was gifted with enormous power and influence over the minds and behavior of great numbers of people. He could charm the pants off a snake with his hypnotic presentations replete with spellbinding words fair to the ear of throngs of enraptured folk who behaved as if they were ecstatically enthralled in the presence of Merlin the magician, particularly when they heard bewitching words of feral violence. The point is, all this traffic around virulent racial myth that infected the minds of many demonstrated the proposition that men and women who seem to be great may be crazed human beings who have the power to engage in concrete historical action that results in life or death, depending on what side of hateful myth a person happens to be: right or left, yes or no, in or out, either a proponent or a victim of a belief that seems to be true and inviolable.

After comparing Nazi arrogance with the critical sensibility of empirical science, and affirming science as a fallible human enterprise that exposes and corrects its own errors, Bronowski looked long into the camera, as if he were attempting to inhabit and haunt the soul, the spirit, the mind, the psyche, of every viewer. Raising a handful of muck out of the pond in which he squatted, he whispered gravely into the ears of anonymous viewers: "I owe it as a scientist to my friend Leo Szilard, I owe it as a human being to the many members of my family who died at Auschwitz, to stand here by the pond as a survivor and a witness. We have to cure ourselves of the itch for absolute knowledge and power. We have to close the distance between the push-button order and the human act. We have to touch people" (*AM*, 374).

There it was at long last, out in the open. This was great theatre, to say the least, but it was considerably more than a theatrical performance. Dressed to the hilt, crouched low in the shallows of a ghastly pond outside the Nazi's most infamous factory of thanatos, Jacob Bronowski was caught on camera lifting the muddy remains of his beloved family out of the muck and the mire, reminding the human community in the most poignant way of the Socratic distinction between learned ignorance and the arrogance of ignorance: the former accruing to those who realize that uncritically accepted belief is not true knowledge, though it seems so, the latter accruing to those who possess the blind certainty that passionately held opinion and phantastic belief is truth.

Encouraging viewers to sustain a humbling awareness of human imperfection, of flaws and fallibility, Bronowski scorned dogmatic belief and the illusion of certainty that closes the mind and clears the way for collective tragedies of a monstrous kind. Imploring viewers to honor the learned ignorance that fosters tolerance, the scientific gentleman squatted in that muddy pond in a dramatic effort to leave his viewers with an indelible impression of the need to wed the will-to-power to a critical understanding of the magnitude of power and its profound, rarely discernible, potentially disastrous effect on the lives of people. Many of whom, I should add, like the men, women, and children who seemed to be shit and went to the ovens, are simply caught-up in the daily grind: a contemporary version of hunting and gathering that keeps a questionable species alive.

I previously stated my view that Aristotle made a big mistake when he argued in a sightless way that "reason more than anything else *is* man." Viewing things within the clinical confessional, this is another dogma, a ranking dogma of philosophers at home in the dominant rationalist tradition. For clinical confessions reveal that irrationality is a free-floating radical that identifies a crazed species of men and women whose ambiguous gifts make the species seem like an evolutionary error. Perhaps Jacob Bronowski was attuned to this crazed notion and that explains why he concluded his commentary on the ascent of man with the following cautionary refrain: "Our actions as adults, as decision makers, as human beings, are mediated by values, which I interpret as general strategies in which we balance opposing impulses. . . . The ascent of man is always teetering in the balance. There is always a sense of uncertainty, whether when man lifts his foot for the next step it is really going to come down pointing ahead" (*AM*, 436). This important question of values and opposing impulses, this sense of uncertainty in making decisions and taking steps that could lead forward or backward, brings me to the importance of being earnest about dogmas of the therapeutic and clinical ethics in postmodernity.

DOGMAS OF THE THERAPEUTIC

When I refer to dogmas of the therapeutic, I have in mind an inherited pantheon of normative rules and regulations that not only *seem* to be true or valid, but also *seem* to be inviolable. Collectively, these seemingly true and inviolable rules are the sacred commandments of the clinical profession: they are handed down from generation to generation uncritically, they usually are conveyed to novice clinicians by authoritative superiors during internship or basic training, and the imperious way in which they are conveyed, the tone of voice that declares this is incontestable truth, leaves no doubt that the dogmatic commandments must be obeyed at all costs. Some rules and regulations are more important than others, just as there are greater and lesser deities in the pantheon of Greek gods and goddesses. Violation of the most important rules may result in ostracism by peers, loss of professional license to practice and, depending on the severity of a therapist's moral conscience, guilt and shame accompanied by self-censure. Violation of lesser rules may result in a loss of income as a result of a noticeable loss of perspicacious patients who smelled a rat.

The proscription against sexual relations with patients is the third dogma of the therapeutic. Freud revealed his inheritance of the third dogma in his discussion of the transference of intense feelings to the phantastic person of the physician, when he wrote presumptively: "It is out of the question for us to yield to the patient's demands deriving from the transference" (*IL*, 443). But Freud was not alone, in fact, untold legions of post-Freudian therapists inherited variants of Hippocrates' (460–377 B.C.) solemn oath that in the clinical situation, sexual relationship of any sort with male and female patients is forbidden. Profoundly influenced by this historical dogma when he wrote his *Theory of Psychoanalytic Technique*, the esteemed teacher and psychoanalyst Karl Menninger instructed generations of readers to view the analysand's erotization of the clinic as an immoral and obstructive resistance to treatment. Writing authoritatively, as we have seen, Menninger also maintained that if a therapist were to yield to a patient's erotization of the clinical situation, this would uniformly harm, rather than help, the patient.

The second dogma commands that clinicians do no harm to patients in their clinical care. Practically everyone knows that this dogma rests in the ancient Hippocratic oath—a sacred oath of service upon which every reputable clinician stands in principle, if not in clinical practice.

The first dogma, preeminent among its peers, is so fixed and immutable that it rarely is mentioned, because it is the polestar of the clinician, as well as the logical foundation, the raison d'être, of clinical practice in its manifold forms and varieties. I am referring to the widely held assumption that life is richer, more valuable, and better than death. Alternately put, life is good and it should be affirmed and embraced; death is evil and it should be repulsed and defeated. Consistent with this dogma and the universal injunction to flee from death, in his groundbreaking postmodern study of the birth of the clinic, including the dialogical clinic that begot the cultural character called "Freudian man," Foucault laid claim to the notion that humankind's "obstinate relation to death prescribes to the universal" experience of death "its singular face, and lends to each individual the power of being heard forever"—the power of being heard, I would add, in the mental health clinic.[5]

In the past, the first dogma has been challenged by those who believe that in severe cases in which life-functioning is compromised irrecoverably, whether death is imminent or not, the personal choice to terminate one's life in order to achieve death with dignity is the most desirable option. Interestingly, in the classic version of the Hippocratic oath—the original version that has physicians swearing to Apollo, god of medicine and healing, and Asclepius, physician-son of Apollo, to whom the snake-entwined rod or caduceus is attributed—a newly anointed physician promises neither to give a deadly drug, nor to even suggest this sort of remedy. In the modern version, however, there is a dramatic change of mind: a modern medical *metanoia*. While promising to "tread with care in matters of life and death," and being thankful for the power to save the lives of one's fellows, the power to take lives is not only openly acknowledged and conceived as an "awesome responsibility," but the healer swears to use this power with "great humbleness" and "awareness of . . . frailty."[6]

Regarding the philosophic point at hand, in antiquity, after receiving a death sentence from his Athenian jurors, Socrates took the first dogma to task during a quiet conversation with jurors who voted for his acquittal. Acknowledging that the death he faced seemed to be the worst evil visited on humans, Socrates suggested that death might actually be a blessing, such that the widely held belief that death is evil might be mistaken. Perhaps death is a wonderful, sound, dreamless sleep, he mused imaginatively, or it might be a journey to Hades, where he would experience the great joy of speaking with Homer or critically examining Sisyphus (*AP*, 40d–41c).[7] Whether Socrates was correct or not in his rejection of the dogma that death is evil, only time will tell. Who knows, the result may be different for each of us. But this is precisely the point: we do not know, although it seems that we do.

In spite of his disdain for uncritically accepted opinion and belief, Socrates was not exempt from entanglement in a spider's web of dogma that has not only survived the proverbial test of time, but has survived with the honor accorded human virtues. The proposition that "the unexamined life is not worth living" is a founding dogma of the Socratic mystique: this golden rule of Socratism is acquired by every college kid straight off in Philosophy 101 (*AP*, 38a). This golden rule may seem to be true or valid at first sight, but I can easily imagine a neurosurgeon who never spent one moment examining his life, given clinical preoccupations or a natural disinclination to engage in self-reflection. Yet he saves lives in the operating theatre every day: countless lives throughout his own unexamined life. In this situation, would we be willing to argue that this devoted surgeon's life is not worth living? Perhaps not, due to the fact that his unexamined life is devoted to fulfilling the life-affirming mandate of the first dogma; in fact, this surgeon seems to be a soldier of life stationed in the clinical trenches, where he is engaged in a daily struggle to defeat death in life.

Clearly, there are greater and lesser dogmas and we are dogged by some dogmas more than others. Identifying and confronting dogma, one's own as well as the dogmas of others, is tricky business. One thing is certain, after Eddie took his plunge from an apartment window, I hoped that Socrates was correct in his critical assessment of the first dogma, such that Eddie was in Hades engaged in enlightening conversation with Sisyphus. But inside, deep within my limbic brain, with neither critical thought nor hesitation, I felt that by losing his grip on life, Eddie lost something richer, more valuable, and better than death. This feeling was automatic, involuntary, instinctive, due to the fact that I am genetically programmed for survival and I worship at the altar of the first dogma. Every fiber of my being is wrapped in the first dogma and in a real way, my clinical life is devoted to bequeathing this dogma to patients in one form or another, notwithstanding the fact that my knowledge of death amounts to nothing. Unless I am mistaken, this is an excellent example of what Thomas Szasz was referring to when he stated boldly that "psychotherapeutic interventions are not medical but moral in character," that the bountiful variety of so-called psychotherapies are "illusory, fake, or metaphorical," that psychotherapy, properly conceived as a rhetorical interaction, is "secular ethics."[8]

In fine, a dogma is a normative proposition that seems to be true and inviolable; however, like the tip of an oar in the water that seems to be bent, but actually is refracted, its seeming bent, doesn't make it bent, although our eyes are deceiving us to the degree that we would bet the rent on the oar being bent. Wittgenstein had similar notions. In fact, in his philosophic work, Wittgenstein was dogged by dogma and the issue of unjustified certainty in the human estate. His last book, a first draft of notes written during the final year of his life, was titled *On Certainty*. In this remarkable little book that recorded brilliant conversations with himself, Wittgenstein clearly was engaged in the philosophic therapy he developed in the aftermath of Freud's psychiatrization of culture, mostly trying to get philosophic thought disorders out of his own system (see appendix). In some places, like the following, he appeared to be speaking about dogma directly: "From its *seeming* to me—or to everyone—to be so, it doesn't follow that it is so. . . . Certainty is . . . a tone of voice in which one declares how things are, but one does not infer from the tone of voice that one is justified. . . . I did not get my picture of the world by satisfying myself of its correctness; nor do I have it because I am satisfied of its correctness. No: it is the inherited background against which I distinguish between true and false" (*OC*, #2, #30, #94).[9]

For example, I once participated in a mandatory clinical in-service for therapists working in the hospital's inpatient and outpatient psychiatric service. This particular in-service was offered to train therapists in techniques to deal with unruly patients who might assault them. All of the techniques being taught were defensive, none were offensive, for the training was premised on the unspoken, uncritically accepted second dogma of the therapeutic: clinicians must never harm patients. This normative rule seemed to be valid without exception, so valid and inviolable that the rule was implied, rather than stated, and simply accepted by everyone present at the training session, with neither thought nor hesitation. Not too crazy about dogmas; not inclined to travel mindlessly down a road given by those who have gone this way before, without inspecting the road for potholes or questioning the direction; not inclined to play footsie while I am being assaulted; I did the honest thing by telling the unvarnished truth. "Anyone who assaults me is going out the window," I stated abruptly, in an emotionally reactive, testosterone-enriched response that left no doubt about my personal boundaries or my readiness to react offensively to an assault on my person.

My boorish attitude was frowned upon by fellow clinicians, male and female alike, all of whom couldn't conceive of harming a patient even if they became victims of a patient assault. We lived in different worlds and the simple truth is, I may not have belonged in this good company of clinicians given the person I am and where I came from. I mean, when a person comes of age in the Appalachian hollow discovered and settled by old, cantankerous Ebenezer Slocum, he acquires a predisposition to do whatever is required to survive, physically and emotionally. The point is, I have never been able to accept the obligation of allowing myself to be harmed in order to spare a person harming me from being harmed by me.

Of course I am blowing this whole thing out of proportion because the dogma prohibiting harm to patients really has to do with causing direct or indirect harm to patients during the application of a clinical treatment, whatever mode or manner of clinical treatment it happens to be. It is an excellent oath of service, one that I uphold and actually live by every day. Still, a dogma is a dogma and I am not crazy about dogmas, even if openly rejecting a dogma meant forsaking a job that is a darn good substitute for tooling out in the state of nature with a club and killing a wild boar to put food on the table in the manner of testosterone-enriched ancestors: the hunters who copulated with the gatherers after bringing the tasty wild boar back to the campsite and passing it around. Unfortunately, my emotional reaction made me seem like a wild boar, but I remained on the job in the hospital's version of the clinical trenches struggling against the *déjà-là* of death, although I also remained constant in my disdain for dogma amid a discreet coppice of neurons, dendrites, and synapses, so that the legal department at the hospital, responsible for liability issues resulting from harm to patients, never realized what chemicals were popping or what the invisible ghost in my machine was capable of plotting.

Functioning clinically as a philosophically minded pragmatic existential therapist who questions dogma instinctively, while seizing every opportunity to benefit patients by using clinical enchantments strategically, I am mindful of the power and the influence of dialogical therapists. I am also driven to help patients heal emotional wounds, affirm life, create authentic selves, and generally flourish on the planet, while raging against death in its biological and psychological manifestations. Committed to this vocation and these clinical goals by choice, I am not committed to accepting dogmas of the therapeutic blindly or unquestioningly, however sacred these clinical commandments might be. Nevertheless, I am a psychological man, my patients have the power of being heard forever, and I choose to honor an implied professional contract that obligates me to do everything in my power to safeguard patients from harm, while I am involved in the fallible human act of providing a professional service in a mental health clinic that may become enchanted.

I would like to think that this is the rational decision-making of a dedicated dialogical therapist who is playing a minor role in the evolutionary drama that placed a biological organism with the capacity to learn in the unique position of encouraging rational intellect to override the genetically wired reflex driving the behavior of insects, turtles, rabbits, rats, horses, chickens, chimpanzees, and snakes. Unfortunately, perfecting this business of self-mastery and rational decision-making based upon learning is easier said than done. This is why we have conversations about dogmas and death camps, as well as critiques of dialogical therapy: to stimulate critical thinking, to bear witness to attitudes and behavior that are life-affirming and life-denying—essentially, to remember who we are and who we might become. With this in mind, contra Wittgenstein, it falls to me to say that something *seeming* to a person, or to everyone, to be true, often justifies the conclusion that it is true, however mistaken this phantastic conclusion may be. In fact, a certain tone of voice declaring how things are indicates unequivocally that a person feels justified, and sometimes, when a human being feels justified, anything goes!

CLINICAL ANARCHISM

From time to time, while functioning as an opportunistic existential therapist who attempts to manage clinical ethics in the enchanted clinic, I have entertained the possibility of justifying a responsible anarchism that keeps clinical options open, while being neither ruthless nor unscrupulous. I am using this language purposefully with the estimable Einstein in mind, because in his famous thought experiments leading first to Special Relativity Theory and later to the more encompassing General Theory of Relativity, Einstein was the model of an anarchistic scientist who thought against the inherited Galilean and Newtonian dogmas of his time. In 1949, responding to critics in the wake of his enormous earlier success, Einstein allowed that a scientist must appear to be "a type of unscrupulous opportunist" to rational philosophers; and in the richly imaginative, pragmatic mind of Einstein this was true and perfectly acceptable.[10] Later, during the 1970s, after acquiring this language and learning from Einstein, the anarchistic philosopher of science Paul Feyerabend argued contentiously that "successful *participation*" in empirical science "is possible only for a ruthless opportunist who is not tied to any particular philosophy and who adopts whatever procedure seems to fit the occasion," rather than remaining restricted by the inherited, commonly accepted, simple-minded, "stultifying" rules and procedures of a "puritanical rationalist"; alternately put, anarchism is better suited than rational method to generate progress in scientific inquiry, accordingly, participants in scientific inquiry are well advised to keep all options open and to work with reference to the first principle of anarchism: "Anything goes."[11]

In the mental health clinic, while actively engaged in therapeutic dialogue with patients whose lives are compromised by one or another disabling disorder, I am not focused on the methods and presuppositions of scientific inquiry; rather, I am focused on the life and death, the health and well-being, the flourishing and the withering, of human beings who have morbid symptoms, concrete problems, implicit trust in their therapist, and the capacity to become charmed or spellbound by fair words. Faithful to an implied contract that obligates me to perform a clinical service in exchange for a monetary fee, some form of healing—a remission of symptoms, a release of petrified potential, reconciliation with self and humanness—some salutary effect on a patient's life, remains the indefeasible goal of pragmatic existential therapy as I conceive it. Toward that end, every dogma of the therapeutic can be challenged—every rule, every method, every presupposition—but I stop short of saying "anything goes," this principle of clinical action appearing to be the anarchistic ethical stance of a strategic therapist who once openly confessed: "Therapeutic work becomes unpredictable—sometimes the therapist is part of the system she creates, and sometimes she is alone with the knowledge that there are no rules, no rites, no obligations. There is nothing but liberty because there are no rules" (*SL*, xv).[12] In fairness to the author of these remarks and with great respect for her honest confession and authentic ethical motives, she followed this anarchistic proclamation with the suggestion that dialogical "therapy may be nothing more than a search for a moral way of living."

During the early 1990s, when these anarchistic remarks were first published, the nihilistic realities of postmodern culture were being digested and processed far and wide: nihilistic realities, I should add, involving the withering of objectivity and truth, the once-powerful king and queen of clinical and philosophic life. Mind you, cultural nihilism, particularly a widespread critique and revaluation of truth, was prophesied by the iconoclastic Nietzsche, who took a venomous bite out of Socratic man, the same cultural character who had been seeking, but failing to find, wisdom, truth, and the best possible state of his collective soul for more than two millennia. Importantly, while the hysterical Nietzsche raged against Socratism, due to the loss of meaningful myth resulting from the perennial quest for truth, he experienced a remarkable foreboding. Divided against himself—at once a seeker of truth combating the lover of myth, and a needy lover of myth at war with the seeker of truth—Nietzsche prophesied that when traditional values are disvalued we shall discover what value these values really had.[13] Oftentimes, to make the point clearly, we do not realize the real value of what we have until we lose it. This applies to all sorts of persons, places, and things, from the quest for truth to mom and dad.

More to the point of searching clinical anarchism, in the modern era there were historical precursors of an anarchistic ethic built upon the guiding principle that there are neither rules nor obligations, such that anything goes. This is particularly evident in the risky existential thinking of Jean-Paul Sartre, a French literary philosopher largely responsible for bringing atheistic existentialism to flower during the twentieth century. In 1946, to be precise, seven years after the death of Freud, but only one year after the Gestapo quit Paris and the Fuehrer had his comeuppance with the Fates and the Furies in a bunker in Berlin, Sartre gave a scandalous public lecture during which he compared morality to art and moral choice to the painting of a creative artwork. There are no a priori rules for a painter to follow when creating a work of art, Sartre declared, no previously established aesthetic values, no previously defined images to make, no artworks an artist is told he ought to paint, no irresponsible paintings that an artist creates; furthermore, in view of the fact that creative artists are never reproached for their failure to follow preestablished rules when they paint an artwork of their own free choice and invention, in an existential ethic of action and self-commitment, the creative person who paints a normative picture of himself, thereby choosing a course of action that identifies a type of humanity, should not be subject to criticism, for in the aesthetic realm of art and morality we are dealing with an artist's free creation and invention, and in morality as in art, there is nothing but liberty (*EH*, 305–6).[14]

At first sight, Sartre's analogy may seem harmless, for he seemed to be another insufferable philosopher living in an ivory tower divorced from the real world: living by wiling away his time talking about seemingly harmless works of art while the great ocean of empirical truth lay before him. Ultimately, however, the ivory tower has purchase on reality and Sartre had delivered a dangerous public lecture about lived experience, moral choice, and existential commitment, raising important Socratic questions such as, "How should I live?" in the human community as a moral agent among fellow humans. Fortunately, in introductory logic classes, students learn to be wary of analogies, such as Sartre's analogy between moral choice and freely created artworks: a particularly dangerous analogy that runs the real risk of life and limb beyond the ivory tower.

Regarding his mental status and the acuity of his thinking, it is noteworthy that Sartre seemed oblivious to the palpitations of art criticism when he claimed obtusely that artists are never censured for failing to follow preestablished rules. Is it possible that a war-weary French philosopher proposing the analogical intercourse of art and lived morality forgot that the exquisite artworks of pioneering French Impressionists—Monet, Renoir, Pissarro, Morisot, and Cassatt, to name a few—were rejected by the authoritative jury of the Beaux Arts Salon for reasons both technical and moral, as with Manet's large, scandalous *Le Déjeuner sur l'Herbe*, featuring not an idealized classical Venus, but a realistically painted young nude female not only enjoying a picnic with two fully clothed men, but also staring out at the spectator provocatively, drawing him in, under her influence, with a slight grin? After being rejected by the uncompromising Salon, Emperor Napoleon III responded to the nasty public outcry of artists and press by ordering an official 1863 exhibition of these rejected artworks called "Salon des Refuses" or Show of Rejected Artists. Say what you will about aesthetic sensibilities and preestablished values, but this showing did not go well for the artists who were lampooned and lambasted from many quarters. But I think we can forgive this lapse of Sartre and reserve further comment about art history for polite parlor conversation at some future date and time, because there are more important issues to address, as well as lives and limbs at stake.

If I take Sartre's comparison of art and morality seriously, as I should, because it is in the public domain and it has influenced human beings both in theory and in clinical practice—in the recent past, unfolding in the creditable postmodern view of narrative psychology, that a dialogical therapist's clinical interpretations are comparable to the creation of a work of art—it now seems as if Sartre had succumbed to a debilitating *folie* while working against the Nazis in the French resistance. If not a strange madness, the existential philosopher seemed to have forgotten the ride of the Valkyries his countrymen had recently taken when he asserted that a moral agent is like a creative painter, "moral choice is comparable to the construction of a work of art," and works of art are "never" referred to as "irresponsible" (*EH*, 305–6). Peering at the world from a safe perch while Europe was slowly waking from a barbarous nightmare, Sartre stretched his dangerous analogy to the end, observing coolly that we are unable to judge paintings until they are finished and the same creative license obtains with the free invention of morality. In fine, "we never speak of a work of art that is irresponsible. It is the same on the plane of morality. There is this in common between art and morality, that in both we have to do with creation and invention. We cannot decide *a priori* what it is that should be done. . . . It is therefore absurd to reproach us for irresponsibility in our choice" (*EH*, 306).

Putting flesh on the bones of Sartre's existential ethic, an anarchistic ethic in which anything goes, it follows logically that the creation of Nazi morality was like the creation of a work of art, insofar as both Nazi morality and an artwork are freely created inventions. Like the fine impressionist art of Monet and Renoir, Hitler's fine Nazi morality was not an irresponsible morality because there were no a priori rules or preestablished values for the Fuehrer to follow. For this reason, it would be absurd for us to reproach Hitler for the murderous moral choices and genocidal commitments that identified a type of humanity to be lived by others; in fact, because Nazi morality was freely created, it would be absurd for us to accuse Hitler of being irresponsible in constructing a moral culture responsible for savaging six million people, more or less. In the end, like the exquisite artwork of Monet and Renoir, the exquisite morality of Hitler could not have been judged until it was finished, and as everyone now knows, that means we could not have judged Nazi morality after one million were dead, or two million, or three million, because the killing was simply not finished: the last Jew, or Slav, or homosexual was not yet dead!

In truth, I am painting Sartre in the worst possible light, having learned from the pioneering French Impressionists that momentary changes of light are crucial to our shifting impressions of self, world, and other. More importantly, I have characterized myself as a pragmatic existential therapist; as a result, I am responsible for understanding and critically evaluating existential literature and learning. On this head, it falls to me to say that when Sartre was seeing things in the glistening sunlight glancing brightly off the azure water of the Seine around noon at Argenteuil, he valued freedom above all else, and in the existential philosophy he identified as godless, liberty was his god: the a priori value upon which his existential ethic rested, his misleading proclamation regarding the absence of a priori values notwithstanding. Freedom was to Sartre what fanatical fascism was to Hitler. But it wasn't just freedom for the individual that Sartre was hawking, rather, following the apocalyptic war and the end of the occupation of France, Sartre was selling freedom for humankind itself. "Freedom," he declared, is "the foundation of all values. . . . The actions of men of good faith have, as their ultimate significance, the quest of freedom itself. . . . In thus willing freedom, we discover that it depends entirely upon the freedom of others, and . . . the freedom of others depends upon our own. . . . I cannot make liberty my aim unless I make that of others equally my aim" (*EH*, 307–8).

The problem is, there are powerful men and women who are not people of good faith. But that is inaccurate. I mean to say that one person's good faith is not the same as another person's good faith. And that's the rub! When good faiths collide as often they do, you get Belsen, Bosnia, Beirut, Afghanistan, and Iraq: freedom for some, death for others. A death of others, I should add, that is freely created, never finished, and always morally justified by decent fellows.

I have previously introduced Nietzsche's hubristic ode to fascism and as I write, although my ears are abuzz with tinnitus, in inner space, I am able to hear Beethoven's glorious Ninth Symphony, the Choral Symphony, the Ode to Joy, as Nietzsche talks about the "fundamental faith" of "a good and healthy aristocracy" being centered on the elevation of a "choice type of being," by means of "the sacrifice of untold human beings who . . . must be reduced and lowered to incomplete human beings, to slaves, to instruments." Although Beethoven was deafened like Eddie, I imagine him conducting the orchestra miraculously, as Nietzsche follows these fanatical fascistic ideas with the overarching idea that "aristocratic morality is intolerant" in the education of the young, in the treatment of women, and in penal laws regarding deviants; moreover, the intolerance of the aristocracy is not only secured by "hardness," but "intolerance itself [is] a virtue"—a virtue the good and healthy aristocracy will call "justice."[15]

When the music stops, as it always does, if you doubt for one moment that daemonic ideas like those of Nietzsche and Sartre have a direct impact on culture and on human lives, it is worthwhile comparing Nietzsche's rhetoric with the rhetoric of Erich Koch, Reich commissar of the Ukraine, who declared in 1943: "We are the Master Race and must govern hard but *just* [italics mine]. . . . We are a master race, which must remember that the lowliest German worker is racially and biologically a thousand times more valuable than the population here."[16] Now compare the aestheticism driving Sartre's modern existential ethic with the aestheticism driving a narrative psychologist's postmodern view that (a) clinical interpretations are aesthetic experiences, and (b) a dialogical therapist is a creative artist who finds the accuracy or historical truth of the patient's story irrelevant to its clinical impact, in the same way that queries regarding the historical truth of a painting would be irrelevant to an appreciation of the painting's beauty. According to Spence:

> It may be useful to think of an interpretation as being a certain kind of aesthetic experience as opposed to being an utterance that is either (historically) true or false. . . . Truth, within certain limits, is actually irrelevant to an aesthetic experience. . . . The historical truth of the [clinical] interpretation is not necessarily relevant to its clinical impact. . . . Once we have moved into an aesthetic domain, it becomes less important to ask about the historical truth of the [clinical] interpretation, just as we would hardly think of asking about the historical "truth" of a painting. . . . The artistic model, then, is one alternative to the archaeological approach. We no longer search for historical accuracy but consider the interpretation in terms of its aesthetic appeal.[17]

To put a fine gloss on this lengthy reference to Sartre, his anarchistic existential ethic is a dangerous modern aestheticism: not the type of moral agency I would be comfortable teaching my children, your children, or any children in my charge, given my understanding of the fact that I am responsible for wiring in these minds, fundamental cognitive and emotional predispositions toward self, world, and others. In retrospect, I have taught Sartre to privileged college students and to condemned inmates caged in a maximum security prison, while engaging these disparate student bodies in a critical examination of the tenuous relationship of freedom *and* responsibility. When push came to shove, I concluded that Sartre's existential ethic was a radical proposal of ethical freedom, so long as the moral picture freely created and chosen by any man, woman, or child, is also chosen for humankind, as if a crazed psychopath actually cared about the fate of a fellow human or the fate of humankind (*EH*, 291). But ask yourself if you would actually teach Sartre's existential ethic to children. Would you really send your children into the world with a clear conscience knowing that their minds were informed by the authoritative claim that there are no irresponsible moral choices? This is not a philosophic argument, rather, it is an acid test of ideas, call it an imaginary thought experiment that envisions and tests the existential implications of ideas: the unfolding of ideas in action and the consequences of these enactments, not in theory, but in the real human world of the daily grind.

For the sake of argument, if I grant that there are neither rules nor obligations in the mental health clinic, I shall also argue that this anarchistic assault on clinical norms is trivially true. After all, we are the reflexively conscious, intellective animal burdened with the task of creating the images and the values that define the moral universe in which we want to live; and if I follow the lead of well-intentioned pragmatic philosophers who argue that there are better or worse values, better or worse images, better or worse moral beliefs—let us say better or worse rules, rites, and obligations—I shall regard some values as better than others because over time, they seem to be indispensable for human survival and for human flourishing.[18] For example, a rule or a law stating that we ought to do whatever we can to enable human beings to survive and flourish—say a law that promotes life, liberty, and the pursuit of happiness—seems considerably better than a law that promotes and facilitates the construction of gas chambers and crematoria to kill and turn to ash the remains of millions of innocent people the dominant majority perceives as subhuman and undesirable: something akin to shit or rats. The former rule or law affirms life to the greatest degree, the latter is a life-destructive lapse into barbarism.

I realize that my existential ethic places a cardinal value on life itself, although I am unable to justify it, except to say, if we do not value life itself, there is little else to value. This is "bedrock," this is where "my spade is turned," as Wittgenstein would say when justifications regarding obedience to a rule are exhausted. Still, it should not escape the reader's attention that turning a spade in this direction and subsequently spreading the news to credulous humans is the way we create and embrace dogma. Yet, if death is affirmed as a cardinal value, widely chosen as a form of life, and willed to become a universal law, to use a Kantian turn of phrase later appropriated and reworked by Sartre, it follows logically that in the long run, there will be no one left to affirm anything as good or true or beautiful, however madded and perverse these interpretations may be.

In the final analysis, if moral images are human creations, then the problem for agonistic therapists searching for a moral way of life may be the problem of learning to distinguish life-affirming from life-destructive moral paintings, while committing ourselves to the pursuit of life-affirming values as a form of clinical life. Unfortunately, when distinguishing values that are life-affirming from values that are life-destructive, there may be wide disagreement over cases. After all, one person's spiritual is another person's diabolical and developing a keen eye for rules, rites, and obligations that withstand rational criticism, while facilitating the survival and flourishing of the clinician and clinic patients, is one of the challenges involved in undertaking the difficult work of becoming a moral agent. This brings me back to the curious notion that dialogical therapy may be nothing more than a search for a moral way of living.

One problem with this particular moral quest is that it is currently informed by the nihilism infecting the hysterical discourse of postmodernism. Focused on this insidious disease like a surgical laser cutting to the core of a malignant tumor, postmodern critic Jean Baudrillard maintained insightfully that we are experiencing the catastrophic death of rationality. Whether we are aware of this metastatic condition or not, on Baudrillard's account, we are not only "witnessing a type of absolute liberty," involving "disaffection, disobligation, [and] disenchantment," we are also being conditioned to gradually assimilate "the interchangeability of previously contradictory or dialectically opposed terms," thereby mindlessly incorporating and learning to exist with reference to,

> the . . . interchangeability of . . . the true and the false in every media message; of the useful and the useless at the level of objects; and of nature and culture at every level of meaning. All the great humanist criteria of value, all the values of a civilization of moral, aesthetic, and practical judgment, vanish in our system of images and signs. Everything becomes undecidable. This is the characteristic of . . . the principle of neutralization and indifference. This is . . . not the brothel of prostitution but the brothel of substitution and interchangeability.[19]

Participating in this widespread historical process that results in the death of rationality, while psychologizing within the brothel of interchangeability, the agonistic author of the search for a moral way of living stated that in her clinical practice: "Contradictions are not experienced as mutually exclusive. The real and the imaginary, the good and the bad, the communicable and the incommunicable are all the same" (*SL*, xv). Now it might be the wiser course to avoid using these important words if one insists on using them in a way that obscures rather than enlightens. I mean, if a person actually believes the real and the imaginary, as well as the good and the bad, are the same, these words have lost discriminating function, practical use, and intelligibility. Moreover, it would not take a genius to understand that if this union of opposites had currency in daily practice, it would warrant Freud's conclusion that humankind is suffering from a collective neurosis: a clinical conclusion consistent with Nietzsche's moral philosophic view that the earth is a madhouse![20]

If it is reasonable to conceive words as tools, then words have a function, like tools in a toolbox: they are used to perform certain tasks enabling us to get on with the business of life. I use a hammer for certain tasks and I use a screwdriver for others, and I would be up against it on the job site if I thought a hammer and a screwdriver were the same, particularly when I tried to use a screwdriver to pound nails, or a hammer to turn a screw around its axis. More to the point, if I lived in a world in which I had been educated to believe that the good and the bad are the same, I might have congratulated Diane's father for successfully incesting his twelve-year-old daughter, incest being good, the words "good" and "bad" being the same. Of course your disagreement would have no merit, for there would be no basis for discriminating judgment, good and bad simply are the same. If I said "good" to incest and you said "bad," we would look at one another blankly and both of us would say "whatever!" for the terms "good" and "bad" would have no intelligible function in our language or in our normative judgments, in fact, moral judgment might cease—something similar to what we are now experiencing cross-culturally, although oftentimes we fail to see it.

Regarding Diane's father, rather than throwing him in jail, I would throw him a party, for this good man had sex with his kid successfully for years on end, managing to derive a lot of pleasure from the experience he initiated by putting a loaded pistol to his daughter's head. This is another example of good behavior to add to the tally of coequal good and bad, including the good deed of betraying Diane to her mother, making Diane appear to be the responsible perpetrator who seduced her father. But good sexual perpetrators are similar to bad sexual perpetrators. It's all the same! Of course, if Diane's mother were thinking clearly and understood that the good and the bad are the same, rather than disconnecting with a daughter who was sexually active with her husband for years on end, she would have praised her daughter, not only for perfecting the *ars erotica* at such an early age, but also for doing such good work in bed with her husband. Perhaps she would have asked her daughter for some lessons in the erotic arts so that she could please her good man as well, thereby taking concrete practical steps to insure that she remained in his good graces.

By the way, if future dialogical therapists are educated to believe that "the real and the imaginary" are the same, that it makes no difference whether they use "real" or "imaginary" during a therapy session when they are engaged in clinical dialogue with one of my terrified patients, who happened to believe that snakes were crawling all over the floor ready to strike her legs, before writhing their way to her thighs and chest and head, they are free to tell this patient the snakes are real, for real and imaginary are the same! Once again, the acid test of this hysterical nonsense is: Would you teach this to your children? Would you actually teach your child that the good and the bad are the same, that the real and the imaginary are the same?

I realize that I am ridiculing others and being ridiculous myself and this may not redound to my favor. But these are daemonic ideas that happen to be part of a hyper-enlightened world in the making. This is a postmodern world, according to one moral philosopher, in which "we have —very largely, if not entirely—lost our comprehension, both theoretical and practical, of morality."[21] Mind you, this is the same moral philosopher who argued contentiously that therapists are unable to engage in moral debate, insofar as the clinical goal of securing the well-being of patients is given in advance and outside the scope of critical thinking, the sole issue for therapists being the manipulative means used to achieve this measurable end. To a great extent, I sometimes think Alasdair MacIntyre's conclusion is valid. I would only add the thought that if I read the postmodern condition correctly, what we risk losing during the twenty-first century is not only our comprehension of morality, but rational comprehension itself.

When I speak this way, I have in mind the insidious nihilism currently infecting the mental health clinic, as well as other cultural institutions. "Nihilism" is a term derived from the Latin *nĭhil*, the simple meaning of which is "nothing." Used in clinical reference, I am suggesting that Freud's view of the therapeutic relationship—his final view that this important clinical relationship is based on "a love of truth" and "a recognition of reality," such that the therapeutic relationship "precludes any kind of sham and deceit"—has been negated and replaced by an aberrant normative picture of the clinical relationship in which truth and reality count for nothing (*TI*, 248). But let me pause to show you exactly what I mean.

NOTES

1. Jacob Bronowski, *The Ascent of Man* (Boston: Little, Brown and Company, 1973), 374; cited in the text as *AM*.
2. Carl P. Ellerman, "Searching for Thomas Mann: A Parable of Myth and Truth," *The Journal of Value Inquiry* 31 (1997): 528.
3. Friedrich Nietzsche, *Beyond Good and Evil: Prelude to a Philosophy of the Future*, trans. Walter Kaufmann (New York: A Vintage Original, 1966), 202.
4. Heinrich Himmler cited in William L. Shirer, *The Rise and Fall of the Third Reich* (New York: Simon and Schuster, 1960), 1259.
5. Michel Foucault, *The Birth of the Clinic: An Archaeology of Medical Perception*, trans. A. M. Sheridan Smith (New York: Vintage Books, 1975), 197.
6. Louis Lasagna, "Modern Version of the Hippocratic Oath," *Definition of Hippocratic Oath*, www.MedicineNet.com (accessed 5 April 2009).
7. Plato, *Socrates' Defense (Apology)*, trans. Hugh Tredennick, in *Collected Dialogues*; cited in the text as *AP*.
8. Thomas S. Szasz, *The Myth of Psychotherapy: Mental Healing as Religion, Rhetoric, and Repression* (Garden City, NY: Anchor Books, 1978), xvii, 4, 8.
9. Ludwig Wittgenstein, *On Certainty*, ed. G. E. M. Anscombe and G. H. von Wright, trans. Denis Paul and G. E. M. Anscombe (New York: Harper Torchbooks, 1972); cited in the text as *OC*.
10. Albert Einstein, "Reply to Criticism," trans. Paul Arthur Schilpp, in *Albert Einstein: Philosopher-Scientist*, vol. 2, ed. Paul Arthur Schilpp, *The Library of Living Philosophers*, vol. 7 (La Salle, IL: Open Court Classics, 1970), 684.
11. Paul Feyerabend, *Against Method: Outline of an Anarchistic Theory of Knowledge* (London: Verso, 1984), 18, 20, 25, 28.

12. Cloe Madanes, *Sex, Love, and Violence: Strategies for Transformation* (New York: W. W. Norton & Company, 1990); cited in the text as *SL*.

13. Friedrich Nietzsche, *The Will to Power*, ed. Walter Kaufmann, trans. Walter Kaufmann and R. J. Hollingdale (New York: A Vintage Giant, 1968), 4.

14. Jean-Paul Sartre, "Existentialism Is a Humanism," in *Existentialism from Dostoevsky to Sartre*, ed. Walter Kaufmann, trans. Philip Mairet (New York: Meridian Books, 1960); cited in the text as *EH*.

15. Nietzsche, *Beyond Good and Evil*, 210.

16. Cited in Shirer, *Rise and Fall of the Third Reich*, 1225.

17. Donald P. Spence, *Narrative Truth and Historical Truth: Meaning and Interpretation in Psychoanalysis* (New York: W. W. Norton & Company, 1982), 268–70.

18. I am referring to the distinguished American philosopher, Hilary Putnam, whose pragmatism and ethical realism are elucidated in a number of contemporary works including *The Many Faces of Realism* (LaSalle, IL: Open Court, 1987), *Realism with a Human Face* (Cambridge, MA: Harvard University Press, 1992), and *Ethics without Ontology* (Cambridge, MA: Harvard University Press, 2005).

19. Jean Baudrillard, "Symbolic Exchange and Death," in *Jean Baudrillard Selected Writings*, trans. Charles Levin, ed. Mark Poster (Stanford, CA: Stanford University Press, 1988), 126, 128.

20. Friedrich Nietzsche, *On the Genealogy of Morals*, trans. Walter Kaufmann (New York: Vintage Books, 1967), 93.

21. Alasdair MacIntyre, *After Virtue: A Study in Moral Theory* (Notre Dame, IN: University of Notre Dame Press, 1984), 2, 30.

9

Therapeutic Sensibility

A DISEASE OF OUR TIME

In his autobiographical *Memories, Dreams, Reflections,* Freud's errant disciple, C. G. Jung, began a sober reflection on life after death by forewarning readers that he could "do no more than tell stories—'mythologize'" (*MD,* 299).[1] When he spoke these words during the latter 1950s in a series of conversations with his biographer, Aniela Jaffé, Jung was more than eighty years old and his words were carefully chosen. For Homer and later Greek poets used *mythos* when referring to a story, a tale, or a narrative. In fact, in the antique tongue of poets like Homer and philosophers like Plato, *mythos* also meant word or speech: practically anything a human being offered by word of mouth. In time, when the Fates and the Furies turned their backside to Greece and graced Romulus with their favors, *fābŭla,* the Latin equivalent of *mythos,* and a word from which our expression "fable" is derived, meant story, tale, or legend.

Explaining his reason for telling a story or mythologizing about the hereafter, the founding father of analytical psychology advised expectant readers that his ideas about life after death came from "memories," "images," and "thoughts" he could not "document" or justify with empirical evidence; continuing these cautionary remarks as if he were a modern analytic philosopher resolved to keep language, idea, and speech in scruple, Jung also warned his readers that he was unable to say whether the thoughts he planned to offer were true or false, although he could not deny that certain memories, images, and thoughts were in his mind, waiting to be spoken: spoken, I should add, in the fashion of a fabulous story that arose from the depths of a human being's rich mythopoeic imagination (*MD*, 299).

Suddenly, in a seemingly strange turn of mind, Jung launched into a fierce critique of critical rationalism and its contemporary cultural character type, scientific man. Accusing critical rationalism of eliminating myth and being "the disease of our time," Jung indicted scientific man for a variety of reasons, including a penchant for: (a) focusing exclusively on the intellect and consciousness, thereby prejudicially limiting, injuring, even crippling humankind's full psychic life; (b) believing erroneously that critical reason was able to answer all the important questions of life; (c) paying scant attention to "the mythic side of man" and "the strange myths of the psyche"; (d) conceiving mythologizing as "futile speculation"; (f) ignoring the emotional side of man and "the healing and valid activity" of storytelling, of mythologizing, of creating meaningful fables from the deep unconscious (*MD*, 300). After equating the domination of critical rationalism with the impoverishment of modernity, and the healthy integration of life with an awareness of the meaningful myths arising from the deep unconscious, Jung drew his scathing indictment to a clinical conclusion in a subsequent final chapter entitled "Late Thoughts." Worshipping at the altar of myth, while arguing reverentially in favor of the healing storytelling activity of the unconscious, Jung identified the clinical burden of his therapeutic thinking when he declared: "Meaninglessness inhibits fullness of life and is therefore equivalent to illness. Meaning makes a great many things endurable—perhaps everything. No science will ever replace myth, and a myth cannot be made out of science" (*MD*, 340).

I am singling out Jung to initiate a discussion of clinical nihilism because Jung's assault on critical rationalism is clearly stated and in the view of former and current disciples, the apotheosis of meaningful myth is persuasive. In clinical circles, however, Jung was not alone in arriving at an understanding of the psychological importance of meaning in human experience and he certainly was not a lone voice crying in the clinic when he spoke about the emotional side of human beings, the therapeutic role of storytelling, or the constructive influence of myth and fiction in daily life and in clinical practice.

For example, while trapped in a living nightmare, but able to carefully observe the cognitive-emotional condition and behavior of fellow inmates at the extremes of human experience, Viktor Frankl gained a unique perspective on the importance of maintaining a grip on meaning, including the meaning of suffering, if a person hoped to survive in a thanatic lifeworld like Auschwitz, Belsen, or Treblinka. Following his liberation from extremity at the end of World War II, Frankl literally equated meaninglessness and illness in his pioneering existential therapy, not only arguing that human beings possess a unique will to meaning, but also maintaining that when humans lose or despair of meaning they are afflicted with a disabling existential neurosis. Frankl was so intensely focused on the unique role and psychological importance of meaning in human experience that he chose the expression "logotherapy" to identify his clinical orientation, having generously interpreted the Greek term *logos* (λόγοs) to literally mean "meaning." Regarding his clinical strategy as an existential therapist, Frankl could not have been clearer: "Logo-therapy . . . focuses on the meaning of human existence as well as on man's search for meaning. According to logotherapy, the striving to find a meaning in one's life is the primary motivational force in man. That is why I speak of a *will to meaning* in contrast to the pleasure principle . . . on which Freudian psychoanalysis is centered."[2]

Earlier, in 1929, while the living nightmare experienced by Frankl was gathering power and political potential in Deutschland, due to the constant clamor of a virulent racial mythology that rose like metastatic cancer from diseased depths of the unconscious, Otto Rank, another errant disciple of Freud, wrote *Truth and Reality*, the third volume of his tripartite *Outlines of a Genetic Psychology on the Basis of the Psychoanalysis of the Ego Structure*. Thinking less of a will to meaning, than a will to illusion and treating the stories, tales, and narratives of religion, philosophy, and other human endeavors as illusional, while arguing in favor of "a view of life that is therapeutic" but characteristically un-Socratic, Rank concluded reflectively:

> With the truth, one cannot live. To be able to live one needs illusions, not only outer illusions such as art, religion, philosophy, science and love afford, but inner illusions which first condition the outer. . . . From this conception there results a paradoxical but deep insight into the essence of the neurosis. If man is the more normal, healthy and happy, the more he can accept the appearance of reality as truth, that is, the more successfully he can repress, displace, deny, rationalize, dramatize himself and deceive others, then it follows that the suffering of the neurotic comes not from a painful reality, but from painful truth.[3]

I realize that I am reveling in the past while focusing readers' attention on modern rhetoric concerning the role and function of myth and meaning, of truth and illusion, in the human estate. But this pedantic digging in the past has contemporary significance. In fact, the important issues discussed by Jung, Rank, and Frankl have a life, a fateful life, I think, in postmodern time.

For example, as I write these thoughts, Christmas is fast approaching and I am facing a deadline for submitting the final manuscript of *Enchantments* to my publisher; however, a popular magazine delivered with the Sunday newspaper is sitting restively on my desk where I placed it three days ago. In spite of the deadline and work remaining in the concluding chapter, the preface, and the bibliography, I made a firm decision to incorporate pertinent thoughts from one of the magazine's lead articles into this chapter: a chapter on therapeutic sensibility I finished one month ago.

The colorful Sunday supplement does not contain scholarly discourse, in fact, it is widely circulated and written for the *hoi pŏlloi*: not the single one, but the many, the masses, the common man reverenced in Aaron Copland's American classic *Fanfare for the Common Man*. With Christmas at hand it seemed natural to find references to the holiday season; less natural to find an article written by a best-selling author whose purpose was to persuade adults to believe in Santa Claus. But that is precisely the message of the text: a persuasive text that reads like the discourse of Jung and Rank, and to a lesser degree, Viktor Frankl.

According to the author of "Why We Should Believe in Santa Claus," an author who was writing a brief essay to influence the minds of the many: "There are times when we need to pretend to believe in things we know not to be true. We know that the world is a place of suffering and hardship, and we know too, that justice and kindness and love and such things will not always prevail against these hard realities. Myths help us to get by. The day they all die and we tell our children exactly how things are, the world will be a poorer, less enchanted place."[4]

Prescinding from consideration of problems involved in literally trying to pretend to believe something one knows is untrue, the verb "to know," when used in scruple, also carrying something akin to a guarantee, the message of this discourse seems innocent enough. In one way or another, we are all struggling to move respective boulders on a Sisyphean mountain, not exactly in Hades, but somewhere east of Eden, in a shared world experienced as "a place of suffering and hardship." With this in mind, who would fault this best-selling author's therapeutic sensibility: a seemingly rational desire to use or to support the use of *mythopoiesis* in a valiant effort to protect innocent children, adults, and oneself from the harsh realities of life? But there is more here than meets the eye as the reader will see in this and in ensuing chapters: much more that greets a mind informed by Santayana's memorable correlation of forgetting and repeating history. Furthermore, if anyone doubts that the "deep thinking" and enlightened discourse of philosophers and psychologizers trickles down to the common man who resides in the culture of the masses, the better part of wisdom would be to disabuse oneself of all doubt. For sooner or later, as we can see from this lead article in a widely circulated, colorful and inviting, Sunday magazine, the high-falutin discourse of philosophers and psychologizers, like Jung and Rank, has a way of becoming persuasive discourse written as a fanfare for the common man.

Less likely to be read by the masses until it leaches into common culture at some unknown point in the future, is the philosophic work of postmodern critic, Jean Baudrillard, who appropriated C. G. Jung's comparison of meaninglessness and illness in an essay "On Nihilism," an important chapter of *Simulacra and Simulation*. In difficult, but compelling prose that delivered an intellectual's agonistic struggle and anguish, Baudrillard maintained that during the twentieth century, postmodern men and women experienced a devastating loss of meaning. As if he were making a clinical point or diagnosing a collective illness for which there is neither a remedy nor a cure, in the fashion of Freud who plowed this terrain in *Civilization and Its Discontents*, Baudrillard observed:

> The true revolution of the nineteenth century, of modernity, is the radical destruction of appearances, the disenchantment of the world and its abandonment to the violence of interpretation and of history. . . . The second revolution, that of the twentieth century, that of postmodernity . . . is the immense process of the destruction of meaning, equal to the earlier destruction of appearances. . . . The dialectic stage, the critical [third Hegelian] stage is empty. . . . There is no therapy of meaning or therapy through meaning. . . . Melancholia is the inherent quality of the . . . disappearance of meaning. . . . And we are all melancholic. . . . Theoretical violence, not truth, is the only resource left us. . . . This is where seduction begins.[5]

Crazed by human indifference produced by a nihilistic loss of meaning and the collective disease of melancholia; stunned by the "collective stupefaction" of the masses manufactured by the processes of simulation and dissimulation operative in our engulfing media-culture; Baudrillard wrote a postmodern footnote to Rank's analysis of truth and illusion when he claimed that a "will to spectacle and illusion, in contrast to every will to knowledge and power . . . is alive in the hearts of people, but haunts just as well the processes of events. . . . To manifest one's being is necessary; to be enraptured is absolutely vital.[6]

Like Baudrillard, Jung was an erudite scholar; unlike the postmodern intellectual, Jung was a practicing psychiatrist who learned early psychoanalytic lessons at Freud's knee. But in his indictment of critical rationalism and scientific man, I believe Jung was reciting memories, dreams, and reflections of one of Nietzsche's books. I am referring to *The Birth of Tragedy*, a brilliant first book in which a young philologist with a budding existential mind-set identified the therapeutic sensibility of psychological man during a vigorous critique of (a) antique Socratism, (b) the single-minded modern search for knowledge and truth, and (c) the critical rationalism animating the quest of theoreticians who embrace modern science without thought of its deleterious effects on the inner life of fellow humans.

Published in 1872, three years before the birth of Jung and one year before Freud graduated with honors from the Leopoldstädter Kommunal-Realgymnasium, the equivalent of a distinguished American high school, Nietzsche argued for a rebirth of myth: a healing, medicinal myth that arises from the depths of an illusion-making artistic consciousness. Complaining that "myth . . . is . . . paralyzed everywhere" as a result of a stultifying Socratism that mistakenly views truth as a virtue, error as evil, and knowledge as a remedy for humankind's ills, Nietzsche insinuated himself into history as the philosophic midwife of psychological man: a modern cultural character type whose need for medicinal meaning, however fictive or fabulous, would supplant the uncompromising quest for truth animating Socratism and its modern successor, the Enlightenment mystique, a late seventeenth- and eighteenth-century complex of optimistic attitudes, ideas, values, and beliefs whose handmaiden is empirical science (*BT*, 111).[7]

On the world stage, in his sanity and in his madness, the existential-minded Nietzsche pulled to birth from the womb of the future, the prototype of a cultural character who revalued the Socratic quest for truth and found it reasonable to place a higher value on meaningful myths, medicinal fictions, and healing illusions. Accusing scientific theorists of being overly optimistic, thus terribly misguided, Nietzsche argued heretically that these modern truth-seekers undermine meaningful myths rather mindlessly, in the fashion of their nihilistic forefather, Socrates, who was rightly indicted for corrupting the young in view of his critical philosophic activity that destroyed meaning-giving myths and left nothing worthy of belief in its wake. To make matters worse, scientific theorists also mistakenly believe they are able to perfect the human condition through knowledge, as if it were possible to control and shape the destiny of humankind by the sustained application of critical reason and the experimental method of empirical science. Given Nietzsche's existential point of view and the therapeutic sensibility his existentialist thinking nurtured, the love of knowledge appeared to be a fateful delusion, something akin to a *folie à plusieurs*—a major madness of the many in modernity. For scientific knowledge is unable to heal the emotional wounds of human existence: the fabled thorns and thistles awarded to Everyman when Adam and Eve were expelled from paradise and condemned to wander agonistically east of Eden.

Science is arguably deficient as a vehicle for healing the wounds of humankind's Sisyphean existence, although the manufacturer of Prozac would have a thing or two to say in rebuttal of that position. But Nietzsche was unabashedly excessive and not interested in finding Aristotle's golden mean between excess and deficiency in his thinking and written work. As a result, while engaged in the historical act of midwifing psychological man, while at the same time cultivating a therapeutic sensibility, Nietzsche established a rationale for a *sacrĭfĭcĭum intellectus*: a fateful sacrifice of Socratic quest that would inform the healing art of dialogical therapy during the twentieth century. Specifically, in 1872, in spite of existing in pre-Freudian time—a historical era that had not yet witnessed the birth of psychoanalysis—Nietzsche planted the fertile seed of cultural *and* clinical nihilism, while also writing the following first draft of C. G. Jung's myth-minded polemic. Arguing boldly, after taking a psychological measure of his modern time and earlier history, the burgeoning existential philosopher observed:

> Almost everyone, upon close examination, finds that the critical . . . spirit [of Socratism and science] . . . has so affected him that he can only make the former existence of myth credible to himself by means of . . . abstractions. . . . The images of myth have to be the unnoticed omnipresent demonic guardians under whose care the young soul grows to maturity and whose signs help the man to interpret his life and struggles. . . . By way of comparison . . . picture the abstract man, untutored by myth; . . . there we have the present age, the result of that Socratism which is bent on the destruction of myth. And now the mythless man stands hungry . . . and digs and grubs for roots. . . . If we could imagine dissonance become man—and what else is man?—this dissonance, to be able to live, would need a splendid illusion that would cover dissonance with a veil of beauty. This is the true artistic aim of Apollo, in whose name we comprehend all those countless illusions . . . that at every moment make life worth living at all and prompt the desire to live on in order to experience the next moment. (*BT*, 135–36, 43)

Extending the existential implications of his therapeutic sensibility fourteen years later in *Beyond Good and Evil*, while Freud was studying hypnotism with Charcot in the neurological clinic of the Salpêtrière, Nietzsche subtitled his new book *Prelude to a Philosophy of the Future*. Deepening his existential orientation, while delivering the prophetic message that in the future, psychology would be the discipline that addresses humankind's fundamental problems, Nietzsche not only swam against the onrushing tide of Socratism, most notably, the quest for truth undertaken by the princely Newton and lesser foot soldiers of modern science, he also further illuminated the therapeutic sensibility of psychological man. Writing boldly with a pen that was distinctively Darwinian, the existential philosopher declared: "The falseness of a judgment is . . . not necessarily an objection to a judgment. . . . The question is to what extent it is life-promoting, life-preserving, species-preserving, perhaps even species-cultivating. And we are fundamentally inclined to claim that the falsest judgments . . . are the most indispensable for us. . . . To recognize untruth as a condition of life—that certainly means resisting accustomed value feelings in a dangerous way."[8]

Like C. G. Jung, I am telling a story or mythologizing when I suggest that Socrates would have wept if it were possible for him to have heard Nietzsche and Jung repudiating his founding quest for truth: the fateful use of the gift of reason to critically examine all manner of uncritically accepted opinion and belief. In the cautious mind of Socrates this quest for truth was no small adventure; for his war-torn, troubled time had taught him that ideas are dangerous, insofar as ideas have the dire consequence of shaping people's lives, as well as the structure and the destiny of the *polis*. Walking purposefully among his fellows in the streets, marketplaces, gymnasiums, and social gatherings of Athens, attired in something akin to a bed sheet and sandals, Socrates engaged in unending circular conversations about everything under the sun, exchanging fair words with anyone he could engage and everyone who happened to engage him. Although he led his dialogical partners in a conceptual circle, the end of which was to arrive where they started, as if nothing useful had been gained, this was neither idle chatter, nor an empty intellectual game, as Camus observed myopically during his discussion of Sisyphus, while arguing that philosophic problems, excepting suicide, are games.[9] For Socrates was convinced that the spoken word, the exchange of ideas, the intercourse of minds, is both gratifying and grave.

Convinced that ignorance is evil, because ignorance leads to errors of thinking and false judgments that affect human life irreparably, Socrates detested the arrogance of ignorance: the blind, haughty, uncritically accepted assumption that one possessed true knowledge about the gods, good and evil, virtue or justice—any conceivable topic his combative conversations raised. Given his fierce animus regarding the arrogance of ignorance, he developed an unfailing talent for detecting this corrosive evil in dialogical partners. In fact, whenever he became involved in philosophic conversation he expected confrontation with arrogance and conflict with ignorance, and he extended a crafty invitation to discuss seemingly simple questions about wisdom, justice, and virtue in order to lure haughty individuals into an inescapable labyrinth of conflicting words and contradictory ideas, creating the illusion that an answer to a perplexing question—discovery of the central passageway out of the labyrinth—was the thing they were mutually seeking in conversation. But this was blindness on the part of the dialogical partner, who had taken the bait and now was trapped! For the seductive old man in the bed sheet and sandals was using fair words to position himself strategically, to hear and to challenge the arrogance of ignorance inevitably displayed.

Like Sisyphus, who was superbly conscious of his existential situation after spending year after year pushing his boulder in a futile manner in Hades, Socrates understood his agonistic life and he knew what to expect from dialogical partners: principally, cognitive abortions he could refute and discard with ease. Whenever the arrogance of ignorance was uncovered, the mental healer took it upon himself to lead the person afflicted with ignorance on a circular adventure around the land of unjustified opinion and uncritically accepted belief, arriving where they started, at the unknowing self. But now, the dialogical partner had acquired some insight and knew himself for the first time. Specifically, he knew that he was ignorant, that he possessed what any fool could possess: mere opinion (*doxa*), rather than true knowledge (*episteme*).

Ideally, after being led around the circle of inquiry masterfully by a skilled, crafty wizard with words, and arriving at self-knowledge and a curative change of mind (*metanoia*), the arrogance of ignorance would be replaced by learned ignorance: the humble human wisdom of the person who knows that he does not possess knowledge, that he does not actually know what he thought he knew before rounding the dizzying circle of self-examination. While learned ignorance does not translate into definitive answers to important existential questions, for those in whom Socratic therapy is working authentically, learned ignorance results both in care for the fellowship of the spoken word and in the moderating influence of an examined life.

I have a poignant example of Socratic therapy in the irreplaceable gift of a letter from an inmate in the maximum security prison where I engaged in Socratic inquiry for many years. This particular man, a memorable murderer, as well as a devoted student, slipped me the following letter on the occasion of his long-awaited parole. This was our final contact and in several ways it was a sad, but joyful farewell. In retrospect, the gifted Plato could not have written a better testimonial to the inestimable value of Socratic therapy or a more incisive refutation of Aristophanes' satirical depiction of Socrates as a buffoon suspended in midair in a basket.[10] "Dear Dr. Ellerman," this reflective murderer began:

> When I first came to prison I wasn't much as a man. I didn't know how to be myself so I was whatever anyone wanted me to be. I just didn't know much about life or people, so I could not see what was really being said. Now I can at least tell when to look at what is being said, break it down, then see how real it could be. My mother visited me last week and told me how much I had changed. I told her I was taking philosophy, I was so proud and so was she.
>
> Through you I have found how I came to be in this awful place. Words can be used in many ways that I never knew. You take time out of your life to show us how to use them in a right way and when others are using them in a way that is not meant to be. I understand what it is for you to come in here and not know if you will leave. However I am glad that I had this place to learn in. Six years of study have made me a better person than I was, so I have been given something I will use for the rest of my life.
>
> Meeting you was one of the most important things that ever happened to me. You opened my eyes. Before I met you I never thought of anything as

true or false. It never occurred to me. You have given me the key to really understand what is correct from incorrect reasoning. To me this is the best that one can do for another, for to reason correctly is to live correctly.

The sad truth is, my grateful student was convicted of murdering a man who tormented him for years on end by calling him "retarded" . . . until this psychological beating came to a sudden end when something snapped within the dummy's head. Don't be taken aback by my use of "dummy," for my devoted student was called "dummy" by his family, friends, and peers throughout childhood. Regarding former teachers, suffice it to say he was a farm boy who simply fell through the cracks.

As fate would have it, while I was teaching logic in the prison one memorable spring semester, I noticed that my seemingly retarded student was able to verbalize correct answers to complex questions of deductive logic, such as queries regarding the formal relationship of categorical propositions in Aristotelian syllogisms. But he was unable to accurately draft the syllogisms prisoned in his mind. Perplexed by the discrepancy between speech and hand, and suspecting a perceptual handicap of one sort or another, I made a number of appeals to prison authorities and in due course, my dumfounded student was tested and correctly diagnosed with a dyslexic disorder.

From time to time, I find it reasonable to entertain the belief that if this truth were known early on, not only known, but properly used to benefit this misunderstood victim of ignorance and error, the loss of life by murder, and the incredible waste of life by incarceration, might never have happened. But who can predict what would come to pass if truth were known? After all, we are considering the crazed life of humans and an absurd, emotionally reactive life of this sort can rarely be compared to an Aristotelian syllogism: a deductive argument consisting of categorical propositions forming premises that seem to provide indisputable proof of the truth of a conclusion. Besides, I am going on and on about truth and in the twenty-first century, we still do not have a decisive answer to Pilate's infamous query "What is Truth?" In fact, it seems as if the best we can do with this question is to tell stories or mythologize. In an attempt to bring this and other tormenting questions of logic, semantics, and ontology to a satisfactory resolution, thereby contributing to discourse that dismantled traditional presuppositions and added another member to the team of that which is meaningless, the distinguished Harvard philosopher W. V. O. Quine argued correctly that we depend on our conceptual scheme for a variety of reasons and we may even improve it while we use it, however, when all is said and done:

We cannot detach ourselves from it and compare it objectively with an unconceptualized reality. Hence it is meaningless . . . to inquire into the absolute

> correctness of a conceptual scheme as a mirror of reality. Our standard of appraising basic changes of conceptual scheme must be, not a realistic standard of correspondence to reality, but a pragmatic standard. Concepts are language, and the purpose of concepts and of language is efficacy in communication and in prediction. Such is the ultimate duty of language, science, and philosophy, and it is in relation to that duty that a conceptual scheme has finally to be appraised.[11]

In this pragmatic spirit, and with remembrance of a rehabilitated murderer whose will to meaning found a home in the Socratic hope that the human ability to reason correctly results in the ability to live correctly, I shall confess that when I let my imagination roam and I stumble on a vision of life after death in the mythic manner of C. G. Jung, I have a clear image of Socrates sipping his hemlock, succumbing to its toxin, and being ferried to Hades by the creepy old ferryman, Charon. Things being what they are in the misty depths of the underworld, Socrates happens to meet Nietzsche and Jung long after concluding his wish-fulfilling conversations with Sisyphus, who is mighty tired from endlessly pushing his rock, although I can see that the surface of the rock has worn down a bit from abrasion. Enraged with these modern myth-minded gentlemen, Socrates attacks them with a rhetorical vengeance as he often did whenever he met a person who possessed the arrogance of ignorance, particularly if he thought the malefactor were spreading ignorance and error throughout the land. Whatever reversals and denouement might have occurred if my fanciful storytelling had a chance to develop its dramatic potential, say in a postmodern stageplay about the travail of Sisyphus and Socrates in Hades, there is reason to believe that Socrates would have been gentler with Freud if he happened to meet him in the bowels of the earth. For there were times when Freud's attitude of mind was consistent with the critical rationalism bequeathed to humankind by the wizard of Athens: a charming linguistic wizard whose quest for truth was given new life in the eighteenth century during a noteworthy era commonly referred to as the Age of Enlightenment.

As far as I know, Freud never used my imaginative expression "Enlightenment mystique," but he summed the essence of the eighteenth-century mind when he wrote simply and directly of himself and like-minded peers: "We believe that it is possible for scientific work to gain some knowledge about the reality of the world, by means of which we can increase our power and in accordance with which we can change our life," change our life, I would add optimistically, for the better (*FI*, 55). Conceiving himself as a man of science, a theoretical man who believed in "the primacy of the intellect," Freud held fast to the optimistic hope that one day in the distant future, humankind would outgrow its infantile need for the emotional consolations of religious illusion, in favor of rational knowledge which offers an *"education to reality,"* even if taking this "forward step" means that human beings must undertake the Sisyphean task of learning to endure "the great necessities of Fate against which there is no help" (*FI*, 53, 49–50).

When I say that Freud embraced the Enlightenment mystique, as a handy way of contrasting Freud's attitude of mind with the myth-minded cognitive set of Nietzsche and Jung, I am not suggesting that Freudian theory was devoid of myth or that Freud did not engage in mythmaking on a grand scale (see appendix). Contrarily, he made much of Oedipus and Electra and these dramatic fictions sprang from the mythopoeic imagination of Sophocles, not from the empirically minded, fallible thought experiments of Galileo, Newton, and Einstein. Furthermore, in published accounts of therapeutic interactions in his consulting room, Freud appears to have crafted clinical observations to fit the mold of his favorite fictions. Proceeding in this fashion and functioning self-consciously as the preeminent theoretician of psychoanalysis, Freud was involved in the ancient, still often-repeated attempt to *save the appearances* (σώζειν τα φαινόμενα) of his pet theories, assumptions, and beliefs. Working this way, like the ancient astronomer Eudoxus, Freud drafted clinical explanations of his patients' symptoms and behaviors that conformed to previously established and accepted, fixed psychodynamic conceptions, notwithstanding the hard fact that a variety of different explanatory hypotheses would similarly save, account for, or "render the phenomena equally well," to use the expression of the highly regarded French philosopher of science Pierre Duhem.[12]

Granting his rich mythopoeic imagination and the full flowering of storytelling in his brainchild, psychoanalysis, at the moment, I wish to focus attention on the attitude of mind advanced by Freud in *The Future of an Illusion* and the attitude of mind displayed by Jung in *Memories, Dreams, Reflections*. What I have in mind is a critical comparison of disparate attitudes of mind, the adoption of which carries concrete consequences, not only in theory, but in life as well. Regarding everyday life and shared reality, it is worth remembering that theory has purchase on reality, if I can use that term in a postmodern era whose theoreticians are prone "to escape in indefinite speculation, beyond any reference to the real."[13] From my vantage point in the mental health clinic, it seems quite clear that in the real world of the daily grind, where men and women are struggling to secure and maintain a place in nature's competitive food chain, the attitude of mind that animates and informs psychological theory may influence great numbers of people for good or ill, particularly when noble psychologizers are possessed by a zealous desire to benefit their fellows by offering a cure for the ills of humankind.

I am thinking of the attitude of mind of a theoretician who is caught up in the drama of psychological man, a cultural character type said to hunger, strive for, and need a healing story, tale, or narrative—any myth that lends itself to therapeutic use—absent a concern for knowledge and truth or an education to reality. On the other hand, I have in mind the attitude of mind of a theoretician who is selling Socratic man, a cultural character type who is obsessed with the danger of ideas and devoted resolutely to an uncompromising quest for truth, the logical goal of which is an education to reality: the kind of education that works to undermine false belief and human error. Obviously, I am comparing the myth-minded attitude and unrestrained therapeutic sensibility of Nietzsche and Jung with the critical rationalism and more moderate therapeutic sensibility of Freud, who not only claimed that in the clinical situation, the therapist is "a model" for and "a teacher" of his patients, but also maintained that the clinical or "analytic relationship is based on a love of truth—that is, on a recognition of reality . . . that . . . precludes any kind of sham or deceit" (*TI*, 248).

More to the point, Freud understood that religious illusions are meaningful and emotionally valuable, in fact, "the most important item in the psychical inventory of a civilization" (*FI*, 14). Nevertheless, when he was not mythologizing and otherwise surrendering Socratic quest and the Enlightenment mystique for his own brand of storytelling, Freud evidenced a share of common sense nourished by a rational understanding of the fact that there is a great danger in a renunciation of reality testing, perhaps a greater danger in a blind disavowal of the perennial quest for truth. In the clinical extreme, this flight from reality may be likened to the danger that infected the mind of patients diagnosed with Meynert's Amentia: the "state of blissful hallucinatory confusion" mentioned by Freud during his discussion of religious illusions that have narcotic effects but are incapable of correction, unlike the corrigible hypotheses of empirical science or the uncritically accepted myths, fictions, opinions, and beliefs that Socrates, the philosophic wizard of Athens, used his razor-sharp critical reason to undress (*FI*, 43).

Perverse as it may sound to an ear conditioned by the modern psychiatrization of culture—an ear accustomed to hearing every nuance of human emotion and behavior translated into one or another disorder—at this pass in human history, if my inner daemon encouraged me to speak against the tide, I would find it reasonable to warn the reading public that an unheralded disease of our time is a widespread therapeutic sensibility, not Socratism or critical rationalism, as Nietzsche and Jung imagined. I say this with some passion, while leaning on lessons learned during years of clinical practice, because I have good reason to say, when the clinical storytelling and meaningful mythologizing of dialogical therapists meets the needy "mythic side" of enchanted, meaning starved, story-loving patients, there is a great risk of producing in these patients a psychological healing, as well as a mindless credulity: a readiness on the part of patients to believe any memory, dream, or reflection; any story, tale, or narrative; practically anything offered by word of mouth or speech, without critical thought, empirical evidence, or care for truth or reality.

Given (a) widespread traffic in mental health clinics, (b) random enchantments of the clinic, and (c) the power and suggestive influence of dialogical therapists, whether they are mistakenly perceived and experienced as phantastic persons or not, an unrestrained or immoderate therapeutic sensibility that affirms the healing work of meaningful myths, healing fictions, and other remedial stories, thereby playing havoc with critical rationalism, the perennial quest for truth, and an education to reality, has produced a pervasive clinical nihilism that is potentially dangerous and worthy of scrutiny. Adding insult to this injury, it falls to me to say that an unrestrained therapeutic sensibility, however noble, benevolent, and otherwise well-intentioned, is morally suspect when it becomes a masquerade of truth. A masquerade of truth takes place when a dialogical therapist saves the appearances or renders the phenomena well by creating and telling a good, coherent explanatory story about the symptoms, the emotional impairments, the lived experience of vulnerable patients who may be enchanted with the clinic and naturally seduced into mistakenly believing that a charming therapist's healing myths are veridical, his gross fictions, true.

The intriguing question is whether or not this masquerade of truth harms the patient in one way or another, in spite of its utility in effecting a vaunted, but elusive psychological healing or cure. At the end of analysis, the answer to this question may be more or less ambiguous, leaving us on the backside of Jacob Bronowski's assertion that our actions are mediated by values or general strategies that attempt to balance opposing human impulses. Stepping outside the clinic and thinking collectively as Freud did when pondering our prospects in *Civilization and Its Discontents*, it may not be overly grandiose to say with Bronowski that the ascent of man teeters in the balance of these strategic decisions and ensuing actions, the ambiguity in question being the gross uncertainty of ascent or descent, of pointing forward or back, whenever these decisions are made either mindlessly or mindfully in the single or the collective case.

NIETZSCHE'S MADNESS

In full confession, Nietzsche was once a favored iconoclastic mentor from whom I learned much, particularly during formative years when I was feeding an insatiable philosophic hunger. Unfortunately, Nietzsche was a bright star who became a self-annihilating supernova: a physically and mentally tormented intellectual sunk in upon himself in the kind of gravitational collapse mental health clinicians refer to as psychotic illness. Sad to say, between 17 January 1889 and 13 May 1890, due to a strange set of circumstances, Nietzsche received inpatient treatment at the Jena Psychiatric Clinic under the supervision of Dr. Otto Binswanger. Although he stabilized to a degree, during his inpatient hospitalization, clinical treatment was ineffective and Nietzsche never recovered his mental faculties, although his peculiar derangement and his published work gave him the power of being heard forever.

From time to time, when enveloped in memories, dreams, and reflections of my own, I imagine that if Nietzsche had been a patient of mine I would have made much of his double will, for he was at once a Socratic man and a psychological man: a conflicted human being who possessed a fierce will to truth in conjunction with a therapeutic sensibility informed by an equally potent will to illusion, falsehood, and error. Divided against himself, openly admitting that he was a *doppelgänger* with two, perhaps three faces, all of which provided separate worlds of experience, Nietzsche was quite capable of arguing in favor of myth and fiction, while also claiming self-referentially: "At every step one has had to wrestle for truth; one has had to surrender for it almost everything to which the heart, to which our love, our trust in life, cling to otherwise. That requires greatness of soul: the service to truth is the hardest service."[14] On the other hand, between March and June of 1888, the same year he referred to himself as a wrestler for truth, Nietzsche spoke with the voice of a psychological man who stated clearly: "Assuming the *true* world, it could still be a world less valuable for us; precisely the quantum of illusion might be a higher rank on account of its value for our preservation."[15]

Crazed and conflicted, Nietzsche harbored hope of reconciling opposites: the psychological man's need for healing myth with a Socratic man's critical quest for myth-annihilating truth. When all is said and done, Nietzsche's life may have been a madding journey because he failed to become a music-playing Socrates: a healthfully integrated human being who tried unsuccessfully to reconcile the ambiguous, competing virtues and vices of myth and truth—the cognitive markers of his double-will. Addressing his wished for reconciliation in *The Birth of Tragedy*, Nietzsche invented the fascinating fiction of an artistic, music-playing Socrates to concretely image a fanciful reconciliation of the artist-liar with the great-souled wrestler for truth (*BT*, 106). Tragically, although he was a psychologically minded existential philosopher who actually played the piano, his reconciliatory third face remained an imaginary way of being an artist-philosopher: a myth and fiction loving wrestler for truth whose embodiment Nietzsche never achieved in real life. As a result, in the wake of a magnificent body of work that secured the modern existential turn in literary philosophy, Nietzsche collapsed on a street in Turin on or about 4 January 1889, reputedly sobbing, while embracing a tired old horse being flogged by a coachman.

Concealed in this enigmatic collapse is the crazy notion that Nietzsche was the deranged "double" or *doppelgänger* that haunted Dostoevsky's psychological fictions; and in a curious way this should come as no surprise, for Nietzsche not only claimed that Dostoevsky was "the only psychologist . . . from whom I had something to learn," he also ranked Dostoevsky as one of "the most beautiful strokes of fortune in my life."[16] Accordingly, in Turin, Italy, on 4 January 1889, Nietzsche lost contact with reality, while sustaining contact with Dostoevsky's fiction. Astonishingly, in *Crime and Punishment*, Dostoevsky's crazed antihero, Raskolnikov, dreamed that when he was a child walking with his father, they saw a tired, old sorrel mare being whipped and beaten to death. In his dream, Raskolnikov cries out, runs to the dead horse, and "throws his arms around her dead, bloodstained muzzle and kisses her, kisses her eyes, her lips."[17] Like Theodor Reik who learned much from Dostoevsky's psychologizing in *Crime and Punishment*, Nietzsche incorporated Raskolnikov's nightmare and while literally acting out the nightmare of a fictional character on a street in Turin, he turned within and finally embraced a long night of madness, like a supernova become a black hole in the silent interstices of intrapsychic space.

While illuminating Nietzsche's double will and his identification with Dostoevsky's "double," I am not suggesting that Nietzsche had a multiple personality or a Dissociative Identity Disorder, although the reputed drama of Nietzsche's collapse in Turin has features of theatricality often reported by patients who present with multiple personalities. Reporting on my clinical experience of imaginatively entering and creatively fashioning an integrative resolution of the dissociative drama enacted by hypnotically susceptible patients whose amnesic experience suggests alter conscious states, I warned of the possibility of patient and therapist being entangled in a *folie à deux*, not to mention the danger of the clinical community being involved in a clinical delusion shared by many. Regarding my phenomenological treatment of dissociative identity disorder, I reported my finding that successful treatment may result from neither believing nor disbelieving the story of multiplicity told by patients during the clinical confession; rather, in clinical practice, "I effect a neutralized apprehension of the patient: the experience of an *as if* consciousness that may be likened to watching a theatrical performance unfolding."[18]

Appearing to be a madman who embraced a horse in Turin, Nietzsche was clinically evaluated on 10 January 1889 by Dr. Wille, director of the Basel Psychiatric Clinic. On 17 January 1889, he was escorted by his mother and a medical attendant to the Jena Psychiatric Clinic, where he was evaluated further by Otto Binswanger, who recommended inpatient care. Delusional, ranting and raving at the piano that he was "the successor of the dead God" and "the clown of the new eternities," Nietzsche may have demonstrated Plato's suspicion that protracted philosophical inquiry runs the risk of madness.[19] Not divine madness that comes from a search for truth that elevates the soul and gives a person a vision of mysteries known by the gods alone, but the disorganizing human madness in which a person is permanently deranged or beside himself. In this case, while trying to become a music-playing Socrates, Nietzsche did not realize that his protracted attempt to reconcile opposites—the wrestle for truth and the need for myth—could drive the sanest man nuts! Although I can only hazard a guess, it occurs to me that the trick to avoiding Nietzsche's madness lies in understanding that some opposites cannot be reconciled. With some luck, a person might become reconciled to the ethic or the habit of living with ambiguity. This may not elevate the soul, in the sense of bringing one closer to the mysteries of the gods; but the better part of wisdom may lie in understanding that living with ambiguity is part of the absurdity of human existence and also part of the enchantment, if a person has the sight to see it and an ear for discordant music.

Needless to say, I am not sure that this story of Nietzsche's madness is true, strictly speaking. But it is a fabulous story: a *mythos* of a man's psyche built upon legends and lore regarding the disease of a time. Whether my story is true or not, in reality, Nietzsche was discharged from the Jena clinic on 13 May 1890. He died on 25 August 1900 after a decade of derangement and physical deterioration. At the same time, the triumph of the therapeutic that Nietzsche foresaw was proceeding apace across the border in Vienna, but not cleanly. For psychoanalysis demonstrated irrefutably that a member of the crazed species can believe he is a fierce wrestler for truth, while he is being embraced by the gross seductions of myth.

NOTES

1. C. G. Jung, *Memories, Dreams, Reflections,* trans. Richard Winston and Clara Winston (New York: Vintage Books, 1963); cited in the text as *MD*.
2. Viktor E. Frankl, *Man's Search for Meaning: An Introduction to Logotherapy* (New York: Washington Square Press, 1965), 153–54.
3. Otto Rank, *Truth and Reality,* trans. Jessie Taft (New York: W. W. Norton & Company, 1978), 42–43.
4. Alexander McCall Smith, "Why We Should Believe in Santa Claus," *Parade,* 13 December 2009, 24.
5. Jean Baudrillard, *Simulacra and Simulation,* trans. Sheila Faria Glaser (Ann Arbor: University of Michigan Press, 2000), 160–64.

6. Jean Baudrillard, "Fatal Strategies," in *Jean Baudrillard Selected Writings*, ed. Mark Poster, trans. Jacques Mourrain (Stanford, CA: Stanford University Press, 1988), 200–201.

7. Friedrich Nietzsche, *The Birth of Tragedy* in *"The Birth of Tragedy" and "The Case of Wagner,"* trans. Walter Kaufmann (New York: A Vintage Original, 1967); cited in the text as *BT*.

8. Friedrich Nietzsche, *Beyond Good and Evil: Prelude to a Philosophy of the Future*, trans. Walter Kaufmann (New York: A Vintage Original, 1966), 11–12.

9. Albert Camus, *The Myth of Sisyphus and Other Essays*, trans. Justin O'Brien (New York: Vintage Books, 1961), 3.

10. Aristophanes, *The Clouds*, in *Five Comedies of Aristophanes*, trans. Benjamin Bickley Rogers (Garden City, NY: Doubleday Anchor Books, 1955), 159.

11. Willard Van Orman Quine, "Identity, Ostension, and Hypostasis," in *From a Logical Point of View: 9 Logico-Philosophical Essays* (New York: Harper Torchbooks, 1961), 79.

12. Pierre Duhem, *To Save the Phenomena: An Essay on the Idea of Physical Theory from Plato to Galileo*, trans. Edmund Doland and Chaninah Maschler (Chicago: University of Chicago Press, 1969), 8.

13. Jean Baudrillard, "Symbolic Exchange and Death," in *Jean Baudrillard Selected Writings*, 126.

14. Friedrich Nietzsche, *The Antichrist*, in *The Portable Nietzsche*, ed. and trans. Walter Kaufmann (New York: Vintage Books, 1963), 632. Nietzsche's diagnosis of his dual personality appears in *Ecce Homo*, trans. Walter Kaufmann (New York: Vintage Books, 1967), 225.

15. Friedrich Nietzsche, *The Will to Power*, ed. Walter Kaufmann, trans. Walter Kaufmann and R. J. Hollingdale (New York: A Vintage Giant, 1968), 313.

16. Friedrich Nietzsche, *Twilight of the Idols*, in *Portable Nietzsche*, 549.

17. Fyodor Dostoevsky, *Crime and Punishment*, trans. Michael Scammell (New York: Washington Square Press, 1963), 62.

18. Carl P. Ellerman, "The Phenomenological Treatment of Dissociative Identity Disorder," *Journal of Contemporary Psychotherapy* 28, no. 1 (1998): 72.

19. Letter of Franz Overbeck to Peter Gast (15 January 1889), reprinted in the epilogue in *Selected Letters of Friedrich Nietzsche*, ed. and trans. Christopher Middleton (Chicago: University of Chicago Press, 1969), 353.

10

Clinical Nihilism

THE MASQUERADE OF TRUTH

From time to time, I have had the disappointing experience of trying to duplicate culinary recipes not only seen on popular TV cooking shows, but also printed in cookbooks written by celebrity chefs. I say "disappointing experience," because there often is a discrepancy between what I have seen or read and the mockery of the masterpiece I produce in culinary practice. I am never sure of the reason for the demonstrable difference, but after several repetitions and an equal number of failures, each time having taken pains to follow the celebrated chef's directions scrupulously, I lean in the direction of faulting the televised instructions or the written recipe, although when the soufflé sinks, I receive no comfort in my suspicion that there is a subtle difference between what celebrity chefs show or write and what they actually do in culinary practice.

Similarly, it may be fair to say that there is a discrepancy between what therapists report in professional literature and what they actually do in clinical practice, as some who have tried to duplicate a method or a strategy published in the literature will attest. Perhaps it is not too much to say that in the human estate, and thus in professional literature, it may be natural for an honest person to put his best foot forward, while in actual practice, there is neither a video camera to see, nor an independent ear to hear, what transpires behind the closed door of the clinical confessional. It is also worth noting that clinic patients are rarely offered the opportunity to talk back in the cookbooks of clinical practice by giving a countervailing view of their therapist's personal manner, interpersonal style, ethics, and treatment strategies, not to mention the abiding success or dismal failure of their fateful or uneventful dialogical experience. This lacuna in the literature distinguishes clinical theorizing from more reliable scientific experiments that talk back by confirming or disconfirming crucial predictions of fallible hypotheses. In the final analysis, absent independent confirmation or disconfirmation of clinical reportage, there may be "a distressingly wide gap between what therapists write and what they do. . . . In the literature, the techniques can seem straightforward and virtually foolproof. However, attempting to produce the same dramatic, consistent, and positive outcomes with real people in one's own practice can be a very different matter."[1]

But the critical point I wish to make is that this natural human business of putting one's best foot forward in professional literature does not always obtain, even when therapists have engaged unsuspecting patients in a masquerade of truth: the existential act of creating and telling a good myth or story that explains the symptoms, the emotional impairments, the lived experience of men and women who may be enchanted with the clinic, under the spell of a clinician, and easily seduced into believing that a charming therapist's healing myths are veridical, his gross fictions, true.

On my reading, clinical colleagues and I may put our worst foot forward in the literature of clinical practice, although we appear to believe that our worst foot is our best. This clearly shows the extent to which the therapeutic sensibility is embedded viscerally, thus mindlessly, in contemporary clinical life, particularly in clinical ethics. This state of affairs also confirms Philip Rieff's astute prediction that in the era of psychological man, the era during which dialogical therapy will triumph, human beings may go "too far, beyond the old deception of good and evil, to specialize at last, wittingly, in techniques that are . . . 'therapeutic,' with nothing at stake beyond a manipulatable sense of well-being. . . . Psychologial man . . . will be . . . a user of any faith that lends itself to therapeutic use. . . . If 'immoral' materials, rejected under earlier cultural criteria, are therapeutically effective, enhancing somebody's sense of well-being, then they are useful."[2]

For example, according to a highly respected existential therapist who published an illuminating account of dialogical encounters in the mental health clinic, therapeutic explanation enables patients to order experience coherently so that they acquire a sense of personal mastery and increased control of their lives. Consistent with Socrates' disparaging commentary regarding the art of rhetorical persuasion being driven not by a quest for truth, but by what a person listening will think is true or hear as plausible, Irvin Yalom argued that the "precise *content*" of an insightful explanation—the information a patient hears and learns—is less important than the "provision of insight" by a therapist (*EX*, 342–44).[3] I would like to translate this clearly so that readers understand precisely what is being said and what is at stake in this sort of clinical masquerade.

It is not *what I say* to my patients that is important, but *that I say* something: anything that facilitates an emotionally impaired patient's personal mastery and control of lived experience. From a clinical point of view, when therapeutic sensibility is all aflame, the important thing is not what people learn, but that they learn something that empowers them and enables them to function with a sense of well-being in the field of human action and interaction.

In an imaginary conversation with this particular existential therapist I hear Socrates pausing to say: "You mean it is more important to speak persuasively in order to influence the mind of a patient with fair words than to use correct words to speak to the patient whose ideas, judgments, and beliefs you are shaping? Is there no interest in the truth of what you are saying? Is there no concern that your persuasive words are founded critically on some search for knowledge and justification?"

Believing he had this first thrust of a Socratic *elenchus* (critical cross-examination) covered, Yalom wrote as follows:

> To the extent that it offers a sense of potency, insight is valid, correct, or "true." Such a definition of truth is completely relativistic and pragmatic. It argues that no explanatory system has . . . exclusive rights, that no system is the correct, the fundamental, or the "deeper"— and therefore better—one. . . . Therapists may offer the patient any . . . number of explanations to clarify the same issue . . . and each may be "true" in that each . . . begets a sense of potency. . . . They are all based on imaginary . . . structures. . . . They are all fictions, all . . . are effective to the degree that they afford a sense of personal mastery and thus inspirit the dormant will. . . . If an astrological or a shamanistic or a magical explanation enhances one's sense of mastery, and leads to inner personal change, then it is valid. (*EX*, 343–44)

Many years have passed since these thoughts were written and I still wonder why there was not the least outrage that a widely published existential therapist would shape the minds of trusting patients by offering astrological, shamanic, or magical explanations—any myth, fiction, or faith that lends itself to therapeutic use—while also educating other therapists to follow this clinical example. No anger in the therapeutic community that a dialogical therapist would knowingly and willingly condition the minds of patients to ignorance, while also educating other therapists to spread ignorance across the land. No public outcry that by virtue of dialogical encounters in the mental health clinic, ignorance would be passed on to legions of children parented by legions of clinic patients given reputed insight filled with false phantoms. Not one word of caution regarding the fact that the education of the mind establishes cognitive-emotional predispositions that determine historical action.

"What ignorance?" "What false phantoms?" "What education?" "What cognitive and emotional predispositions?" you rightly ask! If I follow the money by looking for the cash value of Yalom's ideas, specifically, the way these nihilistic ideas have a concrete life in the real world of lived experience, I could tell you that in the primitive, animistic world of shamans or sorcerers, where taboos and sympathetic magic ruled the day, misogyny and gynophobia played a stunning role; in fact, women often were demonized in a way that might have made their life miserable. In retrospect, the malignant Augustinian experience of women as unclean or filthy had a prior primitive life in the tribal experience of shamanic natives, in whose minds there existed a stark fear of uncleanliness: an existential condition pregnant and pulsing with illness and death. As a result, the mental set of shamanic natives included a horror of unclean, polluted women, particularly menstrual and birthing women, but also young girls entering puberty. For example, menstruating women were believed to be a cause of death if touched; this included touching their person, their clothes, or the utensils they used for cooking. Walking in the shadow of dangerous persons was tabooed and the shadow of an unclean menstruating woman was thought to possess this deadly power and influence. As a result of these false beliefs that now apparently lend themselves to therapeutic use, a seemingly unclean woman was subjected to temporary seclusion, confinement, or exile. Indeed, the fear of unclean women was so profound in the primitive mind that shamans performed rites of purification to save an individual, perhaps the whole tribe, from certain death in the event of physical contact with an unclean female.

Interestingly, this primitive demonization of women, common in shamanic cultures, has been so infectious in Western culture that Jesus was depicted as the offspring of an immaculate conception. In "The Madonna's Conception through the Ear," Freud's authorized biographer, Ernest Jones, explored variations of the myth that Jesus was introduced into the Virgin Mary's ear by the breath of the Holy Spirit.[4] The crucial idea animating this myth is that the mother of God must be absolutely clean in spirit, in flesh, and in shadow. There must be no reference to her impure genitals, certainly no hint of sexual congress with a man, not even a vague possibility that the son of God had a remote association with a filthy birth between urine and excrement.

Please understand: in this day and age, I would not expect a therapist in his right mind to offer a symptomatic patient a shamanic explanation of emotional illness based on the patient's having stepped in the shadow of an unclean woman. Nevertheless, Yalom is responsible for openly stating: "If . . . a shamanistic or a magical explanation enhances one's sense of mastery, and leads to inner personal change, then it is valid." In my mind, at least, this rhetorical flourish is as irresponsible as Nietzsche's hubristic assertion that in a healthy artistocracy, countless human beings can be sacrificed and reduced to incomplete human beings or slaves or instruments!

Baldly put, it is one thing to blithely assume that no explanatory system is the correct one. It is quite another thing to fail to come to terms with the inescapable truth that (a) human beings make many mistakes, (b) some explanations that save the appearances are false, incorrect, or demonstrably mistaken, and (c) in matters of the *polis,* as well as in therapeutic use, explanations riddled with errors of thinking, mistaken inferences, and false conceptions, may do a lot of damage to innocent human beings. Still, in spite of a lengthy history of human experience that has exposed human error of every magnitude—such as the belief that the well-being of a mentally ill qua daemonically possessed human being could be restored by drilling a hole in his head, out of which a demon will escape, thereby terminating a destabilizing possession—Yalom presented himself in the literature as an existential theoretician who believed that "no explanatory system is the correct . . . and therefore better—one." As if the intricate, infinite knowledge and technological prowess required to construct and launch a vehicle that would escape the earth's gravity and, after navigation and guidance through interplanetary space, safely place a human being on the moon, while also effecting a safe return, somehow issued from an explanatory system that was not the correct one: perhaps a myth or a fiction comparable to, certainly no better than, astrology, shamanism, or daemonic possession.

At this hyper-enlightened stage in the life of mind we may have reached a dead end, the kind of uncertain dead end Jacob Bronowski had in mind when he depicted the ascent of man as "teetering in the balance": the fateful balance, I would say, of important decisions and choices we shall make regarding who we become as a biological organism at once gifted and burdened with responsibility for the integrity of our values and our hard-won knowledge, while engaged in the collective existential act of being "nature's unique [evolutionary] experiment to make rational intelligence prove itself sounder than the reflex" (*AM*, 436–37).

Thinking optimistically, as a pragmatic person would, and like Bronowski, not willing to retreat into "falsely profound questions" or truly mistaken answers, I shall make the choice of treating a dead end as an opportune moment to speak about a return to common sense. In so doing, there is a grudging admission that common sense may be historical, like judgments that seem natural and self-evident at a particular moment in time, such that what is a commons of the mind today may not be a commons of the mind tomorrow. Nevertheless, in the *Lebenswelt,* the world of lived experience, including the daily grind as I see it unfailingly through a Sisyphean lens—there are some basic ways of being human, particularly ways of being human together, as well as attitudes of mind, that may be indispensable for survival, for well-being, for human flourishing. In the final analysis, it may serve our collective purposes better if these indispensable modes of being, values, and conceptual tools are given a proper measure in our existential cookbooks, so that we are not "wandering in Cloud Cuckoo Land," where there is a distressingly wide gap between our literature and our life—the concrete life of daily practice (*EO*, 85).[5] To an extent, while speaking this way, I am lauding the notable thinking and dedicated work of the distinguished American philosopher Hilary Putnam, professor emeritus at Harvard, the house of humane learning where William James helped to originate and advance American pragmatic philosophy.

Specifically, after spending fifty years in a philosophical labyrinth with the best and the brightest, and failing to find a passage out, Putnam found it reasonable to address misguided philosophers with a plea for "recovering our common sense," particularly in ethics, thereby following classic American pragmatists in believing that ethics has to do with working out concrete, fallible, provisional resolutions to real-life problems, with a view toward the flourishing of the many (*EO*, 3). In this context, Putnam stressed the fine point that in the lived world there are very few ready or easy solutions to messy human problems; however, "there are better or worse ways of approaching a given practical problem" (*EO*, 28). When all is said and done, with a return to common sense in mind, the essential philosophic work, as well as the essential work of moral agents and mental health clinicians, is to identify the better and separate the better from the worse, at the same time, having a keen eye for certain "ways of thinking," certain attitudes of mind, as I have been saying, that in the human community "are indispensable" for survival and for the flourishing, not of the few, but of the many (*EO*, 16).

With a tip of the hat to Putnam and the plea for a renewal of common sense, I shall confess that I am not critiquing Yalom alone when I make reference to clinical nihilism, for he is a single voice that exemplifies a larger, broader, potentially dangerous therapeutic sensibility that has a nihilistic life in professional literature and in clinical practice: a therapeutic sensibility and a masquerade of truth I am responsible for sharing.

It goes without saying that the clinical dance I am calling a masquerade of truth is contrary to the attitude of mind informing Socrates' claim that in his life and work, "I am not permitted to acquiesce in falsehood and suppress the truth."[6] The masquerade is also inimical to the attitude of mind informing Freud's Socratic claim that "the analytic relationship is based on a love of truth—that is, on a recognition of reality . . . that . . . precludes any kind of sham or deceit," however groundless in actual practice Freud's Socratic idealization of truth may have been. The point is, when engaged in conversation with dialogical partners in Athens, absent a modern therapeutic sensibility, Socrates would not have cared one wit about the sense of personal mastery acquired by means of some obscure mythical explanation that countenanced false phantoms. Rather, with an eye on the danger of ideas, such as the absurd idea that "no explanatory system is . . . correct . . . and therefore better," Socrates would have used rational argument to critically examine the truth value of an astrological, shamanic, or magical explanation in an effort to determine whether the content of these explanations could be justified and was worthy of belief.

Unfortunately, clinical theory often floats on a sea of intellectual obfuscation that justifies reckless rhetoric. For example, the definition of truth articulated by Yalom, a definition of truth packaged and seductively sold as "pragmatic," violates the authentic sense of pragmatic truth developed by the reputable pragmatic philosopher William James: an *epistemological realist* who would have viewed Yalom's use of "pragmatic" as slanderous, insofar as a pragmatic philosopher who says that an astrological, shamanic, or magical explanation is true, also agrees to the existence of the referential objects or processes the explanation is asserting. "When the pragmatists speak of truth," according to James, "they mean exclusively something about the ideas, namely their workableness. . . . The pragmatist, if he agrees that an idea is 'really' true, also agrees to whatever it says about its object. . . . The existence of the object, whenever the idea asserts it 'truly,' is the only reason . . . why the idea does work successfully" (*MT*, xxxv, xxxix).[7]

Strictly speaking, if a classical pragmatist tells a particular person, say Professor Quine, that an astrological, shamanic, or magical explanation is true, he is implicitly advising Prof. Quine to accept whatever these primitive explanations say about Quine in the historical context of lived experience. For the sake of argument, this would include the insight that Quine is ill because he has inadvertently stepped in the shadow of a menstruating woman: an unclean, polluted woman whose shadow is the bearer of illness and death. I say this with assurance because an authentic pragmatist understands himself as a realist, whose interpretations work because they effectively lead to one or another historical reality that exists independent of the ideas spoken or asserted. Listen carefully to James's clarification of this important proposition as if you were a student attending one of his seminars at Harvard during the fall semester of 1885, when Freud was studying with Charcot in the neurological clinic of the Salpêtrière:

> This notion of a reality independent of . . . us, taken from ordinary social experience, lies at the base of the pragmatist definition of truth. With some such reality any statement, in order to be counted true, must agree. Pragma-

> tism defines "agreeing" to mean certain ways of "working," be they actual or potential. Thus, for my statement, "the desk exists" to be true . . . , it must be able to lead me to shake your desk, to explain myself by words that suggest that desk to your mind, to make a drawing that is like the desk you see, etc. (*MT*, 217–18)

I fully realize that some shamans were pulling the wool over the eyes of fellow natives in Aboriginal cultures, just as a dialogical therapist interested in bettering the lot of his fellows pulls the wool over the eyes of a patient if he knowingly tells a finely crafted story or offers a fabulous fictive insight filled with false phantoms. The structural anthropologist, Claude Levi-Strauss, made this quite clear when he explored primitive cultures and cast a sober eye on enchanting shamans and their purported magic. According to Levi-Strauss, one shaman pressed his lips to the lips of a physically ill native and pretended to suck a strange object out of the native's belly, a foreign object that explained the man's illness. In truth, the sorcerer had previously secreted the stone in his own mouth and he was able to produce it at will at the opportune moment, convincing the native and astonished onlookers that he had managed a cure of illness. Of course the charming sorcerer believed this hoodwinking would work; the sick savage believed in the power of the sorcerer; the tribe had faith in its influential shaman and fully expected a cure.[8] But this consensual interaction is beside the philosophic point, to wit, an authentic pragmatist is a realist who believes his interpretations work because his interpretations lead to intersubjective realities that exist independent of the rhetoric, including the fair words used in the explanation of emotional illness. In fine, whatever Yalom may have thought about the validity of his clinical fictions, William James would not have countenanced the use of "pragmatic" in the existential therapist's misleading nihilistic definition of truth.

In addition to mistakenly laying claim to a pragmatic conception of truth that conflicts decisively with more careful conceptions developed by critical philosophers, Yalom packaged and sold his definition of truth as "relativistic"; however, Yalom's use of "relativistic" is not consistent with basic axioms of relativity theory, one pertinent example being that relativity theory does not exclude objectivity or truth. Contrarily, with reference to Einstein's important, often ignored, *Principle of Invariance,* relativity theory honors objectivity—the invariance of laws of nature, such as the constancy of the speed of light—thereby neither abandoning nor pluralizing truth as Yalom suggested.

Commenting on the concept of objectivity in "Einstein's Conception of Reality," an essay written for a collection of essays celebrating Einstein's seventieth birthday, Henry Margenau—former professor of physics at Yale and staff member at Einstein's academic home, the Institute for Advanced

Study at Princeton—stated unequivocally that invariance is the nucleus of relativity theory, such that objectivity becomes equivalent to the invariance of laws of physics. Simply put, while perceptions of a falling object may be different for an observer at rest and an observer in motion, laws of nature, such as the speed of light, are the same for both observers. "To the layman, and sometimes the philosopher," Margenau argued correctively, relativity theory is "a set of laws which allow for variability from one observer to another. This . . . is linguistically implied by the word relativity which does not characterize the theory as centrally as it should. The true state of affairs can be seen when attention is directed to the . . . postulate of objectivity, which requires that the basic laws (the differential equations . . . used in the description of reality) shall be invariant."[9]

Margenau was not alone in understanding that Einstein had formulated a complex mathematical theory premised on his unshakeable belief that there are universal laws of nature, valid or invariant in any system, whether the system is motile or resting. Seen correctly, the principle of invariance undermines the use to which "relativistic" truth has been put by reckless theoreticians who wish to deny objectivity and truth in nihilistic theories. For example, the noteworthy philosopher of science Hans Reichenbach was well versed in relativity theory; his published works include *The Theory of Relativity and A Priori Knowledge, Axiomatization of the Theory of Relativity, The Philosophy of Space and Time*, and *Philosophical Foundations of Quantum Mechanics*. As if he were responding directly to the view that a relativistic therapist may offer patients several contradictory causal explanations, all of which may be true simultaneously, Reichenbach maintained that relativity theory neither abandons, nor pluralizes truth. More precisely:

> The word "relativity" should be interpreted as meaning "relative to a certain definitional system." That relativity implies plurality follows because the variation of definition leads to the plurality of equivalent descriptions. But we see the plurality implied is not a plurality of different views, or of systems of contradictory content: it is merely a plurality of equivalent languages and thus of forms of expression which do not contradict each other but have the same content. Relativity does not mean abandonment of truth; it only means that truth can be formulated in various ways.[10]

Hopefully, readers understand that I am not supporting the pragmatic theory of truth or relativity theory in favor of other competing theories; rather, I am documenting these theories of philosophy and physics to show that they often are blindly and mistakenly used by dialogical therapists to justify nihilistic clinical theories both in professional literature and in clinical practice. In my mind, if a dialogical therapist has abandoned the perennial quest for truth and chooses to use a fictive explanation in the clinical trenches, believing that no conceivable explanation is true and therefore better, it would be more honest to simply state the empirical finding that a tall tale has functional utility, or a whopper works to promote emotional well-being, rather than looking for cover in a responsible theory of philosophy or physics, particularly a complex mathematical theory that is often misunderstood when it is parsed outside its original mathematical frame.

With this in mind, in a prior formulation of the absurd sensibility of existential therapy, while engaged like Jung in an attempt to justify "the healing and valid activity" of storytelling or mythologizing, I stated forthrightly: "An existential therapist must acquire wisdom in judging the character of patients whose well-being hangs in the balance of therapeutic myth and . . . truth. Some patients will need more fiction than truth, more illusion than reality, a state of affairs that forces a prudent therapist to continually weigh . . . stark realism against the contrary vision that human beings need illusion because they are unable to live with truth."[11]

Ethically questionable as this clinical strategy might be, frank confession of the masquerade of truth works against the discrepancy between clinical literature and clinical practice. Equally important, the honest admission and ownership of the clinical masquerade seems more honorable than the attempt to justify it by laying personal responsibility for storytelling at the door of theories of philosophy and physics that have nothing whatsoever to do with the reckless rhetoric informing nihilistic clinical theories. Still, honesty of this sort has the smell of honor among thieves!

Elaborating on the imperatives of a therapeutic sensibility in "Pragmatic Existential Therapy," I reported my finding that a useful clinical strategy may involve replacing destructive fictions with life-affirming deceptions. I supported this view in a variety of ways, even drawing upon evolutionary psychology for support, particularly the proposition that self-deception and the ability to deceive other organisms are biological adaptations enhancing reproductive success. Although this and other theses of evolutionary psychology have been referred to as "the grace of guile," there are times in the human estate when imprinting of this sort is better seen as a fault not lying gracefully upon us.[12] Speaking pragmatically, but in a nihilistic way outlawed in the soul of Socrates, I viewed vital lies and fictions as instruments of clinical action. Pulling back the covers, I illuminated this feature of dialogical therapy as follows: "Creative fictions that facilitate adaptation, imaginative myths that activate choice and commitment, positive illusions that liberate self-creation may be promoted . . . because they have the virtue of enabling *some* demoralized patients to: (a) experience increased self-esteem, (b) develop mastery and control of life circumstances, (c) project positive future outcomes of action. In short, clinical experience . . . indicates that the co-creation of illusion enables some patients to experience a happier, healthier, more meaningful life."[13]

I shall take a moment to exemplify this clinical masquerade by recalling one of the first patients I treated when I was a novice intern acquiring clinical skills, while learning a thing or two about the art of talking people into and out of things, to use the cunning formulation of Freud.

EXOTIC DANCING

Margo was a very depressed exotic dancer who reported the reason for her depression straight off: her beloved dog had died, she was alone and very conflicted about acquiring a new dog now that her deceased pet was in "doggie heaven." To patients with more serious Sisyphean struggles, this is a minor matter, a ripple in the stream of life, a silly trifle light as air. But human beings become emotionally bonded to their pets in incredible ways and to this woefully depressed woman, who customarily danced around a stage wearing next to nothing, her dog was everything. He provided reliable companionship, comfort, and meaning, whether Margo's clothes were on or off. Complicating her depression was the nagging belief that she would literally betray her deceased dog by giving her love to another animal. What should a dialogical therapist do?

At the time, I realized that there were significant questions to be asked about the absence of meaningful human relationships in Margo's life, not to mention questions about her choice of an unsavory profession, particularly if she happened to be involved in illicit drugs and prostitution. But Margo did not come to the clinic for a life-changing intervention; rather, she came with symptoms of depression and she wanted a quick fix, not a lengthy exploration of her life or intensive work toward intrapsychic rehabilitation. Therefore, rather than confronting my depressed patient in Socratic fashion by dragging her out of a cave of juvenile fictions and stripping her of everything, save an endless quest for truth, I engaged opportunistically in a psychologically healing masquerade of truth, not only pretending to embrace her fiction, but offering the supplemental fiction that her beloved dog was now residing happily in doggie heaven, looking down at her sadly, because she was so anguished by the pain of losing him. Amid her tears, I tried my best to change her thinking with hope of getting her unstuck and altering her mood in a favorable way. In retrospect, I extended her myth creatively by telling her something akin to the following fanciful story: "Your dog loves you unconditionally and he wants you to be happy. He knows that a new pet will make you happy. Given his love and devotion, he wants you to feel better and to move forward in life with a new dog to love and care for."

Mind you, I wasn't shooting in the dark when I presented this fabulous therapeutic fiction to my patient, for my existential orientation was grounded in the direct clinical act of getting a person unstuck in life and moving toward the future in a meaningful, healthy way. Besides, there were clear directives being bandied about in clinical literature, one illuminating example of which was based on the aforementioned insights of Otto Rank, the clinical thane of illusion, as well as contemporary cognitive psychology that housed bold, iconoclastic empirical research suggesting: "The normal human mind is oriented toward mental health and . . . construes events in the manner that promotes benign fictions about the self, the world, and the future. The mind is . . . intrinsically adaptive, oriented toward overcoming rather than succumbing to the adverse events of life. In many ways, the healthy mind is a self-deceptive one. . . . A persistent voice from cognitive psychology [and] . . . a substantial amount of knowledge now testifies to the prevalence of bias and illusion in normal human thought. . . . These illusions . . . appear actually to be adaptive, promoting rather than undermining good mental health."[14]

Needless to say, if this formulation of the human condition is true, truth-seeking philosophers become mourners at the grave of Socrates and the old man wearing a bed sheet and sandals looks increasingly like a bumbling idiot who worked against the adaptive thrust of human evolution, not only creating his own brand of nihilism in the streets and marketplaces of Athens, but also deserving his indictment for corrupting the young. Still, this may be hasty thinking on a slippery slope to "Cloud Cuckoo Land," where the existential implications of thought issue in concrete historical action inimical to the flourishing of the few and the many. For the moment, suffice it to say that these neo-Darwinian thoughts supported a fabulous cognitive intervention with Margo, my memorable exotic dancer. This was a masquerade of truth to be sure, a clinical dance grounded in the rational-emotive therapy of Albert Ellis, an iconoclastic thinker like Nietzsche, who made much of the important understanding that emotional disturbances of all manner and sort issue from thinking, particularly thinking enveloped in self-defeating language, ideas, and beliefs, such as Margo's belief that that she would betray her deceased dog by giving her bountiful love to another animal.

At the time of its inception, Ellis's founding work in rational-emotive therapy was un-Freudian, thus heretical. Nevertheless, Ellis's thinking had the wind at its back and ultimately, after evolving at sea, it arrived in safe harbor as cognitive-behavioral therapy, the current darling of many dialogical therapists and third-party insurers alike. One important feature of Ellis's therapeutic method—a feature consistent with my own clinical experience—is his empirical discovery that the most effective clinical strategy is "exhortative-persuasive," in fact, "the more direct, persuasive, suggestive, active and logical," rather than emotion-based and emotion-laden, the "more effective at undermining and extirpating the basic causes . . . of the emotional difficulties of most—though by no means necessarily *all*—individuals who come for psychological help" (*RE*, 11, 37).[15] Another important aspect of rational-emotive therapy is Ellis's conception of an emotionally disturbed patient's thinking as auto-suggestive internal self-talk consisting of sentences that are variously irrational, illogical, unrealistic, impossible, superstitious, thus always self-defeating. In effect, Ellis recognized that the dual between therapist and patient was a linguistic or rhetorical struggle of suggestion that pitted the patient's habitual, emotionally disturbing, internal auto-suggestions against the strategically designed counter-suggestions of an exhortative-persuasive dialogical therapist. This clearly was Freud's "talking people into and out of things" redux, but with an interesting and important developmental difference. For the philosophically minded Ellis focused decisively on the Socratic-like task of persuading patients to "un*say* and un*think*" uncritically accepted language, ideas, and beliefs variously conceived as "hogwash" or "arrant nonsense" likely grounded in childhood indoctrination (*RE*, 20, 22, 94).

Not a man to mince words, Ellis literally conceived the patient's self-reinforcing auto-suggestions as "propaganda"; similarly and brilliantly, he not only conceived the dialogical therapist as a "counter-propagandist," he also conceived the therapist's strategic suggestions as "counter-propaganda" (*RE*, 95). Of course in professional literature, to once again distinguish clinical literature from clinical practice, the successful counter-propagandist was identified as an exhortative-persuasive dialogical therapist able to "induce more rational views" than the irrational, self-defeating views the emotionally disturbed patient was continually "self-instilling" or auto-suggesting (*RE*, 94–95). I am reasonably sure that in a good number of cases this may be true, but not in all cases as we have seen in my masquerade with Margo: a cognitive dance supported by the cognitive psychologist's discovery that benign fictions are adaptive and useful in the dialogical process of restoring mental health.

In the clinical trenches, with these nifty conceptions in tow, the task at hand may not be easy, but it certainly is straightforward. Specifically, given a vision of clinic patients as having an emotional disturbance grounded in uncritically accepted, self-defeating language, ideas, and beliefs—this being conceived as a "philosophic rather than psychiatric disturbance"—the therapeutic task of the clinical counter-propagandist is to suggestively challenge, refute, and change a patient's previously learned, now auto-suggested, self-defeating propaganda (*RE*, 94). In a strange, perhaps inimitable way unintended by Ellis in professional literature, this is exactly what I had in mind when I charmed Margo into believing that her loving pet in "doggie heaven" would not harbor a feeling of betrayal, but a gratifying feeling of relief, if she would acquire and bestow her abundant love on a new dog or better, a talking parrot, whose voice might replace the deathly silence at noon or the lonely obsessing during the wee hours of the morning.

Granted, this clinical interaction may not sound like a move forward in the ascent of man that is "teetering in the balance" of critical choices and decisions relating to a species' collective responsibility for the integrity of knowledge. But with a charming intern's therapeutic sensibility aflame, and fair words at the ready, I initiated a suggestive process of counter-propaganda that worked like Merlin's magic, mindful of the nagging truth that in professional literature, as well as in clinical practice, the quest for truth was already dead or slowly dying.

THE CRAZED COGITO

More often than not, while I am doing cognitive work with symptomatic patients whose minds were indoctrinated early on by self-defeating language, ideas, and beliefs, the regular auto-suggestion of which functions like sticky glue that fastens the chemical code of morbid symptoms to serotonin and norepinephrine receptors, I descend into the *milieu intérieur* in the manner of Descartes and while in a state of doubt about my clinical method, I ask myself whether the promising propaganda I am counter-suggesting is true or false, regardless of the propaganda's rich therapeutic potential. Beleaguered patients never know that I have taken a Cartesian dive into the epicenter of rational consciousness, for I am able to maintain this internal self-talk while lending a strategic ear to a patient's plight, as if I were a *doppelgänger*, daemonically possessed by a separate clinical and philosophic personality.

For the most part, in spite of the internal drama, while fitting clinically created belief to the logical possibilities of previously conditioned belief, or tailoring therapeutic fiction to various threads of tormenting fiction, I am engaged in a clinical struggle to find life-affirming language, ideas, and speech that will enable patients in my care to get unstuck, thereby achieving a remission of symptoms, a release of latent potentials, and constructive forward movement in life. Occasionally, in spite of Ellis's admirable intention to counter-suggest ideas that are more rational than the irrational ideas patients have been auto-suggesting, the art of cognitive therapy involves a clinical masquerade that pits self-affirming counter-propaganda against self-defeating propaganda, adaptive suggestion against maladaptive auto-suggestion, therapeutic indoctrination against harmful childhood indoctrination, regardless of the rule of reason or truth and falsity.

I would like to think that there are limits to the clinical creation of good stories, meaningful myths, and benign fictions used to promote the psychological health or well-being of symptomatic patients; however, as we have seen, the limiting line is not finely drawn and can range from shamanic explanations to the dogs of heaven. Ultimately, the limits of language, the boundary of benign fiction, depends on the ignorance or the acquired wisdom of each therapist, understanding wisdom as inner guidance determined by the circus and circumstance of life: the cash value of intellect, educational preparation, life experience, cultural interests, capacity for insight, moral values, and emotional disorders of the mental health clinician. Whatever the cash value might be, allowing for enormous differences in the calliope of circumstances conditioning the reputed wisdom of individual therapists, one thing seems certain, and that is a problematic uncertainty regarding the actual direction a patient will travel in life, while being guided by a clinical intervention that carries in its brain, breast, and bowels, a world of existential implications and unpredictable concrete consequences.

In retrospect, I am disposed to believe that I discharged my clinical responsibility to Margo, insofar as I persuaded this depressed woman to acquire a new dog and soon thereafter, she experienced a remission of morbid symptoms. In truth, this is as easy as it gets in the trenches. Accordingly, treatment was terminated and the patient went her way with a bill for professional services, but without a felt need for further assistance from a therapist.

Mind you, the remission of symptoms is a principal goal of the contemporary clinical quest for mental health, as well as a fairly accurate measure of the emotional well-being of clinic patients, at least in the collective mind of third-party insurers who are skillfully maneuvering a boulder on the mountain of profit and loss. On the other hand, the therapeutic intervention in question is a conspicuous example of a clinical interaction that resulted in a previously mentioned critique of the moral vacuity of dialogical therapy. This was a tough-minded critique offered by a hard-nosed moral philosopher who viewed the therapist as a manipulative character type who treats clinical ends as given, while remaining focused exclusively on the means to achieve these ends, specifically, effective techniques or clinical strategies capable of changing clinical symptoms into constructive energy, or maladjusted individuals into better-adjusted or well-adjusted women and men. In the harsh view of this contemporary Socratic man, given a therapeutic mind-set predisposed to treat ends as given—the predetermined ends of therapy being a remission of morbid symptoms—dialogical therapists "neither . . . do or are able to engage in moral debate."[16]

In retrospect, while developing a clinical treatment plan for Margo, I engaged in a moral debate of sorts: internal self talk that contrasted deontological conduct honoring rule-driven behavior (quest for truth) with teleological conduct focused on positive results to be achieved (remission of symptoms) by constructively enhancing Margo's silly fiction of doggie heaven. Additionally, I assessed my patient's educational preparation, as well as her capacity for self-reflection and insight in view of her mood disorder and storage of a veritable warehouse of uncritically accepted juvenile beliefs. Judging that the quickest course of action in this seemingly harmless matter was to play her game by pretending to validate the juvenile worldview that held her captive, as if she were a mind-fettered prisoner in Plato's cave and I were a puppeteer responsible for casting the appearance of things in murky shadows on the wall of the subterranean cavern, I supplemented her fiction and asked her to seriously consider the action I believed she needed to take in order to achieve a remission of symptoms. In the end, the clinical goal of symptom relief was achieved in short order, however, the philosopher was right: the clinical goal was set in advance and the ends of treatment were already given long before I laid eyes on this exotic dancer and put my ear to her plight.

Perhaps I am being as harsh as the hard-nosed moral philosopher when I advance the claim that a noble therapeutic sensibility may lead to clinical nihilism, not in the literature, of course, but certainly in practice, allowing for the discrepancy between what is written and what is said during dialogical interactions in rogue or respectable clinics spread far and wide throughout the land. Fortunately, a doubting therapist may sit in a comfortable armchair next to a warm fireplace with a snifter of Chambord and after an hour of relaxing reverie, or a terse moment of intense preparation, he can take a Cartesian dive into the *milieu intérieur* and after comparing and contrasting the philosophic and therapeutic sensibilities, ask himself responsibly: "In the effort to search for a moral way of living, in the midst of complex human problems that are intrinsically messy, what wisdom can I bring to bear in the effort to separate the better from the worse course of action?"

If I happened to suddenly perish from some unknown cause and found myself in Hades in deep conversation with Socrates and Sisyphus, I would certainly ask the Athenian gentleman the same question. The problem is, he would deflect the question by asking "What is wisdom?" and I would be no further ahead. Unwilling to answer direct questions that put him on the spot, Socrates confessed his ignorance to the bitter end. Holding fast to the strategy of having nothing to teach, he persisted in the activity of leading the souls of others by dismantling their uncritically accepted opinions and beliefs, as if he were chosen by the gods to engage in an annihilating style of life that made him a benefactor of humankind.

I have long believed that the confession of ignorance was another masquerade of truth: a philosophic dance that enabled a crafty old man to persuade his dialogical partners to develop *sophrosune* (σωφροσύνη): moderation, temperance, or prudence in thinking and behavior. But the confession of ignorance also hinged on the declaration that wisdom resides in an ethereal realm as a possession of the gods. Whether this is true or not, I cannot say. But for lesser mortals, who have complex questions that demand concrete answers, or pressing problems that cannot be referred to the gods, there may be something to gain by reinforcing the understanding that human wisdom is eminently fallible, particularly wisdom about wisdom, and this obtains in all times and places, whether we are on earth or in some fabulous yonder like Hades, in the throe of the ascent or the descent of humankind.

DEATH AND CREDULITY

From time to time, when I am removed from the clinical trenches and no longer directly responsible for patient care, I imagine Sisyphus taking a momentary pause from his futile labor to have a rejuvenating belly laugh at my ridiculous treatment of Margo. While imagining Sisyphus having a hearty laugh at my expense, I am delighted to think that I might have provided him with a little lift during his unending struggle in the underworld. But Socrates would have been appalled, even angered by my decision to embrace a silly fiction that involved acquiescing in ideas I believed to be false. After all, he was indicted, tried, and condemned to death for not believing in the gods of his fellow Athenians and he sipped a cup of toxic hemlock to honor the principles of a philosophic life, all the while knowing that his faithful friend, Crito, had arranged his escape from prison and safe exile from the sun-drenched shores of Aegean Athens. But we are dwelling in the twenty-first century in a technetronic civilization; biological man is fast succeeding psychological man in the clinical effort to salve the wounds of existence; and the ancient Socrates is neither the first nor the last word of wisdom useful in guiding us through contemporary struggles. In fact, the Athenian gentleman may have had a thing or two to learn in his vaunted quest for wisdom, truth, and best possible state of the soul; for who would deny that there is virtue in trying to better the lot of one's fellows? On closer scrutiny, however, the concrete act of "bettering" is neither as clear nor as self-evident as it may seem—a state of affairs that may have occurred to Karl Popper, who argued pointedly: "Our greatest troubles spring from something that is as admirable and sound as it is dangerous—from our impatience to better the lot of our fellows."

If an evolutionary biologist were to contemplate the grave and constant in human evolution, my masquerade with Margo would appear to be a trifling matter: of lesser moment than the insignificant contribution to the gene pool that issues from the successful perpetuation of an individual's DNA. As the controversial, Pulitzer Prize–winning evolutionary biologist E. O. Wilson observed: "Self-existence, or the suicide that terminates it, is not the central question of philosophy," as Camus claimed in *The Myth of Sisyphus*. "In evolutionary time the individual organism counts for almost nothing. In a Darwinist sense the organism does not live for itself. Its primary function is not even to reproduce other organisms; it reproduces genes, and it serves as their temporary carrier."[17] Wilson's impeccable insight notwithstanding, my brief therapeutic intervention with Margo was not as harmless or as unimportant as it seems; and I am loathe to leave the reader with a false impression, although this scruple does not always obtain when I am treating patients who have commerce with the dogs of heaven.

While discerning readers will not be persuaded by the logic, since it is flawed rather than impeccable, there is a compelling argument to make about a therapist's personal responsibility in reinforcing an attitude of *credulity* in the mind of vulnerable patients.[18] I may have been a well-intentioned clinical alchemist determined to turn my patient's leaden depression into a golden agate of well-being in the shortest time possible. Nevertheless, by adding import and substance to the uncritically accepted belief that dogs of heaven could have thoughts, feelings, and wise guidance for the living on earth, I reinforced a mindless credulity in my patient: a willingness to believe anything, no matter how irrational or absurd, with insufficient empirical evidence or rational justification. In the important business of establishing rational grounds for belief and passing on to others a responsible method of fixing belief, particularly future generations of children destined to depend on adults for wise guidance, both in daily life and in the life of mind, the clinical alchemy I practiced with Margo is suspect insofar as it reinforces an uncritical acceptance of belief that characterizes an arrested, potentially dangerous, primitive stage of cognitive development.

Perhaps this sounds silly or melodramatic? After all, I am talking about a few clinical hours with a woman who was depressed about the death of her dog. This is much ado about nothing! So I ought to give up the dog and move on to something more important.

Granted, Margo was not going to leave the clinic and dance around town spreading a dangerous fiction that could topple Western civilization. But consider this critical rejoinder: when a credulous person shares a fiction with a person who happens to be in a position of power, influence, and authority—say a respected dialogical therapist with a flair for using fair words—and the therapist engages in animated conversation that validates the fiction by returning the impression that the fiction is true, value and significance accrue to false belief and a process of infecting other minds with fiction may ensue. When this happens, uncritically accepted belief is transmitted to other people who may be more or less credulous themselves. Sooner or later, the transmission of a beloved fiction from person to person, from family to family, from city to city, and so on, results in a veritable army of true believers. When this happens, the potentially dangerous combination of credulity and false belief may reach critical mass.

The potential harm in reinforcing credulity is magnified when one considers how often fictive beliefs inhabiting credulous minds result in historical action in the social, political, and juridical spheres of life: concrete historical action among people who are ripe and ready to receive whatever whacky wisdom or inane instruction an uncritically accepted social, political, religious, or juridical fiction has to offer. Equally noteworthy is the possibility that the ruling elite, who either believe in or see through the fiction, may use a grand fiction as a "noble lie": an "opportune falsehood" that enables them to manipulate an army of credulous believers in order to achieve one or another political end held fast in their line of vision.[19] Given a widespread attitude of credulity, a grave and constant willingness to believe anything with insufficient evidence, anything is possible! Conceivably, a whole country could be persuaded to wage war in a foreign land on the basis of this sort of mental screwing.

There is reason to believe that collective nightmares are less likely to occur in a culture inspired by an uncompromising quest for truth, for Socratic quest militates against credulity, insofar as it demands rational grounds for fixing belief. Of course the trouble with Socratic quest, given the interminable questions, the critical cross-examination, the unacceptable answers, is that belief is never fixed; and this produces crazy-making problems of a different kind. More to the point, a hideous variety of historical precedents established the crude fact that Socratic quest, indeed, the life of mind, can go up in flames as it did during the 1930s and 1940s following an eerie medieval book burning engineered by Propaganda Minister Goebbels, during which the groundbreaking scientific work of Einstein and the pioneering psychoanalytic work of Freud were torched and turned to ash. Unfortunately, this particular burning of books augured a cremation of human flesh, the weight of which tipped the scale of genocide. But this is not a rare, isolated example of death and credulity in the rise and fall of civilizations.

Simply put, from time to time, the dogs of heaven bite! Sometimes they merely bark and bark loudly all night, but other times they bite fiercely and will not let go without a struggle. In the best of all possible worlds, the bite leaves a minor flesh wound; but on other occasions, when the dogs of heaven are rabid, as was the case with the myths and fictions enveloping Einstein, Freud, Goebbels, and Hitler, the bite leaves a collective illness or a corporate madness that is difficult, if not impossible, to treat. Then trouble may be heaped upon trouble.

Often, death follows credulity as winter follows autumn, night follows day, confession follows sexual secrets, and punishment follows confession. More recently, to press the point, the dogs of heaven were not only barking, but biting fiercely in the Middle East, the cradle of civilization, where enraptured Muslims embracing truth, goodness, and Allah persevered in an age-old struggle with contemporary Crusaders, who were educated to embrace truth, goodness, and Christ. This endless human struggle, built on and nourished by a variety of myths and fictions, not to mention a vast array of political lies and opportune falsehoods, keeps us attuned to the fact that there may be widespread death and destruction during a masquerade of truth that determines concrete historical action in the social, political, and juridical spheres of life.

Considering evolutionary time, these brief moments of death and credulity in the arc of civilizations are trifles light as air, but of greater moment than the masquerade of truth informing my clinical intervention with a depressed patient who was madly in love with a dog of heaven. Regarding these things, Hegel's dialectical wisdom is still precious: "We may rest assured that it is the nature of truth to force its way to recognition when the time comes, and . . . it only appears when its time has come, and hence never appears too soon, and never finds a public that is not ripe and ready to receive it."[20] I would only add to Hegel's thesis, by way of antithesis, that it is the nature of falsehood to force its way to recognition when the time comes; and it manifests itself when its time has come, although it may be too late to help a disillusioned or disenchanted public that is finally ripe and ready to receive it.

NOTES

1. Jay S. Efran, Michael D. Lukens, Robert J. Lukens, *Language, Structure, and Change: Frameworks of Meaning in Psychotherapy* (New York: W. W. Norton & Company, 1990), 14–15.

2. Philip Rieff, *The Triumph of the Therapeutic: Uses of Faith after Freud* (New York: Harper & Row, 1966), 13, 27.

3. Irvin D. Yalom, *Existential Psychotherapy* (New York: Basic Books, 1980); cited in the text as *EX*.

4. Ernest Jones, "The Madonna's Conception through the Ear," in *Psycho-Myth, Psycho-History: Essays in Applied Psychoanalysis*, vol. 2 (New York: Stonehill Publishing, 1974), 268.

5. Hilary Putnam, *Ethics without Ontology* (Cambridge, MA: Harvard University Press, 2004); cited in the text as *EO*.

6. Plato, *Theatetus*, trans. F. M. Cornford, in *Collected Dialogues*, 151d.

7. William James, *The Meaning of Truth* (Ann Arbor: University of Michigan Press, 1970); cited in the text as *MT*.

8. Claude Levi-Strauss, *Structural Anthropology*, trans. Claire Jacobson and Brooke Grundfest Schoepf (New York: Anchor Books, 1967), 162.

9. Henry Margenau, "Einstein's Conception of Reality," in *Albert Einstein Philosopher-Scientist*, vol. 1, ed. Paul Arthur Schilpp, *The Library of Living Philosophers*, vol. 7 (La Salle, IL: Open Court Classics, 1969), 254.

10. Hans Reichenbach, "The Philosophical Significance of the Theory of Relativity," in *Albert Einstein Philosopher-Scientist*, vol. 1, 295–96.

11. Carl P. Ellerman, "The Absurd Sensibility of Existential Psychotherapy: Clinical Application of Survivors' Experience of Treblinka and Other Death Camps," *Journal of Contemporary Psychotherapy* 27, no. 2 (1997): 128.

12. Loyal Rue, *By the Grace of Guile: The Role of Deception in Natural History and Human Affairs* (New York: Oxford University Press, 1994).

13. Carl P. Ellerman, "Pragmatic Existential Therapy," *Journal of Contemporary Psychotherapy* 29, no. 1 (1999): 61.

14. Shelley E. Taylor, *Positive Illusions: Creative Self-Deception and the Healthy Mind* (New York: Basic Books, 1989), xi, 6–7.

15. Albert Ellis, *Reason and Emotion in Psychotherapy* (Secaucus, NJ: The Citadel Press, 1977); cited in the text *RE*.

16. Alasdair MacIntyre, *After Virtue: A Study in Moral Theory* (Notre Dame, IN: University of Notre Dame Press, 1984), 30.

17. Edward O. Wilson, *Sociobiology: The Abridged Edition* (Cambridge, MA: The Belknap Press of Harvard University Press, 1980), 3.

18. Philosophic discussions with students, particularly prison inmates, were greatly enhanced by the clarity with which the nineteenth-century English philosopher W. K. Clifford presented the subject of credulity in "The Ethics of Belief," in *Philosophy: The Basic Issues* (New York: St. Martin's Press, 1982), 45–50.

19. In Book III of *Republic* (389b, 414b), during an extended discussion of the ideal state, Plato envisioned the ruling elite as healers of a sick *polis*; analogously, he envisioned physicians as healers of sick persons. Conceiving falsehood as a "remedy" or a useful "form of medicine," Plato granted the healers of the *polis* and healers of persons the right to manipulate and deceive by using "opportune falsehoods" or the instrument of a "noble lie," if this would facilitate the struggle to heal a sick *polis* or sick human beings.

20. G. W. F. Hegel, *The Phenomenology of Mind*, trans. J. B. Baillie (New York: Harper Torchbooks, 1967), 129.

11

The Therapeutic Artiste

THE AESTHETICS OF CLINICAL ENCHANTMENT

In the aftermath of Sartre's public lecture of 1945, during which the existential philosopher adumbrated a liberating aesthetic ethic that compared moral choice to the construction of a work of art, meta-psychologists began to argue similarly that in the mental health clinic, the dialogical interaction of therapist and patient is an aesthetic experience that could be likened to the creation of a work of art. I cannot say with certainty that these postmodern theorists actually read Sartre's published lecture on humanistic elements of existentialism; however, I can confirm that by the 1980s, meta-psychologists were raising critical questions about the ambiguities of clinical confession and clinical interpretation.

For a handy visual perspective on the dis-ease in meta-psychology, art aficionados may consider the extent to which the nineteenth-century representational realist Gustave Courbet would have been ill at ease with the swirling splashes of paint appearing in the creative artwork of the twentieth-century abstract expressionist Jackson Pollock. While Pollock was inspired to liberally drip his paints onto a canvas resting on the studio floor, with neither interest in figurative representation, nor intent to paint the natural order of things present to the human perception, Courbet's aesthetic sensibility was conditioned by the opposing view that "painting is an essentially concrete art, and can consist only of the representation of things both real and existing."[1]

As a result of their discomfort with ambiguity, meta-psychologists argued persuasively that a patient's interpretation of the past, the presumptive historical past narrated in clinical confessions, in conjunction with the therapist's interpretation of the patient's interpretive confessions, creates insurmountable ambiguities of meaning and truth. Consequently, it is useless to follow Freud's example of thoughtfully descending into a patient's psyche with the goal of digging in the past and uncovering the historical truth of childhood experience. In the final analysis it is more productive to treat the clinical encounters between dialogical therapists and symptomatic patients as a creative experience in which the value of what is spoken and heard is judged by aesthetic standards, such as (a) the beauty, coherence, meaningfulness, and satisfaction of the story a therapist and patient are co-creating, and (b) the favorable impact of this creative storytelling on clinical results (*NT*, 264–97).[2]

In a mental health clinic built on aesthetic standards of this sort, the measurable standard of progress in patient care is whether or not a good story, a beautiful myth, or a meaningful fiction works to achieve a remission of symptoms, well-being, or other evidence of psychological health in a therapist's dialogical partners. Alternately put, in the postmodern clinic, in a strategic effort to replace a knowledge-based quest for historical truth with the cognitive-emotional satisfaction elicited by clinical stories arising from artistic invention, the critical question a therapeutic artiste must ask himself is this: "Will my imaginative interpretation of a patient's clinical confession produce a good, coherent, meaningful, satisfying story, and will my creative storytelling effectively fulfill the clinical goal of securing the patient's psychological health or emotional well-being, Socratic quest for truth, Freudian dig for truth, and historical truth itself, be damned!"

Unless I am suffering an illusion, in this case being played upon by a remarkable ambiguity of meaning and truth, this is not a mindless nihilism designed to produce anarchy in the clinic, although anarchism plays a leading role in postmodern enchantments of the clinic. In fact, I am not stretching hard truth beyond a reasonable limit when I offer the satiric suggestion that in a meta-psychological way, therapists may be conceived as professional storytellers in the tradition of Hans Christian Anderson, the Brothers Grimm, and other inspired authors of fairy tales that have captured the receptive minds of millions of credulous children. Concerning this state of affairs, I am mindful of the fact that thirty-six years after going to the end of a historical nightmare in Buchenwald and Dachau, the eminent child psychologist Bruno Bettelheim made much of the enchantment offered by fairy tales, noting carefully that by virtue of their ability to enchant the mind, agonistic fairy tales that depict the confrontation of a hero or a heroine with ultimate concerns, such as life and death or good and evil, enable a human being to understand and imaginatively master meaningful aspects of humankind's existential predicament.[3] Of course

Bettelheim was writing about the creative process of enchanting the malleable minds of children who are dealing with oedipal, narcissistic, and sibling conflicts. He was not referring to the clinical process of enchanting the mind of adults who are responsible for the moral and intellectual development of the impressionable children they have begotten and now are guiding to maturity.

One of the meta-psychologists who carefully examined the dialogical interaction of therapist and patient, while critically evaluating an aesthetic model of clinical practice, conceived contemporary therapists as creative storytellers who are best served by realizing that the historical truth or falsity of a clinical story is irrelevant to its cognitive-emotional impact, in the same way, I would add, that queries regarding the historical truth or falsity of one of Pollock's action paintings would be irrelevant to a cognitive-emotional appreciation of the painting's beauty. Extending the implications of the aesthetic model of clinical practice, while searching for an elusive anchor to contain anarchistic chaos in the clinic, psychiatrist Donald Spence offered the provocative notion that "artistic truth" applies to evocative paintings and to clinical interpretations, the satisfaction of which renders both paintings and clinical interpretations objects of beauty, in spite of the fact that an abstract painting fails to faithfully represent reality, while a therapist's interpretation of clinical confessions fails to faithfully represent or accurately correspond, fit, or agree with, historical reality (*NT*, 268–69).

Viewing therapeutic stories as artistic creations, with any number of imaginative stories able to satisfy aesthetic criteria of meaning, coherence, and beauty, Spence advanced a provocative model of clinical practice that abandoned Freud's presumptive search for truth and with it, an attitude of mind cued to an education to reality, in favor of a seductive clinical aestheticism in which a story's imaginative appeal and therapeutic impact are cardinal virtues. In a mental health clinic based upon these aesthetic standards, the therapeutic artiste "commits himself to a belief in the truth of his painting—by which we mean its artistic truth—but we need say nothing about its truth as a representation of the real world. . . . Art, after all, is only loosely tied to reality" (*NT*, 274).

Failing to offer the discriminating judgment that some fine art, such as the representational art of Courbet, is tightly tied to reality, while other fine art, like the modern abstract paintings of Pollock, is not, Spence painted a meta-psychological picture of aesthetic interactions in the mental health clinic that faithfully depicts a masquerade of truth, insofar as unsuspecting patients with morbid symptoms are dancing in the dark with seemingly trustworthy therapists, while being duped into believing that the nonrepresentational stories they are told are true to reality. According to Spence:

> The analyst . . . commits himself to a belief in his hypothesis and is inclined to use it in a pragmatic fashion, as a way of making something happen. He is less committed to a belief in its truth value—either because he has no clear way of knowing whether or not it actually occurred or because he is proposing something that has no clear correspondence with an event in the patient's life. . . . The more appropriate question concerns . . . its artistic truth, its significance as a kind of creative endeavor, a putting together of known facts about the patient in a new form that carries a high probability of making something happen in the analytic space. (*NT*, 275)

Committed Freudians or skeptical therapists trained in other schools of clinical expertise might think that any consideration of artistic truth is patent nonsense because in the real world of action and reaction in the clinical trenches, the creative activity said to be artistically true has nothing to do with putting paint on a lifeless canvas. Rather, in the clinical trenches, artistic truth applies to what dialogical therapists ultimately say and do to the living, breathing, emotionally reactive human beings in their care. Still, snubbing one's nose at artistic truth suggests a hasty conclusion may have been reached, particularly if a thoughtful therapist takes a moment for scrupulous self-examination and carefully considers the creative imagination and free invention involved in actively sketching in language, ideas, and speech subjective impressions offered during clinical interactions with emotionally wounded patients.

Mind you, we have not yet begun to deal with the thorny problem of confirming or disconfirming a therapist's impressionistic painting: the subjective impressions spoken, heard, taken home, and processed by the patient long after the clinical hour comes to an end. Does a painstaking empirical process of confirming or disconfirming clinical hypotheses actually take place in the clinical trenches? Or is it more likely the case that mental health clinicians creatively invent and offer fruitful hypotheses, fitting fictions, or good therapeutic stories that explain the life, the thinking and behavior, the morbid symptoms, of their patients, with hope that these imaginative impressions will resonate favorably in the receptive mind of agonistic men and women who may or may not be enchanted. In either case, as Spence confessed, the therapist never knows whether the details of a therapeutic story "actually occurred" or whether a clinical hypothesis has "correspondence with an event in the patient's life."

The thorny issue of verification aside, if a therapist sees some merit in the aesthetic model of clinical practice and believes this way of thinking may have practical use during dialogical struggles in the trenches, the better part of wisdom—and the way to find Aristotle's golden mean between excess and deficiency in thinking and behavior—may be to fault the aesthetic model for being unbalanced in favor of artistic truth. Specifically, if it is reasonable to speak of artistic truth in fine artworks and in clinical stories, it follows that it is reasonable to speak of *artistic falsehood* in artworks and in clinical stories, as well. After all, truth and falsity are normally conceived as a complementary pair, like "right" and "left," this being a complementary couple taken for granted when a person dons a pair of lambskin gloves to keep hands warm during the icy days of winter. Perhaps a better, more dynamic way to conceive the complementary coupling of truth and falsity would be to imagine marital partners who have an icy relationship during the dog days of summer. They may be married, all right, but they have a cold, highly conflictive, oppositional relationship that keeps them at odds.

Whatever analogy is used for perspective, I am obligated to say that aesthetic models of clinical practice pay scant attention to artistic falsehood, while seeking to liberate therapists from problems of hard truth and objective reference, the correlation of which is captured nicely in Aristotle's quaint notion: "To say of what is that it is not, or of what is not that it is, is false, while to say of what is that it is, or of what is not that it is not, is true."[4] I would also suggest that liberation from Aristotelian truth in the aesthetic clinic has contributed to the cultural creation of "*the desert of the real itself*," once again using Baudrillard's evocative image of a postmodern condition in which "truth, reference, [and] objective cause have ceased to exist." In this parched desert, where hard liquor is cheap, but hard truth has dried-up from disuse, one reason for failing to focus on artistic falsehood, while championing artistic truth, may be that the proverbial devil lurks in this detail. I mean the diabolical detail of painting an *ugly picture* or telling an *ugly story* that is artistically false because it fails to have a therapeutic impact or worse, it has a direct impact that brings harm to an emotionally reactive patient in clinical care.

I am mindful here of Dr. Klein, a previously mentioned patient who had an inferiority complex cued to his perception of being born with a pygmy's penis. In spite of other gross impairments that made interpersonal relationships difficult at best, Dr. Klein became a wonderful patient whose treatment I was committed to for a number of years. He was remarkably intelligent, highly verbal, extremely analytic, willing and able to engage in critical self-examination, and by the end, he presented as a very likeable man of the highest character. During one memorable clinical hour, while I was trying to buttress his esteem by coauthoring a beautiful story about his considerable achievements as a medical doctor, hoping that human achievements writ large would compensate for a body part born small, he replied quite soberly and correctly, I might add: in the medical profession, "if you fail to act with honor you could see the results in the f——ing morgue!"

By acting with honor, Dr. Klein meant that a doctor who has responsibility for the life and death of fellow human beings must engage self-consciously, self-critically, and continuously, in the scrupulous process of identifying, understanding, and correcting false judgments, particularly false judgments that lead to mistaken procedures, otherwise human error and countless mistakes are likely to continue unabated with disastrous results. Of course, if a doctor doesn't have a concept of the falsity of judgments, opinions, and beliefs, thereby blithely believing that everything he thinks and does is hunky dory, his patients will ultimately find themselves in a world of trouble as Dr. Klein suggested when he made his memorable vulgar reference to the morgue.

For this reason, and with a view toward honor in the aesthetic clinic, stationed as it now is, in the desert of the real, I am pleased to say there are historical precedents for focusing on (a) artistic falsehood in fine art, and (b) ugliness as the evaluative standard or scale of measurement, this wise guidance coming from knowledgeable and experienced creative artists themselves.

RUNNING WITH DEGAS

As if he were offering his considerable artistic experience and informed aesthetic judgment to this discussion of truth and falsehood in art and clinical practice, it came to pass that one evening when the masterful nineteenth-century artist Edgar Degas was dining with the masterful French symbolist poet Stéphane Mallarmé, Degas stated boldly, as was his custom: "Art is falsehood!"[5] In another place and time, using a specific artistic experience to support his conclusion, Degas observed: "Art is the same world as artifice, that is to say, something deceitful. It must succeed in giving the impression of nature by false means, but it has to look true. Draw a straight line askew, as long as it gives the impression of being straight!"[6]

It is tempting to pause here to offer the reader an extensive comparison of the shared thinking of Degas and Socrates, strange as that may seem, given the vastly different historical eras and disparate occupations of these noteworthy gentlemen. I have in mind a comparison of (a) Degas's view of the deceitfulness of art and the way a skillful artist enables something to look or falsely appear to be true, and (b) Socrates' incisive view of the art of rhetoric, that is, the art of a skilled orator or politician who uses language, ideas, and speech to influence the mind of others, but in so doing, is not engaged in a search for truth, because the deceitful rhetorician is presenting that which is "plausible" or that which "will be thought" to be true—the art of rhetorical persuasion depending on what is seemingly true and convincing.[7]

Keeping this brief comparison in mind, I would like to continue running with Degas, who once again thematized the falsehood of creative art, this time during a conversation with the impressionist painter Walter Sickert. Reflecting on his own creative work, as well as the work of other artists, Degas confessed: "One gives the idea of the truth by means of the false."[8] Offering a concrete example of the falsehood of art at the Louvre, during a tour with his friend and noted illustrator Georges Jeanniot, Degas asked Jeanniot if he happened to notice that the Medici Venus was "out of the vertical"; explaining what he saw, while also pointing out that artists use fantasy, imagination, and memory to achieve a liberation from "the tyranny of nature," Degas maintained that the Medici Venus "is in a position which she could not hold if she were alive. By this detail, a fault according to people who know nothing about art, the Greek sculptor gave his figure a splendid movement, while still retaining the calm which characterizes masterpieces."[9]

For clinical perspective, "nature," in Degas's reference to "the tyranny of nature," is analogous to a patient's historical reality, while tyranny, to sustain Degas's political metaphor, resides in a therapist's domination by the dogma that clinical interpretations must faithfully represent historical reality, as though therapeutic storytelling should attempt to do the same work as a realistic painting of Courbet. On the other hand, if we conceive the artist as an individual who is free to use fantasy, imagination, and memory to achieve liberation from the tyranny of nature, we might also consider a therapist as an individual who is free to use fantasy, imagination, and memory to achieve liberation from the tyranny of faithful representation. The former liberation may result in an aesthetic masterpiece; the latter liberation hopefully results in the creation of good or beautiful clinical stories that lead to a remission of morbid symptoms or well-being: in short, a favorable resolution of presenting problems, regardless of the absence of Aristotelian truth and objective reference.

Perhaps it is not offending reason to run with the metaphors and offer the view that Jackson Pollock achieved liberation from the tyranny of nature by means of dynamic action painting that allowed him to freely drip, splash, and pour paint on a canvas. This was a form of artistic liberation neither sought nor desired by Courbet, who was controlled by the dogma that painting is a faithful representation of things real and existing. Similarly, dialogical therapists achieve liberation from traditional clinical authority when they abandon any attempt to faithfully represent historical reality in clinical stories, in favor of an aesthetic model of gathering the subjective impressions of patient and therapist, then using these imaginative impressions to inventively create therapeutic stories, myths, or fictions, whose meaning, coherence, and beauty resonate with patients in life-affirming ways suggestive of positive clinical results.

Returning to the aesthetic views of Degas, a man of bountiful self-expression who was never shy to state his mind, it came to pass that he elaborated on the theme of artistic falsehood during the late 1890s, in a conversation with art critic François Thiebault-Sisson. Reflecting on his lengthy experience as an artist—a fine artist who rendered exquisite impressions of graceful racehorses, young ballerinas in awkward repose, and mature women at their toilette—Degas spoke as follows:

> The most beautiful and the best-wrought drawing is always less than the precise . . . absolute truth and thus leaves the way open to all that is fraudulent. You know the . . . very worthy drawing in which Fromentin captures the stride of a galloping Arabian steed; compare it with reality and you will be struck far less by what it expresses than by what it lacks. The natural disposition and true character of the animal are absent from this enthusiastic improvisation by a very clever hand. The same is true of renditions of . . . the human form in motion. Draw a dancing figure; with little skill, you should be able to create an illusion for a short time. But however painstakingly you study your adaptation, you will achieve nothing more than an insubstantial silhouette, lacking all notion of mass and of volume and devoid of precision.[10]

Having run with Degas in an Aristotelian state of mind, thereby attempting to find a way to rectify a deficient, unbalanced focus on artistic truth in meta-psychological theory, we may be ready to say something concrete about how to conceive artistic falsehood while dealing with patients in a mental health clinic supported by aesthetic standards. But there are two caveats, the first of which is, we are not actually referring to paints, canvases, and action painting, strictly speaking. Rather, we are speaking about live subjects: emotionally impaired, often emotionally reactive human beings, some of whom are enchanted with the clinic and trust their therapist to use his knowledge and skill in active dialogue that leads to symptom relief or other evidence of well-being. Secondly, while attempting to see the clinical world through the aesthetic eyes of an eminent painter, it might serve us well to remain cognizant of the fact that Degas was an artist who had a retinal disorder that put him in the agonizing position of painting fine artworks while becoming blind. Sad to say, it is certainly possible that Degas's aesthetic vision was as impaired as his eyesight. Having offered these caveats, I am emboldened to say that Degas was highly skilled with paints and canvases; as a result, he was able to offer an intriguing clue to identifying falsehood in art. Specifically, in 1897, in another conversation with Thiebault-Sisson, while anguishing over the irreversible process of losing his sight, Degas observed:

> In art . . . one is never entitled to disregard what is true. But this truth . . . may be rendered only if one does not seek out ugliness as a matter of principle and so much so that one remains blind to all else. . . . The true realist dissimulates nothing but places things where they belong; he classifies the features that go to make up his composition according to their degree of interest; in this way, he makes a series of choices and if his choices are judicious, this is style. This was how Chardin worked, who while treating the most vulgar motifs with admirable conscientiousness, nonetheless succeeded in lending them elegance, grace and distinction.[11]

Given this interesting run with Degas, I can now say that if we use his standard of evaluating paintings we may begin to think about *ugliness*, as well as *beauty*, in the aesthetic clinic. Simply stated, "ugliness" is an expression I would use in references to artistic falsehood, a clinical state of affairs that complements "beauty," an expression I would use in references to artistic truth. When I think and speak this way, however abominable it may be to clinicians committed to a quest for hard truth and the kind of objective reference Freud referred to as an "education to reality," I have in mind ugly clinical interpretations, ugly clinical stories, or ugly clinical myths that may or may not be coauthored with emotionally impaired patients. Having previously reported that a beautiful, artistically true clinical story was felicitously conceived as good, coherent, satisfying, and meaningful due to its favorable impact on clinical results, I shall now say by comparison, that an ugly, artistically false clinical story may be conceived as bad, incoherent, unsatisfying, and meaningless due to its failure to impact clinical results or worse, its harmful impact on patients in clinical care.

In sum, clinical ugliness is produced when a creative story, an imaginative interpretation, or an inventive myth either fails to have a therapeutic impact or succeeds in having an impact, but it is an unfavorable, counterproductive impact that harms an emotionally reactive patient. Moreover, at the extremes of dialogical experience, if a therapist happens to tell an ugly story it is possible to see the results in the morgue, to borrow the viewpoint of Dr. Klein. On the other hand: (a) if an aesthetically minded clinician does not pursue ugliness as a matter of principle, understanding that in the mental health clinic, a dialogical therapist is never entitled to disregard what he takes for hard truth; (b) if a resourceful clinical confessor addresses features of a patient's painful confession according to the highest degree of meaning, thereby placing fair words where they belong in a therapeutic artwork; (c) if a pragmatic therapist makes a series of creative choices that have consequences in a patient's life, and if these free choices happen to be sound, life-affirming or constructive; (d) an artistic therapist may treat the most vulgar life history with admirable conscientiousness, actually succeeding in the enchanted clinic with elegance, grace, and distinction.

IN LECTURE AND IN LIFE

Professor Spence was not alone in advancing a meta-psychological theory whose aestheticism put the screws to Socratic man, while also placing the aesthetic clinic deep within the desert of the real. More radical, perhaps, Jungian psychologist James Hillman revisioned psychology as fiction. Nominated for a Pulitzer Prize for his distinctive ideas, Hillman argued anarchically that psychology is an imaginative process of open ideation not based on laws, axioms, or hypotheses tied to evidence, experimental test, verification, or falsification (*RP*, 150).[12] In the context of this risky anarchistic aestheticism, the clinician searching for a quest for hard truth in dialogical interactions with symptomatic patients will find himself confused, while an imagination comfortable with ambiguity will find an interesting guide to playing doctor with symptomatic patients who expect a bit of truth for their money. Regardless of the patient's naïve expectations or the seriousness of the mental illness being treated, "we practitioners," Hillman argued, are free to "go on mythologizing, deriving our tough-minded empirical facts from an extraordinary form of fiction: the case history, the anamnesis, the 'write-up,' by means of which the details of a life are composed into a story, receive a vision, and thereby a mythical person becomes the personification of a fate which issues into the therapeutic process" (*RP*, 155).

While working in the clinical trenches, engaged in a daily struggle against illness and death, I am often struck by the difference between theory and practice: the enormous difference between lecturing about a subject and actually putting into practice the subject of the lecture. In fact, it often seems to me that in the postmodern life of mind—a hyper-enlightened mind that often lacks common sense—there is a lost or forgotten sense in which a real human being, not a mythical person, experiences the fateful consequences of suicide, sexual crime, or a momentous historical process resulting in the grief of many. For this and other demonstrable reasons, in theory and in practice, in lecture and in life, I find myself in harmony with Ernst Cassirer, a modern neo-Kantian philosopher, as well as an exiled German Jew, who came to understand firsthand during a hellish holocaust that "the mythology of a people does not *determine* but *is* its fate, its destiny as decreed from the very beginning."[13]

Regarding concrete reality, the cognitive focus of an existential psychology worthy of the name; and with remembrance of Jacob Bronowski's urgent plea that we must learn to touch people, in a respectful way, I would add, that doesn't leave the people we treat in the pseudo-existential state of hyper-enlightened abstraction; it falls to me to say that the cattle cars streaming out of railway stations throughout Nazi-occupied Europe during the Second World War were not filled to the suffocating brim with mythical men, women, and children. The shit, the vomit, and the corpses on cattle car floors were not an extraordinary form of fiction! In fact, when the cattle cars finally arrived and crossed the threshold of monstrous decision, and a harsh voice shouting "left" or "right" was heard, the historical consequence was life or death: a momentary reprieve or brutal extermination. For the select, it was the gas and the ovens and this was a real grim fate, not a fabulous fairy tale of the Brothers Grimm.

To change the focus dramatically, with respect for the handful of remaining survivors who lived this nightmare and millions of the dead whose nightmare came to a horrible historical end, I have treated hundreds of unrepentant perpetrators, many of whom did not seem to have the vaguest notion that they were creating victims when they foisted the tyranny of the penis on innocent children. As a mental health clinician attempting to conduct a responsible private practice; as an aspiring moral agent trying to cultivate a bit of common sense; when treating these children I have asked myself a few pointed questions. "Are these traumatized children mythical people? Is the fate of six-year-old Allen, a patient forced to turn his backside to his father, an abstract fate? Is the incestuous fate of Diane, a patient whose father held a gun to her head and forced her to give him oral pleasure, simply the personification of a fate issuing in a therapeutic process in clinical space: a creative process of open ideation not based on fallible hypotheses tied to evidence, experimental test, verification, or falsification?"

In the end, I suppose the crucial question is this: Can a dialogical therapist actually go to the end of meta-psychological theories in practice, in the clinical trenches, not with mythical people, but with living, breathing human beings who present with serious life problems and morbid symptoms, not to mention suicidal ideation, method, and intention. Is it possible for a mental health clinician to actually put into practice an aesthetic vision of psychology as fiction and successfully engage in an intimate dialogical process within the erotic underworld of the clinical confessional? In short, if we take seriously the postmodern psychologizer's aberrant notion that dialogical therapy is creative art, sans ancient Socratic quest or its modern Freudian iteration, can a therapist use an aesthetic model of therapy in clinical practice and function responsibly, while working to produce psychological health or well-being in the grossly impaired patients in his care?

It goes without saying that I am guilty of being a literalist of the imagination in this discourse on clinical aestheticism, but I am purposefully challenging the mythology of meta-psychologizers, as well as my own clinical method, because myth and method have a good chance of becoming the destiny, the fate, the historical reality, of masses of people: "crowds of neurotics," as Freud realized early on, "whose number seemed further multiplied by the manner in which they hurried, with their troubles unsolved, from one physician to another." If this is true, and clinical experience gives me ample reason to think it is true, postmodern versions of aestheticism are not only a more recent enchantment of the clinic, but in some respects, the enchantment of therapist and patient, of storyteller and hearers of stories alike.

Regarding the enchantment of the therapist, I can honestly say that when a clinical story succeeds, when a meaningful myth or a fabulous fiction actually works to generate constructive change, say symptom relief in a chronically symptomatic patient, a clinical storyteller can literally feel as if he has created a fine work of art. Not in an artist's studio, as though he were a reincarnation of Courbet, Degas, or Pollock, but in the clinical consulting room where fair words are colorful paints and the patient's morbid illness is the weathered canvas of clinical creation.

Unfortunately, I do not have the experience of being an authentic painter, a real wizard, a true magician, or a transcendent miracle worker, but I have had the good fortune of being a successful storyteller; and I imagine that the gratification I experienced while telling a clinical tale or two is similar to the emotional exhilaration that accrues to individuals who have mastered the art of wizards, the craft of magicians, and the illusions of miracle workers, in spite of the fact that in the mental health clinic, gravity goes hand in hand with gratification, while ugliness may be coupled daemonically with beauty.

NOTES

1. Gustave Courbet's observation on art is quoted without source details in John Canaday, *Mainstreams of Modern Art* (New York: Simon and Schuster, 1959), 103–4.
2. Donald P. Spence, *Narrative Truth and Historical Truth: Meaning and Interpretation in Psychoanalysis* (New York: W. W. Norton & Company, 1982); cited in the text as *NT*.
3. Bruno Bettelheim, *The Uses of Enchantment: The Meaning and Importance of Fairy Tales* (New York: Vintage Books, 1977), 3–19.
4. Aristotle, *Metaphysics*, in *The Basic Works of Aristotle*, ed. Richard McKeon, trans. W. D. Ross (New York: Random House, 1941), Bk. IV, #25.
5. A recollection of Degas from Ernest Rouart, quoted in *Degas by Himself: Drawings, Prints, Paintings, Writings*, ed. Richard Kendall (Edison, NJ: Chartwell Books, 1994), 305.
6. An aphorism of Degas from Henri Hertz, *Degas* (Paris: Libraire Felix Alcan, 1920), quoted in Kendall, *Degas*, 319.
7. Plato, *Phaedrus*, trans. R. Hackforth, in *Collected Dialogues*, 260a, 261a, 272e.
8. An aphorism of Degas from Walter Sickert, "Degas," *The Burlington Magazine*, vol. 176, no. 31 (November 1917), quoted in Kendall, *Degas*, 319.

9. A recollection of Degas from Georges Jeanniot, "Souvenirs de Degas," *La Revue Universelle,* 15 October and 1 November 1933, quoted in Kendall, *Degas,* 299.

10. François Thiebault-Sisson, *Degas, Form and Space,* ed. J. Guillaud and M. Guillaud (New York: Rizzoli, 1984), quoted in Kendall, *Degas,* 245.

11. Thiebault-Sisson quoted in Kendall, *Degas,* 245.

12. James Hillman, *Re-visioning Psychology* (New York: Harper Perennial, 1992); cited in the text as *RP*.

13. Ernst Cassirer, *The Philosophy of Symbolic Forms,* vol. 2, *Mythical Thought,* trans. Ralph Manheim (New Haven, CT: A Yale Paperbound, 1966), 5.

12

Normality in the Light of Madness

FAILURE AND FRUSTRATION

Following the example of the erudite depth psychologist C. G. Jung, one way to answer a tantalizing question is to tell a story. I am not referring to a speculative metaphysical question about life after death, of which I know nothing and would not dream of answering by mythologizing in the manner of Socrates, who harbored the hope that he would have interesting philosophic conversations with Sisyphus in Hades, or Jung, who believed that the unconscious offers clues to immortality. Rather, I am referring to my unanswered question about the use of meta-psychological theories in clinical practice, the direct answer to which begins with the story of Samantha and the frank confession that I had the frustrating experience of treating her intermittently for a number of years.

During this time, given the successful application of cognitive-behavioral therapy and an anxiolytic medication prescribed by her psychiatrist, Samantha's Generalized Anxiety Disorder was contained, notwithstanding the fact that chronic symptoms of anxiety originated in a childhood fear of death and were strongly reinforced during middle years by daily reflections of the harsh realities of aging. This gain of orthodox treatment aside, Samantha refused to accept my recommendation of alcohol detoxification: a proposal arising from the undeniable fact that my clinical intervention was largely ineffective in treating her chemical dependency. Whatever the reasons for my failure, and I can think of plenty, I had the clinical tools to treat Samantha's psychoactive substance disorder. Many years earlier, fresh out of school, I acquired experience in an alcohol-drug treatment clinic, where I was not only responsible for individual, group, and family therapy, but also served as an impaired professionals monitor for the New York State Board for Professional Medical Conduct. In truth, I hated the work and often felt like a Gestapo agent when tasked with accompanying patients to the men's room and securing urine samples. In any event, neither this early experience, nor subsequent experience, mattered in the least when I was treating Samantha's substance addiction. But I am pleased to report that in spite of my abject failure, she achieved a sustained abstinence from alcohol as a result of AA and structured treatment in an outpatient clinic devoted exclusively to alcohol-drug rehabilitation.

In retrospect, until I created a beautiful story that began to work—a good, credible, artistically true story built upon a dramatic shift from (a) the concepts, perceptions, and lived experiences that identify a patient who has a mental illness to (b) the concepts, perceptions, and lived experiences that identify a woman who, in her own words, has a "pleasant pastime"—orthodox conversations with Samantha were fruitless and terribly frustrating. Simply stated, nothing I said generated a favorable resolution of Samantha's *process addiction*: not even a small constructive change in an extremely gratifying computer-dependent cyberexistence Samantha's psychiatrist and I treated as an incorrigible mental illness. (For the reader's information, I am distinguishing substance from process addictions in this passage, conceiving the former as a compulsive use of mood-altering psychoactive substances, such as alcohol, cannabis, and cocaine, while understanding the latter as a compulsive involvement in mood-altering behaviors, such as sex, gambling, eating, and work.)

When I reflect on this frustrating case and paint a displeasing picture of clinical failure I am acknowledging the fact that in a sustained effort to help Samantha control the compulsive use of a computer to access the internet in order to seek, find, and conduct meaningful relationships—committed cyberrelationships built on her imaginative creation and dramatic employment of fictitious personas—I tried everything in my power unsuccessfully: every strategic approach, every conceptual construction, every fitting diagnosis and corresponding treatment was tried. But nothing worked! Whatever else I might say, Samantha was never enchanted with the clinic and without the power to persuade that builds around a solid enchantment, I felt as though I had been snubbed by a petulant deity who turned a gigantic rump to his creation. Until I changed the clinical canvas and began to paint an entirely different picture that offered unorthodox impressions of her compulsive behavior, thereby producing in this patient something akin to a gestalt switch—a dramatic change of formula, feeling, cognition, and perception—I was simply unable to talk Samantha out of an intensely gratifying cyberexistence she wished to extinguish and maintain.

On the clinical sofa, talk therapy was frustrating as well, but the patient's frustration was not the same as mine. Samantha's clinical confessions revealed the fact that she was enthralled with her cyberrelationships, but also emotionally disturbed by compulsive behavior she experienced as illicit, abnormal, and immoral. In spite of her stated desire to change, from time to time, Samantha felt the need to take a lengthy break from formal treatment due to the embarrassing fact that her addiction to these erotically charged, power-intensive cyberrelationships interfered with her ability to consistently engage in therapeutic work we coauthored during the clinical hour. Briefly stated, therapeutic work consisted in the development of mutually agreed upon concrete steps designed to help Sam withdraw from compulsive engagement in a full-blown cyberexistence we jointly targeted for extinction.

Ultimately, with therapeutic dialogue having reached a dead end and my clinical vision exhausting its potential, I decided to turn in an unorthodox direction and paint a dramatically different picture for my patient. As Degas "opened up a new world of fantasy" in his beautiful ballet pictures, given the fact that "few of these scenes can be identified with actual productions or the names of reigning ballerinas," I opened up a new world of fantasy during heterodox treatment of Sam, given the fact that little of the language, ideas, and speech informing this aesthetic turn can be identified with the actual content, categories, or names of reigning illnesses appearing in the American Psychiatric Association's *Diagnostic and Statistical Manual of Mental Disorders*.[1]

Prior to placing clinical orthodoxy on the shelf, I came to know Samantha as a professional woman in her fifties, who was not only the parent of two children, but also responsible for the social and emotional development of other peoples' treasured offspring: young children who were diagnosed with Pervasive Developmental Disorders like Autism, as well as disorders of learning, motor skills, and communication. The interesting thing is, Samantha was the type of woman who could live next door, appear to be a friendly neighbor, go to work dutifully every day, and never be seen or experienced as crazed or crazy. But Sam knew better, in fact, she openly confessed to having a "tendency to do things to an extreme!" Coupled with family of origin dynamics that held her captive, the tendency to gravitate toward the extremes resulted in an intractable addiction to cyberrelationships that demonstrated Baudrillard's incisive claim: "All normality sees itself today in the light of madness."[2] While Baudrillard's contemporary impression is consistent with my conclusions about the crazed species, not to mention Freud's harsh judgment that the ego of the normal person approximates the ego of the psychotic, more or less, not everyone sees normality or reality the same way, as representational painters discovered when a new breed of radical painters took their paints, brushes, canvases, and easels outdoors and forsook the artificial light of the studio to paint impressionistic portraits in the sun. This difference in sun and shadow, a distinct difference in visions of normality and reality, is the therapeutic rub, as we shall see in a brief story of a memorable clinical experience whose excellence may be measured on the scale of artistic truth and artistic falsity: an aesthetic weight and measure useful in evaluating beautiful and ugly clinical interpretations, good and bad clinical stories, meaningful and meaningless clinical myths, as well as other pleasing and displeasing *objets d'art*.

THE PERFECT STORM

Things being what they are in the intriguing world of sibling rivalry, young Samantha was unable to successfully compete with her older sister, "the star" in a family of origin drama that had a stranglehold on Sam's psyche. As a result of her failure to measure-up to her sister's looks, social skills, and academic accomplishments, particularly in her father's eyes, Samantha learned to live in the shadow of an "adventurous" sister, as well as in the shadow of others who seemed smarter, prettier, more talented, or otherwise "better" than she perceived herself to be. Quite naturally, therefore, during empty years of marriage, she found herself living in the shadow of an accomplished husband and a bright, attractive teenage daughter who was fast becoming better than her mother in an inimitable adolescent way. In fact, prior to commencing treatment with me, Samantha was not only living in her daughter's shadow, she was actually living within Nina's life, as if Nina's being and existence were her mother's and not her own.

Clinical experience suggests that many mothers are enmeshed with teenage daughters, particularly mothers who are disillusioned with their lives. Mothers strongly enmeshed may become embroiled in a relentless struggle to control every aspect of their daughter's life to the extent that they stir a boiling cauldron of anger, rebellion, and estrangement: a toxic brew that poisons the love of mother and daughter and often leads to pleas for corrective treatment in the mental health clinic. But Samantha was not only enmeshed with her daughter, she was obsessed with (a) the weight, shape, and general appearance of Nina's body, leading to compulsive monitoring and control of the quantity and quality of food Nina consumed, and (b) Nina's sexual appeal and emerging romantic experience with teenage boys. Clinical confession revealed the fact that Samantha's obsession with Nina was influenced by the following fateful question she asked in the still of one long, lonely, empty, meaningless night: I may be in my fifties and have no real prospects, but "what would I do if I were fifteen?" This introspective query was merely the tip of a proverbial iceberg which, when fathomed, revealed a perfect storm of elements that coalesced to produce a meaningful, exciting, arguably pathological cyberexistence long in the making and virtually impossible to control.

The perfect storm included an "unfulfilling, unsatisfactory life": the routine existence of a dysthymic woman who suffered from the deflating belief that "I'm not really good at anything," as she confessed while evaluating herself during a painful clinical confession. Marriage to a narcissistically depressed, hypercritical, browbeating man, who pounced on every opportunity to inflate his deflated esteem by educating his spouse to believe that she was not good at cooking, gardening, decorating, paying the bills, or anything else, for that matter, resulted in mutual disenchantment and withdrawal from sexual relations, after which, an erectile dysfunction became the final nail in this coffin. Emotional and physical distancing left Samantha with a persistent "desire for a man's attention and affection," as well as an urgent "craving for passion": an unsatisfied craving routinely medicated with alcohol, which in turn, resulted in cravings for alcohol when Sam was unable to satisfy her substance addiction. Adding rich context to this crazed condition, Samantha entered menopause with the morbid disposition that accompanies the harsh perception that she had "lost physical appearance." In her mirror, to be clear about Sam's lack of confidence and eviscerated esteem, she received daily confirmation of the irretrievable loss of a woman's magnetic power to attract the penetrating gaze that trumpets a man's erotic interest. As a result of this dismal self-perception and the immutable belief that she had no present or future prospects, the onset of menopause resulted in the crushing belief that "life is over." This faulty fiction issued in the dread of becoming a cranky old hag who lived an empty life of misplaced hope, withered dream, and lost promise. At the same time, Nina was just beginning to flower like a radiant rose flourishing in the morning sun. She had new life, rich possibilities, romance, and the urgency of love's glorious consummation in her youthful hands. In *The Second Sex*, Beauvoir captured this existential situation beautifully in an impressionistic vision of the unhealthy relationship of mothers and daughters:

> The older the child gets, the more does resentment gnaw at the mother's heart; each year brings her nearer her decline, but from year to year the young body develops and flourishes; it seems to the mother that she is robbed of this future which opens before her daughter. Here is the source of irritation some women feel when their daughters first menstruate: they begrudge them their being henceforth real women. In contrast with the repetition and routine that are the lot of the older woman, this newcomer is offered possibilities that are still unlimited: it is these opportunities that the mother envies and hates; being unable to obtain them for herself, she often tries to decrease or abolish them. (*SS*, 520)

Phenomenological evidence gathered in the clinic supports Beauvoir's claim that resentful mothers may try to decrease or abolish their daughter's opportunities; but Sam went in an entirely different direction. Given her attitudes, beliefs, life experiences, and perceptions, she became a crazed mother who began to exist vicariously through her daughter's increasingly voluptuous adolescent experience. Discarding her parental role, as if it were a faded flower withered in winter; becoming blind to Nina's well-being, while failing to consider the emotional and physical consequences of her dereliction of parental responsibility; Samantha became consumed by the need to keep Nina's body as attractive as possible, in order to create opportunities for romantic relationships that would enable her to use her daughter's experience to fulfill her own desperate need for passion.

The clinical problem is that Samantha's attempt to fulfill her needs by vicarious participation in Nina's life took a startling pathological form. She clearly had "an empty hole" in her life, but she filled the hole by becoming a voluptuary of the imagination: a maddened woman who embraced a secret life of erotic intrigue that brought into sharp relief vivid fantasies of passionate encounters between Nina and her new boyfriend, Donald, during which Samantha became Nina in the arms of Donald, as if she were the adolescent maiden enthralled with adolescent pleasure.

Samantha's secret life included compulsive behaviors such as listening to Nina's landline telephone conversations; reading text messages on Nina's cell phone; approaching her daughter's bedroom stealthily and listening to Nina's intimate face-to-face conversations with Donald and other boys. Increasingly parasitic and pathological, Samantha became a voyeur who would silently leave her house in order to watch Nina and Donald engage in sexual activities through a basement window that offered a view of the family playroom. More importantly, as an omen of seemingly insane things to come, Samantha discovered that her computer was a handy tool for spying on and surreptitiously scripting Nina's progress with Donald, not to mention other suitors who became captives of her illness.

"Progress" is the correct word here, for behind the appearance of a normal life, Samantha was a crazed woman doing everything in her power to progressively script Nina's romance with Donald, as if this budding relationship were a live drama and she were the writer and the *auteur* or creative director of a masterpiece in the making. In order to pursue her creative activity an underworld of intrigue was set in motion, not in real life, but in electromagnetic cyberspace.

Having come into possession of their passwords by trickery and deceit, Samantha developed the habit of accessing confidential messages emailed by Nina and Donald. She not only spied, she also created dramatic tension by scripting storylines and emailing thoughts and feelings that produced the dramatic climax she desired in herself. In a continuing series of provocative emails that evidenced a pathological flight from reality—an insidious process in which the ontological difference between self and other began to collapse—Samantha pretended to be Nina messaging Donald and Donald messaging Nina. Beginning to lose herself in the process of becoming an author in search of characters she could become, Samantha gave Nina and Donald clues about and insights into the other's thinking, feelings, and behavior, thereby ingeniously guiding the young couple toward dramatic emotional responses and desired behavior.

While engaged in compulsive cyberplay, Samantha was admittedly "taking time away from real life," "escaping from reality," suppressing her "fear of getting older," and "giving in to impulses"; however, she also had "a sexual outlet" and she was receiving "enjoyable pleasure." Most of all, she was becoming an empowered cyberself who could easily manipulate Donald and use him as a pawn to move in the direction of embracing Nina with a knight's passion. In fact, Samantha experienced considerable gratification in her newfound power to arouse Donald's ire and one afternoon, she openly confessed: "I like making Donald mad!"

Unfortunately, Samantha never experienced a sense of power with men: she was "invisible" to her father, "mousy" during adolescence, sexually assaulted by a cousin when she was in her early twenties, and her spouse was physically and emotionally distanced. But in cyberspace, she began to acquire the power to manipulate and control other human beings and as everyone knows, in the human animal, power is not only heady stuff, but when an impotent individual comes into possession of power, however petty it might be, the tendency to abuse power may tip the scale to an extreme, this having been the case in the life of a woman who had a tendency to do things to an extreme.

Given Samantha's pathological relationship to her daughter and her compulsive use of the computer to gain access to cyberreality, it is not surprising that a responsible psychiatrist treated her as if she were in the throe of a psychotic illness. In fact, by the time she found her way to my office with a fascinating confession of "losing myself" in cyberidentities, cyberrelationships, and cybersex in cyberworld, in short, losing herself in a full-fledged cyberexistence that seemed perfectly disordered at the time, Sam was prescribed a potent antipsychotic medication, a psychotropic to treat an incorrigible Obsessive-Compulsive Disorder, and a separate serotogenic agent to deal with symptoms of depression and anxiety. Quite a witch's brew concocted to deal with the mental illness of a woman who, during her first confession stated forthrightly: "I'm having a hard time being myself!" Sometime later, more ominously, "I'm trying to be Nina!" After that, evidencing a further fragmentation of self, "I'm losing myself in Nina!" Finally, seemingly psychotic, "I'm becoming Nina!"

Interestingly, in days of yore, prior to the psychiatrization of culture by Freud, his disciples, and their clinical successors—I should say, prior to the prevailing perception that many human attitudes and behaviors are markers of psychiatric disorders—behavior of this magnitude, minus computer technology, was not unknown. In the opulent world of psychomythology, an aesthetic underworld of wondrous myth and collective meaning, a mother's special relationship to her daughter has been widely interpreted as the archetypal drama of a woman and her alter ego: specifically, an older woman whose younger daughter is her *double*. For example, in his authoritative guide to Greek mythology, while developing the drama of Demeter—the *mater dolorosa* who grieved long and hard over the loss of her daughter, Persephone, who had been captured, raped, and tricked into marrying Hades, the dark god of the underworld—H. J. Rose referred to Persephone as "the younger double of her mother."[3] Similarly, Simone de Beauvoir maintained that mothers have significant claims on their daughters, in fact, "in her daughter the mother . . . seeks a double. She projects upon her daughter all the ambiguity of her relation with herself" (*SS*, 517). In a dense elucidation of the meaning of the term "Kore," an antique name used to personify goddesses like Persephone, Athene, and Artemis, historian and distinguished scholar Carl Kerenyi maintained that Demeter and her daughter, Persephone, "are to be thought of as a *double figure*"; in addition, Kerenyi noted: "Mother and daughter form a living unity in a borderline situation—a natural unit which . . . carries within it the seeds of its own destruction."[4] In 1917, earlier than these accounts of Demeter and Persephone, the classical philologist Walter Otto wondered about the meaning of the extremely intimate connection of this mythological mother to her daughter, concluding: "'Demeter, mourning her daughter, is mourning some nature that is essentially akin to her, that makes the impression of a younger double'."[5]

Stating this psychomythic vision in a different way in his focused analysis of "The Psychological Aspects of the Kore," C. G. Jung asserted suggestively: "Every mother contains her daughter in herself and every daughter her mother, and . . . every woman extends backwards into her mother and forwards into her daughter. This participation and intermingling give rise to that peculiar uncertainty as regards *time*: a woman lives earlier as a mother, later as a daughter."[6] Appropriating Jung's impressionistic sketch in a volume of studies on archetypal images that allegedly shape human existence, Helen Luke referred to the experience of mothers and daughters in a way that spoke to Samantha's mental illness. "On the archetypal level," to be precise, "the daughter is the extension of [the mother's] very self, carrying her back into the past and her own youth and forward to the promise of her own rebirth into a new personality. . . . Loss of the daughter in older women is . . . loss of the young and carefree part of oneself, the opportunity for the discoveries of meaning which are the task of the second half of life. . . . The great majority of women today . . . have extreme difficulty in giving up this unconscious clinging to youth. . . . To such women the menopause brings long drawn-out disturbances of the body and the psyche as the conflict grows more acute and remains unresolved."[7]

If I were an archetypal therapist, I might have developed a clinical strategy based on the understanding that my patient and her daughter were a postmodern version of Demeter and Persephone. But I happen to be a pragmatic existential therapist focused on lived experience. From this concrete point of view, as I previously stated, Sam was married to a man who was hypercritical of his spouse, controlling to a fault, and generally insensitive to Sam's needs: psychological needs for acceptance, esteem, intimacy, creative self-expression and other aspects of self-actualization and well-being. Save the security provided by his generous income, Sam felt as though none of her needs were fulfilled in this marriage; however, following a clinical discussion of live options she was not prepared to end the marriage, fearing any action that would threaten her economic stability. Equally important, due to the fearless moral inventory she had undertaken while actively stepping in AA, she did not want to have a "real" extramarital relationship, although she would love the attention, a little romance, and some sexual pleasure. This is where cyberworld and the spirit of the time enter the picture: the picture of a new normality seen in the light of madness. In this case, the madness of a crazed woman who stated bluntly: "I can't get my needs met in another way!"

CYBERSELF AND CYBEREXISTENCE

For better and for worse, the technetronic era in which we live offered Sam the opportunity to become obsessed with and compulsively involved in the creative activity of inventing dramatic characters: fictive selves, alter egos, or personas with distinct identities, character traits, and life histories. Not on paper, as she would if she had been a disciple of Anais Nin or some other modern author of female erotica. Rather, unbeknown to me, during a break in treatment of one year's duration, during which time Samantha used our clinical work to successfully wean from existing vicariously within Nina's life, Samantha invented, lost herself in, and became Jillian, Clarice, and Meg—on the internet during dramatic encounters with other human beings who also had meaningful lives in cyberspace.

Strange as it may seem to orthodox clinicians who have a keen eye for psychopathology, by inventing, becoming, and living in the life of these fictitious characters—actually investing herself cognitively and emotionally in the evolving experience of cybercharacters she had created—

Samantha could be likened to a brilliant method actor who breathes real life into a fictitious role by actively calling upon and using personal thoughts, memories, dreams, wishes, and fears: countless personal experiences, according to Stanislavski, that enable an actor to "feel the situation of the person in a part so keenly . . . he actually puts himself in the place of that person," then not only "ceases to act," but "begins to live the life of the play."[8] Samantha never thought of herself as a method actress and this was never mentioned during the clinical hour, although Stanislavski's concept had a direct application. On several occasions, however, in a failed attempt to help Samantha wean herself from an addiction to cyberrelationships, thereby initiating an authentic process of self-creation that would enable her to fulfill latent potentials in reality, I suggested that she was a masterful creator of dramatic characters who could come to life in a novel or a short story: a creative work of fiction she clearly had the talent to write and possibly publish. The idea of a course in creative writing was discussed and as a result of clinical planning, Sam did her homework and researched suitable college courses with the thought of moving constructively in this direction. Unfortunately, my attempt to persuade this imaginative patient to use her creative gift productively never materialized and she continued to participate in meaningful cyberrelationships, not by acting or playing the part of Jillian, Clarice, and Meg, but by experiencing the situation of these personas so acutely that she began to live the fictitious lives she was creating.

Ultimately, to make a fine point finer, during a memorable clinical hour, while she was reflecting on the traits of Jillian, Samantha looked me in the eye, held my stare, and confessed: "I am this person Jillian!" It was late in the day and I was chomping at the bit to go home, but the hair on my arms stood up, stiffened, and presented arms, as if each hair were a sentinel guarding a fortress and its treasure. With my left eye on Stanislavski and my right eye on some psychotic or dissociative process; with my right ear poised to hear the kind of bizarre or nonbizarre delusion that does not yield to empirical evidence or rational suggestion and my left ear ready to receive information regarding a disturbance of the normally integrated functioning of consciousness, memory, identity, and perception; I carefully engaged Samantha in various tests of reality, at which point she admitted: "I'm losing real life . . . I'm wasting my life . . . these internet relationships are superficial!"

This seemingly accurate assessment of the difference between creating or reading about a fictitious character and literally being a fictitious character is a distinct difference arguably lost to Nietzsche when he apparently believed he was Dostoevsky's literary character Raskolnikov and embraced a whipped horse in Turin. This difference between imaginatively creating a fictitious character and becoming the fictitious character one has imaginatively created points to the profound difference between Sam acting "as if" she were Jillian and Sam believing she is Jillian, or my treating the universe "as if" it were created in six days and my literally believing the universe was created in six days. More to the important point at hand, Samantha's cyberpartners were constantly being duped, insofar as Sam led them to believe quite erroneously that Jillian, Clarice, and Meg were the real thing. They had no idea that Sam was lying through her teeth, that every conversation was a fabrication, that virtually every detail offered about her person, her life history, and her current experience, was creative fiction—the product of a ripe imagination overflowing with counterfeit riches.

It always amazed me that after countless invitations to meet Jillian here or there, and an equal number of refusals and excuses, some of which were lame, others being so theatrical and farfetched that only a fool could believe them, none of Samantha's cyberpartners smelled a rat. But when Sam looked into her mirror and tested reality, thereby coming into possession of the fact that her manipulative cyberrelationships were deceiving other human beings in harmful ways, she had the feeling that her cyberexistence was deeply immoral and she experienced some guilt and shame. You see, some of Sam's cyberpartners became emotionally involved with her phantastic characters in a serious way, I mean, they actually fell in love with Jillian, Clarice, and Meg: fictitious characters whose creator was involved unscrupulously in a seductive game of capture and surrender. Although she realized the harm she was doing to others, particularly when reality testing and facing the fact that her internet relationships were "superficial," a wee bit of guilt and shame did not motivate Sam to engage in a therapeutic process that would: (a) release forlorn cyberlovers from the spell of her fictions, or (b) complete the therapeutic process of weaning from an addiction to a compelling cybergame.

As time wore on and clinical thoughts merged with larger concerns about species-life and contemporary civilization, I realized that this troubled patient, as well as her tricked and deceived cyberpartners, had been captured by a powerful new reality: "the rise . . . of a Virtual Reality," according to Baudrillard, "that rests on the deregulation of the very reality principle."[9] To some of its cultured despisers, this displacement of reality is a historical disease; indeed, in the eyes and impressionistic sketches of Baudrillard, we are in the collective throe of a viral infection that is spreading a new type of evil across the globe.

Prior to the onset of the third millennium, stating this as clearly as his hystericized discourse would allow, Baudrillard articulated a new standard of postmodern evil in his passionate argument that by virtue of "the technologies of virtual reality, of the digital and the screen," humankind is experiencing a gradual etiolation of objective reality and with it, an eclipse of the imaginary and illusion that formerly were complements of objective reality and truth; in this ever-increasing, all-consuming, addictive global process, in which the technical and artificial is replacing the real and natural, "real life is sacrificed for the digital hyperrealization of all its possibilities," such that what once was real "exceeds" itself and is "no longer governed by any rule"; pressing the point, to be certain that readers understood his fateful message, Baudrillard argued that the hyperrealities of cyberspace have become a "dark, incurable malady," the "ultimate plunderer of reality," a virulent "viral agent that has infected real life" irreversibly.[10]

When I assimilated Baudrillard's impressions of postmodernity and began to think seriously about his novel concept of evil, while also dealing with Samantha's illness in a mental health clinic operating on orthodox DSM-IV standards, it occurred to me that many individuals who had been naturally conditioned to experience technetronic reality as normal and routine were not experiencing hyperreality in a malefic way. Stretching the point, I also thought that a younger generation of men and women who came of age in a historical era in which traffic in cyberspace is natural and quite common, would see an arrested intellectual like Baudrillard as an old fogy, whose vision of evil is inconsistent with the progressive spirit and technetronic genius of the time. In this impressionistic painting, an individual with a modern sensibility is not prepared to comfortably experience a technetronic reality that is literally giving birth to a radically new human sensibility: a naturally conditioned attunement to and feeling of being-at-home in a technetronic civilization offering possibilities of cyberidentities, cyberrelationships, cybersex, and other novel experiences. In cyberspace, to put it bluntly, a modern man like Baudrillard is bound to feel *unheimlich*: unfamiliar, ontologically ill at ease, anxious, uncanny, or "not-at-home," to borrow Heidegger's existential language concerning a startling, uncomfortable way of being-in-the-world.[11]

Similarly, with reference to my existentialist point of view and my own modernist sensibility, Samantha's cyberexistence was a waste of precious time: a loss of real life that compromised her need to identify and fulfill authentic possibilities of being. An old fogy in my own way, I viewed Samantha's obsession with and compulsive involvement in fictitious cyberrelationships as a disorder or an illness that required clinical treatment so that this terribly impaired woman would invest her energy in developing a real life that included a solid authentic self, genuine human contact, and concrete historical relationships. Toward this end, in the wake of much reality testing, Sam's stated interest in replacing the artificial with the real, and her abiding feeling of being involved in a secret life that was illicit, abnormal, and immoral, I made a good faith effort to have a favorable impact on the failed relationship with her spouse during marital therapy. Unfortunately, Sam's husband remained harshly critical of his wife; in fact, I was forced to call one marital session to an abrupt end when his criticism of Sam became ugly and intolerably abusive. In addition to his nasty serpentine behavior, Samantha now experienced her spouse as "a brother." In fact she "cringed" whenever he initiated sexual intimacy and on one occasion, literally fled the bedroom with a panicky feeling of disgust.

Gradually, as more time wore on and nothing I tried had a therapeutic impact on Sam's cyberaddiction, I conceded defeat, but in a mute Sisyphean way: an attitude of mind that never surrenders in the face of futility, but achieves reconciliation with the act of pushing a weighty boulder by willfully embracing it and making it one's own. On this craggy mountain in clinical Hades, I began to critically question my orthodox point of view, as Sisyphus might have questioned the way his feet were displaced on the rough mountainside or the angle of his shoulder and the way it was ineffectively braced against his massive boulder. One morning, anticipating Sam's scheduled appointment and straining against the weight of failure, I took a Cartesian turn and asked myself an important direct question: "At this stage of history, given the technetronic media culture that has engulfed us, does this patient's active involvement in cyberrelationships identify a mental illness that requires pharmacological and dialogical treatment?" Continuing this line of thought in the *milieu intérieur*, where Descartes gave new meaning to rational inquiry by trying to doubt everything, including his own existence, it occurred to me that if I abstract myself from the psychiatrization of culture and the concomitant presuppositions of the modern mental health clinic, I could argue against myself by entertaining the thought that the technetronic evil Baudrillard decried is giving this woman the opportunity to creatively invent cyberpersonas, whose dramatic interactions in cyberspace provide a fulfilling experience she is not able to have in "real" life. In fact, with the invention of Jillian—a talented, attractive, twenty-something cybergirl, whose creation and employment enables Sam to feel empowered and have the adventurous experience of stepping out of the shadow of others—she is admittedly "able to relive who I always wanted to be!" Certainly, this fulfilling experience is worth something, and may be naturally therapeutic, in spite of my modern existentialist assumption that Samantha's cybergirls are imaginary characters in a fictive drama, the continuation of which precludes her from identifying and fulfilling authentic possibilities of being in her concrete historical existence.

Unlike Sabrina and similar patients I have treated, Samantha was unable to become "a strong, creative person" with her abusive, controlling spouse; but she became a powerhouse when she was Jillian. In fact, in cyberspace, she determined the dramatic action, as if she were a powerful *auteur* responsible for creatively imagining and setting in motion, the plot, reversals, and denouement of hyperreal dramas that also had an interesting and exciting life of their own. Well into menopause Sam feared aging and when viewing herself in the morning mirror she could literally fall into a frenzy after spotting a new wrinkle on her face. But this irrepressible fact of life was sublimed through the creative invention and identification with cybergirls who were young, pretty, and desirable all the time. In real life, to be concise, Sam was psychologically starved: she needed, but could not find, intimacy, sexual pleasure, creativity, confidence, and esteem. But fulfillment of these needs was cyberpossible, a crude fact of life that left Sam asking: "If I give it up, what will I have?" Naturally, I often answered, "a real life" and I struggled with a passion to help her achieve it. But Samantha was enchanted with meaningful cyberrelationships, not with her clinician; as a result, my words were not fair or charming and the metaphors and the metonymies I used lacked the magical power to influence and persuade.

As clinical failure continued apace, the cyberrealization of self continued to replace Samantha's empty historical existence; however, this compulsive activity required anonymous others who had a cyberexistence as well. Sam was able to find complementary partners for her cybergirls rather easily, but I was never certain of their ontological status, never sure whether the unseen others had created fictitious identities like Sam or were exposing a real self that had a birth and a death, a role and a function, in concrete historical reality. In cyberworld, of course, the distinction between ontologically real and fictitious was not viable in any absolute sense, for in our novel technetronic media culture, "reality itself founders in hyperrealism, the meticulous reduplication of the real," by means of television, computers, or some other technology; attempting to explain his complex thinking, Baudrillard observed:

> The hyperreal . . . manages to efface . . . this contradiction between the real and the imaginary. Unreality no longer resides in the dream or fantasy, . . . but in the *real's hallucinatory resemblance to itself*. . . . This does not mean that reality and art are . . . extinguished through total absorption in one another. Hyperrealism is . . . their mutual fulfillment and overflowing into one another through an exchange at the level of simulation. . . . Today, *reality itself is hyperrealistic*. . . . Now the whole of everyday . . . social, historical . . . reality is incorporated into the simulative dimension of hyperrealism; we already live out the "aesthetic" hallucination of reality. The old saying "reality is stranger than fiction" . . . has been surpassed. . . . There is no longer a fiction that life can confront. . . . Reality has passed over into the play of reality. . . . Today, the real and the imaginary are confounded . . . and aesthetic fascination is simply everywhere. It involves a . . . sixth sense for fakery, montage, scenarios, and the overextension of reality. . . . It is an aesthetic reality, to be sure, but no longer by virtue of art's premeditation and distance.[12]

THE PLAY OF REALITY

During the latter stage of Samantha's clinical treatment I was visited by an unwanted guest, specifically, the unshakeable suspicion that Baudrillard and I, as well as other arrested modernists, were out of step with the spirit, the cognitive-emotional sensibility, and the technetronic reality of the time: a momentous time of new birth, transition, and transformation involving the future of a whole civilization. This was not new thinking on my part, but a nagging disposition I adumbrated much earlier in 1990, exactly fourteen years after Baudrillard bemoaned hyperreality, but fourteen years prior to his formulation of a crotchety standard of evil. Specifically, while drafting a contemporary version of the agonistic conflict between modern humanists and scientific rationalists in "New Notes from Underground," this battle having been joined by Dostoevsky in his original *Notes from the Underground* of 1864, I noted in a reconciliatory way:

> Technetronic civilization has become an autonomous monolith: an inarticulate foreign entity, an engulfing strangeness in our midst, an artificial creation, controlling and creating us. . . . In every realm of life, whether work, play, war, or worship, at every level of being and becoming, in acts of birth, feeding, mating, and death, the human animal has been removed from the natural, swallowed whole by an artificial Moloch, as if the evolutionary human experiment were some Jonah sucked deep within the belly of a whale. . . . It is irreversible; and it is awesome! . . . There is magic here. Breathtaking magic! Unimaginable surprise and astonishment await us in the near future. For aborning on this planet whirling aimlessly through cosmic space is a civilization of the miraculous: a ghoul without a soul, to be sure, but an erudite zombie with a genius for discovery and a wizard mind for the marvelous.[13]

Now, in a new millennium, while asking myself whether or not a patient's involvement in cyberrelationships identifies a mental illness that requires pharmacological and dialogical treatment, I was once again visited by the vision that the technocentric wizards of the time were providing new cyberforms and cyberstructures to replace the superannuated forms and structures of the modern world-order previously existing. Haunted by a therapeutic sensibility that urged me to do something useful to help my patient achieve an experience of well-being—something useful that would help her resolve the persistent feeling that her enthralling cyberrelationships were illicit, abnormal, and immoral—I made a critical decision to tell Samantha the simple story that her cyberexistence was *the new normality* in a new millenium. You see, it seemed to me that Samantha was not actually different from many other individuals who were having meaningful cyberexperiences or fulfilling themselves cognitively, emotionally, even sexually in cyberrelationships. In fact, there is an arresting sense in which Samantha's cyberexistence is madness only to those who are unable to accept a new, transforming technetronic condition that has an irreversible life of its own and is destined to leave mourners of an old world order in its wake. In my mind, at least, "The New Normality" could be the title of a good, satisfying story: a coherent account of contemporary reality that had the look of beauty and the smell of aesthetic truth.

It goes without saying that this was a profound reversal of the previously presented clinical story: a radical change of storyline that would not only alter the clinical conversation irreversibly, but also have an unknown impact on Samantha's cognitive-emotional state and on clinical results as well. But the new story had an internal logic: not a respectable logic that results in a clinical hypothesis tied to empirical test, verification, or falsification, but an aberrant logic tied to aesthetics and pygmy ethics. Specifically, I understood that I was now playing the part of a therapeutic artiste involved in a strategic effort to replace a knowledge-based interest in orthodox truth—the established truth offered in the American Psychiatric Association's *Diagnostic and Statistical Manual of Mental Disorders*—with an interest in the cognitive-emotional satisfaction elicited by an imaginative story about the new normality in a rapidly changing technetronic time. In this aesthetic context, I was not concerned with the historical truth or falsity of my story, rather, I was solely concerned with artistic truth and the controlling question: Will my imaginative story of the new normality be experienced as a good, coherent, meaningful story, and will my creative storytelling effectively fulfill the clinical goal of securing Samantha's emotional well-being?

Understanding that I would be treating future clinical encounters with Samantha as a creative experience in which the value of what is spoken and heard is judged by aesthetic standards, such as (a) the beauty, coherence, meaningfulness, and satisfaction of the story we are co-creating, and (b) the impact of creative storytelling on clinical results, I would no longer make reference to psychopathology or offer the clinical impression that I am required to engage in the therapeutic effort of dialogically confronting and eradicating an authentic mental illness. Rather, in the future, when addressing Samantha therapeutically, in an effort to help her reconcile herself to ego-dystonic behavior she experienced as illicit, aberrant, and immoral, I would demonstrate my understanding of her intelligible effort to fulfill perfectly normal human needs for love and affection, meaning and creativity, esteem and sexual gratification, thereby enabling her to understand that, like other organisms struggling for survival on a burnt cinder whirling aimlessly in cosmic space, she had used biological intelligence to seek and find an environment in which to successfully fulfill important needs: in this all-too-human case, physical and psychological needs that went begging for many years.

In the new story I was preparing to present, Samantha's compulsive behavior would be seen as less an illness than a lust for life, less an impairment than a will to meaning, less a mental disorder than a crazed triumph of the human spirit over a lifetime of psychological adversity. If my simple story had aesthetic appeal and resonated meaningfully in Samantha's cerebral hemisphere, like an artwork experienced as an object of beauty, it would not matter in the least whether the creative picture could be likened to a representational painting of Courbet or an abstract painting of Pollock—drips and splashes of paint that fail to faithfully represent reality. After all, as the temperamental Degas observed: "The most beautiful and the best-wrought drawing is always less than precise . . . and thus leaves the way open to all that is fraudulent."[14] Similarly stated, but with a sharper edge characteristic of the self-critical artist: "A picture is something that requires as much trickery . . . as the perpetration of crime, so create falsity and add a touch from nature."[15]

Adding intellectual merit to my therapeutic story that Samantha's cyberexistence was the new normality, and giving this coherent story the theoretical appearance of being aesthetically good, true, and beautiful, notwithstanding Samantha's belief that she is Jillian and the other fictitious characters she created, was the fact that I neither pulled my story out of thin air, nor painted this new, aesthetically pleasing clinical picture without precedent. You see, I realized that the spirit of the time—the disillusioning spirit of postmodern time—included a profound historical change in the way "self" was conceived and understood. The postmodern perception not only conflicted with the modern view that human beings house an authentic core self furnished with personal beliefs, intentions, and rational choices, it also included the radical perspective that "self" is a fiction.

Exploring this perspective in *The Saturated Self*, a study of profound dilemmas of identity in postmodernity, psychologist Kenneth Gergen maintained that in our media culture, technology is saturating us with an enormous variety of disparate images, languages, behaviors, plots, and possibilities of being human. This social saturation is resulting in a fragmentation of self: a loss of the skin-encapsulated core identity that was one of the hallmarks of the modern imagination and modernist analyses of the human condition. Readers may try to envision what is left with the loss of core identity by imagining the difference between an artichoke that has a central heart or core after its leaves are stripped and an onion that has no solid core, merely concentric layers of eliminable leaves that may be likened to a multiplicity of disconnected social relationships, distinctly different possibilities of behaving, and utterly disparate ways of speaking, hearing, and being. On Gergen's account of the saturated postmodern self, our multiple, disconnected relationships,

> pull us in myriad directions, inviting us to play such a variety of roles that the very concept of an "authentic self" with knowable characteristics recedes from view. The fully saturated self becomes no self at all. . . . Selves as possessors of real and identifiable characteristics—such as rationality, emotion, inspiration, and will—are dismantled. . . . Under postmodern conditions, persons exist in a state of continuous construction and reconstruction. . . . As we absorb the views, values, and visions of others, and live out the multiple plots in which we are enmeshed, . . . we no longer experience a secure sense of self, and . . . doubt is . . . placed on the very assumption of a bounded identity with palpable attributes. As saturation continues, . . . one senses the raptures of multiplicitous being. . . . The final stage in this transition to the postmodern is reached when the self vanishes fully into a stage of relatedness. One ceases to believe in a self independent of the relations in which he or she is embedded.[16]

After choosing to see Samantha as a saturated woman who was (a) playing a variety of roles, including dramatic parts with her husband, children, students, fellow teachers, friends, and multiple cyberpartners, (b) continuously constructing and reconstructing disparate identities while playing these different roles in different venues, (c) no longer experiencing a secure sense of self, while living out the multiple, disconnected plots in which she was enmeshed, and (d) experiencing the rapture of multiplicitous being when she was method acting in cyberworld with other saturated selves, I presented my new clinical story to her during our next regularly scheduled clinical hour. She listened carefully as always and clearly understood the suggestion that she was not only trying to fulfill perfectly normal human needs in her cyberrelationships, but also participating in a style of life that was the new normality in an engulfing technetronic era. Samantha's understanding of my story gave me hope that the picture my story painted would ultimately be experienced as a thing of beauty: a good, satisfying, meaningful story with therapeutic impact. As the clinical hour drew to an end, I asked her to carefully consider our discussion during the forthcoming week, silently hoping that when the door closed behind her and she became caught up in the daily grind, the picture I had painted would not be seen as an ugly representation of reality or experienced as incoherent drivel. Finally, we confirmed our next appointment and went our separate ways.

When Samantha returned the following week she was excited and eager to speak. "That was quite a session," she said, referring to our last fateful encounter. "It took power from it," she blurted out, referring to her illicit cyberbehavior. "It no longer had a forbidden quality, it was more like a pleasant pastime, and I was less inclined to do it!"

I would be understating the case if I said I was surprised, but I would also be deceiving readers if I failed to mention the fact that when I dreamed up the idea of the new normality I also had the fleeting thought that if I told this story successfully it might function as a *paradoxical intention*. This is one of the interesting and important clinical strategies introduced by Viktor Frankl during the post–World War II years when he developed his conception and clinical practice of existential therapy. Specifically, out of Auschwitz, Frankl noticed that when his patients anticipated becoming anxious and struggled against it, they were more likely to become anxious. Similarly, if an individual intends to sleep and tries to fall asleep, the less likely sleep will come. If a person struggles against a phobia or tries to suppress an obsessive idea, the direct struggle and the direct attempt to suppress may actually reinforce the fear and the obsessive idea, making the desired remission of symptoms virtually impossible to achieve. Paradoxically, with a change of intention, a reversal of the clinical situation may naturally happen. For example, if an anxious person embraces anxiety rather than resisting it; if a sleepless person accepts sleeplessness, rather than trying to fall sleep; if a phobic individual invites the feared object, or the obsessive person exaggerates the idea holding him captive, "*the wind is taken out of the sails*" of anxiety, sleeplessness, phobias, and obsessive ideas, as though these controlling existential conditions had lost their overwhelming power.[17]

In the case of Samantha, I have entertained the thought that when I gave the impression of normalizing her cyberrelationships, thereby appearing to implicitly consent to her compulsive behavior, I announced a dramatic change of mind and clinical intention that initiated a complementary change in my patient: a cognitive-emotional change and a reversal of intention that began to thaw a long-frozen clinical situation. Believing that I consented to her compulsive behavior and no longer had the therapeutic intention of working with her to eradicate a mental illness or oppose her illicit relationships, Samantha was now free to creatively participate in these relationships absent the negative picture of mental illness and her own disapproving belief that these pleasurable relationships were illicit, abnormal, and immoral and ought to be resisted. Paradoxically, when Samantha stopped struggling against her compulsive behavior, mostly in thought, if not in behavior, the wind was taken out of the sails of her cyberexistence and a reversal of the clinical situation was set in motion. Given Samantha's enthusiastic account of her new experience, including the report that she now had "less guilt" about her behavior, one may reasonably conclude that my story of the new normality deprived her cyberrelationships of some of their power, in as much as some of the wind, the psychic energy, the enthrallment with the forbidden that grounds eroticism, was taken out of the sails of Sam's cyberexistence. Temporarily, at least, like a drawing that is less than precise, thus leaving the way open to all that is fraudulent; like a beautiful picture that requires as much trickery as the perpetration of crime, my artful story may have created falsity with a touch of nature added, but it also created the opportunity for Samantha's previously proscribed pathological experience to become less intense, compulsive, and guilt-ridden, thus more manageable and controllable, as if it were a "pleasant pastime."

When this memorable clinical hour drew to an end, having noticed and clinically noted Samantha's demonstrable state of well-being, I raised my eyes from the yellow pad in my lap, looked directly at my patient, and while holding her eyes with mine, I said ironically, half believing, half disbelieving: "I guess my work is done, therapy was successful!" I don't mind telling you that we laughed . . . we openly laughed, not hysterically, but in an intimate, intelligent, searching way, each having a separate experience of hyperreality, hypertherapy, and hypertruth.

When the laughter died down and Sam began to speak of her desire to begin weaning from multiple medications, the poet Rilke popped into my mind, particularly the scathing indictment of inauthenticity in his prose work, *The Notebooks of Malte Laurids Brigge*. Now Malte was a fictitious character to be sure, but Rilke made it clear that "if a man is a deep writer, all his works are confessions" (*ML*, 8).[18] In this case, Malte confessed that a person may look for a mirror with the idea of washing off the makeup or removing what is false in an effort to be real. However, it may happen that some of the makeup, some of the disguise, remains in place and is forgotten. When this occurs, a person's eyebrows may be exaggerated or the corners of the mouth may appear to be twisted. In this freakish way of appearing or manifesting oneself, a human being is a laughable mockery: a man or a woman who neither exists authentically, nor becomes a good actor (*ML*, 194).

Mind you, when he finished writing *Malte* in 1910, Rilke was not a saturated man; rather, he was a modern litterateur who believed in the artichoke: the idea that human beings have a core self that could manifest itself authentically or inauthentically, depending on a person's comportment toward self and others. In this regard, as if she were not only acknowledging, but literally repudiating the inauthenticity of her cyberexistence, Samantha drew me away from fleeting thoughts of *Malte* when she confessed: "I want to be proud of myself, I want something meaningful, something acceptable." Following this pivotal confession, we scheduled an appointment for the following week and once again went our separate ways with much to think about and much more work to do.

At the time of this writing, Samantha was admittedly "phasing out" of her pleasant pastime. In addition to "closing out" some internet accounts, she was purposefully "setting up" and playing a part in dramatic scenarios, the denouement of which was designed to bring an end to her cyberrelationships. In a smart, concerted, self-directed effort to "replace negative behaviors with positive ones," she not only joined a gym with her sister, where she now went after work when cyberbehavior was most likely to occur, but Sam and her sister started working together on separate personal problems each targeted for change. At long last, Samantha and her sister had commenced the adventure of becoming sisters in a life-affirming way, taking classes in yoga and relying on each other for support and accountability. Most of all, as I write these words, I have the sense that Sam is motivated and engaged in the therapeutic process of reconciliation with self, world, and others. In fact, it seems to me that she has made an important psychic turn, for she has now asserted the firm conviction, "I can make my life better": her real life, I should say, not her cyberexistence. In spite of an underlying fear of death and an eye on wrinkles, she has also articulated her new belief that "it's okay to be fifty-six!" This was a huge change of mind: a major *metanoia* that is one of the foundation blocks of a new beginning in the autumn of real life.

In an intriguing way, as intriguing and paradoxical as Pirandello's exploration of the creative idea that a literary character could search for an author, the power of a cyberpersona began to manifest itself in Samantha's relationship with her spouse in concrete historical reality. I am thinking of Jillian's healthy, life-affirming self-assertiveness when I offer the suggestion that Samantha may have been the author of a powerful, self-assertive cybercharacter, but when she initiated the therapeutic process of empowering herself, it seemed as if the character Jillian quickened or enlivened herself by actually becoming the author who created her. Alternately put, feeling the situation of her author so keenly, a cybercharacter put herself in the place of her author, thereby ceasing to be a fictitious character due to the fact that she found a life in concrete historical reality.

If I wanted to tell a good story or mythologize about the future, while not departing from the intuitions informing this account of normality in the light of madness, I would suggest that in the life and time of Samantha, everything will turn out well. I would say this with the hope that there will not be a distressing discrepancy between what is written and what actually happens in life and in clinical practice. But after the death of Eddie, I became uncomfortable speculating about the fate of my patients and I am not in the position of confirming that the unconscious is giving me clues about an unknown state of affairs of which I know nothing.

NOTES

1. Daniel Catton Rich, *Edgar-Hilaire-Germain Degas* (New York: Harry N. Abrams, 1985), 19.

2. Jean Baudrillard, *Simulacra and Simulation*, trans. Sheila Faria Glaser (Ann Arbor: University of Michigan Press, 2000), 145.

3. H. J. Rose, *A Handbook of Greek Mythology* (New York: A Dutton Paperback, 1959), 91.

4. C. Kerenyi, "Kore," in C. G. Jung and C. Kerenyi, *Essays on a Science of Mythology: The Myths of the Divine Child and the Divine Maiden*, rev. ed., trans. R. F. C. Hull (New York, Harper Torchbooks, 1963), 107, 109.

5. Walter F. Otto, "The Meaning of the Eleusinian Mysteries," trans. Ralph Manheim (New York: Eranos Yearbooks BS XXX 2, 1955), quoted in C. Kerenyi, "Epilegomena," in *Science of Mythology*, 179.

6. C. G. Jung, "The Psychological Aspects of the Kore," in *Science of Mythology*, 162.

7. Helen M. Luke, "Mothers and Daughters: A Mythological Perspective," in *Mirrors of the Self: Archetypal Images That Shape Your Life*, ed. Christine Downing (Los Angeles: Jeremy P. Tarcher, 1991), 80, 82.

8. Constantin Stanislavski, *An Actor's Handbook*, trans. and ed. Elizabeth Reynolds Hapgood (New York: Theatre Arts Books, 1903), 56, 73, quoted in Jay Martin, *Who Am I This Time? Uncovering the Fictive Personality* (New York: W. W. Norton & Company, 1990), 108.

9. Jean Baudrillard, *The Intelligence of Evil or the Lucidity Pact*, trans. Chris Turner (Oxford: Berg Publishers, 2005), 17.

10. Baudrillard, *Intelligence of Evil*, 18, 27, 35.

11. Heidegger, *Being and Time*, trans. John Macquarrie and Edward Robinson (New York: Harper & Row, 1962), #189.

12. Jean Baudrillard, "Symbolic Exchange and Death," in *Jean Baudrillard Selected Writings*, ed. Mark Poster, trans. Jacques Mourrain (Stanford, CA: Stanford University Press. 1988), 144–46.

13. Carl P. Ellerman, "New Notes from Underground," *Inquiry: An Interdisciplinary Journal of Philosophy* 33, no. 1 (1990): 24–25.

14. A remembrance of Thiebault-Sisson quoted in Richard Kendall, ed., *Degas by Himself: Drawings, Prints, Paintings, Writings* (Edison, NJ: Chartwell Books, 1994), 245.

15. This remark of Degas's is from P.-A. Lemoisne, *Degas et son oeuvre* (Paris: n.p., 1946–1949), quoted in Kendall, *Degas*, 318.

16. Kenneth J. Gergen, *The Saturated Self: Dilemmas of Identity in Contemporary Life* (New York: Basic Books, 1991), 7, 15–17.

17. Viktor E. Frankl, *The Doctor and the Soul: From Psychotherapy to Logotherapy*, trans. Richard Winston and Clara Winston (New York: Vintage Books, 1973), 224.

18. Rainer Maria Rilke, *The Notebooks of Malte Laurids Brigge*, trans. M. D. Herter Norton (New York: W. W. Norton & Company, 1958); cited in the text as *ML*.

13

Conclusion: After the Fall

SLEEPING WITH BEAUTY

When the gifted American playwright Arthur Miller offered a thinly veiled account of his humiliating experience with Marilyn Monroe in the controversial stageplay *After the Fall,* he suggested that there is a stiff price to pay for existential choices and a particularly tough price to pay for sleeping with beauty, particularly if beauty is a false manifestation and the person seduced by beauty is blind to reality. This was not new thinking, but it has wide application and I am confident that many readers have had at least one memorable experience of falling under the spell of a person, place, or thing that appeared to be beautiful, but was a false manifestation that resulted in some physical harm or psychological damage. There are lesser disenchantments as well. For example, fifteen years ago, while I was beginning to contemplate the decision to resign my clinical position in the psychiatric service of the hospital in favor of full-time private practice, I had another itch that drove me to purchase a new Corvette off a Chevy dealer's showroom floor. This was my first Corvette and it was a thing of beauty, although the ugly truth is, like Eddie, but in a vastly different way, I was blind to reality.

At first sight, the polo green metallic body with a beige ragtop and matching interior made an elegant presentation that was difficult to resist. Low to the ground and fleet of foot, with a 5.7 liter engine pushing 300 horsepower at 5,000 rpm, her forward thrust was an experience in perfect harmony with an astronaut's defiance of gravity. Perhaps the best way to put it is to say, when she took off, like a rocket launched in obedience to

Newton's laws of motion, the thrust pressed my back hard against the contoured seat in the cockpit, as if I were in the throe of lift-off during the inaugural stage of a dangerous journey to a distant planet in cosmic space. To change the figure and bring this experience down to earth, when she leaped forward and was off and running, at each moment seeming to redistribute her weight from left to right and from front to rear simultaneously, her wide rubber paws barely tickled the pavement as she graced the road like a wild American cougar in hungry pursuit of prey. Closer to home, she was so sleek that when I washed her in my driveway every Saturday morning, using my right hand to gently run the soapy sponge over her gracefully arched front fenders and finely sculpted hind quarter, I felt a strange embarrassment, as if I were in the throe of an erotic experience in public.

Unfortunately, this particular Corvette was a lemon and the erotic car washes soon became a sour experience because there was something internally wrong with my flawed thing of beauty. Something dangerously wrong was hardwired, never correctly diagnosed, and never fixed, in spite of countless trips to the Chevy dealer's service department for an accurate diagnosis and cure. In spite of the appearance of beauty, my iconic sports car would spit, sputter, and stall, sometimes in the driveway out of harm's way, other times in heavy traffic, the final time when I was slowly turning left into an intersection on a country road, while another car I could not see due to a sharp curve in the road, was speeding toward me. I cannot say with assurance that God exists and loves me, but a fatal collision was avoided and I found myself eternally grateful to live to see another day. In the wake of this potentially disastrous experience, I became totally disaffected and I withdrew my libido from the sleek, sexy sports car I had married. Repulsed by the sight of false beauty, I engaged in the dramatic action of hiring an attorney to assist me in getting a divorce by formally applying the "lemon law" on the books in New York State.

Because I am a private person not given to engaging in or speaking about intimate experiences in public, the documents relating to my legal case contain no mention of the fact that in my thoughts, while experiencing this mechanical dysfunction and disturbing dysphoria, I often compared the flawed engine of my Corvette to the flawed psyche of a beautiful woman. Someone like Marilyn Monroe: a rare beauty who happened to have an incurable personality disorder. Whenever my imagination ran riot with this analogy, it seemed to me that my classic American sports car had a beautiful exterior, in fact, she possessed irresistible beauty: the kind of beauty that could drive a passionate car-loving man crazy with desire. But internally, thus quite invisible to the naked eye, this irresistible beauty could become a volatile, emotionally reactive, rage-filled explosive entity who not only engaged in reckless behavior, but also had an intense, unstable, impossible relationship with her lover: sometimes loving, other times hating, often loving and hating simultaneously, while attempting to destroy herself and her lover at the same time.

Needless to say, a prudent person would avoid an intimate relationship with a beauty of this sort if he had the ability to see through false appearances and grasp reality. Failing foresight, I mean the kind clairvoyance that would give a guy a fighting chance against a calamitous future, a person who seeks to satisfy an itch by undertaking an intimate relationship with dysfunctional beauty will soon be in a world of trouble as Arthur Miller discovered and many of my clinical case histories show. On the other hand, things being what they are in the world of jurisprudence, the case against my dysfunctional Corvette went well, for I had carefully documented every unsuccessful trip to the local dealer's service department and this record of trial and error and ultimate failure provided all the empirical evidence I needed to secure a divorce.

Ultimately victorious, I returned the graceful green metallic sports car whose beauty was a grand illusion: a false manifestation that possessed the power to glide in beauty like the night. Like the night, I should explain following Lord Byron obliquely, because her internal defects were obscured by the darkness denied to beauty seen more clearly in noon's harsh, ungracious light. In return for the keys and a summer of disenchanting discontent, I received a check from the Chevy dealer for every penny I had spent—a sad, but satisfactory resolution that included my vow to never again be seduced by this false beauty.

In spite of my sacred vow, three years later, I ordered a brand new Corvette from the General Motors factory in Bowling Green, Kentucky. Some readers will undoubtedly think I was stark raving mad, while others will survey their own experience and agree with me when I say: the seductions of beauty are sometimes so powerful that human beings commonly return to the scene of the crime, once again attempting to embrace beauty in whatever form and manifestation tweaks temptation or lights desire. Fortunately, I have driven this beautiful black convertible without incident for twelve years, but only during the summer months and never in the rain. Apparently, it was constructed well on the assembly line, although I understand that when dealing with beauty and its subtle manifestations, things do not always turn out this way.

Parenthetically, my repeated references to manifestations of dysfunctional feminine beauty might appear to be part of the historical demonization of women that has plagued the tempestuous relationship of the sexes in both primitive and civilized cultures. To correct this mistaken impression, readers are invited to imagine the handsome, internally impaired, iconic Dr. Jekyll and envision the ugly, monstrous Hyde in my references to the iconic, mechanically dysfunctional Corvette and the iconic, emotionally dysfunctional Marilyn Monroe.

Regarding the clinical issues at hand, agonistic therapists have confessed that in the mental health clinic, one disturbing price paid for sleeping with beauty is the increased risk of harming emotionally ill patients who are enchanted with a good therapeutic interpretation or a beautiful clinical story. Spence never referred to this destructive state of affairs as a violation of a dogma of the therapeutic, but like Hawthorne and other authors who warned their readers that they were toying with some sort of danger, Spence took pains to warn his readers of the danger involved in treating patients with reference to loose-fitting aesthetic standards. Specifically, "if clinical interpretations are creative rather than veridical," such as my inventive story of Samantha's cyberrelationships being the new normality in a new millennium; "and if the analyst functions more as a pattern maker than a pattern finder," in other words, if a dialogical therapist is a creative storyteller, rather than a clinical explorer who embarks on an archaeological journey to dig for and discover sedimented layers of historical truth

> We may be faced with a glaring absence of general rules. . . . The rules for [a clinical story] being true are just as much out of reach as the rules for any other kind of artistic masterpiece. . . . If there is less established theory than we like to assume, . . . it makes each analyst even more alone than he is already; if there are almost no guidelines, then the risk of going wrong is sizably increased. If [we] are correct in seeing an interpretation as primarily a creative act, then the analyst, . . . is engaged in an artistic struggle with the patient and with all of his colleagues. Seen in this light, the impossible profession becomes even more so.[1]

Unless I am mistaken, this fitting mention of "the impossible profession" is a direct reference to Freud's illuminating discussion of the professional standards and expectable flaws of dialogical therapists who, as I have previously stated, may be false manifestations appearing to be someone or something they are not. Written in 1937, two years before he died, Freud claimed that therapy is "a particular art," while therapists are all-too-human like their patients; reflecting on his lengthy clinical experience and admitting honestly that the personal "defects" of the clinician may not only "interfere with his making a correct assessment of the state of things in his patient," Freud also claimed forthrightly that the flaws of therapists may also interfere with their ability to react to patients "in a useful way" (*TI*, 247–48). Absent the self-analysis of the therapist, an honest, insightful, self-reflective encounter that digs for and uncovers the therapist's imperfections, Freud argued that dialogical therapy is one of our "'impossible' professions": not only a clinical profession presumptively based on a love of truth, but an interpersonal art sure to render "unsatisfying results," given the flaws and defects of therapists and patients alike.

Noteworthy is Freud's view that dialogical therapy is a particular art. Because he was a modern man who believed his psychoanalytic theory was veridical in the sense of having some correspondence or agreement with the realities of being human, when he referred to therapy as an art, he did not mean the clinical art of an analyst who uses creative imagination to invent a good story that on the best day of the week might effect a psychological healing—God willing! Given his invention of a rich variety of enchanting psychoanalytic mythologems, the image of a creative artist habituated to telling beautiful stories may be an accurate representation of clinical reality in Freud's consulting room. Nevertheless, when he referred to therapy as a particular art, Freud was thinking of the persuasive art of a modern Socratic man: a scientific man of the Enlightenment who struggled for truth, provided an education to reality, and accepted the responsibility of being a model for and a teacher of his emotionally impaired patients.

Some of Freud's standards may be high-minded and out of reach, like the well-being of my unsighted patient, Eddie, who viewed things from an apartment window high above the streets of the city and in his mind's eye, thought he saw a route to the Promised Land. I would like to think that Eddie's deadly fall led to the land of milk and honey, however, chances are good that I shall never be certain of his final destination. But I am absolutely certain that Freud's clinical standards reveal an attitude of mind that contrasts sharply with postmodern theory that has painted the radical picture of a creative clinical storyteller who is liberated from functioning with reference to the validity of therapeutic stories, the historical truth of therapeutic pictures, and the agreement of clinical interpretations with reality.

More precisely, (a) the nihilistic notion that clinical interpretations are creative rather than veridical, (b) the anarchistic idea that there is an absence of general rules in clinical practice, and (c) the agonistic view of the lonely therapist involved in an artistic struggle with patients and colleagues, are critical features of a coherent, influential, postmodern picture of the impossible profession that amounts to a rejection of discourses of modernity built on Socratic quest and Enlightenment rationalism. In other words, whether we know it or not, we are sleeping with another thing of beauty that may be flawed and potentially destructive. Adumbrating this point of view in a comprehensive study of postmodern theory, Best and Kellner maintained that in the diverse discourses of postmodernism:

> Modern theory—ranging from the philosophical project of Descartes through the Enlightenment . . . —is criticized for its search for a foundation of knowledge, for its universalizing . . . claims, for its hubris to supply apodictic truth, and for its . . . fallacious rationalism. Defenders of modern theory, by contrast, attack postmodern relativism, irrationalism, and nihilism. . . . Postmodern theory provides a critique of representation and the modern belief that

> theory mirrors reality, taking instead "perspectivist" and "relativist" positions that theories at best provide partial perspectives on their objects, and that all cognitive representations of the world are historically and linguistically mediated. . . . Toynbee described the [postmodern] age as one of anarchy and total relativism. He characterized the . . . postmodern age . . . [a]s a "Time of Troubles" marked by the collapse of rationalism and the ethos of the Enlightenment.[2]

A TIME OF TROUBLE

Readers who have had the pleasure of perusing Toynbee's voluminous *A Study of History* do not need to be told that in the idioms of this great British historian, a time of trouble is a time of testing that may result in the gradual disintegration of civilizations. Similarly, in the archetypal cycle of the hero Toynbee used to model his study of the rise and fall of civilizations, a time of trouble is a time of trials and tribulations or rites of passage, the success or failure of which determines whether an agonistic hero has the intellect, the will, the power, and the skill to venture into the unknown, confront some daemonic challenge, and survive a severe test required to achieve an important goal or capture a precious treasure: a golden egg, a beautiful princess or a handsome prince, an education, travel to a distant planet, perhaps a decent job offering the ability to feed a starving family after years of tormenting quest.

My reason for focusing on the time of trouble in the cycle of the hero is simple, yet unsettling. Specifically, given disintegrative aspects of the postmodern turn, not only the collapse of rationalism, but the disfranchisement of the Enlightenment mystique—a cultural paradigm championing the optimistic belief that (a) rational laws are working in and governing the universe, (b) human reason is fully capable of discovering these laws, and (c) human beings can use lawful scientific knowledge to make progress in perfecting the human condition—there is good reason to say we are currently in a time of trouble: grave trouble in the life of mind to identify the challenge categorically. Perhaps it is too late and our postmodern disorder is now incurable. But if this hasty judgment of futility is mistaken, our success in surviving the challenge of living with this disquieting personality disorder—I am referring to anarchism, nihilism, and irrationalism—may hinge on our having a rude awakening in the arms of a disenchanting experience that forces us to see this contemporary manifestation of truth and beauty as ugly and terribly harmful. While fully expecting a rendezvous with disenchantment some time in the future, our current time of trouble involves a momentous philosophical struggle, for our epoch is a time of intellectual trials and cognitive tribulations that a learned historian like Toynbee may record one day in the distant future, when writing a voluminous study of the genesis, growth, breakdown, and disintegration of postmodern civilization.

Anchored in the present moment, while focusing critical attention on a disturbing time of trouble in the mental health clinic, I would like to offer the simple warning that as postmodern theory insinuates itself insidiously in clinical practice, there is a real danger of excess that carries the risk of harming both patients and the enchanting art of dialogical therapy itself. After the fall—the fall into anarchy, nihilism, and irrationalism—there is a real danger of excess unless there is a countervailing trend supporting a search for wisdom in clinical theory and an ethic of moderation in clinical practice. Toward this end, I have found it worthwhile to entertain the thought that there is a profound difference between (a) clinical theory and clinical practice, (b) a mythological person and a historically existing person, (c) a philosophy of life and lived experience itself.

In retrospect, the intense, unpredictable experience of treating emotionally wounded patients enabled me to clearly see that it is one thing to theorize about enchantments of the clinic, quite another to become responsible for actually managing the tumultuous emotional life of a diverse population of suggestible patients who are fixed in a clinical enchantment. Breuer had this rude awakening when he presided over the delivery of the child he had fathered in the heart and mind of Anna O; I discovered the same when I was treating my "star" patient, Sabrina, whose painful enchantment remained constant long after the termination of treatment. With admiration and respect for Freud and Ferenczi and their dedicated work to better the lot of their fellows, it is one thing to have a theoretical understanding of the fact that a human being's tendency to blind belief and uncritical obedience may be transferred to the phantastic person of the therapist; it is a much graver thing for a zealous therapist to take direct control of another human being by deliberately establishing clinical conditions that elicit blind belief and uncritical obedience. For clinical action of this sort rests upon mindless self-assurance, overweening confidence, or the arrogant conviction that the human person who manifests himself as a phantastic person while working in the impossible profession actually possesses the wisdom to manage the blind belief and uncritical obedience of fellow human beings.

Clinical experience suggests that the artful practice of enchantment requires much wisdom, insofar as the clinical struggle against emotional illness is not cut and dried as many "how to" manuals for treating this or that disorder imply. From time to time, I am obliged to ask myself: "What is the wisest course of action in this particular case, with this particular man or woman, given these specific circumstances?" Often, a patient's well-being seems to hinge on a definitive answer that may not be forthcoming, leaving an ordinary mortal holding the bag of clinical decision.

Beyond this sobering responsibility, how can an honest therapist ask his patients to exercise wisdom in their lives if he hasn't the slightest idea what wisdom might be? To ask wise judgment of a patient, while not having a clear idea of wisdom oneself, seems like corrosive hypocrisy; and a therapist flawed in this way is bound to have difficulty shaving or applying cosmetics in the morning, while glancing at the distorted reflection staring back from a looking glass that has an uncanny way of leading an inauthentic person back to himself.

Fortunately, clinical experience teaches that a therapist does not have to define wisdom to find a measure of wisdom to use as a guide; similarly, a person does not need a precise definition of a venomous snake to be bitten fatally if he happens to be in harm's way. Of course it helps to have a precise image of a venomous serpent in order to know what to embrace and what to avoid while successfully guiding oneself and others through the intricate and perplexing passageways of life. Failing a precise definition of wisdom, the protracted process of thinking about wisdom may do the work of instilling a bit of wisdom in a person's soul or mind or psyche. I believe Socrates had this in mind when he took it upon himself to become involved in the art of leading souls in Athens; I also think Heidegger held this view when he challenged the common complaint that we cannot do anything with philosophy. Admitting honestly that we really cannot do anything with philosophy, Heidegger argued that this is not the final word, because the activity of philosophizing does something to those who choose to involve themselves with it (*IM*, 10).[3]

This was a brilliant maneuver on the part of a modern existential philosopher who had learned the sophistic craft of toppling his opponent by standing a forceful argument on its head. Yet in 1935, at a crucial historical moment when the grim reaper was about to make a collective call on Western civilization, Heidegger used his influential voice to speak about the spiritual decline of the West; but after offering this vision of a modern time of trouble in conjunction with the corrective view that philosophy does something to those who concern themselves with it, Heidegger spoke to his eager students about their native Fatherland becoming an endangered nation caught in pincers between Russia and America. Then with reckless hubris, profound and sightless as Nietzsche's, while casting persuasive words into the open ears of impressionable students at the University of Freiburg, the esteemed, influential headmaster applauded the promising new spiritual energy that was emerging into being within Germany by virtue of the sociopolitical activity of Hitler and the Nazis (*IM*, 31–32). Mind you, this wisdom was openly aired just two short years after Hitler became chancellor of the Reich and Propaganda Minister Goebbels announced an introductory course in Germany's new existential philosophy by staging a massive burning on Unter den Linden of all the freely created books housed at the University of Berlin. Everything was clear, the blinders were off, there was no need for further enlightenment!

I commonly ask patients to identify lessons learned from painful life experience. This is an important therapeutic exercise that helps a wounded person identify the hard-won wisdom acquired while moving a massive boulder in Hades. But Heidegger showed no remorse and he remained unapologetic to the end. So it is not clear that this eminent philosopher who searched for wisdom learned anything at all from his error of blindly embracing a serpent. Nevertheless, if there is reason to believe that engaging in philosophic reflection does something to a person who devotes himself to it with passionate intensity, it does not follow that philosophic reflection does something life-affirming, rather than life-destructive. Simply put, there is no telling whether philosophic reflection will make a crazed human being better or worse! This is the lesson of Heidegger's historical experience with the serpents of a bygone era—the lesson of a brilliant philosopher's gross seduction during a demonic era when some of the best and the brightest became devil's advocates. This failure of protracted philosophic reflection may also be an important aspect of Socrates' aforementioned personal confession that "wise" is an expression appropriate only to a god. Obviously, if this is true, in matters clinical and nonclinical, a sharp eye for excess, as well as moderation in thinking and behavior, may be beneficial.

Reflecting on personal experience in the ivory tower and in the clinical trenches, I am mindful of the fact that it is one thing to offer a seminar in a scholarly academy where I am free to comfortably speculate about everything under the sun, including the troubling, consequential idea that dialogical therapy is mythologizing not tied to evidence, empirical test, verification, or falsification. But it is quite another thing to actually invent and become personally responsible for telling a whopper about the dogs of heaven to an enchanted patient who hears my charming words, fails to see through the masquerade of truth, believes the words are true, and extends the existential implications of my therapeutic story in some unforeseen, unexpected, perhaps harmful way—not in the life of mind, but in concrete historical reality, where stories have a fateful life involving direct and indirect consequences to self and others.

Similarly, it is one thing to compare moral choice to a work of art during a philosophical lecture that advances the contentious notion that there are no irresponsible moral choices; it is quite a different thing to actually use this dangerous idea to guide the moral development of children. At the time, Sartre may have been blind to reality, I mean, the clinical reality that a good number of children educated in this nihilistic way will be programmed to visit their morality on other people, while enacting the predicates of an adolescent Conduct Disorder, followed later by an Antisocial Personality Disorder, the respective traits of which are: (a) aggression to people and animals, willful destruction of property, lying, theft, and the violation of established rules, and (b) behaving in ways that are grounds for arrest, aggressive assaults on others, irresponsibility, and a glaring absence of remorse.

Perhaps one acid test of excess is the fact that I cannot imagine telling symptomatic patients at the onset of treatment that they will be paying hard-earned money each week so that I can engage in the effort of inventing a coherent myth or a satisfying story about their emotional illness, this creative activity being a lonely artistic endeavor that has neither guidelines nor rules, thus increasing the risk that the story I tell them will be wrong and possibly result in some irreversible harm to their person. I cannot imagine preparing a symptomatic patient for treatment at the end of an initial psychiatric evaluation by saying: "My storytelling will place me in conflict with other clinical storytellers who would undoubtedly create different myths and fictions, none of which will be true in the strict sense of agreeing with the historical experiences that shaped your life. Still, a powerful enchantment may occur while I am hearing your confession and preparing to use the information I gather to co-create a clinical story about your emotional illness. Perhaps an erotization of the clinic will occur, as well, and this experience may be worth your dime. But when you cross the threshold of the mental health clinic and take a seat on my sofa you are not purchasing a quest for truth. Rather, you are buying my attempt to create and tell a beautiful, satisfying, imaginatively appealing story that will have a therapeutic impact on your dysfunctional way of thinking, feeling, and behaving. If all goes well during our enchanting encounter, you are likely to become involved in a masquerade of truth that will find you embracing a beautiful story. If nothing ugly is encountered along the way and the story you hear glides in beauty like the night, our dialogical experience will result in your feeling better and my clinic notes will contain 'remission of symptoms' as a closing line."

If this disenchanting conversation took place at the onset of treatment, during a full disclosure of the aesthetic realities of clinical practice, I venture the guess that talk therapy would fast become an impossible profession and the therapeutic artiste would be driven out of the storytelling business post haste. Regarding this very real possibility, mental health clinicians will have no trouble understanding that my satirical remarks are consistent with the serious disposition of corporate insurers who seem to have sniffed the hard truth about the aesthetics of persuasive therapy subject to third-party reimbursement. The result has been the installation of a controlling structure whose authoritarian demands include preauthorization of clinical treatment, strict limits on the number of annual visits, submission and regular review of clinical treatment plans, and a cap on the amount of money reimbursed for dialogical treatment, regardless of modality.

Deferring comment on the demonstrable excesses of corporate insurers, the unassailable truth is, dialogical therapists may find themselves literally engaged in the struggle of life against death in the clinical trenches. This is a huge responsibility and when the struggle is taking place, while a patient's life is on the line and I am a lonely clinical storyteller riveted to the moment, it does not feel like there is anything aesthetically beautiful or fabulously mythical about it, in spite of the fact that the great literature of the Western and Eastern worlds abounds with enchanting stories of mythical heroes and heroines who had overwhelming responsibilities, difficult times of trouble, gargantuan trials and tribulations, as well as priceless victories against fire-breathing dragons and other manifestations of fate and fury. In the end, therefore, it may be true to say with the great mythographer Joseph Campbell: "Freud, Jung, and their followers have demonstrated irrefutably that the logic, the heroes, and the deeds of myth survive into modern times. . . . The latest incarnation of Oedipus, the continued romance of Beauty and the Beast, stand this afternoon on the corner of Forty-second Street and Fifth Avenue, waiting for the traffic light to change."[4] Similarly, in mental health clinics across the globe, the latest incarnation of Asklēpĭŏs, the brilliant, zealous, heroic god of healing, is sitting in clinical armchairs inventing good stories that will have a therapeutic impact on symptomatic patients who are sighing on their sofas.

But there is a real difference between life and literature: a profound difference between actually experiencing the consequences of one's clinical choices and writing an enchanting story about the way in which the overzealousness of Asklepios resulted in his death. In sum, there is a profound existential difference between (a) participating in the life of mind while developing philosophical and psychological theory, and (b) liberally applying these theories while treating live subjects who happen to be emotionally vulnerable, severely symptomatic patients. When I am participating in the life of mind and dealing with the ambiguities of ideas, though I may be terribly disconcerted, I find myself in a dramatically different existential position than I am when I become intensely involved in the concrete historical activity of using language, ideas, and speech to help patients whose time of trouble includes suicidal ideas, florid symptoms, and a desperate inability to solve the pressing problems that have a stranglehold on rational thought and constructive action. For this and other reasons, I drafted the following conclusion to an earlier essay on the dangers of myth-minded aestheticism: "Those who dwell on earth poetically and intellectually are guardians of culture and caretakers of the mind. By virtue of their signal vocation as artisans of language and architects of ideology, they share a unique personal responsibility for the idols of our ethics and the ethics of our idols; for the blindness of our vision and the vision of our blindness; for our reason and our madness, our decadence and our dreams; for the satyrs and the sirens soliciting our seductions and our screams" (*SM*, 530).[5]

Like Jacob Bronowski's inspired public appeal for personal responsibility when dealing with values and beliefs that may have an impact on humankind's evolutionary step forward or back; like Freud's honest self-appraisal and public confession of the defects of persuasive dialogical therapists who are in the delicate business of suggestively talking people into and out of things; this was a cautionary note about human flaws and fallibility: not only a note about personal responsibility, but also a plea for moderation when dealing with ideas that have the power to shape the life of mind or directly influence the lives of people. My appeal for responsibility and moderation appeared in the conclusion of a literary-philosophic essay concerning the peculiar blindness of the great Nobel Prize–winning litterateur Thomas Mann. Like Nietzsche, from whom he learned much, C. G. Jung, whose depth psychological views he shared, and Heidegger, who blindly embraced a serpent, Mann was a modern celebrant of myth until he realized too late that there was a price to pay for blindly sleeping with this apparent beauty. During the apocalyptic 1930s and 1940s, the incalculable price was a mythologically generated global war built on a good story whose coherent elements, satisfying to many, included a savage racism, a deathly mystique of the hero, and a romantic mysticism that evoked a powerful Germanic obsession for autochthony or rootedness in a transcendental *Volkgeist* (*SM*, 528).

With this in mind during our own postmodern era of cultural and clinical trouble, it may be wise to remember that the historian Toynbee believed the growth of a civilization hinged on the availability of creative personalities or creative minorities whose pioneering aptitudes and ideas the dominant majority could assimilate by imitation. Additionally, Toynbee not only claimed that broken-down civilizations may be victims of self-inflicted wounds or suicide, he also maintained that the withdrawal of *mimesis* by the dominant majority was a decisive factor in a civilization's decline and fall.[6] But after careful thought, it is also reasonable to entertain the thought that a civilization and its institutions could break down and disintegrate because the dominant majority actually succeeds in imitating the creative personalities who were the artisans of language and the architects of ideology—the poets, the philosophers, and the politicians of a historical world spirit or *Geist*. In certain cases, a civilization's suicide could issue from the dominant majority's successful imitation of a creative minority, such that a withdrawal of *mimesis* would result not in the breakdown and disintegration, but in the rescue and cure of corporate life.

A MEETING OF THE MIND

In conclusion, to tie a loose end, I shall swim against the tide by suggesting that postmodern theoreticians are living in a world of babble. Generated in part by a "fanaticism of language," this is a world of babble in which commonsense notions of objectivity and truth lost value and mooring (*IE*, 68). But if I were a dyed-in-the-wool gambler, I would risk my Corvette on the wager that if a postmodern psychologizer were accused of murder like many of my former students; likewise, if a postmodern incarnation of Theodor Reik were accused of being a quack by a dissatisfied patient whose morbid symptoms failed to remit; in each case, in the blink of an eye, the falsely accused individual would abandon aesthetic truth and every published approval of stories not tied to evidence, experimental test, verification, or falsification. In reality, the falsely accused would immediately abandon their hyper-enlightened views and shout out instinctively, "*Not true*!" thereby availing themselves of the simplistic intuitions informing Aristotle's quaint notion: "To say of what is that it is not, or of what is not that it is, is false, while to say of what is that it is, or of what is not that it is not, is true."

Falsely accused of murder or malpractice, a hyper-enlightened theoretician would fast become a man of common sense who now finds it essential to speak out publicly in self-defense of truth and falsehood, of evidence and verification, hoping in some way to promote an attitude of mind that would result in a correct decision regarding his innocence. Granted, he might never concede that when considering better or worse values—existential values that point ahead or back in evolutionary time—the true-false system seems better suited to the conduct of life than a form of life that does not include Aristotle's simplistic distinctions, notwithstanding the fact that whenever philosophers offered an explanation of Aristotle's quaint notion, thereby attempting to explain in precise terms exactly how language, ideas, and beliefs agree with or correspond to reality, they could do no more than tell a flawed philosophic story. Reflecting on this disordered state of affairs as he approached an end of time and the end of a luminous philosophic career, Wittgenstein offered the therapeutic view that we cannot explain this sort of thing without babble. When all is said and done, giving grounds for an important form of life comes to an end and the end is the way we human beings comport ourselves, the way we conduct our lives, the way we act in common while working the daily grind. Specifically, the end of explanation "is not an ungrounded presupposition," rather:

> It is an ungrounded way of acting. . . . Why do I not satisfy myself that I have two feet when I want to get up from a chair? There is no why, I simply don't.

> This is how I act. . . . The reason why the use of the expression "true" or "false" has something misleading about it is that it is like saying "it tallies with the facts or it doesn't," and the very thing that is in question is what "tallying" is here. Really, "The proposition is either true or false" only means that it must be possible to decide for or against it. . . . As soon as I think of an everyday use of [a] sentence instead of a philosophical one, its meaning becomes clear and ordinary.[7]

In the everyday world of the daily grind, a daily drama of survival enacted with rapacious self-interest by an anonymous majority of men and women anxious to secure a place in nature's competitive food chain, we would be hard-pressed to relinquish the true-false system as a pragmatic form of life. For the availability of a conceptual tool that allows us to do the practical work of making decisions for or against what is said and heard seems indispensable to successfully dealing with self, world, and others, not to mention the fact that the fruitful idea of hypotheses tied to evidence, experimental test, verification, or falsification is compellingly coherent to anyone falsely accused of murder or in the case of Theodor Reik, a lesser crime.

I realize that I am rambling on like a crazed clinician, speaking as if the enchanted clinic must be wed to an anachronistic attitude of mind that reflects a quest for truth and an education to reality. But in the throe of a time of trouble, I have been speaking about the therapeutic sensibility and its fitful relationship to truth not from a misguided fidelity to Freud, who failed to live up to his best intention, as I did when I purchased Black Beauty. Rather, I am speaking about these complex things, often in a simple-minded manner, because I know firsthand that behind the closed door of the clinical confessional there is no way of knowing whether the suggestive power and influence of a lonely therapeutic artiste is being used in a way that offers the best chance of benefiting emotionally wounded patients. As we have seen, this is one reason why Freud recommended the self-analysis of dialogical therapists who, by virtue of inalterable humanness, happen to be flawed like their patients, more or less.

Beyond Freud's professional recommendation, following his examination of the logic of suicide in *The Myth of Sisyphus*, in fact, in the aftermath of the carnaticum of the corporate body that defined the barbarism of his time, Camus came to understand that in the human community: "Whatever we may do, excess will always keep its place in the heart of man. . . . We all carry within us our places of exile, our crimes and our ravages. But our task is not to unleash them on the world; it is to fight them in ourselves and in others."[8] Concerning this fight, I may look in the mirror and see my father and recognize his flaws in myself. But I have a clear looking glass at long last and I see my situation, my capacity for excess, in a way my beloved father failed to see in himself. This puts me in the position of revolt: rational revolt against malignant excess, which in all times and in all places, crushes hope that there is a moderate way of being-in-the-world—something other than a time of troubles and a litany of history's unsung humiliations.

In the final analysis, in the impossible profession as I have come to know it, management of the phantastic, storytelling therapeutic artiste is self-imposed and self-directed. Unless it is a lark, moral agency of this sort begs some awareness of and respect for the virtue of self-mastery (*enkrateia*): an ancient Greek virtue in short supply in a postmodern culture that maintains the carnival of clinical practice that came to birth and flourished with the seminal struggles of Freud. Corny as it sounds during this hyper-enlightened era of anarchy, nihilism, and irrationalism, moral agency based in self-mastery has more than a little to do with caring to cultivate the human sensibility that motivated Socrates' agonistic struggle for wisdom, truth, and best possible state of the soul. In this self-reflective, self-critical, self-regulating struggle, where learned ignorance and the examined life have a place of honor, all the agonistic arguments, conflicts, condemnations, punishments, and deaths take place deep within the self. This is a crazed self that longs to sleep with beauty, but often awakens to find itself embracing a phantom: a false manifestation effected by the subtle secrets and stealthy shadows of night.

On the lighter side, like young Alcibiades, who was enchanted with Socrates and experienced him as a "satyr" or a "wonderful piper," whose charming words had the "magic power" to stagger and bewitch philosophically minded Athenians who participated in the fellowship of the spoken word—I too have the feeling that I have been bitten by something more painful than the bite of an adder (*SY*, 215b–d).[9] As Alcibiades said of himself: I have been bitten "in the heart, or the mind, or whatever you like to call it, by Socrates' philosophy, which clings like an adder to any . . . mind it can get hold of, and does exactly what it likes with it" (*SY*, 218a). Insofar as this adder's bite leads to "philosophical frenzy," as Alcibiades confessed, it might be similar to having a frenzied relationship with a reincarnation of Marilyn Monroe, Dr. Jekyll, or an enchanting sports car.

Whether this is true or not, the preceding pages demonstrate that I disagree wholeheartedly with Alcibiades who, in his eulogy of Socrates at a supper party or symposium devoted to speeches on love, compared himself to a man who had been bitten by a snake, but would not tell anyone how it feels except another individual who had been similarly bitten. For he feared making a fool of himself and reasoned that if he happened to become a fool while under the influence of this painful bite, only a person with similar experience would understand and sympathize.

Of course during clinical training, young interns are taught to distinguish sympathy from empathy and they are wisely instructed to develop and use the latter power during therapeutic encounters with patients. But I can say from personal experience, when driving Black Beauty in the open air on a warm, sunny Sunday afternoon, listening to Miles, Brubeck, Wagner, or Verdi, a passionate car-loving man doesn't need sympathy or empathy, for everything seems right with the world. All of which brings me to a meeting of the mind with Voltaire: a man of the Enlightenment who championed civil liberties and despised dogma, but never drove a Corvette. Instead, during the 1750s when he wrote *Candide*, Voltaire rode a fine horse, perhaps a black beauty that may have played a greater or lesser role in his understanding that this may not be the best of all possible worlds, but there is much to be gained from the simple task of cultivating one's garden.[10] When all is said and done, I do not believe that Socrates or Freud would disagree with Voltaire. Although neither the ancient Athenian philosopher, nor the modern Viennese psychoanalyst thought to use the wonderful prosaic image of cultivating one's garden when referring to the virtues of self-examination and self-analysis respectively.

NOTES

1. Donald P. Spence, *Narrative Truth and Historical Truth: Meaning and Interpretation in Psychoanalysis* (New York: W. W. Norton & Company, 1982), 292–94.

2. Steven Best and Douglas Kellner, *Postmodern Theory: Critical Interrogations* (New York: The Guilford Press, 1991), 4, 6.

3. Martin Heidegger, *An Introduction to Metaphysics*, trans. Ralph Manheim (Garden City, NY: Anchor Books, 1961). References to this work are cited in the text with the abbreviation *IM*.

4. Joseph Campbell, *The Hero with a Thousand Faces* (New York: Meridian Books, 1967), 4.

5. Carl P. Ellerman, "Searching for Thomas Mann: A Parable of Myth and Truth," *The Journal of Value Inquiry* 31 (1997); cited in the text as *SM*.

6. Readers who wish to follow this set of ideas directly, but are not disposed to read six volumes, may refer to Arnold J. Toynbee, *A Study of History: Abridgement of Volumes I–VI*, ed. D. C. Somervell (New York: Oxford University Press, 1963).

7. Ludwig Wittgenstein, *On Certainty*, ed. G. E. M. Anscombe and G. H. von Wright, trans. Denis Paul and G. E. M. Anscombe (New York: Harper Torchbooks, 1972), #110, 148, 199, 200, 347.

8. Albert Camus, *The Rebel: An Essay on Man in Revolt*, trans. Anthony Bower (New York: A Vintage Book, 1956), 301.

9. Plato, *Symposium*, trans. Michael Joyce, in *Collected Dialogues*; cited in the text as *SY*.

10. Voltaire, *Candide*, in *"Candide," "Zadig" and Selected Stories*, 2nd ed., trans. Donald M. Frame (New York: A Signet Classic, 1963), 101.

Appendix: Freud's Ghost

To a certain extent, the damage suffered by Freudian analysis was the result of a rigorous critique of the *ghost in the machine* by scrupulous analytic philosophers who engaged in a rugged no-holds-barred battle against enchantments of the intellect resulting from the use and abuse of fuzzy language. I am referring to the abstract concepts of philosophy, theology, and psychology whose speculative use reified an invisible mind, soul, or psyche within the human body: a ghost in the fleshy machine whose reputed existence resulted in the widespread belief that there is a nonphysical entity within the physical body that functions outside conscious awareness, for good or for ill.

Noteworthy was the Freudian concept of the unconscious, the alleged province of fluctuating libido, historical repressions, and sexual wishes, all of which allegedly function with great consequence to the person whose unconscious mind was being excavated and exposed on clinical sofas across the European and American continents during the first half of the twentieth century. To his credit, Freud did not mince words about the existence of the ghost: "We call a psychical process unconscious whose existence we are obliged to assume—for some such reason as that we infer it from its effects—but of which we know nothing."[1] Given the nature of the inference it followed that prior to being psychoanalyzed, a person is never truly aware of the functioning of his pleasure-seeking id, reality-testing ego, or moralistic superego, because all the inferred activity takes place mysteriously within the ghostly interior unless there is a telling event, such as a parapraxis or slip of the tongue: a meaningful misarticulation that seems to support the inference that an internal ghost with psychical processes is alive and kicking in intrapsychic space with its own hidden motives and intentions that have leaked out in a verbal misarticulation that involves interference with or a suppression of the speaker's conscious intention.[2]

Regarding the philosophic assault on Freud's psychological translation of the ghost in the machine, Wittgenstein argued that the Viennese psychoanalyst was often given to "speculation—something prior even to the formation of an hypothesis," in spite of his mistaken belief that he was a legitimate man of science (*CF*, 44).[3] Targeting speculative metaphysics and the reification of abstract concepts in psychoanalytic theory, Wittgenstein maintained that Freud's references to the unconscious are neither grounded in evidence, nor capable of being evidenced empirically; rather, Freud's references to the unconscious have the attraction of "mythological explanations" that when accepted, make things seem clearer, in spite of the fact that these references are vacuous (*CF*, 43). In a mocking way—and I offer this conjecture with good reason, because the temperamental Viennese philosopher did not suffer fools kindly—Wittgenstein borrowed Freud's clinical language when suggesting that the actual results of psychoanalysis may be likened to a "delusion," whereby a person is persuaded to surrender one way of thinking in favor of another: an erroneous way of thinking that when accepted, "makes certain ways of behaving and thinking natural," while also enabling a person to journey through life in an easier way (*CF*, 44–45).

Wittgenstein's conclusion prefigures the sophisticated thesis put forward twenty years later in *The Triumph of the Therapeutic*, specifically, the thesis that the application of therapeutic techniques with manipulatable patients has the single goal of producing a "sense of well-being," such that psychological man, a cultural character type that came of age in the era of Freud, is "a user of any faith" or fiction or delusion, to use Wittgenstein's mocking expression, "that lends itself to therapeutic use."[4]

In the camp of analytic philosophers who carried the torch of Wittgenstein into the battle against bewitchments of language and intellect, the alleged existence of the ghost in the machine was stuff-and-nonsense: a historical dogma advanced by soul-searching religionists like Augustine, dualistic philosophers like Descartes, and speculative psychologizers like Freud, each of whom inherited and bequeathed the fiction that human beings have physical or bodily states and processes, as well as nonphysical states and process that somehow connect and interact mysteriously within the drawn interior of reflexive self-awareness. Although the existence of a ghostly entity capable of surviving the death of the physical machine may be consoling to those in whom a fear of death is flourishing, the internal specter and its private, invisible states and processes can be inspected neither by introspection, nor by empirical experiment. In short, the internal ghost is the grand fiction of dualistic thinkers who inherit, reinforce, and continue to bequeath to succeeding generations, one or another form of the myth that human beings lead separate lives: one conscious, the other strangely out of awareness.

If the existence of a soul, mind, or psyche is an enchanting myth—a good story whose telling is unnecessary in monistic explanations of human functioning based exclusively on the physiology of the brain—then the Freudian edifice premised on the segregated structures and dramatic functions of an internal unconscious mind comes tumbling down like Humpty Dumpty, as if psychoanalytic theory were a fragile egg cracked open during a precipitous fall. And a fall from grace, or something like it, is precisely what came to pass during the second quarter of the twentieth century.

This was a momentous historical era, not only a time of regressive Hitlerian holocaust, but also a time during which a progressive transfer of human expectation from the ancient promise of otherworldly salvation after death to the promise of secular salvation in life came into sharper view, ironically, as a result of Freud and the clinical hope of bettering the life of fellow humans by healing mental illness. In retrospect, during the second quarter of the twentieth century, in spite of the deathly barbarism and the death of humane expectation wrought by two world wars, the transfer of human expectation caught summer wind and set sail in a war of human liberation waged in part by Freud: an imaginative genius who advanced the modern myth of the ghost in the machine by seeking a cure of psyche rather than a cure of soul. Although this revolutionary shift of human expectation had its virtues, in 1949, in *The Concept of Mind*, an admittedly abusive assault on the historical dogma of the ghost in the machine, Oxford philosopher Gilbert Ryle referred to Freud as "psychology's one man of genius": a man whose influential teaching is "profound" and whose "allegories" are "damagingly popular" (*CM*, 324).[5]

In the view of Ryle and in the post–World War II culture that followed, the ghost of Freud lived on, although Freud succumbed to cancer in 1939. For better and for worse, Freud and his disciples, both loyal and errant, had successfully psychiatrized Western culture. Increasingly, and persisting to this day, an astonishing number of human attitudes and behaviors were being conceived as mental illnesses of one sort or another. In fact, during the second quarter of the twentieth century, the illustrious Wittgenstein taught his students to conceive (a) the bewitchments of language as an illness or a disorder, (b) philosophy as the therapeutic treatment of this illness, and (c) the philosopher's own linguistic problems as maladies that hopefully will disappear with proper treatment.[6] As if he were a philosophic foot soldier in Wittgenstein's therapeutic army, Ryle confessed to being motivated primarily by an attempt "to get disorders out of my own system," not to mention the secondary goal of facilitating in other disordered individuals, insight into a "malady" and "benefit from my medicine" (*CM*, 9).

In the end, Ryle critiqued Freud, modern psychology, and the historical dogma of the ghost in the machine simultaneously, admitting that if we abandon the dogma of living in two separate worlds, one physical, one mental, one material, the other immaterial, we shall finally surrender the notion that there is a "locked door" to the mental world and an important "key" to this nonphysical kingdom as yet undiscovered; after all, Ryle continued in a passage that plunged a dagger into the heart of Freud's belief that he was a dedicated man of science engaged in a quest for truth: "A researcher's day cannot be satisfactorily occupied in observing nonentities and describing the mythical" (*CM*, 320–21).

Parenthetically, this arcane philosophic discussion about the ghost in the machine is now in the public domain; in fact, rejection of the ghost is common discourse delivered regularly to the public in mass-market publications. For example, in a recent *Newsweek* article entitled "Sad Brain, Happy Brain," the jubilant author not only focused on the new discipline of cognitive neuroscience, whose empirical evidence arrives by means of advanced neuroimaging technology; he also asserted boldly that "the brain is the mind is the brain," a monistic point of view carrying the direct implication that it no longer makes sense to separate the physical brain from a separate nonphysical entity called "mind," such that contemporary "neuroscientists consider it settled that the mind arises from the cooperation of billions of interconnected cells," while humankind's richest, most soulful experiences, "could be reduced to mechanical or chemical bits."[7]

In spite of his critique of Freud, Wittgenstein understood the origin of his inspired view that he was a therapeutic philosopher treating disordered language or linguistic illnesses, in fact, he claimed ambivalently that at one time, he was "a disciple" or "a follower of Freud"; moreover, having a living sense of history informed by the belief that Freud had advanced a momentous cultural revolution of historic proportions, during the 1940s, Wittgenstein claimed that the influence of psychoanalysis in Europe and in America was "enormous": so prodigious, he thought, that a lengthy period of time would have to elapse before modern man lost "subservience" to whatever harm psychoanalysis created (*CF*, 41).

Perhaps the harm of Freud was his remarkable ability to package and present ideas in a persuasive way that had the power to make myth and fiction appear to be truth. Taken at its flood, therefore, Freudian "analysis is likely to do harm," according to Wittgenstein, because a patient in analysis is presented with interesting discoveries about himself, but if his critical faculty is not acute, he will neither see, nor see through, the myth the analyst is persuasively presenting. In the clinical consulting room, therefore, considering the power and influence of the therapist and the suggestibility of some vulnerable patients, "there is an inducement to say, 'Yes, of course, it must be like that.' A powerful mythology" is working when clinical enchantments of this sort take place (*CF*, 52).

What the esteemed philosopher failed to grapple with is a number of serious existential questions regarding the assumption that Freudian analysis, and by extension, other forms of dialogical therapy, may do harm if the patient's critical faculty is not acute. Speaking to this issue in the time of Freud, and writing as if the critical faculty, rather than a therapeutic myth or fiction, is harmful, one of Freud's errant disciples developed a therapeutic view of life based on the un-Socratic notion that the quest for truth itself is harmful or destructive! "With the truth," Otto Rank stated frankly, "one cannot live. To be able to live one needs illusions"; paradoxically, "the neurotic . . . is not the voluntary happy seeker of truth, but the forced, unhappy finder of it."[8]

If I wished to extend the implications of Rank's therapeutic view of life, thereby accurately envisioning dialogical therapists as mental health clinicians who are dedicated to the noble goal of producing a sense of well-being in fellow humans, I would liken these clinicians to citizens of an inverted world where everything runs backward.[9] This inverted world is something akin to the wonderland Alice discovered when she fell through a looking glass and found herself negotiating relationships in a society where everything was lived in reverse. In this case, if a person lived in a looking-glass world where therapeutic myth, fiction, and illusion had a place of honor, he would be experienced as abnormal, perhaps mentally ill or neurotic, if he condemned falsehood, while undertaking a Socratic quest for truth. In the best of all looking-glass worlds, this misguided man could be committed to a benevolent asylum, where noble dialogical therapists, informed by inverted dogmas of sickness and health, would develop a clinically sound, ethical treatment plan whereby the misguided mentally ill fellow would be mandated to a round of dialogical therapy that would persuade him to surrender his pathological quest for truth, in favor of one or another therapeutic myth or fiction. Absurd as it may seem to Socratic philosophers who have not fallen through a looking glass and thus are not living in a world where everything is inverted and lived in reverse, men and women divorced from a quest for truth would be seen as healthy, emotionally stable, psychically integrated human beings: successful role models for children, whose inquisitive minds are being properly conditioned to participate quite naturally in a therapeutic sensibility nicely conceived as the artful therapy of daily life.

NOTES

1. Sigmund Freud, *New Introductory Lectures on Psycho-Analysis,* in *Standard Edition,* vol. 22, 70.

2. Sigmund Freud, *Introductory Lectures on Psycho-Analysis,* in *Standard Edition,* vol. 16, 80.

3. Cyril Barrett, ed., "Conversations on Freud," in *Wittgenstein: Lectures & Conversations on Aesthetics, Psychology and Religious Belief* (Berkeley: University of California Press, 1967); cited in the text as *CF.* "Conversations on Freud" is a record of conversations between Wittgenstein and his student, Rush Rhees, written by Rhees between 1942 and 1946.

4. Philip Rieff, *The Triumph of the Therapeutic: Uses of Faith after Freud* (New York: Harper & Row, 1966), 13, 27.

5. Gilbert Ryle, *The Concept of Mind* (New York: Barnes & Noble, 1949); cited in the text as *CM.*

6. Ludwig Wittgenstein, *Philosophical Investigations,* 3rd ed., trans. G. E. M. Anscombe (New York: The Macmillan Company, 1969), #109, #133, #255.

7. Michael Craig Miller, "Sad Brain, Happy Brain," *Newsweek,* 22 September 2008, 51.

8. Otto Rank, *Truth and Reality,* trans. Jessie Taft (New York: W. W. Norton & Company, 1978), 42–43.

9. The following satirical comment is a reformulated version of an idea originally offered in my "Notes from the Margins of Being," *Inquiry: An Interdisciplinary Journal of Philosophy* 39, no. 1 (1996): 17.

Bibliography

American Psychiatric Association. *Diagnostic and Statistical Manual of Mental Disorders*. 2nd ed., rev. Washington, DC: American Psychiatric Association, 1987.

Aquinas, St. Thomas. *Effects of Sin, Stain and Guilt*. In *Summa Theologiae*, vol. 27, translated by T. C. O'Brien. New York: McGraw-Hill, 1974.

Aristophanes. *The Clouds*. In *Five Comedies of Aristophanes*, translated by Benjamin Bickley Rogers. Garden City, NY: Doubleday Anchor Books, 1955.

Aristotle. *Nicomachean Ethics*. In *The Basic Works of Aristotle*, edited by Richard McKeon, translated by W. D. Ross. New York: Random House, 1941.

Bataille, Georges. *Erotism, Death and Sensuality*. Translated by Mary Dalwood. San Francisco: City Lights Books, 1986.

Baudelaire, Charles. "Heautontimoroumenos." In *The Flowers of Evil*, translated by Roy Campbell. New York: A New Directions Paperbook, 1958.

Baudrillard, Jean. "Fatal Strategies." In *Jean Baudrillard Selected Writings*, edited by Mark Poster, translated by Jacques Mourrain. Stanford, CA: Stanford University Press. 1988.

———. *The Intelligence of Evil or the Lucidity Pact*. Translated by Chris Turner. Oxford: Berg Publishers, 2005.

———. *Simulacra and Simulation*. Translated by Sheila Faria Glaser. Ann Arbor: University of Michigan Press, 2000.

———. "Symbolic Exchange and Death." In *Jean Baudrillard Selected Writings*.

Beauvoir, Simone de. *The Second Sex*. Translated by H. M. Parshley. New York: Alfred A. Knopf, 1971.

Becker, Ernest. *The Denial of Death*. New York: The Free Press, 1975.

Berggren, Erik. *The Psychology of Confession*. Leiden: E. J. Brill, 1975.

Best, Steven, and Douglas Kellner. *Postmodern Theory: Critical Interrogations*. New York: The Guilford Press, 1991.

Bettelheim, Bruno. *The Informed Heart: Autonomy in a Mass Age*. New York: Avon Books, 1979.

———. *The Uses of Enchantment: The Meaning and Importance of Fairy Tales*. New York: Vintage Books, 1977.

Blake, William. "Let the Brothels of Paris Be Opened." In *The Complete Poetry and Prose of William Blake,* edited by David V. Erdman. New York: Anchor Books, 1988.

Bok, Sissela. *Secrets: On the Ethics of Concealment and Revelation*. New York: Vintage Books, 1984.

Bronowski, Jacob. *The Ascent of Man*. Boston: Little, Brown and Company, 1973.

Calne, Donald B. *Within Reason: Rationality and Human Behavior*. New York: Vintage Books, 2000.

Campbell, Joseph. *The Hero with a Thousand Faces*. New York: Meridian Books, 1967.

Camus, Albert. *The Myth of Sisyphus and Other Essays*. Translated by Justin O'Brien. New York: Vintage Books, 1961.

———. *The Rebel: An Essay on Man in Revolt*. Translated by Anthony Bower. New York: A Vintage Book, 1956.

———. *The Stranger*. Translated by Stuart Gilbert. New York: Vintage Books, 1946.

Canaday, John. *Mainstreams of Modern Art*. New York: Simon and Schuster, 1959.

Cassirer, Ernst. *The Philosophy of Symbolic Forms*. Vol. 2, *Mythical Thought*. Translated by Ralph Manheim. New Haven, CT: A Yale Paperbound, 1966.

Catton Rich, Daniel. *Edgar-Hilaire-Germain Degas*. New York: Harry N. Abrams, 1985.

Cioran, E. M. *The Temptation to Exist*. Translated by Richard Howard. Chicago: University of Chicago Press, 1998.

Degas, Edgar. "From the Memoirs of Thiebault-Sisson." In *Degas by Himself: Drawings, Prints, Paintings, Writings,* edited by Richard Kendall. Edison, NJ: Chartwell Books, 1994.

D'Emilio, John, and Estelle B. Freedman. *Intimate Matters: A History of Sexuality in America*. New York: Perennial Library, 1989.

Dostoevsky, Fyodor. *Crime and Punishment*. Translated by Michael Scammell. New York: Washington Square Press, 1963.

Duhem, Pierre. *To Save the Phenomena: An Essay on the Idea of Physical Theory from Plato to Galileo*. Translated by Edmund Doland and Chaninah Maschler. Chicago: University of Chicago Press, 1969.

Dworkin, Andrea. *Intercourse*. New York: Free Press Paperbacks, 1997.

Efran, Jay S., Michael D. Lukens, and Robert J. Lukens. *Language, Structure, and Change: Frameworks of Meaning in Psychotherapy*. New York: W. W. Norton & Company, 1990.

Einstein, Albert. "Reply to Criticism." Translated by Paul Arthur Schilpp. In *Albert Einstein: Philosopher-Scientist,* vol. 2, edited by Paul Arthur Schilpp. *The Library of Living Philosophers,* vol. 7. La Salle, IL: Open Court Classics, 1970.

Ellerman, Carl P. "The Absurd Sensibility of Existential Psychotherapy: Clinical Application of Survivors' Experience of Treblinka and Other Death Camps." *Journal of Contemporary Psychotherapy* 27, no. 2 (1997): 119–30.

———. "New Notes from Underground." *Inquiry: An Interdisciplinary Journal of Philosophy* 33, no. 1 (1990): 3–26.

———. "Notes from the Margins of Being." *Inquiry: An Interdisciplinary Journal of Philosophy* 39, no. 1 (1996): 3–19.

———. "The Phenomenological Treatment of Dissociative Identity Disorder." *Journal of Contemporary Psychotherapy* 28, no. 1 (1998): 69–79.

———. "Pragmatic Existential Therapy." *Journal of Contemporary Psychotherapy* 29, no. 1 (1999): 49–64.

———. "Searching for Thomas Mann: A Parable of Myth and Truth." *The Journal of Value Inquiry* 31 (1997): 527–30.

———. "A Talent for Life." *The Journal of Value Inquiry* 32 (1998): 191–204.

Ellis, Albert. *Reason and Emotion in Psychotherapy*. Secaucus, NJ: The Citadel Press, 1977.

Ferenczi, Sandor. "Introjection and Transference." In *Sex in Psychoanalysis (Contributions to Psycho-Analysis)*, translated by Ernest Jones. New York: Dover Publications, 1956.

Feyerabend, Paul. *Against Method: Outline of an Anarchistic Theory of Knowledge*. London: Verso, 1984.

Foucault, Michel. *The Birth of the Clinic: An Archaeology of Medical Perception*. Translated by A. M. Sheridan Smith. New York: Vintage Books, 1975.

———. *Discipline and Punish: The Birth of the Prison*. 2nd ed. Translated by Alan Sheridan. New York: Vintage Books, 1995.

———. *The History of Sexuality: An Introduction*. Vol. 1. Translated by Robert Hurley. New York: Vintage Books, 1990.

———. *Madness and Civilization: A History of Insanity in the Age of Reason*. Translated by Richard Howard. New York: A Mentor Book, 1967.

———. *Power/Knowledge: Selected Interviews & Other Writings, 1972–1977*. Translated by Colin Gordon, Leo Marshall, John Nepham, and Kate Soper. New York: Pantheon Books, 1980.

Frank, Jerome D., and Julia B. Frank. *Persuasion and Healing: A Comparative Study of Psychotherapy*. Baltimore: Johns Hopkins University Press, 1993.

Frankl, Viktor E. *The Doctor and the Soul: From Psychotherapy to Logotherapy*. Translated by Richard Winston and Clara Winston. New York: Vintage Books, 1973.

———. *Man's Search for Meaning: An Introduction to Logotherapy*. New York: Washington Square Press, 1965.

Freud, Sigmund. *Analysis Terminable and Interminable*. In *The Standard Edition of the Complete Psychological Works of Freud*, vol. 23, translated by James Strachey, in collaboration with Anna Freud, assisted by Alix Strachey and Alan Tyson. London: The Hogarth Press and The Institute of Psycho-Analysis, 1975.

———. *An Autobiographical Study*. In *Standard Edition*, vol. 20. 1959.

———. "Charcot." In *Standard Edition*, vol. 3. 1962.

———. *Civilization and Its Discontents*. In *Standard Edition*, vol. 21. 1961.

———. *The Complete Letters of Sigmund Freud to Wilhelm Fliess, 1887–1904*. Translated and edited by Jeffrey Moussaieff Masson. Cambridge: The Belknap Press, 1985.

———. *Fragment of an Analysis of a Case of Hysteria*. In *Standard Edition*, vol. 7. 1953.

———. *The Future of an Illusion*. In *Standard Edition*, vol. 21. 1961.

———. *A General Introduction to Psycho-Analysis*. Translated by Joan Riviere. Garden City, NY: Garden City Publishing Company, 1938.
———. *Group Psychology and the Analysis of the Ego*. In *Standard Edition*, vol. 18. 1975.
———. *The Interpretation of Dreams*. In *Standard Edition*, vol. 4. 1975.
———. *Introductory Lectures on Psycho-Analysis* (Part III). In *Standard Edition*, vol. 16. 1963.
———. *New Introductory Lectures on Psycho-Analysis*. In *Standard Edition*, vol. 22. 1964.
———. "Observations on Transference-Love (Further Recommendations on the Technique of Psycho-Analysis III)." In *Standard Edition*, vol. 12. 1975.
———. "On Beginning the Treatment (Further Recommendations on the Techniques of Psycho-Analysis I)." In *Standard Edition*, vol. 12. 1975.
———. "Preface to the Translation of Bernheim's *Suggestion*." In *Standard Edition*, vol. 1. 1966.
———. *The Question of Lay Analysis*. In *Standard Edition*, vol. 20. 1959.
———. "Sexuality in the Aetiology of the Neuroses." In *Standard Edition*, vol. 3. 1962.
———. *Totem and Taboo*. In *Standard Edition*, vol. 13. 1955.
Fromm-Reichmann, Frieda. *Principles of Intensive Psychotherapy*. Chicago: Phoenix Books, 1960.
Fuchik, Julius. *Notes from the Gallows*. Salt Lake City: Peregrine Smith Books, 1995.
Gay, Peter. *Freud: A Life for Our Time*. New York: W. W. Norton & Company, 1988.
Genet, Jean. *The Balcony*. Translated by Bernard Frechtman. New York: Grove Press, 1966.
Gleick, James. *Isaac Newton*. New York: Vintage Books, 2003.
Goodman, Nelson. *Ways of Worldmaking*. Indianapolis: Hackett Publishing Company, 1978.
Haliczer, Stephen. *Sexuality in the Confessional*. New York: Oxford University Press, 1996.
Hawthorne, Nathaniel. *The Scarlet Letter*. New York: Dell Publishing, 1972.
Hegel, G. W. F. *The Phenomenology of Mind*. Translated by J. B. Baillie. New York: Harper Torchbooks, 1967.
Heidegger, Martin. *Being and Time*. Translated by John Macquarrie and Edward Robinson. New York: Harper & Row, 1962.
———. *An Introduction to Metaphysics*. Translated by Ralph Manheim. Garden City, NY: Anchor Books, 1961.
Hillman, James. *Re-visioning Psychology*. New York: Harper Perennial, 1992.
Horney, Karen. *Neurosis and Human Growth*. New York: The Norton Library, 1950.
James, William. *The Meaning of Truth*. Ann Arbor: University of Michigan Press, 1970.
———. *The Principles of Psychology*. Vol. 2. Cambridge, MA: Harvard University Press, 1981.
———. *The Varieties of Religious Experience: A Study in Human Nature*. New York: Collier Books, 1967.

———. "What Pragmatism Means." In *Essays in Pragmatism*, edited by Alburey Castell. New York: The Hafner Library of Classics, 1966.

Janet, Pierre. *L'État Mental des Hystériques*. 2nd ed. N.p., 1911.

Jones, Ernest. *The Life and Work of Sigmund Freud*. Vol. 1, *The Formative Years and the Great Discoveries, 1856–1900*. New York: H. Wolff, 1962.

———. "The Madonna's Conception through the Ear." In *Psycho-Myth, Psycho-History: Essays in Applied Psychoanalysis*, vol. 2. New York: Stonehill Publishing, 1974.

Jung, C. G. *Memories, Dreams, Reflections*. Translated by Richard Winston and Clara Winston. New York: Vintage Books, 1963.

———. "The Psychological Aspects of the Kore." In *Essays on a Science of Mythology: The Myths of the Divine Child and the Divine Maiden*, rev. ed, translated by R. F. C. Hull. New York: Harper Torchbooks, 1963.

Kafka, Franz. "Couriers." In *Parables and Paradoxes*, translated by Clement Greenberg. New York: Schocken Books, 1966.

———. *I Am a Memory Come Alive: Autobiographical Writings by Franz Kafka*. Edited by Nahum N. Glatzer. New York: Schocken Books, 1974.

———. "In the Penal Colony." In *The Penal Colony: Stories and Short Pieces*, translated by Willa Muir and Edwin Muir. New York: Schocken Books, 1976.

———. *The Trial*. Translated by Willa Muir and Edwin Muir. New York: The Modern Library, 1956.

Kant, Immanuel. *Lectures on Ethics*. Translated by Louis Infield. New York: Harper Torchbooks, 1963.

Kendall, Richard, ed. *Degas by Himself: Drawings, Prints, Paintings, Writings*. Edison, NJ: Chartwell Books, 1994.

Kerenyi, C. "Epilegomena." In *Essays on a Science of Mythology*.

———. "Kore." In *Essays on a Science of Mythology*.

Kierkegaard, Søren. *The Concept of Dread*. Translated by Walter Lowrie. Princeton, NJ: Princeton University Press, 1970.

———. *The Sickness Unto Death*. In *"Fear and Trembling" and "The Sickness Unto Death,"* translated by Walter Lowrie. New York: Doubleday & Company, 1954.

Lacan, Jacques. *The Other Side of Psychoanalysis*. Translated by Russell Grigg. New York: W. W. Norton & Company, 2007.

Lasagna, Louis. "Modern Version of the Hippocratic Oath." *Definition of Hippocratic Oath*. www.MedicineNet.com.

Lea, Henry Charles. *A History of the Inquisition of Spain*. Vol. 4. New York: The Macmillan Company, 1907.

Lemoisne, P.-A. *Degas et son oeuvre*. Paris: n.p., 1946–1949.

Levi-Strauss, Claude. *Structural Anthropology*. Translated by Claire Jacobson and Brooke Grundfest Schoepf. New York: Anchor Books, 1967.

Luke, Helen M. "Mothers and Daughters: A Mythological Perspective." In *Mirrors of the Self: Archetypal Images That Shape Your Life*, edited by Christine Downing. Los Angeles: Jeremy P. Tarcher, 1991.

MacIntyre, Alasdair. *After Virtue: A Study in Moral Theory*. Notre Dame, IN: University of Notre Dame Press, 1984.

Madanes, Cloe. *Sex, Love, and Violence: Strategies for Transformation*. New York: W. W. Norton & Company, 1990.

Margenau, Henry. "Einstein's Conception of Reality." In *Albert Einstein Philosopher-Scientist*, vol. 1, edited by Paul Arthur Schilpp. *The Library of Living Philosophers*, vol. 7. La Salle, IL: Open Court Classics, 1969.

Martin, Jay. *Who Am I This Time? Uncovering the Fictive Personality*. New York: W. W. Norton & Company, 1990.

McDougall, Joyce. *Theaters of the Mind: Illusion and Truth on the Psychoanalytic Stage*. New York: Brunner/Mazel Publishers, 1991.

Menninger, Karl. *Theory of Psychoanalytic Technique*. New York: Harper Torchbooks, 1958.

Merleau-Ponty, M. *Phenomenology of Perception*. Translated by Colin Smith. New York: Humanities Press, 1970.

Middleton, Christopher, trans. and ed. *Selected Letters of Friedrich Nietzsche*. Chicago: University of Chicago Press, 1969.

Mill, John Stuart. *Utilitarianism*. Edited by George Sher. Indianapolis: Hackett Publishing Company, 1979.

Miller, Michael Craig. "Sad Brain, Happy Brain." *Newsweek*, 22 September 2008, 51–56.

Mowrer, O. Hobart. *The Crisis in Psychiatry and Religion*. Princeton, NJ: D. Van Nostrand Company, 1961.

Nietzsche, Friedrich. *The Antichrist*. In *The Portable Nietzsche*, edited and translated by Walter Kaufmann. New York: Vintage Books, 1963.

———. *Beyond Good and Evil: Prelude to a Philosophy of the Future*. Translated by Walter Kaufmann. New York: A Vintage Original, 1966.

———. *The Birth of Tragedy*. In *"The Birth of Tragedy" and "The Case of Wagner,"* translated by Walter Kaufmann. New York: A Vintage Original, 1967.

———. *On the Genealogy of Morals*. Translated by Walter Kaufmann. New York: Vintage Books, 1967.

———. *Twilight of the Idols*. In *The Portable Nietzsche*.

———. *The Will to Power*. Edited by Walter Kaufmann. Translated by Walter Kaufmann and R. J. Hollingdale. New York: A Vintage Giant, 1968.

Otto, Walter F. "The Meaning of the Eleusinian Mysteries [1939]." Translated by Ralph Manheim. In *The Mysteries: Papers from the Eranos Yearbooks*, edited by Joseph Campbell. Bollingen Series 30. Princeton, NJ: Princeton University Press, 1955.

Pipher, Mary. *Revivng Ophelia*. New York: Ballantine Books, 1995.

Plato. *Charmides*. Translated by Benjamin Jowett. In *The Collected Dialogues of Plato*, edited by Edith Hamilton and Huntington Cairns. Bollingen Series 51. Princeton, NJ: Princeton University Press, 1969.

———. *Laws*. Translated by A. E. Taylor. In *Collected Dialogues*.

———. *Meno*. Translated by W. K. C. Guthrie. In *Collected Dialogues*.

———. *Phaedrus*. Translated by R. Hackforth. In *Collected Dialogues*.

———. *Republic*. Translated by Paul Shorey. In *Collected Dialogues*.

———. *Socrates' Defense (Apology)*. Translated by Hugh Tredennick. In *Collected Dialogues*.

———. *Symposium*. Translated by Michael Joyce. In *Collected Dialogues*.

———. *Theatetus*. Translated by F. M. Cornford. In *Collected Dialogues*.

Popper, Karl R. *The Open Society and Its Enemies*. Vol. 1, *The Spell of Plato*. Princeton, NJ: Princeton University Press, 1971.

Putnam, Hilary. *Ethics without Ontology*. Cambridge, MA: Harvard University Press, 2004.

Quine, Willard Van Orman. "Identity, Ostension, and Hypostasis." In *From a Logical Point of View: 9 Logico-Philosophical Essays*. New York: Harper Torchbooks, 1961.

———. "Logic as a Source of Syntactical Insights." In *The Ways of Paradox and Other Essays*. New York: Random House, 1966.

Rank, Otto. *Truth and Reality*. Translated by Jessie Taft. New York: W. W. Norton & Company, 1978.

Reichenbach, Hans. "The Philosophical Significance of the Theory of Relativity." In *Einstein Philosopher-Scientist*, vol. 1, edited by Paul Arthur Schilpp. *The Library of Living Philosophers*, vol. 7. La Salle, IL: Open Court Classics, 1969.

Reik, Theodor. *The Compulsion to Confess: On the Psychoanalysis of Crime and Punishment*. Translated by Norbert Rie. New York: Grove Press, 1961.

———. *Masochism in Sex and Society*. Translated by Margaret H. Beigel and Gertrud M. Kurth. New York: Grove Press, 1962.

Rieff, Philip. *Freud: The Mind of the Moralist*. Garden City, NY: Anchor Books, 1961.

———. *The Triumph of the Therapeutic: Uses of Faith after Freud*. New York: Harper & Row, 1966.

Rilke, Rainer Maria. *The Notebooks of Malte Laurids Brigge*. Translated by M. D. Herter Norton. New York: W. W. Norton & Company, 1958.

Rose, H. J. *A Handbook of Greek Mythology*. New York: A Dutton Paperback, 1959.

Rue, Loyal. *By the Grace of Guile: The Role of Deception in Natural History and Human Affairs*. New York: Oxford University Press, 1994.

Ryle, Gilbert. *The Concept of Mind*. New York: Barnes & Noble, 1949.

Sade, Marquis de. *The 120 Days of Sodom*. In *The 120 Days of Sodom and Other Writings*, translated by Austryn Wainhouse and Richard Seaver. New York: Grove/Weidenfeld, 1987.

Saint Augustine. *Confessions*. Translated by R. S. Pine-Coffin. Baltimore: Penguin Books, 1966.

———. *The Soliloquies of Saint Augustine*. Translated by Thomas F. Gilligan. New York: Cosmopolitan Science & Art Service Co., 1943.

Saint Teresa. *The Life of Teresa of Jesus: The Autobiography of St. Teresa of Avila*. Edited and translated by E. Allison Peers. New York: Image Books, 1960.

Sartre, Jean-Paul. "Existentialism Is a Humanism." In *Existentialism from Dostoevsky to Sartre*, edited by Walter Kaufmann, translated by Philip Mairet. New York: Meridian Books, 1960.

Shakespeare, William. *King John*. In *The Complete Works of William Shakespeare, with Themes of the Plays*. New York: Walter J. Black, 1937.

Shirer, William L. *The Rise and Fall of the Third Reich*. New York: Simon and Schuster, 1960.

Simmel, Georg. *The Secret and the Secret Society*. Part 4, *The Sociology of Georg Simmel*, edited and translated by Kurt H. Wolff. New York: The Free Press, 1950.

Smith, Alexander McCall. "Why We Should Believe in Santa Claus." *Parade*, 13 December 2009.

Snoeck, Andreas. *Confession and Psychoanalysis*. Translated by Theodore Zuydwijk. Westminster, MD: The Newman Press, 1964.

Sophocles. *Electra*. Translated by David Grene. In *Greek Tragedies,* vol. 2, edited by David Grene and Richmond Lattimore. Chicago: University of Chicago Press, 1964.

Spence, Donald P. *Narrative Truth and Historical Truth: Meaning and Interpretation in Psychoanalysis*. New York: W. W. Norton & Company, 1982.

Stanislavski, Constantin. *An Actor's Handbook*. Edited and translated by Elizabeth Reynolds Hapgood. New York: Theatre Arts Books, 1903.

Szasz, Thomas S. *The Myth of Mental Illness: Foundations of a Theory of Personal Conduct*. New York: A Delta Book, 1967.

———. *The Myth of Psychotherapy: Mental Healing as Religion, Rhetoric, and Repression*. New York: Anchor Books, 1978.

Taylor, Shelley E. *Positive Illusions: Creative Self-Deception and the Healthy Mind*. New York: Basic Books, 1989.

Tentler, Thomas N. *Sin and Confession on the Eve of the Reformation*. Princeton, NJ: Princeton University Press, 1977.

Tertullian. *On Penitence*. In *Tertullian: Treatises on Penance, Ancient Christian Writers*. Edited by Johannes Quasten and Walter J. Burghardt. Translated by William P. LeSaint. Westminster, MD: The Newman Press, 1959.

———. *On the Pallium*. Translated by Rev. S. Thelwall. In *The Ante-Nicene Fathers: Translations of the Fathers down to A.D. 325*, vol. 4, edited by Rev. Alexander Roberts, D.D., and James Donaldson, LL.D. Grand Rapids, MI: Wm. B. Erdmans, 1994.

Torrey, E. Fuller. *Witchdoctors and Psychiatrists: The Common Roots of Psychotherapy and Its Future*. New York: Perennial Library, 1986.

Toynbee, Arnold J. *A Study of History: Abridgement of Volumes I–VI*. Edited by D. C. Somervell. New York: Oxford University Press, 1963.

Voltaire. *Candide*. In *"Candide," "Zadig" and Selected Stories*. 2nd ed. Translated by Donald M. Frame. New York: A Signet Classic, 1963.

Wilson, Edward O. *Sociobiology: The Abridged Edition*. Cambridge, MA: The Belknap Press of Harvard University Press, 1980.

Wittgenstein, Ludwig. "Conversations on Freud." In *Wittgenstein: Lectures & Conversations on Aesthetics, Psychology and Religious Belief,* edited by Cyril Barrett. Berkeley: University of California Press, 1967.

———. *On Certainty*. Edited by G. E. M. Anscombe and G. H. von Wright. Translated by Denis Paul and G. E. M. Anscombe. New York: Harper Torchbooks, 1972.

———. *Philosophical Investigations*. 3rd ed. Translated by G. E. M. Anscombe. New York: The Macmillan Company, 1969.

———. *Remarks on the Foundations of Mathematics*. Translated by G. E. M. Anscombe. Cambridge, MA: MIT Press, 1967.

Yalom, Irvin D. *Existential Psychotherapy*. New York: Basic Books, 1980.

Index

About the Author

Carl P. Ellerman is a graduate of the University of Rochester and Syracuse University, where he received his PhD with an interdisciplinary concentration in existential psychology and existential philosophy. He is currently a psychotherapist in private practice following years of clinical experience with a severely and persistently mentally ill population in the psychiatric service of an urban hospital, as well as clinical experience in an alcohol-drug treatment center, where he served as an impaired professionals monitor for the NYS Department of Health, State Board for Professional Medical Conduct. He also taught philosophy to inmates in a maximum security prison and to students in a liberal arts college on the East Coast.

Dr. Ellerman has published numerous clinical and philosophical essays including "New Notes from Underground," "The Phenomenological Treatment of Dissociative Identity Disorder," "A Talent for Life," and "The Absurd Sensibility of Existential Psychotherapy: Clinical Application of Survivors' Experience of Treblinka and Other Death Camps." He has appeared on public television for discussions of depression, anxiety, alcohol-drug dependency, and self-mutilation, and has lectured on a variety of clinical subjects, including the inpatient and outpatient treatment of Dissociative Identity Disorder; Paranoid, Borderline, and Narcissistic Personality Disorders; and Pragmatic Solution-Focused Therapy. He is an inveterate writer who lives with his wife in central New York.

www.ingramcontent.com/pod-product-compliance
Ingram Content Group UK Ltd.
Pitfield, Milton Keynes, MK11 3LW, UK
UKHW012035150926
475560UK00001B/21